Mapping Generations of Traumatic Memory in American Narratives

Mapping Generations of Traumatic Memory in American Narratives

Edited by

Dana Mihăilescu, Roxana Oltean and Mihaela Precup

CAMBRIDGE SCHOLARS

PUBLISHING

Mapping Generations of Traumatic Memory in American Narratives,
Edited by Dana Mihăilescu, Roxana Oltean and Mihaela Precup

This book first published 2014

Cambridge Scholars Publishing

12 Back Chapman Street, Newcastle upon Tyne, NE6 2XX, UK

British Library Cataloguing in Publication Data
A catalogue record for this book is available from the British Library

ISBN (10): 1-4438-5672-X, ISBN (13): 978-1-4438-5672-0

TABLE OF CONTENTS

ACKNOWLEDGEMENTS

This volume was edited as part of the UEFISCDI-funded project "Cross-Cultural Encounters in American Trauma Narratives: A Comparative Approach to Personal and Collective Memories," PN-II-RU-TE-2011-3-0149 (October 2011-September 2014), contract no. 64/2011, project coordinator Dr. Roxana Oltean.

INTRODUCTION

Identifying mechanisms of traumatic memory for various generations of trauma survivors has been an increasing focus of scholarship and public attention in recent decades, in the works of scholars such as Mieke Bal, Cathy Caruth, Shoshana Felman, Geoffrey Hartman, Marianne Hirsch, Nancy K. Miller, Dominick La Capra, Michael Rothberg, Leo Spitzer, and others. Marianne Hirsch's concept of "postmemory" (1997, 2012), Peggy Phelan's "performative memory" (1997), Dora Apel's "secondary witnessing" (2002), Alison Landsberg's "prosthetic memory" (2004), Michael Rothberg's "multidirectional memory" (2009), the role of mediation and remediation in the dynamics of cultural memory (Astrid Erll, 2012; Aleida Assman, 2011), and Stef Craps' focus on "postcolonial witnessing" and its cross-cultural dimension (2013) are all essential to current scholarly examinations of generations of post-traumatic memory.

Mapping Generations of Traumatic Memory in American Narratives is a collection of essays that participates in this particular conversation as it explores the performance and transmission of post-traumatic memory in contemporary United States. The essays in our collection expand current directions of trauma studies beyond the narrow focus of early 1990s practitioners and towards the creation of a self-reflective critical paradigm. They examine the dynamics of the transmission of trauma from the personal to the public and from one generation to another; they attempt to reexamine the classic definition of trauma as a singular exceptional event that shatters all systems of representation; they also propose a definition of testimony that goes beyond presence, and draws attention to the potential for cross-cultural ethical engagements. These complex forms of traumatic transmission are examined in this volume in four parts, each with a different focus: trauma and multidirectional memory; the representation of trauma in autobiographical texts; the dynamic of public forms of national commemoration; the problematic instantiation of 9/11 as a traumatic landmark.

Our volume attempts to expand the narrow definition of the term "generation" beyond the genealogical and into the cross-cultural. Thus, the chapters from **Part One. Legacies of Multidirectional Memories: From Pre-Holocaust to Postcolonial Traumas**, build on the work of Michael Rothberg, Stef Craps, and Gert Buelens by exposing the blind spots of a

Western theoretical and diagnostic model in trauma studies, and exploring forms of non-Western/alternative engagements with oppression and suffering. Two chapters explore the Holocaust and the input of Neo-Hoodoo mythology on the traumatic history of African Americans, thus juxtaposing the experiences of (post)colonialism, Auschwitz, and Harlem. More precisely, Adam Brown and Danielle Christmas's chapter focuses on Sydney Lumet's influential and controversial film *The Pawnbroker* (1965) in comparison to Richard LaGavranese's post-neoliberal film *Freedom Writers* (2007). The authors explore the stakes of this kind of Holocaust films for collective understandings of race and class in urban America, highlighting the importance of whether the directors choose a redemptive resolution when exposing the genocidal nature of urban racial and economic suffering. Next, Elisabeth Oyler's chapter examines Ishmael Reed's theory of Neo-Hoodoo, a tradition based on the organization of Haitian VooDoo and building upon an Americanized version of it; the author explains it as "a multicultural and inclusive practice that welcomes all cultures to (re)join, reclaiming a lost cultural history" which is part traumatic, part celebratory, and works towards creating an inclusive cultural future. Anna Sajecki's chapter also focuses on the inscription of trauma into space, examining Annie Proulx's novel *The Shipping News* (1993) in order to decode the manner in which the imprint of a spatial, traumatic narration can be passed down across generations, and how it changes as one starts the process of working through.

Two other chapters from Part One propose a novel path in the field of trauma studies by suggesting that Rothberg's model of multidirectional memory can be extended to also instrumentalize the analysis of trauma in the case of postcommunism. The chapters reflect on the US as a site of East European traumas when they examine the 1903 antisemitic Kishinev pogrom and the early 1990s war from Yugoslavia in Aleksandar Hemon's *The Lazarus Project* (2008), as well as the role of Voice of America radio broadcasts for the investigation of American representations of East European traumas during the Cold War. Dana Mihăilescu's chapter thus reads Hemon's narrative as a work underscoring the difficulty of dealing with urban norms of historical/structural traumas and practices of mourning. She also suggests that the examination of the perspective of displaced individuals in the city leads to the possibility of shifting reductive frames of reference, and opens spaces of negotiation that will hopefully allow for a better future via cross-cultural, multidirectional configurations. The author does this by examining the struggles of immigrants to the US in a multidirectional approach connecting refugees from two widely different historic traumas—the 1992 siege of Sarajevo and the 1903 Kishinev pogrom. On the other hand, Roxana Oltean's chapter focuses on two VOA scripts from 1951 and 1953, which "address the issues encoded by the syntagm 'Stalintowns aplenty'—violence, imposition and obliteration—and engage the wider topic of the communist purges from two perspectives: the politicization of city names and its role in the creation of a totalitarian geography, and the projection of an American/universal counter-space built on ethical principles from surprisingly diverse perspectives." The author's main aim is to read VOA broadcasts and their ideological function in the spirit of Michael Rothberg's suggestion that non-competitive traumas may yield a multidimensionality that opens up the space of ideology to multivocal readings.

Part Two. Trauma, Lineage, and Transmission in Autobiography ponders the complex relationship between the autobiographical mode and traumatic testimony, while reflecting on the interplay between words and images, as well as the role of gender in the construction of the autobiographical subject. Our contributors also expand the sometimes rigid fixation of trauma studies on the strictly theoretical debates about trauma and representation or trauma and temporality as established by several leading figures in the field (such as Cathy Caruth, Shoshana Felman, and Dominick LaCapra). They do so by investigating the constantly shifting dynamics of Nora's already mediated sites of memory (Erl and Rigney). This shift of focus opens wider debates in the humanities that have driven scholars towards the exploration of specific transnational and transgenerational experiences and encounters. Thus, Kate Parker Horigan discusses the conversion the autobiographical discourse of trauma from the first-person story—present in Abdulrahman Zeitoun's Katrina survival story first published online in his own blog—into the story of the heroic immigrant whose individual voice is erased as he is emplotted in a best-selling success story in Dave Eggers' *Zeitoun* (2009). Parker Horigan uses critical discourse analysis to reflect on the public transformation of the character Zeitoun into a useful prop in the construction of competing political discourses, where Islamic masculinity is one of the main variables. The fictionalization of a real-life traumatic event is complicated by its embeddedness in a specific ideology, as Sostene M. Zangari's chapter from this collection also demonstrates. By focusing on crime novelist James Ellroy's interpretation of his mother's unsolved murder, Zangari reads Ellroy's successful series of four crime novels, the *Los Angeles Quartet* (made up of *The Black Dahlia*, *The Big Nowhere*, *L.A. Confidential*, and *White Jazz*) through his 1996 autobiography, *My Dark Places*. In the latter, Ellroy remembers his own reading of his mother's death as a crime in which she was complicit, a perspective that was proposed to him as a child by his father but that was also informed by the particular gender politics of the 1950s. Zangari demonstrates that Ellroy's ambivalent emotions are also reflected in a fictional world dominated by a violent patriarchy whose destruction of the city mirrors the shattering of the psyche of the child whose mother was killed, and whose understanding of the event is manipulated by the same forces that may have allowed for her death. The negotiation between contemporary norms of mourning and the referential expectations of autobiography is next examined in Mihaela Precup's chapter on three memoirs of mourning: Joan Didon's *The Year of Magical Thinking* (2005) and *Blue Nights* (2011), and Joyce Carol Oates' *A Widow's Story* (2011). Precup focuses on the reception—in reviews and online comments sections from amazon.com and other relevant websites—of these three autobiographical texts whose main purpose is recording the death of a loved one and the subsequent period of grief and mourning. The role of the archive in the exploration of trauma is further analyzed by Golnar Nabizadeh in a chapter that interprets the particular reading experience imposed by autobiographical comics (or "autographic comics") whose main representational challenge lies at the intersection of punctual and ongoing trauma—Art Spiegelman's *Maus I and II* (1987, 1991), *MetaMaus* (2011) and *In the Shadow of No Towers* (2004), and Alison Bechdel's *Fun Home* (2006).

The chapters from **Part Three. Commemorating Trauma, Shifting National Icons: Marginal and Mainstream Paths of Remembrance** depart from the examination of the site of punctual trauma and into the exploration of the dynamic mediation of public places of memory. Emma Login's chapter, "Contemporary War Memorials and the Urban Landscape: The Memorialization of Marginalized Groups in Washington, D.C.," reads the visual rhetoric of three memorials from Washington, D.C.—the African American Civil War Memorial, the Japanese American Memorial to Patriotism during World War II, and the American Indian Memorial Initiative—to unveil the negotiations and power dynamics behind their construction and to propose a shift in the policies that dictate official structures of remembrance. In a similar vein, Liz Medoff's chapter, "The Gendered Approach. Talking Trauma in National Monument Discourses," places itself in conversation with theoreticians such as Ann Cvetkovich, Erika Doss, and Jill Bennett in order to walk readers through the ways affect is negotiated in the memorial site of Ground Zero. Sara Polak's chapter, "Prosthetic Memories of Franklin D. Roosevelt's Infantile Paralysis as Narrative Embodiments for Traumatic American War Memory" examines Roosevelt's disability—as it is represented in several films such as *Pearl Harbor* (Michael Bay, 2001), *Hyde Park on Hudson* (Roger Michell, 2012), *FDR American Badass!* (Garrett Brawith, 2012)—that functions as an embodiment of the trauma of war.

The chapters in **Part Four. 9/11 and the Canonization of Trauma** question the place of 9/11 in an international hierarchy of suffering constructed through the formation of a canon of representation established by post-traumatic visibility. Rodica Mihăilă's opening chapter investigates several forms of memorializing the 9/11 terrorist attacks in the recent American novel, as either healing therapy for the nation or oblique critique of American exceptionalism, by focusing on two debut novels published in 2011, Amy Waldman's *The Submission* and Teju Cole's *Open City*. Allison Whitney expands the exploration of various processes of healing by examining Paul Greengrass's 2006 film, *United 93*; she presents both film production and spectatorship as memorial acts, and argues that Greengrass's formal and narrative strategies suggest that to memorialize 9/11 is to remember the cognitive dissonance experienced by the spectator-survivor, thus foregrounding the initial stage of confusion over working through a traumatic experience. Audrey Bardizbanian's chapter considers how the narration of urban space and traumatic memories reflect each other as a way of transmitting both personal experiences and collective traumas in Jonathan Safran Foer's popular but problematic novel *Extremely Loud & Incredibly Close* (2005). By looking at Foer's 2005 novel from a different angle, Brittany Hirth exposes how direct articulation of 9/11 is not always readily accessible in the present, and critiques Foer's method of utilizing the Dresden and Hiroshima bombings within his narrative about 9/11 as stand-ins for the latter's representation. Finally, Jenn Brandt's chapter focuses on the narrative use and function of "othered" bodies in response to 9/11 and the War on Terror—specifically those considered transgressive, terrorist, and/or tortured—in Claire Tristram's *After* (2004) and Mohsin Hamid's *The Reluctant Fundamentalist* (2007). Brandt shows how such transgressive bodies subvert recognizable stereotypical notions of gender, sex, class, and nation in an effort to problematize notions of identity and nation that have been ignored or oversimplified in many discourses of 9/11, thereby destabilizing the processes of nostalgia.

Overall, our volume explores cross-cultural and trans-generational encounters in post-World War II American trauma narratives by mapping out traumatic memory in successive cycles of American narratives generated by major moments of trauma in US history or European history impacting the US through geopolitical consequences or extensive public debate in the US: slavery, ethnic cleansing in Eastern Europe, the Holocaust, post-Cold War configurations, and the 9/11 attacks. We read these narratives as not separate but interconnected, in the sense that they shape the US as a performative site of post-traumatic cross-cultural and transnational dialogue between generations. The corpus of narratives under discussion includes fiction, diaries, memoirs, films, visual narratives, and oral testimonies given in the US. The selection discloses a wide diversity of memories and voices, belonging to East European immigrants, to individuals marginalized because of class, race, ethnicity, gender differences and to a seemingly prosperous multicultural America, the target of the 9/11 terrorist attacks. Given the broad range of topics addressed, the essays in our volume propose a new paradigm of post-traumatic memory which connects not only separate generations, but also separate geographical, cultural and political spaces affected to different degrees by shared historical events which produced considerable loss of life and liberty and which show how the US paradoxically became a space of inherited trauma and possible but always complicated relief for various generations of survivors.

Part One:

Legacies of Multidirectional Memories: From Pre-Holocaust to Postcolonial Traumas

When the Holocaust Comes to Harlem: Traumatic Memory, Race, and Economic (In)Justice in American Holocaust Film

Adam Brown and Danielle Christmas

Sidney Lumet's controversial 1965 film *The Pawnbroker* was one of the first films to situate Nazi Germany's persecution of Jews alongside the experiences of an impoverished community of ethnic minorities in urban America. Almost half a century after its release, debate over the film continues unabated. Wendy Zierler captures one version of this debate when she stresses the "both problematic and salutary" consequences of those narratives (and she counts Lumet's film as a particularly guilty offender here) that juxtapose what she calls "the individual histories of Jewish and black suffering alongside each other."[1] Her concession, however, that "salutary" benefits exist holds promise that, even in her analysis, the limitations revealed in texts like Caryl Phillips's *Higher Ground* (1989) and *The Nature of Blood* (1997) can be overcome.

Counseling caution for a different reason, Laurence Mordekhai Thomas critiques the "invidious" and widespread "rivalry of suffering between the two groups," which has, at least partly, been brought about by what he views as the indifference of white America to both, and a reinforcement of racialized ideas on all sides.[2] Thus, even when put forward with the best intentions, any suggestion that the Holocaust and African American slavery can be compared with one another must be thought through with considerable care. In this chapter, we return to Lumet's pivotal film to re-examine the complexities of situating deeply traumatic historical experiences "next to" one another in film. Our analysis here of the textualities and reception of *The Pawnbroker* maps a trajectory from Lumet's film to contemporary notions of urban race and class politics, and the place of Holocaust representations in those conversations. Similar themes converge in *The Pawnbroker* and contemporary Hollywood intersections of the urban and the Holocaust—for our purposes, we will look at Richard LaGravenese's 2007 drama *Freedom Writers* as one such example—exemplifying what could be called different generations of Holocaust memory, though the narrative and technical strategies employed by Lumet, and transformed by his successors, yield profoundly different results.

In both Lumet and LaGravenese's productions, the specter of the Holocaust, which is used alongside urban American narratives, directly engages with the transformation of American notions of racial and economic oppression. Lumet's film was developed in the context of the 1960s Civil Rights Movement, more specifically the 1964 Harlem race riot, while later urban-Holocaust dramas respond to contemporary American notions of urban race and class; *Freedom Writers* follows Lumet's map, in its structure as an answer to the climactic Los Angeles race riots of the early 1990s. An analysis of these films reflects a social schizophrenia over the role of race versus the role of class in early incarnations of urban conflict—and later films that revive and revise these early tropes—highlighting a collapsing of narratives about one group popularly imagined as white and wealthy (Jews) with another group imagined as brown and violent (urban young adults). The resulting analogies and hierarchies set up between Holocaust persecution and urban American racial tensions have long proven contentious, as is revealed through an analysis of the popular and scholarly reception of Lumet's work in particular. The fraught tension between the convergence and conflation of the distinct traumas of these different groups must also be considered within the broader critique of what has been called the "Americanization" of the Holocaust, or the "Holocaust Industry."[3]

Annette Insdorf has observed that while the first two decades of Holocaust feature films focused on "Jewish victims and Nazi villains," the "second wave," beginning in the mid-1980s, has concentrated on resistance and rescue.[4] Lumet's film and followers, like LaGravenese's *Freedom Writers*, can be seen to fit into each of these waves respectively. Taking on a somewhat apocalyptic tone, Alvin H. Rosenfeld's recent volume *The End of the Holocaust* (which includes chapters on the Americanization of the Holocaust and the influence of Anne Frank's story), warns of the destructive impact of continued and increasing denial, indifference, and misrepresentations—particularly in terms of the "American triumphalism" (by which he means the optimistic resort to heroic deeds and happy endings) of film and other media.[5] While we do not subscribe to an inherently negative perspective on Holocaust film—indeed, we see it as a potentially very effective medium for negotiating Holocaust memory and experience in a complex and nuanced manner—the problems involved in screen narratives remain integral to any consideration of their potentialities. It is for this reason that the web of critiques surrounding a key text like *The Pawnbroker* be subjected to the same level of scrutiny as the prolific body of critics has brought to the film itself.

Elucidating how the Holocaust came to fill "a need for a consensual symbol" for American Jewish identity, Peter Novick's 1999 study *The Holocaust in American Life* makes an important contribution to the ongoing debate over the "uniqueness" versus the "universality" of the genocide.[6] Relating this debate to the "comparability" issue, he writes, "Every historical event, including the Holocaust, in some ways resembles events to which it might be compared and differs from them in some ways (...) to declare the Holocaust unique, is intellectual sleight of hand."[7] In his study of Holocaust popular culture in America, Alan Mintz outlines what he sees as the predominant "exceptionalist" model of Holocaust representation, which is "rooted in a conviction of the Holocaust as a radical rupture in human history that goes well beyond notions of uniqueness," as opposed to the "constructivist" model, which "stresses the cultural lens through which the Holocaust is perceived."[8] The former perspective will clearly be more suspicious of comparative explorations of the kind Novick describes, while the latter constructivist approach is more likely to be at least open to the possibility that such comparisons can lead to illumination and are not automatically labelled a betrayal of Holocaust victims. Although our subsequent analysis of *Freedom Writers*, as one of many examples, will expose significant problems in the embedding of the Holocaust as a framework through which to understand (and resolve) the problems of urban America, our investigation of Holocaust-related cinema in a sense straddles the exceptionalist and constructivist approaches, as we seek not only to critique the problematic implications of the process of "Americanization" that have eventuated, but also to highlight the cultural (and generational) lenses through which the intersection of Holocaust and urban American narratives have been mediated.

In his introduction to *Multidirectional Memory: Remembering the Holocaust in the Age of Decolonization*, Michael Rothberg writes that his study pivots on several central questions, namely,

> What happens when different histories confront each other in the public sphere? Does the remembrance of one history erase others from view? When memories of slavery and colonialism bump up against memories of the Holocaust in contemporary multicultural societies, must a competition of victims ensue?[9]

Located within a more specific context, this chapter seeks to examine these questions through an analysis of the simultaneous depiction of urban America and the Holocaust in film. Critiquing what he views as the "flawed" and commonplace conceptualization of traumatic pasts as existing within a "competitive" framework, Rothberg writes of the need to "consider memory as multidirectional: as subject to ongoing negotiation, cross-referencing, and borrowing; as productive and not privative."[10] Given that the vast majority of scholarship on Holocaust film has frequently focused on the (mis)appropriation of Holocaust memories and experiences to serve various (non-Holocaust-related) political agendas, it might be argued that the literature in this area in part reinforces a "competitive" discourse influenced by, and linked to, the contentious issue of "uniqueness." To be sure, there are certainly more than enough cases where Holocaust films (and texts in various other genres) justifiably give one pause, if not discomfort, in their attachment of Holocaust imagery to generate meanings about other historical phenomena. Yet as our previous discussion of Zierler highlights, a productive conversation incorporating both black and Jewish suffering can—and must—ensue in order to come to terms with the past from all angles. Furthermore, while a great deal has been written about how certain "trivializing" comparisons have negative implications for Holocaust collective memory, we aim to shed light on the problematic consequences of Hollywood's embrace of Holocaust narratives for understandings of urban America. In doing so, we underline the need to both resist "competitive" frameworks that position Holocaust (mis)representations as only impacting one set of historical experiences, and to acknowledge that memory, its mediation, and the consequences of this process, are multidirectional, subject to continual re-negotiation and comprising both problematic and productive possibilities. Both the limitations and potentialities of Holocaust film can be seen nowhere more clearly than in the textualities and reception of a single and singular film: *The Pawnbroker*. While each subsequent section can be read on its own terms, this chapter as a whole is meant to complicate, while also rescuing a valuable film from the often polemical, sometimes reductionist, regularly competing, and always impassioned critics that have raised the volume of discussion beyond understanding.

Cashing in on Jewish Suffering? Contentious Analogies and Christological Imagery in *The Pawnbroker*

Based on Edward Lewis Wallant's 1961 novel of the same name, *The Pawnbroker* focuses on the story of Holocaust survivor Sol Nazerman, who ekes out a miserable existence amidst low-income, urban American ethnic minorities—people he callously exploits through his business. From the outset, the film makes clear that Nazerman has unsuccessfully attempted to repress his memories of the past, exemplified in his refusal to change the page of his store's calendar past the anniversary date of his family's murder, lest he lose temporal proximity to their death in the Nazi camps. Using fragmented "flash cuts" or "shock cuts" to construct an innovative mode of flashback, Lumet stylistically juxtaposes re-enacted footage of concentration camp existence with dismal images of New York slum life. Depicting a society divided by the race- and class-based tensions of 1960s New York City, the plot pivots on Nazerman's relationship with his young, charismatic Puerto Rican shop assistant, Jesus Ortiz, who is desperate to break free of socio-economic restraints and leave his criminal youth behind. Turning to Nazerman for inspiration that does not come, Ortiz reluctantly resorts to helping others rob the pawnshop, but is killed when he defends Nazerman from one of his armed accomplices.

Made in 1962 and released three years later, *The Pawnbroker* was produced at a time when a new set of American social values were being normalized, propelled by initiatives like the Civil Rights Movement. Situated within this complex context, the film merges the repressed trauma of the survivor with the socio-cultural tensions of American society, reflecting Lumet's intense preoccupation with the latter subject, as seen in his earlier powerful film *12 Angry Men* (1957). Notably, during the mid-1960s, pawnshops and their predominantly Jewish owners were often "viewed as the symbol of white colonization of the black inner city" and targeted during the race riots in Harlem (and as we discuss later, in 1990s Los Angeles).[11] Indeed, Alan Rosen points out that the setting of the pawnshop has repeatedly been appropriated throughout cinematic history to "emphasize allegations of Jewish greed or contest them."[12] And while, to the film's potential credit, it complicates these representations in important and unusual ways—humanizing the Jewish pawnbroker-archetype without turning him into the warm-hearted predecessor of Charlie Chaplin's *The Pawnshop* (1914)—*The Pawnbroker* has attracted a great deal of criticism on a number of issues, with scholars and other commentators debating the apparent analogy drawn between the Holocaust and Harlem, the problematic use of Christological imagery, and the reinforcement or subversion of antisemitic stereotypes. This section evaluates and contributes further to these debates.

Speaking to the potential problem of the Holocaust-as-American allegory, the intertwined narrative imagery of the Nazis' persecution of Europe's Jews and "everyday" suffering in New York have drawn the ire of a number of critics. Despite Lumet's claim that "there certainly was no attempt to show Harlem as a modern day concentration camp," many have censured *The Pawnbroker* for doing exactly this.[13] Ilan Avisar, one of the first scholars to write on Holocaust film, classifies the film as an "extreme example of Jewish self-hatred," condemning "the bogus analogy between the horrors of the Holocaust and living conditions in Spanish Harlem."[14] More recently, Lawrence Baron has reiterated this point, writing that the "conflation of American racial discrimination and Nazi extermination distorts the historical reality of each."[15] On viewing the film, there would seem to be considerable evidence to support such sentiments. Lumet's sophisticated use of montage, a metaphor for the protagonist's ongoing psychological trauma, suggests that certain events witnessed by Nazerman in his New York-urban present instantly trigger memories from his European-labor camp past: the sound of barking sparks a memory of his friend, another Jewish prisoner in the camp, being chased by German guard dogs as he attempts to escape over the fence; a fleeting shot of a gang of adolescents assaulting an African American child in the "ghetto" evokes more images of the past. And when Nazerman catches a subway train, his mind returns to his family's deportation in cattle trucks and his son's death on the journey. The metaphorical significance of the film's aligning of the present with the past—and vice versa— is seldom rendered in a subtle manner, neither for Nazerman nor his viewers.

And yet, the film's approach to hand-held camerawork positions the viewer to situate Harlem as slight evidence for the privileged gaze at Jewish trauma, staging Jewish victimhood as the prime (if practically-speaking, out of view) injustice for which American injustice is a vehicle for understanding, rather than presenting urban trauma as co-equal to the Holocaust. In this way, the brief shot of a pile of shoes in a store window, the frequently passing trains outside Nazerman's store, and the striped shadows cast on his body by the pawnshop's bars, might be interpreted as a manifestation of his (distinctively Holocaust-induced) internal conflict more so than what Zierler suggests is a one-to-one parallel between historical contexts.[16] Joshua Hirsch finds traction in this reading of the film; pointing to the distinction between the fragmented shot/reverse shots used in the flashback sequences and the classical short/reverse shot structure of the film's opening title as Nazerman observes the ghetto streets as he drives through Harlem, Hirsch contends that "the formal directness with which the film constructs an epistemology of Harlem could not be more directly opposed to the formal fragmentation with which it constructs an epistemology of the Holocaust."[17] Similarly, Leonard J. Leff stresses additional devices used to discourage—or at least destabilize—connections between the Holocaust and Harlem, among them the impact of the peaceful family scene set in Germany that opens the film; the contrast between the "hallucinatory" cinematography of the camp sequences revealed in fractions of seconds and the dense, sustained composition of New York's *mise-en-scène*; and the scoring of the past and present with classical music and Quincy Jones' jazz respectively.[18]

Similar to the purported analogy between the camps and Harlem, visual allusions in the film to Christian mythology are inarguable, if variously interpreted. Several scholars point to the youthful and aptly named Jesus Ortiz spiraling through a process of temptation and doubt (expressed through his visit to a Catholic Church just prior to robbing the pawnshop), through to his ultimate sacrifice, which redeems not only his own misguided behavior, but—according to many interpretations—Nazerman as well. In the film's final sequence, Nazerman moves from cradling Ortiz's body in a style somewhat resembling Michaelangelo's "Pietà" to slowly impaling his hand on the spike punch he uses to collect receipts, which has often been seen as evoking the stigmata. While commentators at the time of the film's release did not generally find the Christian appropriation of Jewish suffering to be problematic,[19] and even in the 1980s, Nazerman's infliction of pain on himself was uncritically described as "a complex and eloquent physical action that functions as penance,"[20] this was soon to change. For instance, a dismayed Avisar writes of Nazerman's gesture as "obviously an act of crucifixion," which literally Christianizes him through "love, grace, and suffering."[21]

On the other hand, Annette Insdorf makes a compelling counter-argument, writing that Nazerman's act of self-impalement on the spindle must be situated within a broader narrative thread developed in the film. In her reading, "Nazerman's attempt to express his pain ultimately shows his inheritance of a Nazi concept"—again predicating the film's narrative on Nazerman's relationship to the Holocaust, more than an allegory of urban malaise. Setting the "religious overtones aside," Insdorf argues that the "excruciating shot" in which Nazerman impales his hand on the pawnticket spike "conveys how Nazerman's self-inflicted wound makes concrete one of the film's central themes: [Holocaust] survivor guilt."[22]

Despite subtle gestures to opportunities for Nazerman to move past this guilt over the course of the film—in his (extremely) restrained affection for Ortiz or his potential (if unlikely) friendship with social worker Marilyn Birchfield—the alleged redemptive thrust of the narrative is blunted significantly in the film's final minutes, when Nazerman walks with his bleeding hand before him out of the pawnshop and through the crowd of bystanders gathered outside. With no offers of help from those around him, he wanders down the street and around the corner, his continuing trauma seemingly unnoticed by both the people around him and the jarring, enthusiastic trumpeting that plays on the soundtrack. Here,

Lumet distances his film from the final developments in Wallant's novel, which depicts a more sympathetic Nazerman who actually accepts Birchfield's friendship and continues his work at the pawnshop with a new assistant. Lumet's abandonment of this more uplifting conclusion supports the often-overlooked fact that the film's denouement—despite the earlier abundant and troubling use of Christological imagery—can be argued to resist a clear-cut notion of redemption. Amidst the ambiguous tone of the final frame, as Nazerman wanders traumatized through the indifferent crowd, *The Pawnbroker* may come closer than many other (particularly American) Holocaust films to fitting the "anti-redemptory aesthetic" that a number of Holocaust scholars, like Oren Baruch Stier, would call for in the decades that followed.[23]

Even with a more generous analysis of the film's Christological implications in mind, it is still frequently understood as a vehicle for antisemitic stereotypes. Nazerman's cold exploitation of his customers and generally unsympathetic nature leads Avisar to argue that the film uses "the anguish of Jewish history (...) insidiously to strengthen one of the most negative stereotypes of Jews as heartless money-makers."[24] Ortiz's temptation and "fall" has been read as a (if not unreasonable, at least partially excusable) consequence of Nazerman's refusal to take him on as a "disciple" (in another Jewish "betrayal" of the Christian martyr), and links have been made by several scholars between Nazerman's name, indifferent attitude, or exploitative behavior, and his apparent status as a perpetrator of injustice, or "Nazi man." With this and other critiques taken together, there are still unexplored avenues for critique. For instance, Avisar's denouncement of the "insult and offence in [the film's] portrayal of the Jews vis-à-vis the blacks and the Puerto Ricans" raises questions about the representation of other ethnic minorities through the subjectivity of the Jewish protagonist.[25] This includes the sexualization of Ortiz's African American lover Mabel Wheatley, a prostitute who is depicted in one of the film's most pivotal scenes through an arguably porno troped aesthetic, and the demonization of Rodriguez, the thoroughly unsympathetic boss of a crime syndicate. Terri Ginsberg points to the controversial argument put forward by some historians concerned with Jewish American filmmakers that the prevalence of violently racist imagery regarding African Americans in Hollywood cinema is the result of "a displaced allegory-effect of suppressed, often repressed, Jewish anger and indignation over historical, including North American, antisemitism."[26] It is necessary, then, to understand how representations of non-Jews in the film can speak to the social role of non-Jews in its own time, up to the present.

From "Oppressor" to "Whore": Depictions of Non-Jews in *The Pawnbroker*

In spite of what the title of Lumet's film suggests, Nazerman in an important sense only adopts the guise of a pawnbroker, and is actually the (somewhat reluctant) front man for a criminal organization led by Rodriguez—by far the film's most unsympathetic character. While the youthful, enthusiastic, and compassionate Ortiz assists in establishing Nazerman's shortcomings in personality and morality, Rodriguez is situated at the opposite extreme. Indeed, Rodriguez can be read as the "present day Nazi" within Lumet's film—in Insdorf's words, "a new incarnation of an old demon."[27] Curiously, the process of adaptation from book to film centers much of the racial anxiety of the film on African Americans. On the one hand, Ortiz was a light-skinned African American in the 1961 novel, but is Puerto Rican in the film; whereas on the other hand, the crime syndicate boss has transformed from an Italian immigrant in Wallant's text to an African American with a Spanish name in Lumet's.

The demonization of Rodriguez begins from his very first appearance early in the film when he calls Nazerman to ask how business is—although it is clear he has no interest in the answer, and only seeks to torment Nazerman with his power over him. Seated in the dining room of his extravagant home, the intimidating Rodriguez is portrayed through a low camera angle, dressed in a conspicuous white shirt and cravat, and at one point demanding that Nazerman acknowledge a joke he made was funny until the dismal survivor hangs up the phone. The power Rodriguez holds over him is nonetheless reinforced when he has one of his henchmen call Nazerman again and he is forced to answer. Later in the film, Mabel Wheatley, the lover of Ortiz who works as a prostitute, testifies to Rodriguez's reputation for brutal violence. At the instant Nazerman realizes that Wheatley and he share the same boss, a shock cut juxtaposes Nazerman in the present uttering Rodriguez's name and a brief glimpse of the younger Nazerman being spoken to by a Nazi officer in the camp, clearly implying a connection between the two perpetrators. The parallel is reinforced a number of times, as Wheatley claims Rodriguez is "the big man, the boss, about the biggest in Harlem." Further, when Nazerman subsequently confronts Rodriguez with his dismay that the pawnshop is connected with prostitution, the latter is again portrayed through low camera angles as he stands domineeringly over the trembling Nazerman with an aggressive glare. This scene is also the first time flash cuts are used with images only set in the present, suggesting that Rodriguez's threats to Nazerman have brought the trauma of his past back to him more closely than ever. Rodriguez then leaves Nazerman sitting slumped on a sofa with the comment, "Happy dreams, Uncle."

In his last appearance in the film, Rodriguez's threats become reality, as he initiates and then oversees the physical beating of Nazerman. When Nazerman still refuses to sign the papers Rodriguez requires him to, and tells his oppressor that he will have to kill him, Rodriguez refuses. Again standing over him defiantly, he calmly tells his victim in a manner that echoes much survivor testimony regarding Nazi refusals to allow Jews the "freedom" to die of their own volition: "That's what you really want Professor, isn't it? Tell you what, you'll die, but not when you want to." He then exits the store and disappears from the narrative, although his menacing threat still hangs in the air for the remainder of the film. Rosen writes that while Wallant's novel implies that oppression in American society replicates that of European colonialism, Lumet's film suggests that "the agent of oppression comes from within, not from a white European but from a black American who himself comes out of Harlem."[28] He goes on to comment on how, in a shift from "the victim's relation to his own victimization…blacks [in *The Pawnbroker*] are complicit in their own exploitation and persecution."[29]

Following from this, Rosen connects the depiction of Rodriguez with the issue of "collaboration" with one's persecutors, widely criticized at the time of the film's release by Hannah Arendt and Raul Hilberg: "The film suggests that whatever the Jews did, they did as any victim would have done—and does."[30] However, the film gives no indication that Rodriguez suffers, or has ever suffered, persecution of any kind. The evil he perpetrates seems to stem from his own vicious nature, because, as Rodriguez himself declares, "I've got a feel for things." Further, the crucial facet of this issue that Rosen does not consider is the problem of judgment that arises in such assessments of the so-called "collaboration" of the persecuted. Indeed, the passing of moral judgments on Jewish victims forced to cooperate with their Nazi captors remains an emotionally and morally fraught topic, with strong condemnation of such "complicity" being particularly common to Holocaust films.[31] The overwhelmingly negative, two-dimensional depiction of Rodriguez is no exception to this.

Another problematic representation of an African American character is that of Wheatley herself. Given that Wheatley and Ortiz's healthy sexual relations are symbolically used to contrast with the "mechanical," even "necrophilic," sexual intercourse that Nazerman has with the wife of his dead friend, combined with the fact that Wheatley is listed not by her name, but as "Ortiz's girl," in the film's credits, she can hardly be considered a rounded character.[32] In the pivotal sixth flashback sequence of the film mentioned above, Wheatley visits the pawnshop and attempts to use her body to entice Nazerman to give her a better price for her locket. When the woman takes off all her clothes in front of Nazerman, she repeatedly directs him to "look" at her nude body. But obstructing our own ability to "look," the camera cuts to more images of Nazerman's experience in Auschwitz, including a panning shot of several women forced to be camp "prostitutes" (or, more accurately, rape slaves). Juxtaposing the black woman's exposed breasts in the present day with the naked body of Nazerman's wife just prior to his witnessing a Nazi officer raping her, Lumet positions Wheatley as a conduit to Nazerman's repressed memories, ignited by her physical provocation. Nazerman orders the woman out of his store, and his enraged groan and clenched fist serve as a dramatic prelude to his climactic "silent scream."

Joshua Hirsch provides an acutely detailed discussion of this sequence, which he characterizes as "a paradigm of the posttraumatic flashback," yet relegates his brief reflection of the gendered implications of this sequence to an endnote.[33] While Aaron Kerner's analysis of this scene notes that "the female subjects [are] treated as fetish objects as well as subjugated by forcing them into sexual slavery" within the film, this must be taken a step further to acknowledge how both women are objectified through the camera's gaze.[34] The construction of Wheatley's sexuality in the scene, pivoting on the colonialist binary of simultaneous revulsion from the "savage," and desire for and fascination with the "exotic," reveals that the depiction of her behavior arguably reinforces the racialized and sexualized stereotype of the "Othered" Black woman. More problematically still, and reflecting the parallel arguably made between Rodriguez and Nazerman's Nazi tormentor, Wheatley's commands that Nazerman "Look" at her naked body are connected through his memory to the Nazi officer's demands that he watch his wife being raped ("Willst du was sehen?" ["Do you want to look at something?"]). As discussed elsewhere, the common trend of deploying female sexuality that is both intrinsically connected to fascist ideology and used to further male narratives has proven a particularly problematic cultural context for attempts to represent women in Holocaust cinema.[35]

The sultry facial expression and pleading tone with which Wheatley delivers her request for Nazerman to "look," alongside the positioning of the viewer to see her body through the eyes of Nazerman, can further be argued to engage in what has been termed "pornotroping"—a process of representation derived from slavery that transforms a human being into objectified flesh and renders them subject to the (un)pleasure of the viewer.[36] Spillers writes that pornotroping occurs where the African

American body becomes "a territory of cultural and political maneuver," an object of "captured sexualities" embodying both "otherness" and "sheer physical powerlessness that slides into a more general 'powerlessness.'"[37] When pornotroping reduces a body to a sexualized object that embodies nothing but the absence of all power, the process of eroticization overwhelms that which is purportedly being critiqued. In the case of Wheatley's desperate struggle to make ends meet in the present, the fetishistic display of her body while she appeals to Nazerman's "sexual instincts" undermines the film's apparent critique of the social forces that drive a woman to such lengths in search of extra money. Also of significance is that Nazerman is very uncomfortable with Wheatley's presence and tries hard not to look, thus arguably rendering the camera's (and viewer's) gaze more implicitly titillating.

Another often overlooked facet of *The Pawnbroker* is the pedagogical discourse constructed through the relationship between Nazerman and Ortiz—the most central non-Jewish figure in the film, and certainly a more complex figure than the demonized Rodriguez and sexualized Wheatley. Ortiz explicitly positions himself as the "student" of the reluctant Nazerman throughout the narrative; however, the educational process and outcome revealed in this relationship is considerably different from that depicted in *Freedom Writers*, which we will return to. In fact, *The Pawnbroker* can be seen to suggest that finding salutary meaning from the Holocaust is a flawed enterprise. The distance between Nazerman's experiences and the lives of all those around him is particularly evident when Ortiz asks him whether his identification tattoo from Auschwitz signifies a "secret society or something?" Further, none of the film's flashback sequences—roundly criticized by many for purportedly constructing an analogy between the Holocaust and Harlem—are ever recounted by Nazerman to any other character. Presumably, his Jewish sister (also a survivor) knows, but all others, it seems, including Ortiz, cannot know nor understand.

The issue of pedagogy in *The Pawnbroker* was recently taken up by Rosen, who focuses on three scenes in Lumet's film that depict the protagonist "teaching" his would-be protégé different "lessons" that might provide "the assistant with skills that will help him 'get legit'—to give up a life of crime in order to acquire economic, social, and cultural legitimacy—and also school him in a broader circle of cultural awareness."[38] Consisting of monologues and conversational exchanges of various lengths, these "lessons" constitute a form of transaction markedly different from the exploitative pawnbroker-customer relationships (and the extreme power discrepancy between Nazerman and Rodriguez) that pervade the rest of the film. Crucially, however, these "lessons," if they can rightly be characterized as such, are unsuccessful. Driven to despair and following the "wrong lesson" (Nazerman's declaration that "money is the whole thing"), Ortiz resorts to participating in the robbery of the pawnshop and becomes the plan's ultimate victim. To add yet one more to a long list of interpretations of Nazerman's well known "silent scream" as he clutches Ortiz's body, this outcry might well be read as amplifying Ortiz's spoiled attempt to liberate himself from his surroundings; thus mourning the unfulfilled promise Ortiz makes to his mother at the start of the film, "I am going a long way." The suffering of the Holocaust survivor who cannot be liberated from his past thus becomes a metaphor for the poor Latino New Yorker who cannot be liberated from his slum. Further, the scene depicting Ortiz's drawn-out death in the street and the long wait for the ambulance to collect his body—filmed mostly using long shots—reveal him to be still very much encased in the community he so desperately wished to leave. In a sense, Nazerman's inability to escape the memories of his past reflects Ortiz's inability to escape the barriers of race and class he encounters in the present. Even if one accepts the view that Ortiz functions as a plot device to introduce the film's Christological themes, or that at least some tentative hope for Nazerman's future is gestured to, it is clear that no easy salvation exists for Ortiz or any of the other victims of race and class oppression in Harlem. A radically different conceptualization of pedagogy, memory, redemption and the role of the survivor can be found in Richard LaGravenese's 2007 film *Freedom Writers.*

Nazerman's Harlem or Today's Long Beach? Conversion and Redemption in *Freedom Writers*

Freedom Writers is based on the experiences of a class of English students and their teacher at Woodrow Wilson High School in Long Beach, California. Once a high-achieving public school, its quality and safety have been dramatically compromised by an early 1990s state-mandated racial integration program. Into this chaotic and violent atmosphere enters the white, wide-eyed, well-intentioned main character, Erin Gruwell, whose formal dress style and trademark pearls reveal that she comes from a somewhat privileged background. The brand new English teacher is given, in the language of the film, the "unteachables" and "at-risk" students, who are not trusted by the school's administration to learn with "real books." *Freedom Writers* enters the tradition of Richard Brooks's *Blackboard Jungle* (1955) and John N. Smith's *Dangerous*

Minds (1995), by focusing on "an optimistic White novice teacher's struggle to inspire urban high school students. Her delinquent, remedial students become dependent on their teacher, who instils in them a sense of self-respect and motivation to learn."[39] Following this well-trodden formula, all of Gruwell's students, save one, are non-white and before they become "dependent," they approach their new teacher with a skepticism and contempt reserved for racially privileged outsiders. While the intertextual links to similar films are important in reinforcing a generic trend of whites redeeming non-white(s), *Freedom Writers* differs significantly in its appropriation of the Holocaust to this end.

Stylistically, LaGravenese's decision to open the film with scenes of the 1992 Los Angeles race riots recalls Lumet's invocation of urban suffering when he sets the tone of *The Pawnbroker*'s narrative with images of Harlem's poverty-stricken streets. Alongside archival footage of the L.A. riots, the opening sequence of *Freedom Writers* utilizes documentary-style, on-screen text to preface the narrative with the authoritative statement that "gang violence and racial tension reach an all time high." However, while Lumet seamlessly uses shots of his New York setting to move the narrative forward, LaGravenese relegates his urban landscape images to the beginning of his film, making it the scene onto which his narrative of redemption gets mapped. From the opening scene, then, *Freedom Writers* reflects an acute interest in building a narrative of redemption, one for which Lumet arguably does not share an interest (despite some narrow critical accounts of his film).

Further, in contrast to Ortiz's fervent attempts to alter his socio-economic situation in *The Pawnbroker*, the students of *Freedom Writers* seem possessed by a fatalistic acceptance of their deprived status. Indeed, the film offers a very negative depiction of their attitude towards society and their place within it in a number of ways, configuring their suffering as a self-fulfilling prophecy of the continued perseverance of each group in persecuting all others, while (for the most part) marginalizing the role of those with actual social, economic and political power for the desperate situation ethnic minorities face. Early in the film, the African American, Latino, and Asian students offer graphic depictions of their lives as a constant "war" of survival. The school is starkly characterized as the sum of several distinct communities, including "little Cambodia," "the ghetto," and "South of the border"—communities that seem to be inherently violent. Home lives are similarly defined by affiliation and hostility, encapsulated in sentiments like, "My people are a gang," "We fight for territory," and "It comes down to what you look like." Thus defined, the students' race- and class-infused suffering sets the terms of their relationship with Gruwell; it is exactly the nature of this suffering, then, that is impacted by their Holocaust education.

The students' encounter with the Holocaust is precipitated by Gruwell's distress at the in-class exchange of a racist image, which she discovers when one day's lesson is interrupted by the laughter of several students. She is disturbed to find Jamal, an African American student, upset by the picture of a face with exaggerated lips. In response, Gruwell offers an especially angry monologue in response to the image, drawing a parallel between the hand-drawn image and racial stereotypes perpetuated in the propaganda of the Nazi party, which she terms "the most famous gang in history." Gruwell challenges the class's belief that they "know all about gangs." In fact, she explains that "you're amateurs. [The Nazi] gang will put you all to shame." And should the students fail to see the relationship between themselves and the discontented German populace of the 1930s, she explains how like her class, the Nazis "started out poor and angry and everybody looked down on them." This turns into a cautionary tale when Gruwell explains the historical consequences of this subversion of personal responsibility and prejudice: the Nazis "just wiped out everybody else. Yeah, they wiped out everybody they didn't like and everybody they blamed for their life being hard."

Expanding further on the influence of Nazi racial propaganda, Gruwell ends her emotive speech with the statement: "That's how a holocaust happens. And that's what you all think of each other." Not entirely unlike the parallel made between Rodriguez and a Nazi officer in *The Pawnbroker*, Gruwell links a manifestation of racial prejudice in the classroom to the Holocaust in a very problematic manner, as the connection hinges on Gruwell's suggestion that the students are behaving like Nazis, a notion reinforced by most students' initially gleeful responses to the notion of wiping out other groups. The metaphor rests on her account of the Nazis as people reacting to being "poor and angry," an oversimplification that is the film's first gesture at de-historicizing the decidedly different nature of poverty and anger that has led to conditions in Long Beach. Not only does Gruwell's "lesson," as Tara Yosso and David García point out, "falsely equat[e] the [Nazi] regime's violence and an ideology of White supremacy with her students' racial prejudices," it also occurs at the expense of the humiliation of one African American student, Jamal, who had unsuccessfully pleaded with Gruwell to "just let it go."[40]

Discovering that the vast majority of her class have no prior knowledge of the Holocaust, Gruwell becomes committed to the idea that Holocaust history has the power to wholly convert each student into something different and better. Sacrificing everything, including her marriage, Gruwell takes on two extra part-time jobs to purchase student copies of *The Diary of Anne Frank* and fund a field trip to the Museum of Tolerance, followed by a lavish dinner in the company of several Holocaust-survivor guests (who are played by actual survivors). It is precisely at this moment in the film that the students begin to transcend their communities and negative attitudes as a result of this encounter with the Holocaust. Gruwell therefore takes on the role of savior alongside the often universalized figure of Anne Frank and, in a later and even more transformative plot development, the appearance of Miep Gies, the Gentile woman who sheltered the Frank family from the Nazis.

The appropriation of the Anne Frank story is highly significant given its central place in the collective memory of the Holocaust and the "Americanization" of the event. The subject has attracted a substantial critical literature, with scholars analyzing countless adaptations of the diary for the page, stage, and screen. George Steven's Hollywood film *The Diary of Anne Frank* (1959), which concludes with Frank's now well-known optimistic affirmation, "In spite of everything, I still believe that people are really good at heart," is a prime example. Doneson finds the film's optimistic tone immensely troubling,

> The film makers opt to strive for a feeling of audience identification with the Jewish victims for the purpose of creating a universal antipathy toward all persecution. The Jews and the Holocaust, in other words, can be the symbol for the suffering of mankind [*sic*] (...) The universal Christian tenet 'love thy neighbour' forms the basis of the relationship between the Christian and the Jew; it assumes that the majority Christian will act in good conscience on behalf of the minority Jew when the latter is in trouble. At the same time, it is this dependency on the gentile that unavoidably makes of the Jew a passive, weak individual.[41]

Indeed, in addition to its redemptive, triumphalist rhetoric, *The Diary of Anne Frank* goes to some lengths to avoid the Jewish specificity of Frank's experiences altogether. By constructing dubious parallels between elements of the Anne Frank narrative and the various characters in *Freedom Writers*, LaGravenese arguably exacerbates these problems of universalizing meaning, viewer identification, and Christological agendas.

Although Gruwell defines her lessons using "the Holocaust," they are curiously absent of any exploration of the lived experience of the Nazi state, ghettos or concentration camps that are so often framed as the apotheosis of racial hatred. As much as Lumet is invested in layering New York with the concentration camps, LaGravenese is invested in erasing the camps altogether. With the exception of the very brief gesture to survivor anecdotes during the post-museum dinner, the students' Holocaust education is defined in terms of redemption. Crucially, following the brief appearances of these real-life survivors, the pathos of the film implies to the viewer that the Miep Gies on-screen is the historical figure herself, rather than the actor Pat Caroll. When one African American student tells Gies that she is the first person he knows who he can label a "hero," Gies refuses the compliment and instead states that it is Gruwell's students who are the "heroes." Thus, the class transforms from the perpetrators identified by their teacher to heroic rescuers of themselves—even though Gruwell's overwhelming role in their redemption hardly bares this out. In any case, this equation of "rescuers" leaves no room for a sustained acknowledgement of victims of oppression. This, in combination with the reliance on Anne Frank's diary, within which the Holocaust is present only in its oppressive invisibility, and the virtually muted nature of survivor testimony within the film, has the effect of rendering the story of the students' journey as reliant on a heavily sanitized Holocaust to dissolve racial barriers.

A notable difference between the film and its source text, *The Freedom Writers Diary*, is Gruwell's real-life decision to follow up *Anne Frank* with *Zlata's Diary: A Child's Life in Sarajevo,* a diary by a young woman and contemporary genocide survivor, as well as other Holocaust-free lessons. Although the time constraints of cinema may explain the absence of these teaching materials, the production decision to focus so entirely on the Holocaust is just as likely a symptom of the avoidance of histories less familiar to American audiences, which are otherwise so attuned to the urban high school tropes and Holocaust redemption that characterize the film. Further, just as the gentile Geis is the immediate embodiment of Holocaust history, it is interesting to note that the embodiment of the negligible reference to non-Holocaust, racialized history is yet another savior, Jim Zwerg—a white man who participated in the Civil Rights Movement, and who is identified and idolized by Ben, Gruwell's only white student.

The students' encounter with the Holocaust provides them with both solace and some apparently much-needed moral fiber. While they start out in the 1990s L.A. equivalent of Lumet's New York, their struggle to reconcile with poverty and violence does not require Ortiz's version of socio-economic ambition to leave his poor and violent community, or to challenge or alter the power structures that reinforce it. Instead, Holocaust history enables the students to remain in their unsatisfactory socio-economic conditions, yet with an apparently much less troubled attitude towards these conditions. As opposed to Ortiz's tragedy, the students in *Freedom Writers* are freed by the way in which Holocaust history has taught them to abandon racial stereotypes and build mutual, interracial trust. This relationship-building in turn serves as a platform on which the students build intellectual self-esteem because, the film suggests, if they understand nothing else, and nothing else changes, at least they can grasp the racial disenfranchisement that defined Nazi Germany. Without exception, each student undergoes a different form of positive transformation, including several characters deciding to discard a handgun, avoid becoming a teenage mother, stop being involved in crime or, in the case of Eva, the main student figure, tell the truth in court about a murder she witnessed her boyfriend commit.

(Pawn)Brokering American Trauma: The Holocaust Narratives of Yesterday and the Economic Injustices of Tomorrow

In his study entitled *Facing Black and Jew: Literature as Public Space in Twentieth-Century America*, Adam Newton explores the potentialities for African American and Jewish literary narratives of persecution and suffering to comingle, arguing that while simplistic, misleading, or exploitative comparisons need to be avoided, "something *has* conjoined [both groups] in public space, and at the very least, they are entangled in American history and culture, complexly thrown up against one another. How such conjunction and entanglement will be imagined or enacted, of course, is the freighted question—the shape, that is, of 'relations.'"[42] While *The Pawnbroker* has been roundly criticized on many points—and indeed we have expanded on some of its ideologically problematic elements—few commentators have considered at length the way that the film is a significant and substantive—rather than merely a critically problematic—intervention in American discourses of race and class. Neither the naive ambitions of the gentile social worker Marilyn Birchfield, who attempts to comfort and understand Nazerman and can be seen as an earlier incarnation of Gruwell, nor the desperate attempts of Ortiz to gain socio-economic and cultural legitimacy are realized. On the other hand, the appropriation of the Holocaust in *Freedom Writers* leads to a sentimental group cohesion that liberates them from socio-economic suffering, exhibiting a clear-cut and problematic mode of redemption while making the unprecedented horror of history palatable. The ideological differences between the films rest in part in LaGravenese's commitment to tell the story of the "Freedom Writers" in a way that domesticates the Holocaust so thoroughly that the film practically eliminates the need for Jews entirely.

Freedom Writers veers away from the often ambiguous tone of *The Pawnbroker* to embrace an optimistic outcome for the disenfranchised victims of urban America, allowing the Holocaust to erase racial boundaries and differences. In turn, the former film elides economic suffering by showing a group of students for whom inter-ethnic trust obfuscates impoverished and violent surroundings. Whereas Lumet's film underscores the economic injustice that defined the experience of Ortiz and his own thwarted ambitions, *Freedom Writers* makes economic injustice acceptable by appealing to urban youth's familiarity with the notion of racial injustice. In this way, the Holocaust becomes a pillar of the narratives of racial inequality that detract from and thus enable the perpetuation of economic inequality—revealing a different limitation of an overly hopeful desire to find and apply "universal" meaning in and from the Holocaust. After all, when the students return for their sophomore year and a previously silent Latino student explains how his family has become homeless, he makes it clear that Gruwell's uniquely racially safe space is the most encouraging thing in his life. It is his "home." The viewer leaves this anecdote, as they will likely leave the film, with the sentimental impression that the extension of the lessons learned from the Holocaust somehow make going hungry and sleeping in a car more tolerable. As noted earlier, the films examined in this chapter reveal memory to be what Rothberg calls multidirectional. Subject to constant re-negotiation, traumatic pasts can be situated alongside one another, though comparisons and contrasts need to be made with due care and sensitivity. The complexity of Lumet's film reveals both the problematic and productive possibilities involved in this process, while an update like *Freedom Writers* serves as a reminder of the limitations of analogies when they are used to serve a clear-cut redemptive agenda.

Bibliography

Avisar, Ilan. *Screening the Holocaust: Cinema's Images of the Unimaginable*. Bloomington: Indiana University Press, 1988.

Baron, Lawrence. *Projecting the Holocaust into the Present: The Changing Focus of Contemporary Holocaust Cinema*. Lanham, MD: Rowman and Littlefield, 2005.

Brown, Adam. *Judging "Privileged" Jews: Holocaust Ethics, Representation, and the "Grey Zone."* New York: Berghahn Books, 2013.

—. "Screening Women's Complicity in the Holocaust: The Problems of Judgement and Representation." *Holocaust Studies: A Journal of Culture and History* 17.2-3 (2012): 95-127.

Brown, Adam, and Deb Waterhouse-Watson. "Representing Rape in Holocaust Film: Exhibiting the Eroticised Body for the Camera's Gaze." *Aftermath: The Politics of Memory.* Melbourne: Monash University Press, 2013. In press.

Chaney, Michael A. *Fugitive Vision: Slave Image and Black Identity in Antebellum Narrative.* Bloomington: Indiana University Press, 2008.

Doneson, Judith E. *The Holocaust in American Film*, 2nd ed. Syracuse: Syracuse University Press, 2002.

Finkelstein, Norman G. *The Holocaust Industry: Reflections on the Exploitation of Jewish Suffering,* 2nd ed. London: Verso, 2000.

Freedom Writers. Directed by Richard LaGravenese. Los Angeles: Paramount Pictures, 2007.

Friedman, Lester D. *Hollywood's Image of the Jew.* New York: Frederick Ungar, 1982.

Ginsberg, Terri. *Holocaust Film: The Political Aesthetics of Ideology.* Newcastle: Cambridge Scholars Press, 2007.

Gruwell, Erin, and Freedom Writers. *The Freedom Writers Diary: How a Teacher and 150 Teens Used Writing to Change Themselves and the World Around Them.* New York: Broadway Books, 1999.

Hirsch, Joshua. *Afterimage: Film, Trauma, and the Holocaust.* Philadelphia: Temple University Press, 2004.

Insdorf, Annette. *Indelible Shadows: Film and the Holocaust*, 3rd ed. Cambridge: Cambridge University Press, 2003.

Kerner, Aaron. *Film and the Holocaust: New Perspectives on Dramas, Documentaries, and Experimental Films.* New York: Continuum Books, 2011.

Leff, Leonard J. "Hollywood and the Holocaust: Remembering *The Pawnbroker.*" *American Jewish History* 84.4 (1996): 353-76.

Mintz, Alan. *Popular Culture and the Shaping of Holocaust Memory in America.* Seattle: University of Washington Press, 2001.

Newton, Adam Zachary. *Facing Black and Jew: Literature as Public Space in Twentieth-Century America.* Cambridge: Cambridge University Press, 1999.

Novick, Peter. *The Holocaust in American Life.* Boston: Houghton Mifflin, 1999.

Rosen, Alan. "'Teach Me Gold': Pedagogy and Memory in *The Pawnbroker.*" In *The Modern Jewish Experience in World Cinema,* edited by Lawrence Baron, 208-20. Waltham, MA: Brandeis University Press, 2011.

Rosenfeld, Alvin H. *The End of the Holocaust*. Bloomington: Indiana University Press, 2011.

Rothberg, Michael. *Multidirectional Memory: Remembering the Holocaust in the Age of Decolonization*. Stanford: Stanford University Press, 2009.

Spillers, Hortense. "Mama's Baby, Papa's Maybe: An American Grammar Book." *Diacritics* 17.2 (1987): 64-81.

Stier, Oren Baruch. *Committed to Memory: Cultural Mediations of the Holocaust*. Amherst: University of Massachusetts Press, 2003.

The Pawnbroker. Directed by Sidney Lumet. 1964. Los Angeles: Republic Pictures Home Video, 2003. DVD.

Thomas, Laurence Mordekhai. "Suffering as a Moral Beacon: Blacks and Jews." In *The Americanization of the Holocaust*, edited by Hilene Flanzbaum, 198-210. Baltimore: Johns Hopkins University Press, 1999.

Wallant, Edward Lewis. *The Pawnbroker*. 1961. San Diego: Harcourt Brace, 1989.

Weheliye, Alexander G. "Pornotropes." *Journal of Visual Culture* 7.1 (2008): 65-81.

Yosso, Tara J., and David G. Garcia. "'Cause It's Not Just Me': *Walkout*'s History Lessons Challenge Hollywood's Urban School Formula." *Radical History Review* 102 (2008): 171-84.

Zierler, Wendy. "'My Holocaust Is Not Your Holocaust': 'Facing' Black and Jewish Experience in *The Pawnbroker, Higher Ground*, and *The Nature of Blood*." *Holocaust and Genocide Studies* 18.1 (2004): 46-67.

Notes

[1] Wendy Zierler, "'My Holocaust Is Not Your Holocaust': 'Facing' Black and Jewish Experience in *The Pawnbroker, Higher Ground,* and *The Nature of Blood,*" *Holocaust and Genocide Studies* 18.1 (2004): 49.

[2] Lawrence Mordekhai Thomas, "Suffering as a Moral Beacon: Blacks and Jews," in *The Americanization of the Holocaust,* ed. Hilene Flanzbaum (Baltimore: Johns Hopkins University Press, 1999), 198, 207.

[3] Norman G. Finkelstein, *The Holocaust Industry: Reflections on the Exploitation of Jewish Suffering,* 2nd ed. (London: Verso, 2000).

[4] Annette Insdorf, *Indelible Shadows: Film and the Holocaust,* 3rd ed. (Cambridge: Cambridge University Press, 2003), 247.

[5] Alvin H. Rosenfeld, *The End of the Holocaust* (Bloomington: Indiana University Press, 2011), 63.
[6] Peter Novick, *The Holocaust in American Life* (Boston: Houghton Mifflin, 1999), 7.
[7] Novick, *The Holocaust in American Life*, 9.
[8] Alan Mintz, *Popular Culture and the Shaping of Holocaust Memory in America* (Seattle: University of Washington Press, 2001), 38-39.
[9] Michael Rothberg, *Multidirectional Memory: Remembering the Holocaust in the Age of Decolonization* (Stanford: Stanford University Press, 2009), 2.
[10] Rothberg, *Multidirectional Memory,* 3.
[11] Mintz, *Popular Culture and the Shaping of Holocaust Memory in America,* 211.
[12] Alan Rosen, "'Teach Me Gold': Pedagogy and Memory in *The Pawnbroker,*" in *The Modern Jewish Experience in World Cinema,* ed. Lawrence Baron (Waltham, MA: Brandeis University Press, 2011), 208.
[13] Quoted in Mintz, *Popular Culture and the Shaping of Holocaust Memory in America,* 124.
[14] Ilan Avisar, *Screening the Holocaust: Cinema's Images of the Unimaginable* (Bloomington: Indiana University Press, 1988), 122, 124.
[15] Lawrence Baron, *Projecting the Holocaust into the Present: The Changing Focus of Contemporary Holocaust Cinema* (Lanham, MD: Rowman and Littlefield, 2005), 42.
[16] Zierler, "'My Holocaust Is Not Your Holocaust,'" 51.
[17] Joshua Hirsch, *Afterimage: Film, Trauma, and the Holocaust* (Philadelphia: Temple University Press, 2004), 182 n.55.
[18] Leonard J. Leff, "Hollywood and the Holocaust: Remembering *The Pawnbroker,*" *American Jewish History* 84.4 (1996): 375.
[19] Mintz, *Popular Culture and the Shaping of Holocaust Memory in America,* 124-25.
[20] Lester D. Friedman, *Hollywood's Image of the Jew* (New York: Frederick Ungar, 1982), 185.
[21] Avisar, *Screening the Holocaust,* 125.
[22] Insdorf, *Indelible Shadows,* 31.
[23] Oren Baruch Stier, *Committed to Memory: Cultural Mediations of the Holocaust* (Amherst: University of Massachusetts Press, 2003), 17.
[24] Avisar, *Screening the Holocaust,* 124.
[25] Avisar, *Screening the Holocaust,* 124.
[26] Terri Ginsberg, *Holocaust Film: The Political Aesthetics of Ideology* (Newcastle: Cambridge Scholars Press, 2007), 59 n.143.
[27] Insdorf, *Indelible Shadows,* 30.
[28] Rosen, "'Teach Me Gold,'" 214-15.
[29] Rosen, "'Teach Me Gold,'" 214-15.
[30] Rosen, "'Teach Me Gold,'" 215.
[31] See Adam Brown, *Judging "Privileged" Jews: Holocaust Ethics, Representation, and the "Grey Zone"* (New York: Berghahn Books, 2013).
[32] Avisar, *Screening the Holocaust,* 123.

[33] Hirsch, *Afterimage,* 85-86, 105.
[34] Aaron Kerner, *Film and the Holocaust: New Perspectives on Dramas, Documentaries, and Experimental Films* (New York: Continuum Books, 2011), 40.
[35] Adam Brown, "Screening Women's Complicity in the Holocaust: The Problems of Judgement and Representation," *Holocaust Studies: A Journal of Culture and History* 17.2-3 (2012): 95-127; Adam Brown and Deb Waterhouse-Watson, "Representing Rape in Holocaust Film: Exhibiting the Eroticised Body for the Camera's Gaze," in *Aftermath: The Politics of Memory* (Melbourne: Monash University Press, 2013), in press.
[36] Michael A. Chaney, *Fugitive Vision: Slave Image and Black Identity in Antebellum Narrative* (Bloomington: Indiana University Press, 2008), 63; Alexander G. Weheliye, "Pornotropes," *Journal of Visual Culture* 7.1 (2008): 71.
[37] Hortense Spillers, "Mama's Baby, Papa's Maybe: An American Grammar Book," *Diacritics* 17.2 (1987): 67.
[38] Rosen, "'Teach Me Gold,'" 208.
[39] Tara J. Yosso and David G. Garcia, "'Cause It's Not Just Me': *Walkout*'s History Lessons Challenge Hollywood's Urban School Formula," *Radical History Review* 102 (2008): 174.
[40] Yosso and Garcia, "'Cause It's Not Just Me': *Walkout*'s History Lessons Challenge Hollywood's Urban School Formula," 177.
[41] Doneson, *The Holocaust in American Film*, 76-77.
[42] Adam Zachary Newton, *Facing Black and Jew: Literature as Public Space in Twentieth-Century America* (Cambridge: Cambridge University Press, 1999), 4.

NEGOTIATING TRAUMAS VIA CROSS-CULTURAL URBAN IDENTITY CONFIGURATIONS OUT OF GRIEF: ALEKSANDAR HEMON'S *THE LAZARUS PROJECT*

DANA MIHĂILESCU

People from the Balkan region share a troubled existence characterized by what Michelle Levy has called "a present haunted by an undead past," by the recent violent events which escalated in Kosovo throughout the 1990s and have understandably become the focus of much of the region's art.[1] Among the authors from the region who engage fiction and history in the attempt to transcend essentializing myths, one counts the name of Aleksandar Hemon, a contemporary Sarajevo-born Bosnian American author who came to the US in 1992, at the age of 27, not intending to emigrate but finally staying,[2] and using his personal experience of "suffering through most of the nineties' conflicts long-distance" as inspiration for writing fiction.[3]

Hemon's 2008 *Lazarus Project. A Novel* sets out to record Bosnian American narrator/writer Vladimir Brik's trip back to Eastern Europe at the side of his travelling companion, photographer Rora Halilbasic, in view of retracing a young Jewish immigrant's flight from Kishinev to Chicago in the early 1900s, and writing a book about that man, whose name was Lazarus Averbuch. Hemon's novel mainly considers the struggles traumatized immigrants to the US have had to encounter throughout time, the difficulty of dealing with displacement but also what all can gain from the perspective of displaced individuals. I argue that cross-cultural configurations that come to define immigrants to the US throughout time in Hemon's narrative suggest how an Eastern European immigrant's lens offers the possibility of solving the conundrum of responsibility beyond the past vs. present, death vs. life divide, via an alternative agent stance. I examine the book as a work underscoring the difficulty of dealing with urban norms of historical/structural traumas and practices of mourning but also suggesting the gain accompanying the perspective of displaced individuals—the possibility to shift reductive frames of reference and open spaces of negotiation in view of a better future.

The Lazarus Project comprises twenty-two unnumbered chapters in all, each one introduced by a different black-and-white picture against a black background, and there is a permanent balance between photo-type and story-line throughout. The would-be odd-numbered chapters, starting with the initial ones, are dedicated to the past events from 1908 Chicago, when Jewish immigrant Lazarus Averbuch was killed in the house of policeman George Shippy, and later associated with allegations of immigrant Jews' anarchist state in early 20th century America. The overture for all these odd-numbered chapters *in absentia* is represented by pictures from the Chicago Historical Society at the turn of the century. The would-be even-numbered chapters refer to the present-day story of the first person narrator, Bosnian-born Brik, living in Chicago ever since 1992 and writing a column about newly arrived immigrants for *The Reader*, finally deciding to go to Eastern European cities at the side of his countryman and photographer, Rora, in order to do research for the story he wants to write, "about a Jewish immigrant shot by the Chicago police a hundred years ago."[4] This time, the overture of the corresponding chapters is represented by photos of everyday life actually taken by Velibor Božović. Importantly, the chapters about the 1908 events revolve around a flowing type of narrative whereas the present-day chapters widely contain meta-narrative comments about the other project, blurring any attempt at establishing definite lines between past and present. Thus, the novel features two Eastern European immigrants to the US at different moments in time who, as pertinently indicated by Lisa Monarelli, are refugees from historic traumas—Brik and Rora running from the 1992 Sarajevo siege and Lazarus, his sister Olga and friend Isador Maron, from the 1903 Kishinev pogrom.[5]

This cross-temporal dimension of Hemon's novel sustains what Michael Rothberg has called the *multidirectional* character of memory. This is based on the idea that "remembrance both cuts across and binds together diverse spatial, temporal, and cultural sites," hence our recollections are fundamentally the result of a dynamic interaction of different historical and intercultural memories.[6] More precisely, in favoring the encounter of multiple urban sites of grievance, people can keep themselves at bay from the dangers of the uniqueness discourse, likely to create a hierarchy of suffering. As Rothberg has suggested, moving between layers of history allows "an engagement with the fundamental situations that produce violence. By probing the uncomfortable overlap and complicities that mark histories of genocide and colonialism, they leave the possibility of building new places of concord."[7] To remain true to such ethical aspirations of trauma and memory studies, Stef Craps joins Rothberg and relevantly notes that "traumas of non-Western or minority populations need to be acknowledged for their own sake."[8] In keeping with the two scholars' claims, given its construction as such a site of encounter between several layers of history and sites of grievance, Hemon's novel opens the debate over the connections one can establish between the past and present situation of Eastern European immigrants in America and suggests a non-violent agent ethical responsibility available via cross-cultural urban configurations of identity out of grief, as I will show in what follows.

The Story of Lazarus Averbuch—Chicago 1908

Before proceeding with an analysis of the immigrant situation in the US as rendered in Hemon's book, I will first present the main coordinates of Lazarus Averbuch's story as it enweaves itself through images and text from the eleven sections dedicated to the event in Hemon's novel. I believe this presentation is necessary for understanding how immigrants at the time had to confront the urban discourse of American condescending exceptionalism.

Lazarus's story—contained in the eleven pictures included in the novel—begins with the façade view of the place where he is to die, Shippy's residence, followed by an interior view of probably the same house, making up the same image of a high-class location on page 24. Indeed, the commentary around these pictures concentrates on the rich neighborhood making Lincoln Place "a different world," since "these houses are like castles, the windows tall and wide; there are no peddlers on the streets; indeed, there is nobody on the street."[9] This will come in contrast to Lazarus's usual environs, the Sunday Market Place from Chicago's immigrant ghetto, as rendered in a photo on page 166. In this case the opposite image of dense human presence without enough air to breathe alongside need and want reigns supreme. Again, a commentary seems to depict the photo's content in words, and we read, "Where did they all come from? The city has become smaller; the sidewalks are dense with bodies squeezing between pushcarts and horse carriages, milling meaninglessly, in no hurry to get anywhere."[10]

These two pictures alone set Lazarus's story within a clearly delimited background made up of actually two Chicagos, following the criterion of class and ethnic background. The leading native, upper, elite class is characterized by security, richness, privacy. The lower immigrant class neighborhood is a place of a swarming humanity, suspect hygiene, and cutthroat struggle for life. Within this clearly divided structure of American urban society, Lazarus, the Jewish survivor of the 1903 Kishinev pogrom who immigrated to the US seven months before, dares to cross the threshold of Shippy's residence, with the result visually rendered in the photos on page 52 and page 240. The former picture depicts Lazarus sitting on a chair while Captain Evans is behind him, hands on Lazarus's head, arranging it for the photo, Lazarus's body slightly slanted to the left. While the captain gazes at the camera, Lazarus's eyes are half-closed, suggesting a dead person. Signs of undernourishment are imprinted on his skinny face, and also follow from his rather large jacket. In the latter photo, Lazarus's profile is highlighted; this time, a blurry-faced policeman keeps his head straight while Lazarus's trousers are not totally covering his legs, he has no shoes and his partly holed socks show. All these signs are proof that Lazarus had just been undressed, and we could previously read how the police investigators wanted to make sure whether he is an Italian or Jewish immigrant, by looking for "circumcision signs."[11] In other words, the early 20th century Eastern European immigrant to the US appears as a totally helpless being under the complete control of official policemen.

In addition, in the section corresponding to the photo from page 52, Olga's meeting her brother can be read in a descriptive comment on the margin of that picture, representing the view of the photo from the sister's perspective. After the policemen come to her house and ask about her brother's beliefs and whereabouts, she is taken to the station without being told anything. The following troubling scene is what shortly ensues,

> Men are gathered around the chair where Lazarus sits, and she is relieved to see he is alive. She sighs and grips Fitzpatrick's forearm. But one of the men is holding Lazarus's head; her brother's eyes are closed, his face ashen; her heart stops, frozen. Fitzgerald urges her on; Fitzpatrick says, as if delivering a punch line: 'Happy to see him? Give him a kiss...' The crowd titters, transfixed by Olga stepping toward Lazarus, as if she were mounted on cothurni; a short, reluctant step back, then two awkward steps forward to touch his lifeless cheek, whereupon she collapses, unconscious. The crowd gasps.[12]

Thanks to the accompanying theatrical depiction here, the customary police photos help to show that official objectivity was at best doubtful in early 20th century US. In this sense, one cannot ignore the policemen's condescending, humiliating, and dehumanizing treatment of Olga who is never told the truth beforehand but is brutally confronted with the sight of her dead brother. In addition, there is Fitzpatrick's idiotic sarcasm revealing total lack of human sympathy for a person who has just seen her sibling dead. All these details already make the police investigation questionable. This is made possible by the medium of photographs with their awareness of a temporal gap, as perhaps best theorized by Roland Barthes. A wonderful opportunity gets born out of such temporal gaps within the photo, as pointed out by Annette Kuhn and Kirstin Emiko McAllister. They raise our "anxieties about change and loss" and hence "undermine any certainty about what it is possible to know"[13] since a photo is the locus of at least two perspectives—that of the photographer and that of the viewer. In Hemon's novel, thanks to the traumatized perspective of immigrant Olga who had come to the States a few months prior to Lazarus, we can see how photos are the site of acknowledged partiality and instability, a recognition which, following Kuhn and McAllister, requires of people an *ethics of engagement*. Indeed I concur that the coupling of unsettling photos and words in Hemon's book disrupts the possibility of asserting the policemen's truth as the only one and suggests instead the need to give up assimilationist violent paths and take up humanistic cross-cultural ethical engagements.

In fact, henceforth, the questionable character of the police investigation into Lazarus's death is multiplied in Hemon's book. This is for instance related to policemen's incessant beating of Olga's neighbor Isaac Lubel on first arriving at her residence to make him speak about Lazarus's alleged anarchist connections and Isador's whereabouts. Moreover, the police ransack the Lubel abode (as visually suggested by a photo on page 216); they also beat Isaac, who will soon die. His innocent death becomes an important element for criticizing unfair police practices in early 20th century US, based on a prejudiced association of immigrants to anarchism despite lack of proof, and on their use of force outside any right.

Throughout the narrative, the credibility of the Chicago police is totally dismantled given at least three of its unfair practices: its violent abuse of innocent citizens, its dehumanizing, humiliating practices in relation to surviving family members, and its discriminatory counterfactual evidence. As a result, a large part of Lazarus's story is a biased, unfair account promoted by officials out of a generalized sense of suspicion and fear vis-à-vis Eastern European anarchism, but actually largely employing the same type of anarchist violence against these suspicious-looking immigrants. The problem with the mainstream attitude becomes obvious following the *Chicago Tribune*'s covering of Lazarus's second burial which puts forth the discourse of American exceptionalism, of the nation's superiority in comparison to immigrants' backgrounds, suggesting the latter's need to change and assimilate to the American way:

> *Have they not come here to escape the madness of murder, the persistence of persecution in their own lands? Have they not found here previously unimaginable freedoms, not least the freedom to go back to wherever they came from if they so desired? Can they not share in our noble intentions? See they not that they have a singular opportunity to be a part of a people who naturally strive toward liberty and excellence, toward the greatness that would dwarf all the sanguine accomplishments of the past empires?*[14]

According to the mainstream American urban speech above, the backward immigrants are the only ones supposed to change their inferior ways and align themselves to superior America. A hierarchical dominant American culture is here taken for granted, while immigrants are portrayed as less than human, in need of civilizing by adherence to the better society's norms. In the interim, America is described as the land of the immigrant success story, following an over-emphasized trajectory of displacement, travails, redemption, and success.

This press article imagined in Hemon's novel actually replicates the role of urban mass media in highlighting nativist claims on the US in the early 20th century, as sanctioned by many articles published around the first decades of the 1900s in the main journals of America, such as *The Atlantic Monthly*. To give just one example, such an article from 1914, "The Modest Immigrant," by Agnes Repplier, aggressively sustains American exceptionalism by occasioning an attack on the immigrants' lack of gracefulness, and placing mainstream Americans in the position of victims. If immigrants are associated to "arrogance," individual self-concern, and an inconsistent behavior posing the problem of loyalty,[15] mainstream Americans are mainly characterized by their openness to equality, exemplified in the case of citizenship, where the comparison with Europe serves to highlight the equal status of the immigrant in America as opposed to his or her inferior stand in Europe, seen as a favor that the immigrant does not appreciate. Such excerpts suggest how the time's press was in possession of an extreme stand going against Eastern European immigrants, following Repplier's insistence that their difference is irreducible.

Yet, this whole mass-media preached edifice crumbles down if one considers the very event invoked in the article from Hemon's novel—Lazarus's death. America does not prove to be the promised mythical place of immigrant success but one of trauma and annulled hopes via unfounded suspicion and persecution, since this is "the immigrant who escaped the pogrom in Kishinev and came to Chicago only to be shot by the Chicago chief police."[16]

If the photos from pages 0, 24, 52, 166, and 240 try to construct the image of Lazarus the anarchist on the basis of class differences and racial/ethnic engrained features and fail because of the inherent politicized, discriminatory practices revealed therein, the photos on pages 86 and 190 project a different image of Lazarus, the one Olga, his sister, remembers. The image on page 86 depicts a "throng of Jewish girls exercising on the roof of a building, reaching for something in the sky,"[17] a picture from the *Daily News* that Lazarus pinned among other objects which now remind Olga of her dead brother. Isador, Lazarus's friend and companion (both of them depicted in a photo from page 202) later confirms the former's idealistic character, his view of a better world, in relation to the picture from page 190, titled *Chicago at night*. Isador remembers how, "We used to walk by the lake. It was like wilderness to us, its vastness. We could turn our backs to the filth and the grime and the slums. We looked at the waves and the horizon, sometimes we could see the other shore. He wanted to write a poem about what he saw."[18] In these photos, Lazarus appears as a young immigrant dreaming about escaping the grim reality of ghetto life, not happy with the condition of his existence (just as anarchists were not), yet interested in focusing his criticism not on violence but on artistic creation. He saw America as the land of right and freedom, as the photo on page 114 attests, yet his participation in some anarchist meetings and his poor immigrant condition turned him into a certain enemy for the Chicago police in 1908 and his wings got broken. "The land of the right and the free" proved to be largely only a preached ideal, with real existence far much more complicated and prejudiced than suggested in its discourse.

Meanwhile, the contrast between the photo on page 240 and that on page 266 sets the story's tone as not one of loss but of hope. The former image depicts a sitting dead Lazarus while the latter is that of Lazarus's sitting live friend Isador whose existence is saved by Olga's burial-related decision. Equally relevant, Isador's escape to Canada is made possible by another innocent's death, that of Isaac Lubel. Isador will be taken out of Olga's apartment in the same casket as Isaac, and thanks to Olga's choice, he will have the chance to start anew. Thus we learn how a humanist penchant is born out of grief and manages to breed life. Given this, the mono-cultural mainstream American urban superiority proves to be an illusion, actually a case of clear prejudice and disrespect for the other. By contrast, the cross-cultural milieu of traumatized Eastern European immigrants in the US suggests a promising lens that needs to be acknowledged and included in policy-making.

At bottom, then, Lazarus's story is one of death—that of immigrant Lazarus Averbuch—which was most likely carried out because of the Shippy family's internalized, prejudiced, mainstream-spread suspicion and terror in front of so-called immigrant anarchists, but which was re-instrumentalized as a real case of anti-anarchist struggle. But Lazarus's story is also about a resurrection—that of another immigrant, Isador Maron, thanks to the humanist decision of Olga which suggests the openness of a cross-cultural existence by contrast to the closed nature of the mainstream mono-cultural lifestyle.

The Story of Vladimir Brik, 2004 Chicago, and Eastern Europe

Similarly to the case of Lazarus, Brik is an Eastern European immigrant coming to the US after the elapse of almost a century. Despite the temporal gap, however, he confronts the same discourse of American condescending exceptionalism and predominant myth of the immigrant success story. He unveils it at the level of his marriage with American-born Mary Field, a neurosurgeon of Irish extraction who typically believes in the American WASP formula of the country's founding rags-to-riches Benjamin Franklin-type story according to which the key to certain well-being in the States exclusively depends on one's hard work. In Brik's own case, one of the problems to tackle is that he is actually a husband whose wife supports him since, as a neurosurgeon, "Mary was the serious wage earner in the family," while Brik contributed only "symbolically: the lousy English-teaching pay, until I got fired, plus not much per column."[19] As a consequence, Brik applies for a grant in order to write a book about Lazarus Averbuch and, on meeting the Glory foundation people, he is desperately trying to convince them in order to get financed. Meanwhile, he takes the opportunity to unveil the persistent present-day condescending American mainstream attitude to immigrants. First, Susie Schuettler, one of the board members of the foundation tells Brik she likes his immigration columns in *The Reader* for the fresh "foreigner" perspective he brings forth. In other words, though an American citizen and having lived in the new country for over twelve years, he is not perceived as a de facto citizen but he remains a foreigner to many native-born Americans. Prior to this, he noted American benefactors' proneness to help "unintelligible" cultures[20] which attract them in their exoticism, as strange ways in their midst.

Later on, while Brik is on his trip to Eastern Europe and Ukrainian Andriy hopefully asks him about America, Brik chooses not to tell the truth of complicated paths in the US but leaves him with the myth, "I wanted him to think that my life in America was all about *hard work*, rather than an embarrassing mixture of *luck and despair*."[21] Put differently, on Eastern European territory, Brik chooses to use the American official discourse of mythical promise instead of his complicated lived and felt experience according to which life here actually runs on the coordinates of pure contingency. Yet, Brik cannot come to inhabit this American mainstream myth of immigrant success following its impossible demand—the need to "disremember his previous life and start from scratch."[22]

This is what is also expected of Brik from his own wife, and her strict Catholic father, George. Brik's main problem is that, "[m]y country was this remote, mythical place for him, a remnant of the world from before America, a land of obsolescence whose people could arrive at humanity only in the United States, and belatedly."[23] George again uses here the exceptionalist discourse of America. In 2004, this is the case of exoticizing Bosnia as a lesser culture to be assimilated by the superior mainstream, foregrounding the backward, uncultured aspect of the ethnographic other, in which succeeding at "being American" alone would be an indication that "the humanizing process had been completed."[24] This follows a polarized discursive separation and binary logic that distinguishes between a "superior" West and an "inferior" East, which is still present in Western intellectual discourse, and which has been recently exposed in quite a few works on Eastern European life and culture.[25] Especially Andrew Hammond has clearly shown how, in the post-Cold War situation, the Balkans have been construed in journalism, political statements, travel writings, etc. as a zone of backwardness, barbarism and violence that threatens to engulf the civilized and democratic West.[26] Hammond particularly notes how,

> As with nineteenth century balkanism, crucially, this discriminatory, hierarchical mode of continental geography also works through metonym. The construction is not nation- or ethnicity-specific but, via the deployment of the term 'Balkan,' holds as its true object the whole peninsula; balkanism being that cross-cultural discourse which targets a collectivity of negatively-evaluated ethnic groups whose properties may appear at any one point across the region but are always characteristic of the collectivity as a whole. (…) This is the West's concept of the 'eternal

> Balkans,' always fixed and immutable, yet at the same time always worsening, a persistently unprecedented barbarism evoked in a register mingling amusement, absurdity, and absolute terror.[27]

Like Hammond, Hemon's novel sets out to reveal the inherited clichés of the Western gaze on Eastern Europe and immigrants coming from there. It implicitly suggests the unfair distortions and limited discourse of freedom characteristic to the US. In line with this, even if Mary does not condone her father's condescending insistence on Brik's foreignness, she too believes that indulging in hard work alone can lead to her husband's happiness. Instead, Brik suggests the failure of such pursuits and of his marriage since Mary permanently rejects a sharing of their inner feelings which would betray their vulnerabilities. This happens since she leaves the impression of being an emotion-free individual who, on losing a patient, simply tells Brik she feels "he is dead."[28] Then, at the end of the book, when Brik tells her of companion Rora's death, she keeps silent and simply informs him she has a surgery to perform, then hangs up,[29] permanently refusing to open herself emotionally to her husband.

By contrast, Brik finds comfort in the openly pain-sharing encounters with Iuliana from the Chişinău Jewish Center, which I will analyze below, and with Azra, Rora's surgeon sister who fixes Brik's broken arm and bears the loss of her brother with dignity. The most important counter-current to American mainstream discourse thus comes from Rora's and Azra's cross-cultural stories of grief: born in a Muslim Bosnian family, they lost their parents in a bus accident when Rora was six. His sister, Azra, a surgeon who was in Sarajevo during the siege, amputating legs, used to be married to a Serbian husband for seven years before the war; once the conflict started he asked her to follow her wifely duty and join him in shooting her people, which she definitely declined and chose instead to help the injured.[30] Most importantly, at the end of Brik's journey there is another death, that of Rora; based on the stories Rora used to say about the war, Brik concocts a conspiracy theory leading to this one's death—namely, that the Bosnian fighter Rambo had Rora killed since the latter was in possession of photos that could be used as evidence against Rambo, the photos of dead American journalist Miller whom Rambo had eliminated. Azra dismantles all this, saying Miller is still alive and reporting in Iraq, while Rora was simply killed by a boy who wanted to show off his gun and was after the camera, no deeper meaning. This story of absurd death becomes a means to mirror Lazarus Averbuch's own killing; following the above details that Brik had unearthed for writing the book, it might well be that, like Rora, Lazarus was killed for no apparent reason by a suspicious policeman. In light of this, these two disparate cases, one in early 20th century US, one in present-day Eastern Europe, stand proof of the absurdity of war/killing which makes random, innocent victims.

Rora's photographs meanwhile remain and are highly relevant; in their large majority they record blurry images of Eastern European landscapes and roads (the photos on pages 64, 98, 174, 248) to which one adds a slightly blurred view of Chicago's skyscrapers against a pessimistic grayish tone on page 11. These are images of societies ravaged by an absurd man-made history of death and violence. Not surprisingly, among the photos is included a view of two tombstones from a Jewish cemetery in Chişinău, with the name of one Isaac Averbuch printed in Hebrew letters[31]: this can be read as a means to draw our attention to how the human choice for violence in the name of one's cultural superiority only leads to needless deaths. The last photo on page 276 is again a streetscape but this time there is no blurring. Instead the simple quietness of trees and houses suggests an optimistic possibility of starting anew by means of non-violent alternatives of peaceful life among different others. Put differently, life does go on among the ruins, and it is only up to our choices if it is going to be a multiplication of absurd deaths and sufferings, or a more promising site of respectful co-existence. In what follows, I will try to show how Hemon's novel makes this plea by using multidirectional methods, namely overt, *meta-narrative* or *stream-of-consciousness* moments of relapse into the past as well as the use of *overlapping names* and, most importantly, of the largely *identical content* of stories and comments once made by characters in 1908, once by present-day characters.

First, in point of *overlapping names*, we learn that, after Lazarus Averbuch's death, the police discover that "the five sentences that Assistant Chief believed to have been coded instructions are an exercise from an English-class at the Maxwell Street Settlement House. Indeed, Mr. Brik (sic!), a teacher there, describes Lazarus Averbuch as *a faithful and persevering student of a very good character*."[32] The name of narrator Brik therefore resonates with that of another Brik in 1908 who, just like him, was an English teacher.

Then, on page 206, there is a brief mention of Brik's aunt Olga who has the same name as Lazarus's sister. Most importantly, the journalist covering Lazarus Averbuch's death in 1908 for The *Chicago Tribune* is called William P. Miller, and Miller reappears in Rora's narratives about the war in Sarajevo: it is the name of an American journalist sent to Eastern Europe in 1992 as a war correspondent. The two journalists share more than the name: their fundamental characteristic seems to be that of writing articles that mirror the official, governmental prejudiced position. All of W.P. Miller's italicized articles from *The Chicago Tribune* simply echo society's war on anarchism, and even when witnessing how Schuettler picks up, reads and silently pockets the letter Lazarus had been carrying and giving to Police Officer Shippy before being shot, the reporter "notices but asks nothing."[33] Later on, he agrees with the assistant chief about the other-worldly dangerous characters of foreigners like Lazarus. Therefore, rather than being interested in finding out the truth by a fair investigation of all the details, his articles simply prove how the press generally sides with the official government-run agenda and tries to impose this point of view on the masses, becoming an instrument of control. Not far from this image of press as a manipulating instrument, in 1992, war correspondent Miller at first writes overtly biased articles—for instance, after losing at poker, he has to pay back with favors, among them, writing "a story in American papers about Rambo, heroically fighting the Chetniks."[34] Later on, we learn that the same "Miller had to leave Sarajevo more often because New York was sick of yet another story about Rambo and his brave unit," going to Mostar, Gorazde and Doboj.[35] In either case, press appears to be far from the medium it aspires to be, doing independent investigation in search of truth; instead, especially in war or crisis situations, it most often serves a state's official agenda as well as market demands by offering sensational stories no matter what. In drawing attention to this, Hemon's novel echoes Judith Butler's plea from *Precarious Life*, in connection to *The New York Times* 2001 use of Afghan women's photos, that of the danger of turning the press into a blindingly observant organ of official politics, which can fail to notice the others' individuality and unfairly discriminate. By bringing together different temporal zones, the cross-temporal dimension proposed by Hemon offers even more weight to Butler's argument, proving how instances of such prejudice are a long-standing precedent of biased thinking that have led to unfair oppression of certain people throughout time.

Most unsettling for the past-present connection are the two episodes where *identical content* is used, once in a chapter about 2004 adventures, once in a chapter dedicated to 1908 events. Thus, in Chapter 14, Rora talks about Eastern European natural passivity and resigned acceptance vis-à-vis dysfunctional bus timetables for the Cernivitsi-Chişinău route, "Naturally, the ten-o'clock bus to Chişinău did not show up. Nobody said or knew anything; Rora and I just waited with everyone else for a couple of flaccid hours, and then the twelve-o'clock bus showed up. If you wait long enough, *something will happen—there has never been a time when nothing happened.*"[36] These lines seem to set the tone of Eastern European life, as a permanent state of patience for an already determined fate apparently epitomized by passive waiting for something to happen by itself, with no need to interfere or use personal agency to make things happen. This is a characteristic state of many formerly autocratic societies where generalized control of citizens' individual lives has resulted in their internalization of a deterministic viewpoint. Then, in the following chapter, we hear Isador wondering what to do since all of Chicago's police forces are after him, convinced he was Lazarus's anarchist partner that managed to run away the day Lazarus was killed. To this, Lazarus's sister, Kishinev-born Olga answers in keeping with the above Eastern European manner, in the attempt to calm him down, "We will think of something. (...) *Something will happen. There was never a time when nothing happened.*"[37] Except for a minimal change of tense, Brik's and Olga's above comments are identical and make one ponder over the high degree to which history seems to run in cycles.

That there is this difference between the Eastern European preferences for passive waiting *in situ* as opposed to the agency of Eastern European immigrants from US cities is not coincidental if one considers the following similarity between Olga and Brik in relation to the mainstream culture around them. Brik is an immigrant sojourner in Eastern Europe, returning to familiar formerly autocratic locations after having lived in the States for twelve years; Olga is a recent Eastern European immigrant to Chicago, as part of a democratic society, that of America. Both of them are in the position of displaced individuals in contact with a new type of reality. As born and raised in autocratic Eastern Europe, both of them know the discourse of its passivity, yet, given the novel insights provided by life in a new environment, they have distanced themselves from actually embodying it, by contrast to the surrounding people who have continued to live *in situ* all their lives. Not surprisingly, then, in recording this state of facts, Brik suggests his irritation before native people's natural complacency about this absurd "uncertainty of the moment." In contrast to their rejoicing in this situation, Brik places his anger, by noting "I needed everything—a shower, water, to shit, comfort, love, to reach the end of this lousy journey, to write a book."[38] Later on, Olga herself will feel the need to act in order to save Isador, although this will involve accepting to be part of a charade-burial, she will save Isador at the cost of improperly performing the Jewish burial ritual for her brother.

An opportunity to better grasp Olga's choice above will be occasioned by considering the other case of two more or less identical comments in the novel. The former is located in chapter 12, and deals with the meeting between Brik and Chaim Gruzenberg from Czernovitz's Jewish Center in

2004. On that occasion, on hearing of Brik's interest in past historical events, namely if there might be some details of Lazarus Averbuch's family coming here in search of asylum after the Chişinău 1903 pogrom, Chaim draws attention to the different interests of Jews living in North America vis-à-vis Eastern Europe and of Jews continuing to live in Eastern Europe, by stating, "All of you foreigners come looking for your ancestors and roots. (...) You are only interested in the dead. God will take care of the dead. *We need to take care of the living*."[39] Put differently, in the context of an ever-smaller and constantly aging Jewish community in present-day Eastern European cities, the primary interest is the struggle for prolonging survival rather than to primarily preserve the traces of their traumatic past.

Later, in section 17, we are back in 1908, and German Jewish lawyer Taube explains to a grieving Olga why she should publicly participate in the Jewish burial ritual involving an empty coffin. Since her brother's body has been missing, it has given rise to the town's rumors, on the one hand coming from anarchists who try to transform Lazarus into a martyr of their cause, on the other hand, coming from excited Christians who connect Lazarus's absence from the grave with the symbolism of his name, and Jesus' second coming. In order to dispel such rumors and stop both "anarchist hatred and Christian superstitions," Taube asks Olga to acquiesce to being part of this charade meant to provide all proper rituals, *shivah*, and *kaddish*, as a way of burying Lazarus's spiritual body. As Olga definitely refuses to lie to herself and to God, Taube tries to convince her by stating, "God knows our despair. God wants His chosen people to live in peace. God loves life, cares less about death. *We need to live. I want to live, I want my children to live*. Everyone I know wants to live. You have to ask yourself, what is more important to you, life or death. *What is this world about—life or death?*"[40] Like Brik, the foreigner, then, Olga the recent immigrant to early 20th century Chicago has to confront the logic of personal or past loss with the present-geared logic sustained by older immigrants who have been in the new country for a longer period of time, here represented by already-integrated urban German Jews who work towards smoothing everyone's assimilation and acceptance into the new culture by cooperation with the mainstream elite. In both cases, the primary concerns of the already integrated older immigrants from the Jewish community is to concentrate on the living over the dead, on the immediate future rather than the traumatic call of the past, even if they pose God in a different position. Taube foregrounds God's relation to life, Chaim invokes God as the entity taking care of the dead.

In analyzing these discourses, I will rely on Judith Butler's insights from *Frames of War* which start with the Foucault-based assertion that human life and the human being are organized via normative frames established and enforced via repetition. As Butler explains, "[t]he normative production of the subject is an iterable process—the norm is repeated, and in this sense is constantly 'breaking' with the contexts delimited as the 'conditions of productions.'"[41] Starting from here, Butler suggests how this very iterative nature of norms allows for shifts starting with slight differences of reproduction and ending in new configurations. Hence gets born the possibility of another temporality, of an alternative way to follow than the one of the origins of the norms, one which, I argue, happens if one stays in the critical state of "disturbance" and "distance."[42] In Hemon's novel, this stance is epitomized by immigrant characters whose discourses are unsettled by and unsettle in their turn the world of the host country's mainstream and older generations of assimilationist-drawn individuals via cross-cultural encounters.

In this respect, Olga's passionate response is essential in understanding the tortuous paths traumatized immigrants need to follow in a new host country. Her immediate reaction is that of accusing Taube and other present-day rich second or third-generation Jewish Americans of complicity with the mainstream in view of clinging to their decent way of life at all costs, even if it means giving up on traditions and desecrating the name of the dead, "Why don't you and you rich friends stand up to Schuettler and the anarchists and the Christians and whoever wants to take your *gilden* life away from you? Why do I have to spit on my brother's grave because you and your *negidim* friends are scared of death?"[43]

In a similar vein, Brik continues the same type of discussion—first started in Czernivisti with Chaim—in Chişinău, at the Jewish Community Center. This time his interlocutor is 25-year old Iuliana, whose entire attitude is one of grief as to the 1903 pogrom or the Averbuch name, given that her grandmother's maiden name had been Averbuch and she had ended up shot by Romanians in 1942, during World War II, while in her 30s. Considering all these, at the cemetery, the question that Brik poses places him in a largely similar position with that of Olga above, that of the responsibility we owe to the dead. He asks, "If there are more dead than living, *then the world is about death*, and the question is: what are we to do with all the death? Who is going to remember all the dead?"[44]

Put differently, both Brik and Olga sustain a reverse type of logic to that of assimilated Jews like Chaim and Taube. This is obvious from the emphasized passages in the speeches above, which in simplified terms suggest opposite claims: that the world is about life (Chaim, Taube) and that the world is about death (Olga, Brik). More to the point, Chaim and Taube both talk about the need of the living to struggle in order to help the others stay alive and leave the dead to God's grace. In this argument, the individual people who are still alive can and should take care of themselves. By contrast, Olga and Brik seem to sustain that the dead can no longer speak or act, so those alive are responsible to preserve their memory at all costs. The problem in both cases seems to be that of an equally extremist, reductive type of logic: exclusive focus on the struggle for survival in the case of assimilationist older generations of immigrants and, respectively, exclusive focus on the struggle for honoring the dead in the case of grieving individuals.

Yet, are these solutions the only two available when addressing trauma? Is life actually about such clear-cut choices between death and life, as earlier implied by Taube and here by Brik? Can it be also a case of bridging these two possibilities by conjoining the responsibility to remember the dead with the equal need to provide for the living? I believe that this middle-ground path of negotiation is the one that both older and newer generations of immigrants and the mainstream need to learn from one another. This alternative is actually the one Brik finds in Iuliana's answer as to whether the world is about death rather than life. She states, "I think it is about life. I think there is always more life than death. (...) Those who lived are always alive for someone. Those who are alive remember life, not death. And when you are dead nothing happens. Death is nothing."[45]

Iuliana's statement can be placed on a par with those of Taube and Chaim above, since, like them, she believes life has primacy over death. But, in fact, she refuses a binary type of division between life and death and optimistically suggests how somebody goes living beyond death in the memory of those still standing. Then, as Brik tells her how as a Bosnian close to the terrible events of 1992 he feels a terrible rage at the world for letting it happen, Iuliana's take on unfair deaths in futile wars and violent demonstrations is pacifist. Thus, asked about what she feels vis-à-vis the 1903 well-known violent Kishinev pogrom, and about her grandfather's time in the Red Army, her answer speaks volumes, "When I think about the pogrom, (...) I feel love for those people. When I think about my grandfather, I think about how hard it must have been for him, how lonely and happy he was on top of the Reichstag. When I think about those things, I love him."[46] A humanist, constructive struggle for life, also keeping alive the remembrance of those gone is paramount, and called for in this passage in contrast to possible recourse to violence, as initially felt by Brik and Olga following their immediate losses. In that, Iuliana sustains

Butler's idea about the essential precariousness of life, namely the fact that "one's life is always in some sense in the hands of the other,"[47] and one's personal losses make one aware of the value of life, while equally drawing attention to it for Brik and the readers.

Not surprisingly, Olga will later acquiesce to Taube's proposition and publicly bury her missing brother while thinking of writing to her mother and asking her forgiveness for apparently succumbing to Taube's plea, since she feels "I chose life over death. *God will take care of the dead. We have to take care of the living.*"[48] Here, following Olga's choice to assume Taube's exact words, it seems she has taken the extreme path of life and has decided to morally give up on her dead brother. Actually, however, Olga's choice is not a willful inobservance of rituals in the name of ensuring the perpetuation of the comfortable decent lifestyle of older immigrants like Taube, even if it also serves their cause. Her project has a different stake—that of ensuring Isador Maron's survival by getting him protection and a safe passage to Canada where he will disappear without a trace. Put differently, had Olga decided not to follow Taube's proposition, Isador would have most likely been caught within a day or two, unfairly accused of anarchist activities, and most probably ended up dead. Meanwhile, her dead brother Lazarus would remain without a proper Jewish burial and would simply serve as a bone of content and possible emblem used in the name of different ideological causes. By contrast, given her choice, Olga willfully decides to disobey Judaic burial requirements but not as the passive acceptance of Taube's plea in favor of comforting assimilationist purposes but as an active participation in saving one's life, that of her dead brother's friend. Given her iteration with a difference of Taube's norm, Olga manages to redefine the meaning of survival in the sense indicated by Butler. For Taube, survival seems to have meant merely "policing a boundary—the strategy of a certain sovereign in relation to its territory," the blind acceptance of the mainstream ways in order to ensure comfortable life for the middle class.[49]

Following her latter choice, Olga will manage to best settle the dispute between serving life and death, since, at the end of the day, she will return home and terribly feel her brother's absence. Or, as Brik notices in Sarajevo in 2004, in keeping with Iuliana's insights, "Home is where somebody notices you absence."[50] This echoes Brik's same line of thought once he gets to Chişinău and feels the people's overwhelming indifference, saying "[h]ome is where someone might notice your absence"[51] and Lazarus's nostalgic remembrance of Kishinev at the start of the novel, a variant of Brik's words above reading that "[h]ome is where somebody notices that you are no longer there."[52] Applying this to

Olga's case here, it is obvious that even if she fails in observing the Jewish requirement of proper burial, she never fails in celebrating her brother's life, in responsibly remembering him by this acute sense of absence she inhabits. Her trajectory makes us wonder over the complexity of choices one makes, suggesting how one can sometimes not meet the ritual requirements of death and yet be forgiven as long as this action is meant to promote a positive cause, thereby also suggesting an alternative act of mourning.

Most importantly, Hemon's novel opens the debate over the connections one can establish between the past and present situation of immigrants in America and suggests an ethical plea of responsibility available via cross-cultural configurations of identity out of grief. In this equation, Brik's above violent-like reaction about the war in Sarajevo is not only countered by Iuliana's Butler-echoing love claims. Beforehand, while in Czernivisti waiting for the bus to Chişinău, and following Rora's memories of the Sarajevo conflict, Brik admitted how war, at best, has only an initial logic but then turns into an absurd dehumanizing struggle to stay alive at all costs, no matter what happens to the others, "In the beginning, every war has a neat logic: they want to kill us, we want not to die. But with time it becomes something else, the war becomes this space where anybody can kill anybody at any time, where everybody wants everybody dead, because the only way you are sure to stay alive is if everybody else is dead."[53] Butlerian-wise, then, Brik decries the absurdity of war as disavowal of interdependency and erasure of the other as a rightful being.

This leads Brik to remember a contradictory discussion with his American wife, Mary, vis-à-vis the use of the Abu Ghraib photos in the context of the fight against terrorism. Prior to that, he had drawn the readers' attention to the analogy one can draw between the 1908 Chicago events and the post-9/11 American war on terror, between sustaining *the war against anarchism* in 1908 and *the post-2001 war against terrorism.* First, in the post-Hay Market atmosphere of America's war against anarchism of new immigrants, Chicago's reaction to a policeman's shooting a Jewish immigrant and supposedly anarchist Lazarus Averbuch is a mad hunt against poor immigrants, even if proofs might be absent. As a result, immigrants had to suffer, stricter immigration laws were enforced, with "suspected anarchists" persecuted and deported while "scientific studies of the racial profile of degeneracy"[54] abounded. In order to sanction Hemon's correct assertions here, it is enough to note that the 1911 forty-two volume Dillingham report established a distinction between old, "superior" Northern and Western European immigrants and new, "inferior" Southern and Eastern European immigrants. More precisely, the report expressed anxiety about the assimilability of the new immigrants, thus solidifying the US dominant ethnic identity as Anglo-Saxon, traceable to English and Northern settlers, while, as Belluscio rightly notes, it completely neglected African Americans, considered Eastern Europeans as inferior, and emphasized a vision of US identity as white.[55] This makes Brik deplore how "[t]he war against anarchism was much like the current war on terror—funny how old habits never die."[56] In his autobiographical collection of stories, *The Book of my Lives*, Hemon explained this nativist attitude of post-2001 America as part of the neoconservative agenda in which only legal "others" can be accepted and only if they will "adapt to our ways of life, the successful standards of which have long been established."[57]

Keeping this nativist neoconservative approach in mind, Brik explains the different take on the Abu Ghraib photos on his part, as an Eastern European immigrant versus his American wife, Mary, a successful brain-surgeon who supports her immigrant husband and believes in a simplified, ideal myth of immigrant success in the US, provided one works hard for it while being unable to grasp the impact of Sarajevo's ruin on Brik's present-day confused life. For her, these photos are simply a case of decent American kids acting on a misguided belief that they were protecting freedom, a case of good intentions going astray. For Brik, they are an instance of "Americans expressing their unlimited joy of their unlimited power over someone else's life and death,"[58] an instance of the "triumphalist image" Butler was criticizing in *Frames of War*.

Yet, unlike Butler, who uses her comments to criticize American government policies, in Hemon's book the photos are used for showing an immigrant's tensional relation to America, as a new host country, and to its average citizens. They also serve the need to vent one's anger at how some US citizens naively believe in essential good intentions of everyone gone astray, not seeing the evidence—imposing an imperialist superior position on the others. Hence, Brik continues, "I told her that to be American you have to know nothing and understand even less, and that I did not want to be American,"[59] while he smashes the family china. Yet, as the story develops, thanks to his back-and-forth voyages across cultures, Brik replaces this initial radical violence-instilling position and suggests instead a critical stance based on dialogue and informed by the cross-cultural perspective of the immigrant or the one who is in a minority position in a particular location, following his fascination with Olga's and Iuliana's proposed alternatives, those of an agent non-violent, ethical responsibility.

At the end of the line, the past returns with a difference in Hemon's novel, there is no resolution he can find for Lazarus's story because the young man's death cannot be undone. However, by putting past and present events together, the novel suggests how they can communicate in order to make existence bearable via debate and acknowledgment of precariousness and interdependency rather than by following violent paths. At the same time, Hemon's novel joins other Eastern European contemporary books and suggests how Eastern European societies and the American cultural space need to engage in an honest dialogue of mutual recognition by avoiding exclusive criticism of the other's past and present follies and indulging instead in self-critical analysis of traumas at the side of a critical attitude towards the other.

Acknowledgment: This work was supported by the Romanian National Authority for Scientific Research, CNCS-UEFISCDI, under grant PN-II-RU-TE no. 64/2011 titled *Cross-Cultural Encounters in American Trauma Narratives: A Comparative Approach to Personal and Collective Memories.*

Bibliography

Barthes, Roland. *Camera Lucida. Reflections on Photography*. 1980. Translated by Richard Howard. New York: Hill & Wang, 1981.

Belluscio, J. Steven. *To Be Suddenly White. Literary Realism and Racial Passing*. Columbia: University of Missouri Press, 2006.

Butler, Judith. *Precarious Life. The Powers of Mourning and Violence*. London: Verso, 2004.

—. *Frames of War. When Is Life Grievable?*. London: Verso, 2009.

Craps, Stef. *Postcolonial Witnessing. Trauma Out of Bounds.* Houndmills: Palgrave Macmillan, 2013.

Forrester, Sibelian, Magdalena J. Zaborowska, and Elena Gapova, eds. *Over the Wall/ After the Fall. Post-Communist Cultures through an East-West Gaze*. Bloomington: Indiana University Press, 2004.

Hammond, Andrew. "'The Danger Zone of Europe.' Balkanism between the Cold War and 9/11." *European Journal of Cultural Studies* 8.2 (2005): 135-54.

—. *The Debated Lands. British and American Representations of the Balkans*. Cardiff: University of Wales Press, 2007.

Hemon, Aleksandar. *The Lazarus Project*. New York: Riverhead Books, 2008.

—. *The Book of My Lives*. New York: Farrar, Straus and Giroux, 2013.

Kuhn, Annette, and Kirsten Emiko McAllister, eds. *Locating Memory. Photographic Acts.* New York: Berghahn Books, 2006. 2008.

Levy, Michelle. "'Brotherly Wounds.' Representations of Balkan Conflict in Contemporary Balkan Literature." *World Literature Today* 75.1 (Winter 2001): 66-75.

Monarelli, Lisa. "A Book of Shifting Borders." *California Literary Review* February 11, 2009. Accessed October 20, 2013. http://calitreview.com/2539.

Repplier, Agnes. "The Modest Immigrant." *Atlantic Monthly* 116 (September 1915): 312.

Rothberg, Michael. *Multidirectional Memory. Remembering the Holocaust in the Age of Decolonization.* Stanford: Stanford University Press, 2009.

Todorova, Maria. *Imagining the Balkans.* New York: Oxford University Press, 1997.

Wolff, Larry. *Inventing Eastern Europe: The Map of Civilization on the Mind of the Enlightenment.* Stanford: Stanford University Press, 1996.

Notes

[1] Michelle Levy, "'Brotherly Wounds.' Representations of Balkan Conflict in Contemporary Balkan Literature," *World Literature Today* 75.1 (Winter 2001): 67.

[2] Aleksandar Hemon, *The Book of My Lives* (New York: Farrar, Straus and Giroux, 2013), 112-27.

[3] Levy, "'Brotherly Wounds,'" 71.

[4] Aleksandar Hemon, *The Lazarus Project* (New York: Riverhead Books, 2008), 15.

[5] Lisa Monarelli, "A Book of Shifting Borders," *California Literary Review* February 11, 2009, accessed October 20, 2013. http://calitreview.com/2539.

[6] Michael Rothberg, *Multidirectional Memory. Remembering the Holocaust in the Age of Decolonization* (Stanford: Stanford University Press, 2009), 11.

[7] Rothberg, *Multidirectional Memory*, 308.

[8] Stef Craps, *Postcolonial Witnessing. Trauma Out of Bounds* (Houndmills: Palgrave Macmillan, 2013), 3.

[9] Hemon, *The Lazarus Project*, 2.

[10] Hemon, *The Lazarus Project*, 168.

[11] Hemon, *The Lazarus Project*, 26.

[12] Hemon, *The Lazarus Project*, 57.

[13] Annette Kuhn and Kirsten Emiko McAllister, eds., *Locating Memory. Photographic Acts* (New York: Berghahn Books, 2008), 13-14.

[14] Hemon, *The Lazarus Project*, 273, italics in the original.

[15] Agnes Repplier, "The Modest Immigrant," *Atlantic Monthly* 116 (September 1915): 312.

[16] Hemon, *The Lazarus Project*, 41.
[17] Hemon, *The Lazarus Project*, 90.
[18] Hemon, *The Lazarus Project*, 192.
[19] Hemon, *The Lazarus Project*, 16.
[20] Hemon, *The Lazarus Project*, 13.
[21] Hemon, *The Lazarus Project*, 108, emphases mine.
[22] Hemon, *The Lazarus Project*, 127.
[23] Hemon, *The Lazarus Project*, 162.
[24] Hemon, *The Lazarus Project*, 163.
[25] Among these, I mention here Larry Wolff, *Inventing Eastern Europe: The Map of Civilization on the Mind of the Enlightenment* (Stanford: Stanford University Press, 1996); Maria Todorova, *Imagining the Balkans* (New York: Oxford University Press, 1997); Sibelian Forrester, Magdalena J. Zaborowska and Elena Gapova, eds., *Over the Wall / After the Fall. Post-Communist Cultures through an East-West Gaze* (Bloomington: Indiana University Press, 2004); Andrew Hammond, "'The Danger Zone of Europe.' Balkanism between the Cold War and 9/11," *European Journal of Cultural Studies* 8.2 (2005): 135-54; Andrew Hammond, *The Debated Lands. British and American Representations of the Balkans* (Cardiff: University of Wales Press, 2007).
[26] Andrew Hammond, "'The Danger Zone of Europe.' Balkanism between the Cold War and 9/11," *European Journal of Cultural Studies* 8.2 (2005): 135.
[27] Hammond, "'The Danger Zone of Europe,'" 146-47.
[28] Hemon, *The Lazarus Project*, 252.
[29] Hemon, *The Lazarus Project*, 287.
[30] Hemon, *The Lazarus Project*, 253.
[31] Hemon, *The Lazarus Project*, 226.
[32] Hemon, *The Lazarus Project*, 61.
[33] Hemon, *The Lazarus Project*, 25.
[34] Hemon, *The Lazarus Project*, 84.
[35] Hemon, *The Lazarus Project*, 111.
[36] Hemon, *The Lazarus Project*, 175, emphasis mine.
[37] Hemon, *The Lazarus Project*, 194, emphasis mine.
[38] Hemon, *The Lazarus Project*, 175.
[39] Hemon, *The Lazarus Project*, 156, emphasis mine.
[40] Hemon, *The Lazarus Project*, 224, emphasis mine.
[41] Judith Butler, *Frames of War. When Is Life Grievable?* (London: Verso, 2009), 169.
[42] Butler, *Frames of War*, 157.
[43] Hemon, *The Lazarus Project*, 224.
[44] Hemon, *The Lazarus Project*, 236, emphasis mine.
[45] Hemon, *The Lazarus Project*, 236.
[46] Hemon, *The Lazarus Project*, 251.
[47] Butler, *Frames of War*, 14.
[48] Hemon, *The Lazarus Project*, 272, emphasis mine.
[49] Butler, *Frames of War*, 52.
[50] Hemon, *The Lazarus Project*, 278.

[51] Hemon, *The Lazarus Project*, 204.
[52] Hemon, *The Lazarus Project*, 3.
[53] Hemon, *The Lazarus Project*, 185-86.
[54] Hemon, *The Lazarus Project*, 42.
[55] Steven J. Belluscio, *To Be Suddenly White. Literary Realism and Racial Passing* (Columbia: University of Missouri Press, 2006), 31.
[56] Hemon, *The Lazarus Project*, 42.
[57] Hemon, *The Book of My Lives*, 20.
[58] Hemon, *The Lazarus Project*, 188.
[59] Hemon, *The Lazarus Project*, 189.

"STALINTOWNS APLENTY": TOTALITARIAN CITYSCAPES IN TRANSATLANTIC MEMORY[1]

ROXANA OLTEAN

A script for a Voice of America broadcast dated September 20, 1951, entitled "Political Geography"—subsequently changed to "On War of Words"—and attributed to Bertram Wolfe,[2] working at VOA's Ideological Advisory Unit, addresses in a particularly salient way the manner in which cities—and city names especially—encode sites of communist trauma, bearing witness to historical violence while at the same time deferring the origin of the violence to an elusive past,

> All over Eastern Europe, place names have been changed to pay tribute to Communist leaders. In Rumania, Bulgaria, Hungary, Czechoslovakia, Albania, there are towns named Stalin (…). In Czechoslovakia, the town of Zlin, famous for its shoe factories, has been renamed after Clement Gottwald. In Bulgaria there is a Dmitrovo and a Dmitrovgrad, Stalintowns aplenty and even a Tobulkhin.[3]

The ideological drive of VOA scripts in general, and of this script in particular, is both transparent and self-avowed. As Robert Hessen points out, the very purpose of the Ideological Advisory Unit at VOA was to "counteract communist propaganda," which VOA did by broadcasting an officially-endowed American perspective back beyond the Iron Curtain, combating the communist states' jamming, to audiences in various communist states who listened to these broadcasts in their own language, often at great peril to their own safety and liberty, as the broadcasts were deemed subversive and threatening by the communist powers. Thus when Bertram Wolfe applied for the job at VOA, for example,

> Foy Kohler, head of the Voice of America's International Broadcasting Division, was looking for someone who could counteract communist propaganda and expose the imperialist goals of Soviet foreign policy—to create an Ideological Advisory Unit. The unit's chief responsibility would

be to produce radio scripts to be broadcast by the Voice of America in 46 languages worldwide.[4]

And yet, beyond the visible ideological layer of the script, its narrative and rhetorical content make possible the enunciation of postwar Eastern European historical and personal traumas, which spiral back to the place of origin under the form of airwaves, giving a voice to ruptures and abysses of history which would otherwise have remained silent for Eastern European public space. In fact, "Political Geography"/"On War of Words" brings forth in a surprisingly poignant way the manner in which city names encode the historical and personal trauma they seek to efface, and their new names are actually characterized by a belatedness that Cathy Caruth sees as an essential element of traumatic experience. As Caruth reminds us, in the subversive logic of traumatic memory, there is a dimension—irreducible to "the thematic content of the text or to what the theory encodes"—which "stubbornly persists in bearing witness to some forgotten wound."[5]

Similarly, in the logic of traumatic recall, the new city names signal a painful absence made all the more evident by the reality of totalitarian rule, seeking to obliterate all that came before through the imposition of a generic Stalintown. The syntagm "Stalintowns aplenty" is highly suggestive for the investigation of American representations of Eastern European trauma, as it captures the palimpsestic nature of that representation: it both addresses the "heart" of violence and—by the Anglicized name (Stalintown)—also creates a hyperreal city of totalitarianism that contains the essence of historical violence while at the same time translating it into Anglophone reality, referring to a town that does not, of course, exist. "Aplenty" adds a stylistic twist, suggesting the distancing vision of the American perspective on trauma, which also doubles as a discourse of witnessing.

The subject of communist trauma as well as its representation across the Atlantic has been a fruitful topic of debate. Various sites of Romanian communist trauma emerging after the Revolution have been discussed.[6] This chapter aims to contribute to the discussion of the representation of communist trauma to suggest that VOA—overt vehicles for ideological transmission[7]—also became a space of voicing, or of literally and metaphorically airing Eastern European trauma, illustrating this issue with reference to two "points of memory"[8] located in the Sol Stein Papers at Columbia University Library, namely two VOA scripts: "Political Geography"/"On War of Words" (1951), attributed to Bertram Wolfe, and "This is our Answer to the Communist Purges" (1953), by Sol Stein. Both scripts address the issues encoded by the syntagm "Stalintowns aplenty"—

violence, imposition and obliteration—and engage the wider topic of the communist purges from two perspectives: the politicization of city names and its role in the creation of a totalitarian geography, and the projection of an American/universal counter-space built on ethical principles from surprisingly diverse perspectives.

Moreover, in the contrapuntal logic of memory studies, this reading will also seek to explore the interstices of Michael Rothberg's groundbreaking vision of multidirectional memory engaging a series of non-competitive pasts and traumas, contextualized by his questioning of the "competition of victims": "does collective memory really work like real-estate development? Must the claims of memory always be calculated according to their relevance for national history?"[9] Against this vision of competitive memory, which Rothberg discerns in the approach of Walter Benn Michaels, Rothberg argues for multidirectional memory, "subject to ongoing negotiation, cross-referencing, and borrowing; as productive and not private."[10] In this sense, I attempt to suggest an additional multidirectional reading to Rothberg's own rendering of early Cold War America from his analysis of Du Bois's 1949 trip to Warsaw and of Du Bois's text "The Negro and the Warsaw Ghetto" published in 1952 in *Jewish Life*, contemporary with the two VOA scripts to be addressed in this chapter. Rothberg's intricate reading of Du Bois is carried out against a background which appears to stretch out as an impermeable "cold war hysteria": "The period surrounding Du Bois's trip to Warsaw in 1949 and the eventual publication of the article in 1952 comprised the height of cold war hysteria and of Du Bois's persecution by the United States government."[11] This reading will attempt to supplement the syntagm "the height of cold war hysteria" in the spirit of the surprising reversals yielded by Rothberg's own reading, taking a cue from Rothberg's own vision of "unexpected insight into issues of history and memory" and the necessity of "bracketing" "post-cold war sensibilities," but exploring these in a different direction,

> While it is necessary to approach critically the Stalinism of intellectual and activist figures like Du Bois and the editors of *Jewish Life*—especially in considering a moment when anti-Semitic repression was reaching new heights in the Soviet Union—temporarily bracketing our post-cold war sensibilities can produce unexpected insight into issues of history and memory.[12]

One such issue of history and memory contributing to "unexpected insight" into Cold War America, and moving this in yet another direction, is the existence of a communist background shared by Du Bois and

Bertram Wolfe (before Wolfe's subsequent disillusionment with communism),[13] whose interests at certain points coalesced around the New Workers School in New York, where Bertram Wolfe (as director) invited Du Bois to lecture "on the topic 'Lynch Law and Democracy,' or any other similar topic of your own choice, involving the problems of the American Negro," in a letter dated November 21, 1930.[14] In fact, in the same contrapuntal logic giving a dynamic dimension to the static syntagm "Cold War America," a further glance at the biographical and intellectual trajectories of the staff on the Ideological Advisory Unit at VOA suggests the extent to which the US's ideological arm was in fact an eclectic space. Firstly, there is the complicated intellectual and political trajectory of members of staff such as Bertram Wolfe, one of the founders of the Communist Party in the USA, whose gradual but definite break with communism is documented by Hessen.[15] Secondly, members of VOA staff—for example the Director of Religious Programming, Roger Lyons—were subject to McCarthy hearings in 1953, as documented by David Krugler.[16] In this sense, starting from the interstices of Rothberg's reading, my approach will try to open up VOA broadcasts and their overtly ideological function in the spirit of Rothberg's own urge for multidirectional memory and non-competitive traumas to yield a multidimensionality that opens up the space of ideology to surprisingly multivocal readings, functioning as a place to air trauma and engaging a dialogue with other multidirectional memories.

Pursuing the multidimensional direction of the self-avowedly ideological VOA scripts, it is possible to envisage the immaterial space of broadcasting spanning both sides of the Atlantic as a public sphere understood in Rothberg's sense of a "malleable discursive space in which groups do not simply articulate established positions but actually come into being through their dialogical interactions with others."[17] The prevalent (and self-endorsed) impression of VOA as an early Cold War vehicle for an American ideological consensus can thus be supplemented by the awareness of the extent to which this "discursive space" came into being through "dialogical interactions with others," borrowing Rothberg's formulations.

Another significant point of departure within the field of scholarship devoted to the study of American Cold War broadcasting beyond the Iron Curtain lies in the approach suggested by Martin Medhurst, who points out that, since Thucydides and his *History of the Peloponnesian War*, history and rhetoric have been inextricably linked. As Thucydides no longer recalls exactly what each speaker said in speeches just before or during war, he wrote what he believed would have been called for in each situation.

> In the case of Thucydides, one of his goals was clearly to construct an account of the war that would be persuasive to his readers. To accomplish his goal, he turned to the art of rhetoric. What he found in that art was a systematic approach to the construction of character (*ethos*), an inventory of human emotions (*pathos*), and a checklist of rational appeals (*logos*). [18]

Medhurst further contends that platonic dialectics of knowledge/opinion, reality/appearance and the distinction between rhetoric and reality are questionable, "[b]ecause if there is a reality above or outside of human perception, we cannot know it, being creatures of limited symbolic capacities. All of what we call knowledge is symbolically mediated."[19] Following this line of argument, Medhurst points out that the Cold War was a rhetorical construction into which ambiguity was built (as the notion of a cold war in itself is an oxymoron),

> To clarify, I am not arguing that the Cold War was nothing but rhetoric. I am arguing that even in its most material manifestations—armaments, armies, air forces, agreements, et cetera—rhetorical dimensions were necessarily present. I am further arguing that to understand those rhetorical dimensions is to gain a new way of thinking about the Cold War.[20]

Pursuing this direction of unsettling the dichotomy words-things, another approach this reading relies on is Slavoj Žižek's dilution of the opposition between ideology and reality in his musings on the post-ideological status of our contemporary world, but which can shed light on the early Cold War scenario as well as on our relation to that scenario. On the one hand, there is what Žižek calls "totalitarian ideology" which, he argues, goes beyond a view of ideology as "a system which makes claim to a truth" because totalitarian ideology no longer even makes a pretense of truth,

> Totalitarian ideology no longer has this pretension, It is no longer meant, even by its authors, to be taken seriously—its status is just that of a means of manipulation, purely external and instrumental; its role is secured not by its truth value but by simple extra-ideological violence and promise of gain.[21]

On the other hand, Žižek explores ideology less in the sense of the "classic" concept "in which illusion is located in knowledge" but rather in view of the "overlooked, unconscious illusion" that he terms "ideological fantasy,"

> The fundamental level of ideology, however, is not of an illusion masking the real state of things but that of an (unconscious) fantasy structuring our social reality itself. And at this level, we are of course far from being a post-ideological society. Cynical distance is just one way—one of many ways—to blind ourselves to the structuring power of ideological fantasy; even if we do not take things seriously, even if we keep an ironical distance, *we are still doing them.*[22]

In this sense, not only is the dichotomy between ideology and the real destabilized, but there appear nuances in the very notion of ideology. In its "totalitarian" version, ideology functions not because of a purported truth value but due to extra-ideological factors (violence and the promise of gain); in addition, ideology can also be understood as a powerful fantasy structuring the real in spite of any cynical distance. The image of the Cold War as a ground of contention between ideologies predicated in similar ways is thus enriched by an awareness of key asymmetries: on the one hand, a totalitarian ideology enhanced by extra-ideological means, marking the landscape of Eastern Europe and, on the other hand, an ideological fantasy creating a compensatory American/universal space of peace and freedom.

Bringing together these disparate points of departure, the paradox that emerges is that the Anglophone, ideologically-charged recounting of historical events on both sides of the Atlantic, through the VOA scripts, actually acts as the post-factum voicing of a historical East European trauma which otherwise remains muted, locked in a space of repression. Following this reading, the US broadcasts, and VOA as a case in point, act as a space of reflection of Eastern European trauma, aired in a different place/space of expression, yet spiraling back to the place of infliction, beyond the Iron Curtain.

Airing Totalitarian Traumas: "On War of Words"

If, as argued above, the VOA is an institution of power which remains eclectic, as a stage of internal propaganda battles over the Cold War, and if ideology can be a gateway into an understanding of the configuration of the real, it becomes possible to posit the function of VOA scripts as loci from which to essentially voice a "memento trauma," borrowing Hartman's definition, as an ethical act addressed at an "other." In effect, Hartman envisages an act of reading which is ethical "because the readings are addressed, and not only formally (…) to the other as a responsive, vulnerable, even unpredictable being."[23] Although Geoffrey Hartman is careful to point out the danger of "displaced evangelical intensity" inherent in the fact that the "'memento trauma' aspect is not all that far from a 'memento mori,'"[24] the ethical function of the memento trauma can be retained as a necessary correlative of the act of engaging with the script.

Pursuing this line of reading, the VOA scripts act to give an expression to the "expressionless," where even silence has been muted, drawing on Shoshana Felman's rereading of Walter Benjamin's term "expressionless" and its multiple valences,

> I use the word *expresionless* throughout this book in Benjamin's path-breaking sense, but also in the sense of Levinas (…): expressionless (*das Ausdruckslose*) are those whom violence has deprived of expression; those who, on the one hand, have been historically reduced to silence, and who, on the other hand, have been historically made faceless, deprived of their *human* face—deprived, that is, not only of a language and a voice but even of the mute *expression* always present in a *living* human face.[25]

For Felman, one of these sites where this expression is made possible is the courtroom, and while a discussion of the implications of telling as a form of justice is, at this point, beyond the scope of the discussion, her insights into acts of telling as giving expression can inform an interpretation of the function of VOA scripts beyond the ideological purpose (itself not symmetrically opposed to "truth" nor to Soviet ideology) as opening up the possibility of airing trauma. This aspect is particularly striking in the text with which this chapter started, and which describes the attempted muting of the past, voiced and aired in the VOA script. Here, the new cities are meant to capture present history, and the script presents in fact a double vision: on the one hand, historical cities commemorating recent violence and, on the other hand, natural cities commemorating a long past perspective,

> The earth endures. Cities are laid waste and cities are founded. The names of cities are wiped off of the map. Tyrants impose new names on cities, often their own names take the place of names that have been known for centuries. But the earth endures and the memory of man is a stubborn, unfettered thing.[26]

In fact, in Eastern Europe, a double geography is shown to be inscribed into the city: one anchored in an immediate history, the other in a natural form of history, which also acts as a memento of the trauma of violence that ensued,

> All over Eastern Europe, place names have been changed to pay tribute to Communist leaders. In Rumania, Bulgaria, Hungary, Czechoslovakia, Albania, there are towns named Stalin, yet the men who live there, the men whose fathers and fathers' fathers built those towns, still carry around the ancient names in their hearts.[27]

The new names—collectively "Stalintowns aplenty"—do not only mark this present history; they are also actively meant to obliterate a trauma spanning the personal as well as the collective, translated into geographic terms. In this sense, the "Stalintowns aplenty" suggest a geography marked by totalitarian ideology which, returning to Žižek's insight, is transparent in its imposition and relies less on purported truth value than on extra-ideological means of persuasion and coercion, "When the Volga Germans, the Crimean Tartars, the Chechens and the Inguah peoples were wiped out and deported, hundreds of place names expressing their ancient habitation of their homelands had to be changed so that their very memory should be wiped out."[28] In the logic of traumatic recall that seems to inform the rendering of Eastern European geography in this script, the memory to be wiped out, however, can neither be quite remembered, nor quite forgotten. Thus, for example, in this political geography, the only remaining Tartar names are those colonized by literature (Pushkin's poem) or by historical rhetoric (the Crimean War), and yet they inevitably bring up the echo of the other Tartar identities, now rendered expressionless: "In the Crimea, about the only Tartar names that remain are those of Bakhchisaray, immortalized in Pushkin's poem, 'The Bakhchisaray Fountain,' and Balaklava, known for its role in the Crimean war."[29]

Additionally, the new totalitarian history is built on an absence that seeks to cover the suffering and trauma it elicited, now transformed into a void (the names wiped out), by supplementing absence with meaningless repetition, those "Stalintowns aplenty" that sketch a vast geographical propaganda, "New names that have thus far proved safe are repeated endlessly in all the Soviet Republics. Which of them has not a Sovietskoye, or an Oktyabrakoye, or a Komsomolskoye, repeated everywhere with a monotony which is characteristic of so many aspects of Soviet propaganda and Soviet life?"[30].

However, the monotony of Soviet propaganda is soon revealed in the script to encode a repetition of the original violence at the buried origin of the communist city names, as the latter represent an occasion for a prompt association with the perpetrator of violence, hastening the obliteration of natural memory but in fact, in the logic of the script, perpetuating natural memory as lost and buried,

> When Kirov was assassinated in 1934, and Stalin began the great hunt for scapegoats which in the end claimed the lives of thousands and tens of thousands of alleged assassins of Kirov, every republic and province hastened to proclaim its allegiance to the executioner by renaming one or more of its towns Kirov. The latest Soviet Geography lists at least nineteen towns named after Kirov.[31]

The script's rhetorical construction often indicates Stalin himself as the origin of historical violence, and there is an interesting paragraph which stands out in this respect, perhaps because it was subsequently crossed out. Unlike other paragraphs which were crossed out, and which generally provided more illustrations or examples of a pervious point, this particular one seems to place Stalin's personality cult squarely as the cause of the totalitarian ideology of violence, interestingly combining in a rhetorical twist on the one hand a humorous vision of Soviet monotony, perhaps disturbingly underlining the American perspective of witnessing and commenting ("once you have figured out the difference between Kirovskoye and Kirovabad") with, on the other hand, the looming perspective of the Stalinist content and the extent of the trauma of cultural and geographical purging, "When you have figured out the difference between Kirovskoye and Kirovabad, then you will know what Stalin means when he says that 'Soviet culture is national in form but Socialist in content.' Or should it be *Stalinist* in content? Again 'Political Geography' suggests the answer."[32]

The account of a traumatic geography identifies an interesting modulation in the totalitarian monotony, namely the absence of Lenintowns during Lenin's lifetime, contrasted with a proliferation of the "Stalintowns aplenty," suggested by the enumeration which might stop nowhere, echoing the traumatic repetition of the original violence inherent in the establishment of Stalintowns, which also seems to stop nowhere. In fact, Stalinist violence spreads both in time and also across generations, perpetuating the trauma of social and cultural obliteration,

> As long as Lenin lived there was no Leningrad. But even as early as 1939, the smallest Soviet pocket Atlas showed a Stalingrad, a Stalinir, a Stalinabad, a Stalino in remote Kamchatka, a Stalino in the Oblast named Stalin, a Stalino in Turkmenia, a Stalino on the Pergansk Oblast, a Stalino in the Novosibirsk region, a Stalinskil, a Stalinisi, an Ust Stalinsk, not to mention Stalin districts in every city, Stalin factories, Stalin streets, Stalin autos, Stalin Tractors, Stalin Locomotives, and, of course, a Stalin Peak 23,620 feet high, which is 238 feet higher than Lenin Peak.[33]

Perhaps for rhetorical relief, the continuation of this proliferation of Stalin cities—and names—accumulates into a grotesque landscape crowned at a "mere" height of 18,480 feet by the tyrannical and also caricature-like perpetrator of the geographical, cultural and political violence indexed earlier in the script, "And on Elbruz in the Caucasus, a mere 18,480 feet above the level of the sea, there is a statue, bemoustached, ridiculous and fierce, and on its pedestal the words: 'On the highest crest of Europe we have erected the bust of the greatest man of our times.'"[34] Moreover, in addition to the heavy monotony of predictable Stalintowns, there are the names of towns which permanently react to the convulsions of contemporary history, traumatic in that it is based on radical breaks (the re-naming) which only serve to repeat, yet again, the traumatic violence,

> So, in the Caucasian mountains where Stalin was born there was a little town named Batalpashinks. Then it was named after Stalin's crony, Sulimov. When Sulimov was purged, it was named after the chief purger of the moment, Yezhov. When Yezhov was purged, all maps and all memories had to be changed once more. Now they are afraid to name it after a mortal, all too mortal Bolshevik leader, so they have renamed it Cherkessk. Maybe this name will last.[35]

The amnesiac state which seeks to cover the traumas of communist history and totalitarian ideology is presented as a provisory state, in opposition to a state of nature and remembering. Moreover, it cannot erase, at least in this account, the memory of what is projected as a natural geography before the trauma, which acts—the speaker reminds the subjects of trauma—as a memento trauma in itself,

> In all these Stalin cities and around the base of these Stalin peaks there are men who call their mountains and their towns by older, more natural names. In all the satellite countries, ancient names vanish from the books along with ancient cultures and ancient freedoms. But the heart of man is more stubborn than paper, of which none other than Joseph Stalin once wrote: 'Paper will put up with anything that is written on it.'[36]

Thus, the ending note—"how long will this name endure"—prolongs the traumatic state in which the historical wound is inflicted, while also acting as a memento of a past beyond that trauma, as it voices a buried question "that is in millions of hearts,"

> As we hear of the rise and fall of names and consider how many towns in how many lands haven been compelled to adopt the name of one living ruler, we cannot help but ask the question that is in millions of hearts: 'this name that has been imposed upon our home, how long will this name endure?'[37]

An American Fantasy: "This Is Our Answer to the Communist Purges"

At this point, another issue emerges in relation to the re-interrogation of VOA scripts for their multidirectional remembering of Cold War trauma. Returning to the multivocal reading of the early Cold War years opened up by Rothberg himself, and exploring the interstices of Cold War consensus, the discourse of certain VOA scripts in the Sol Stein collection echo another inflexion discerned by Rothberg in Du Bois's text, which Rothberg places in a larger context, against an expanding backdrop, "cold war America, that of the Left and, in particular, the Jewish Left, and that of African American and African diaspora experience in an era of segregation at home and decolonisation abroad."[38] In this sense, in Rothberg's reading, Du Bois is ultimately "trying to find forms to express a postemancipation context of extreme suffering twinned with hope for a different future."[39]

Interestingly, in another VOA script ("The Freeing of the Slaves"), Stein directly engages the issue of American slavery and emancipation in a transatlantic setting and correlates it with the postwar configuration and a postemancipation future, but this is the subject of a separate discussion.[40] Here, the interest in an ethical approach to a universal postemancipation future will be illustrated with a second script by Sol Stein, "This is Our Answer to the Communist Purges" (dated January 30, 1953) which, it will be argued, is not only a presentation of American superiority resulting from a Cold War consensus, in line with VOA's ideological mission. By its universalist ethical aspirations, it also projects an imagined, delocalized alternative to all-encompassing communist persecutions and traumas, in an ideological fantasy, returning to Žižek's term, that structures reality in ways that are different from totalitarian ideology, which relies on extra-ideological means of coercion, as invoked in the geography of totalitarianism in the first script. From this perspective, the fact that VOA in general, and the VOA scripts in the Sol Stein collection in particular, repeatedly invoke the American present as a counterpoint to the communist traumas aired on VOA is also an imperative correlative of recounting another's trauma, which inescapably engages the (American) present.

The significance of the religious or ethical dimension of the script "This Is Our Answer to the Communist Purges" is underlined by the accompanying hand-written note from Roger A. Lyons, Director of Religious Programming at VOA: "Sol: This is the best script on religion I have seen since I have been in this job. Roger."[41] The pervasiveness of religious discourse in the Cold War in general, at VOA in particular, and Roger A. Lyons's role in this, has been the subject of recent reappraisal. Jonathan Herzog for example argues that, "Voice of America fed its religious propaganda to the masses"[42] and investigates the "spiritual offensive" overseen by Lyons at VOA, pointing out two essential messages: "The first highlighted the importance of religious freedom and attacked the Communist animus towards religion. The second emphasized the importance of religion in American society."[43]

However, a brief consideration of the wider context of the script under discussion complicates the overtly ideological mission, yielding the dimension of the text as (also) an American/universal compensatory fantasy pitted against the communist totalitarian world, and extending beyond a Cold War America fraught by its own battles. The text under discussion focuses its message around an account of the testimonial dinner held on January 28, 1953 in honor of Anna M. Rosenberg, sworn Assistant Secretary of Defense in 1950, the highest position held by a woman in the US military establishment. While a discussion of McCarthy's opposition to Anna M. Rosenberg's nomination, documented for example in Griffith's now classic *The Politics of Fear*,[44] is beyond the scope of this chapter, the fact that the text is coalesced around the figure of Anna M. Rosenberg, hardly a Cold War hardliner, and herself a target of American Cold War intimidation tactics and of other ongoing investigations, already pierces the monolithic representation of "religious propaganda" fed to the masses. Interestingly, Lyons himself was a target of McCarthy investigations.[45]

Beyond "spiritual offensive," the religious discourse of the text can thus be read, on the one hand, as a counterpoint to the space of trauma aired on VOA and, on the other hand, as a representation of a postemancipation scenario which is pan-religious and universalist, emerging as an ethical alternative couched in universalist—and not strictly American—terms, audible not only as a discourse of cultural imperialism, but also as a formulation of a cross-cultural ethical engagement, functioning not just as ideology but also as an ideological fantasy.

In this sense, the opening paragraph frames the American event as a counterpoint to all-sweeping religious persecution as well as to the specter of a "decadent democracy" haunting America,

> This is our answer to the persecution of Jews behind the Iron Curtain. This is our answer to our persecution of priests behind the Iron Curtain. This is our answer to all those who have called America a decadent democracy. In these words, Captain Joshua L. Goldberg opened a testimonial dinner, held in New York last week January 28th in honor of a great lady: Anna M. Rosenberg.[46]

In the logic of traumatic recall spanning both sides of the Atlantic, Stein's text spirals from the overt subject—the communist purges—to the American soil and the dramatic content inscribed on it, the private and public trauma occasioned by the Rosenberg case, here presented as a threat to the very heart of American democracy,

> Rosenberg? That name has a familiar ring. There are many Rosenbergs in America. Recently the world was shocked by the infamy of two of them. Julius and Ethel Rosenberg, professional spies, turned over the secrets of the atom bomb to the communist aggressors. And then there are the many Rosenbergs who live the lives of ordinary citizens.[47]

By contrast, using the "infamy" of the Rosenberg spies as a foil, Anna M. Rosenberg is singled out as a virtuous Rosenberg epitomizing American and at the same time universal ethical ideals, and celebrated by "representatives of all faiths,"

> And then, at a position morally opposite to that of the Rosenberg spies, is Anna M. Rosenberg, the guest of honor, to whom the representatives of all faiths now pay tribute.
>
> For over two years, Anna M. Rosenberg, mother of a family, served her country as chief of manpower and personnel of the armed forces of the United States. The contribution for which she would be remembered longest, it was said, was her concern for the spiritual welfare of the young men who have left their families, some for the second time, to enlist in the defense of the free world against aggression.[48]

The tribute to Anna Rosenberg centers around three key religious leaders, united in Stein's text by the resistance to Communist purges, a standpoint which unites faiths in the face of a world dominated by "confusion and tumult." Thus, in Rabbi David DeSola Pool's vision of his young contemporaries, "[v]ery many of them are groping for standards that they may hold on to in a world of confusion and tumult," and Stein quotes his words to the chaplains of the American armed forces, transmitting a message about personal spirituality and responsibility, opposed to a "professional military mentality" and in stark contrast to the ills of both Communism and Fascism, which the Rabbi brings together in antithesis to the "free democratic state,"

> 'The army, Navy and air Force must never be allowed to enforce on [these young men and women] a professional military mentality. We thank God,' he said, 'that ours is not a .... Communist or Fascist state.' He emphasized the necessity of strengthening the spiritual character of the young soldiers. 'Ours is a free democratic state,' he said. 'The optimum soldier is one in whom the human values in life are best safeguarded and preserved.'[49]

Stein's script then shifts to Bishop William C. Martin, "president of the National Council of the Churches of Christ in the United States" to focus on the latter's explanation concerning the role of the priest, minister or rabbi in the armed services, "'The chaplain,' he said, 'interprets to the soldier the wider and deeper meaning of this world conflict so that his hardships and sacrifices are understood to be a part of a global struggle between forces that would enslave man and those that would set him free.'"[50] In Stein's account, Bishop Martin continues his oppositional geography encompassing postwar traumas as well as colonial power structures traversing the world picture, "Unlike the imperialistic countries, we in the United States, said Bishop Martin, have come home from two world wars with nothing but our dead."[51] In this vision, the US stands aside from totalitarian countries significantly conflated with imperialism, interestingly anticipating debates today about the imperialism of Soviet power.[52] Moreover, this geography includes differentiation based on postwar trauma: whereas the US burden is that of the dead, the "imperialistic" trauma looms large, unspoken.

With the account of the next speaker, the script continues to reinforce the American/universal fantasy staged against the violent traumas and wounds inflicted by totalitarian ideology. Stein's account proceeds with the message of "His Eminence Francis Cardinal Spellman, Archbishop of New York" whose words "shocked the large audience into absolute silence,"[53] as the speaker recounts the new violent attack of words levied by the Communists against him—a piece of news which had just pierced the Iron Curtain in the form of a "dispatch from Warsaw." In contrast, Stein emphasizes, Spellman "spoke in praise of charity, of love, and of living by the Ten Commandments."[54] In line with Cardinal Spellman's pacifist and universalist discourse, Stein effectively ends his account of this part of the tribute as a fable about ethical universalism, "Here then were the representatives of the three major faiths of America, a Jew, a Protestant, and a Catholic, joining together in praise of good in a world of evil, in praise of faith in a world to which the Communists would bring despair, in praise of love in opposition to the red dogmas of hate."[55]

In a similar vein, the music at the close of the official ceremony is inscribed by Stein into a similar postemancipation American/universalist fantasy which includes religious and racial communion, as suggested by the succession of "Hebrew song," the "Divine Redeemer," "Ave Maria" sung by "Dorothy Maynor, a distinguished Negro singer," and a final pan-religious hymn: "Then the audience, members of all three faiths, together sang 'Faith of Our Fathers, Living Still.'"[56]

Towards the end of the script, beyond the language of (American) religious promotion in this self-avowedly ideological text, Stein's discourse coalesces into a moralizing tale of which Anna Rosenberg is both a protagonist and an emblem of a "free world." Upon being presented with the award, "Mrs. Rosenberg, choked with emotion, declined to accept this as a tribute to herself. She said she was only a symbol of the men and women in uniform who devote their life and energy so that we and the whole free world may live in peace."[57] In this sense, the central character emerges as an allegory of freedom and unity, couched in pan-religious terms ("Friends under God") and which Stein pits against the communist purges, "This had been an evening of praise. Praise for Mrs. Rosenberg, yes. But above all, praise of religious leaders for each other's efforts. Friends under God, these leaders stood united in their common brotherhood and their quest for peace."[58]

The fable of unity, ethical living and freedom sketches out less a real America (fraught by textual specters—allegations of the "decadent democracy," by the treason of the other Rosenbergs—and also, extra textually, by its own Cold War propaganda battles to which VOA as an institution, VOA staff or Anna Rosenberg were not immune) but rather an imaginary America projected in Stein's VOA script as a fantasy of freedom, responsibility and peace. In addition, this projected space of a "common brotherhood" airs, once again, the traumas ("purges") beyond (and silenced by) the Iron Curtain, back beyond the Iron Curtain. In their turn, in the logic of traumatic compensation and repetition, these serve to air a compensatory fantasy of democracy, "This united strength of the spirit is what Captain Goldberg called America's answer to the persecution of the Jews behind the Iron Curtain, America's answer to the persecution of priests behind the Iron Curtain, America's faith in democracy."[59]

(Post)memories of Communism: Commencement and Commandment

This reappraisal of VOA's airing of communist trauma and the accompanying projection of a universalist fantasy, coalescing around two points of memory located in the Sol Stein Papers, also needs to be placed in relation to the inevitable act of memory that such a reappraisal implies, and more precisely in relation to the field of cultural memory and cultural recall. In the theoretical comments to the collection of essays *Acts of Memory*, Bal emphasizes the cultural component of memory, a component situating memory in a permanent connection with the present and the future,

> Cultural memory has become an important topic in the emergent field of cultural studies, where it has displaced and subsumed the discourses of individual (psychological) memory and of social memory. In other words, the term *cultural memory* signifies that memory can be understood as a cultural phenomenon as well as an individual or social one. (…) We also view cultural memorization as an activity occurring in the present, in which the past is continuously modified and redescribed even as it continues to shape the future.[60]

In this culturally-oriented awareness of the past, two positions can actually be identified with reference to the VOA scripts: the (American) writer of the script, who remembers the original traumas beyond the Iron Curtain and recalls them for the listener, airing the trauma back to its space and place of occurrence; and the post-Cold War reader of the scripts who reopens the transatlantic rendering of the events, re-engaging with them from contemporary perspectives. In this way, the location of the writer of the scripts or the reader of the archives is delegated to that of a postmemory of the Cold War—borrowing the definition from Marianne Hirsch, who argues that living in postmemory, for the children of Holocaust survivors, "is to be shaped, however indirectly, by traumatic fragments of events that still defy narrative reconstruction and exceed comprehension. These events happened in the past, but their effects continue into the present."[61]

As Hirsch goes on to explain, the "post" is a "location in an aftermath," "not a movement, method or idea; I see it, rather, as a *structure* of inter- and transgenerational return of traumatic knowledge and embodied experience."[62] Moreover, postmemory is "a *consequence* of traumatic recall but (unlike posttraumatic stress disorder) at a generational remove."[63] Postmemory, moreover, includes a site of traumatic transfer which can be placed in "resonance" with other sites of trauma and postmemory,

> Certainly, my analysis is in dialogue with numerous other contexts of traumatic transfer that can be understood as postmemory. In fact, the process of intergenerational transmission has become an important explanatory vehicle and object of study in sites such as American slavery; the Vietnam War; the Dirty War in Argentina and other dictatorships in Latin America; South African Apartheid; Soviet, East European, and Chinese communist terror.[64]

In this spirit, by extrapolating Hirsch's observations to another postwar trauma, one can argue that the forms of engagement with the VOA scripts, both in the early 1950s as well as now, are situated in a postmemory which recalls the always deferred original trauma for a then-present context. Firstly, the VOA scripts and their airing at the beginning of the Cold War constitute a 1.5 moment, borrowing both Susan Rubin Suleiman's term and Hirsch's own use of it, denoting both participation in the trauma of communism (and the turmoil of McCarthyism) yet located at almost a whole remove from the moment of infliction, both spatially as well as (sometimes) temporally—given the suppression of news from the Eastern Block, or topics dealing with earlier years of communist abuse, such as the beginning of proliferation of Stalintowns which had already reached significant proportions, the first script tells us, by 1939. Secondly, contemporary engagement with these scripts in the form of archive work is marked by forms of "intergenerational transmission" seeking to reestablish a multidirectional and multidimensional dynamicity to a shared American and Eastern European heritage. Thus, in a double way, the VOA scripts can be read as sites of "resonance" for communist trauma, acting also as sites of traumatic transfer at a 1.5 remove or at full multigenerational removes.

If the main part of this chapter has addressed the scripts themselves and their situatedness at the beginning of the Cold War, it is useful to dwell a little further upon the contemporary moment of engaging not with the actual broadcasts but with the archives. In Hirsch's view of archival work, the latter, one may infer, implies multidirectional readings of points of memory invoked at the beginning of the paper, fostering modes of transgenerational transmission,

> We argue that, rather than giving information about the past, archival images function as 'points of memory' that tell us more about our own needs and desires, our own fantasies and fears, than about the past to which they supposedly bear witness. The notion of small 'points of memory,'

> inspired by Roland Barthes's *punctum*, connects productively to feminist preoccupations with the subjective, the daily, the intimate and embodied, the affective.[65]

Moreover, argues Hirsch, following Sedgwick, these connections and engagements are accompanied by a restorative, healing project, "Such a reparative approach to memory would be open to connective approaches and affiliations."[66]

Bringing these lines of argument together, one can suggest that, by unearthing sites that address, reflect, or air trauma, creating numerous spirals of departure and return across the Atlantic, between the totalitarian world of the 1950s in Eastern Europe and Cold War America, between communist trauma and American ideology, between the Cold War past and the post-Cold War present, an engagement with archives creates much more than a *fort-da*, to-and-fro of memory and interrogation, indicative of a state of stalling in a classical Freudian traumatic mechanism rather than of an act of remembering. In fact, by dwelling on "points of memory," recuperative and restorative work potentially takes place, pointing to connections between non-competing memories and traumas.

The restorative function of points of memory and of the archive in general can actually be even more ample. As Derrida reminds us right at the commencement of *Archive Fever*, our understanding of archive is double from its very (buried) incipience, marked by "two orders of order: *sequential* and jussive" brought forth by the simultaneous understanding of archive as "*commencement*" and "*commandment*,"

> Let us not begin at the beginning, nor even at the archive. But rather at the word 'archive'—and with the archive of so familiar a word. *Arkhne*, we recall, names at once the *commencement* and the *commandment*. This name apparently coordinates two principles in one: the principle according to nature or history, *there* where things *commence*—physical, historical, or ontological principle—but also the principle according to the law, *there* where men and gods command, *there* where authority, social order are exercised, *in this place* from which *order* is given—nomological principle.[67]

Drawing on this double lineage of the archive, explored in its manifestations or obliterations at length by Derrida's *Archive Fever*, VOA archives in general and the two points of memory evoked here in particular represent occasions both to engage with an origin and to engage with a theater of justice. It is interesting to return at this point to Felman's vision of the courtroom as a space of staging (not just healing) trauma and to expand this to the space of the archive. Felman places emphasis on the tight relationship between trauma and justice, and on the possibilities of the law to cope with traumatic legacies, as at the heart of trauma is the impossibility of telling, and this is worse confounded by instances when the law turns out to be oppressive, a characteristic which was evinced in the Nuremberg trials. And yet, Felman argues, the courtroom ends up being invested with the possibility of granting redemption: "One longs for justice and one hopes in legal justice because the only secular redemption comes from the law,"[68] which is why the Nuremberg trials and the O.J. Simpson trial (analyzed by Felman as "trials of the century") "have turned into veritable theatres of justice."[69] Broadcasting back beyond the Iron Curtain, and engaging with VOA archives, can also place communist traumas in a similar theater of justice, fulfilling the functions which, in Felman's view, were carried out (or confounded) by the trials of the century, without the legal implications, of course; however, Felman's own analysis is less concerned with the legal implications than with the effect upon/of traumatic remembering.

Finally, going back to Derrida's discussion of the archive, the latter's function seems to begin in a "post" moment, when spontaneous memory starts to falter,

> Because the archive, if this word or this figure can be stabilized so as to take on a signification, will never be either memory or anamnesis as spontaneous, alive and internal experience. On the contrary: the archive takes place at the place of originary and structural breakdown of the said memory.[70]

While the correlation between archive work and possible forms of redemptive justice remains beyond the scope of the present chapter, it is worth noting that voluntarily remembering—memorializing—is frequently represented as a form of doing justice in a historical sense. To take a Romanian example, an exhibition organized by the Sighet Memorial to the Victims of Communism and to the Resistance, under the High Patronage of the president of the European Parliament, now hosted in Bucharest, bears the title "Memory as a Form of Justice." This notion of doing justice through memory, correlating the act of remembering in an organized fashion with justice, is certainly not a singular case. Archives, too, following Derrida's comments, can be seen as a form of voluntary memory, which becomes necessary when memory as "spontaneous, alive and internal experience" actually breaks down. In this sense, archives—and engagement with them—suggest a form of witnessing which does not necessarily imply presence.

This chapter has tried to identify, on the one hand, new spaces of resonance in the representation of trauma and, on the other hand, to explore the manner in which an overtly ideological medium can be read as a point of memory constituting a surprisingly multivocal discursive space. US VOA broadcasts thus become a space of expression of Eastern European trauma, which spiral back to the place where the trauma was inflicted and perpetrated with the aim of voicing, if not healing. An approach to the content of the VOA broadcasts cognizant of trauma studies theories can also enrich the current state of debate and reappraisals of the role of US Cold War broadcasting beyond the Iron Curtain. In this respect, the two VOA scripts at the center of this reading perform a memento trauma, giving voice to the violence underlying a geography of totalitarianism which would otherwise remain mute and expressionless. This airing of an Eastern European trauma correlated with totalitarian ideology back beyond the Iron Curtain is accompanied by the projection of an ethical American-universalist context readable as an ideological fantasy anchored in the present, yet far exceeding Cold War America not immune to its own propaganda battles. Finally, from today's perspective of a post-Cold War world, the VOA scripts engage us not by airing a communist trauma through the insubstantial medium of radiowaves, but in the substantial form of an archive. Beyond a discussion of VOA broadcasts in terms of ideology and/or truth, or a vision of the VOA as a rudimentary propaganda machine, the ideological, traumatic, always multidirectional and multidimensional content of VOA scripts creates a site of cultural memory which is palimpsestic as it is inscribed by, and a shaper of, past, present and future transatlantic memories subject to restorative remembering.

Bibliography

Bal, Mieke. "Introduction." In *Acts of Memory: Cultural Recall in the Present*, edited by Mieke Bal, Jonathan Crewe and Leo Spitzer, vii-xvii. Hanover, NH: Dartmouth College: University Press of New England, 1999.

Borcila, Andaluna. "Accessing the Trauma of Communism. Romanian Women on US Television News." *European Journal of Cultural Studies*. 12.2 (May 2009): 191-204.

Caruth, Cathy. *Unclaimed Experience: Trauma, Narrative, and History*. Baltimore, MD: Johns Hopkins University Press, 1996.

Cummings, Richard H. *Radio Free Europe's Crusade for Freedom: Rallying Americans behind Cold War Broadcasting, 1950-1960.* Jefferson, N.C.: McFarland & Co., 2010.

Derrida, Jacques. *Archive Fever: A Freudian Impression.* Translated by Eric Prenowitz. Chicago: University of Chicago Press, 1996.

Felman, Shoshana. *The Juridical Unconscious.* Cambridge: Harvard University Press, 2002.

Griffith, Robert. *The Politics of Fear: Joseph R. McCarthy and the Senate.* 2nd edition. 1970. Amherst: University of Massachusetts Press, 1987.

Hartman, Geoffrey H. *The Geoffrey Hartman Reader.* Edinburgh: Edinburgh University Press, 2004.

Herzog, Jonathan P. *The Spiritual-Industrial Complex: America's Religious Battle against Communism in the Early Cold War.* New York: Oxford University Press, 2011.

Hessen, Robert, ed. "Introduction." In *Breaking with Communism: The Intellectual Odyssey of Bertram D. Wolfe*, edited by Robert Hessen, 1-32. Stanford, CA: Hoover Institution Press, Stanford University, 1990.

—, ed. *Breaking with Communism: the Intellectual Odyssey of Bertram D. Wolfe.* Stanford, CA: Hoover Institution Press, Stanford University, 1990.

Hirsch, Marianne. *The Generation of Postmemory: Writing and Visual Culture after the Holocaust.* New York: Columbia University Press, 2012.

Krugler, David F. *The Voice of America and the Domestic Propaganda Battles, 1945-1953.* Columbia: University of Missouri Press, 2000.

Medhurst, Martin J. "Introduction. The Rhetorical Construction of History." In *Critical Reflections on the Cold War: Linking Rhetoric and History*, edited by Martin J. Medhurst and H.W. Brands, 2-19. College Station: Texas A&M University Press, 2000.

Parry-Giles, Shawn. "Militarizing America's Propaganda Program, 1945-55." In *Critical Reflections on the Cold War: Linking Rhetoric and History*, edited by Martin J. Medhurst and H.W. Brands, 95-134. College Station: Texas A&M University Press, 2000.

"Political Geography"/"On War of Words." September 20, 1951. Sol Stein Papers, 1943-2004. MS 1437 Box 48 Folder 7 Series 3. Rare Book and Manuscript Library, Columbia University Library.

Puddington, Arch. *Broadcasting Freedom: The Cold War Triumph of Radio Free Europe and Radio Liberty.* Lexington: University Press of Kentucky, 2003.

Rothberg, Michael. *Multidirectional Memory: Remembering the Holocaust in the Age of Decolonization.* Stanford, Calif.: Stanford University Press, 2009.

Ştefănescu, Bogdan. "Reluctant Siblings: Methodological Musings on the Complicated Relationship between Postcolonialism and Postcommunism." *Word and Text. A Journal of Literary Studies and Linguistics* II.1 (June 2012): 13-26.

Suleiman, Susan Rubin. "The 1.5 Generation: Thinking About Child Survivors and the Holocaust." *American Imago* 59.3 (Fall 2002): 277-95.

"The Freeing of the Slaves." December 24, 1952. Sol Stein Papers, 1943-2004. MS 1437 Box 48 Folder 11 Series 3. Rare Book and Manuscript Library, Columbia University Library.

"This is Our Answer to the Communist Purges." January 30, 1953. Sol Stein Papers, 1943-2004. MS 1437 Box 48 Folder 18 Series 3. Rare Book and Manuscript Library, Columbia University Library.

Todorova, Maria. *Imagining the Balkans*. New York and Oxford: Oxford University Press, 1997.

Wolfe, Bertram. Letter from the New Workers School to W. E. B. Du Bois, November 21, 1930. *W. E. B. Du Bois Papers (MS 312). Special Collections and University Archives, University of Massachusetts Amherst Libraries*. Accessed January 22, 2014. http://oubliette.library.umass.edu/view/full/mums312-b055-i456.

Žižek, Slavoj. *The Sublime Object of Ideology*. London: Verso, 1989.

Notes

[1] Research for this chapter was carried out as part of a team project financed through PN-II-RU-TE grant no. 64/2011, *Cross-Cultural Encounters in American Trauma Narratives: A Comparative Approach to Personal and Collective Memories.*

[2] The script is part of the Sol Stein collection, Rare Book and Manuscript Library, Columbia University, New York. While the script bears Bertram Wolfe's name, the description of the box's content makes no reference to Voice of America scripts written by collaborators other than Sol Stein, nor is this script referenced in discussions of Bertram Wolfe's work at the Voice of America. At the time this chapter was published, Bertram Wolfe's authorship of this script still remained to be certified by custodians of the Sol Stein Collection.

[3] "Political Geography"/"On War of Words," September 20, 1951, Sol Stein Papers, 1943-2004. MS 1437 Box 48 Folder 7 Series 3, Rare Book and Manuscript Library, Columbia University Library, 1.

[4] Robert Hessen, ed., *Breaking with Communism: The Intellectual Odyssey of Bertram D. Wolfe* (Stanford, Calif.: Hoover Institution Press, Stanford University, 1990), 22.
[5] Cathy Caruth, *Unclaimed Experience: Trauma, Narrative, and History* (Baltimore, MD: Johns Hopkins University Press, 1996), 5.
[6] Borcila, for example investigates Romanian women's experience of communism as a first site on which communist trauma is predicated on American TV. See Andaluna Borcila, "Accessing the Trauma of Communism. Romanian Women on US Television News," *European Journal of Cultural Studies*, 12.2 (May 2009): 191-204.
[7] Cold War broadcasting activity aimed beyond the Iron Curtain (i.e. broadcasts issued by Voice of America, the US government's ostensible foreign policy tool, along with Radio Free Europe and Radio Liberty, where federal financing was covert until the scandal in the late 1960s revealing RFE and RL to be largely CIA-owned), are frequently discussed as part of the US arsenal of ideological weapons in the Cold War. The role of radio broadcasting in the propaganda battle is persuasively documented and explored, both in view of its positive effects for democracy-building. See for example Arch Puddington, *Broadcasting Freedom: The Cold War Triumph of Radio Free Europe and Radio Liberty* (Lexington: University Press of Kentucky, 2003) or Richard H. Cummings, *Radio Free Europe's Crusade for Freedom: Rallying Americans behind Cold War Broadcasting, 1950-1960* (Jefferson, N.C.: McFarland & Co., 2010), or for the manner in which the radios, taken together or separately, contributed to an ampler American offensive David F. Krugler, *The Voice of America and the Domestic Propaganda Battles, 1945-1953* (Columbia: University of Missouri Press, 2000) or Shawn Parry-Giles, "Militarizing America's Propaganda Program, 1945-55" in *Critical Reflections on the Cold War: Linking Rhetoric and History*, eds. Martin J. Medhurst and H.W. Brands (College Station: Texas A&M University Press, 2000), 95-134.
[8] The term "point of memory" is borrowed from Hirsch and it is used in the sense of material evidence from the past serving to open up historical memory to its own context as well as to transgenerational communication. See Marianne Hirsch, *The Generation of Postmemory: Writing and Visual Culture after the Holocaust* (New York: Columbia University Press, 2012).
[9] Michael Rothberg, *Multidirectional Memory: Remembering the Holocaust in the Age of Decolonization* (Stanford, Calif.: Stanford University Press, 2009), 2.
[10] Rothberg, *Multidirectional Memory*, 3.
[11] Rothberg, *Multidirectional Memory*, 117.
[12] Rothberg, *Multidirectional Memory*, 117.
[13] For a discussion and documentation of Wolfe's engagement with the communist cause and his subsequent anti-communism, see Robert Hessen, ed., *Breaking with Communism*.
[14] See Bertram Wolfe, Letter from the New Workers School to W. E. B. Du Bois, November 21, 1930, *W. E. B. Du Bois Papers (MS 312), Special Collections and University Archives, University of Massachusetts Amherst Libraries*, http://oubliette.library.umass.edu/view/full/mums312-b055-i456.

[15] See endnote 13.
[16] See David Krugler, *The Voice of America and the Domestic Propaganda Battles, 1945-1953*.
[17] Rothberg, *Multidirectional Memory*, 5.
[18] Martin Medhurst, "Introduction. The Rhetorical Construction of History," in *Critical Reflections on the Cold War: Linking Rhetoric and History,* eds. Martin J. Medhurst and H.W. Brands (College Station: Texas A&M University Press, 2000), 3-4.
[19] Medhurst, "Introduction. The Rhetorical Construction of History," 4-5.
[20] Medhurst, "Introduction. The Rhetorical Construction of History," 6-7.
[21] Slavoj Žižek, *The Sublime Object of Ideology* (London: Verso, 1989), 30.
[22] Žižek, *The Sublime Object of Ideology*, 33.
[23] Geoffrey Hartman, *The Geoffrey Hartman Reader* (Edinburgh: Edinburgh University Press, 2004), 293.
[24] Hartman, *The Geoffrey Hartman Reader*, 294.
[25] Shoshana Felman, *The Juridical Unconscious* (Cambridge: Harvard University Press, 2002), 13.
[26] "Political Geography"/"On War of Words," 1.
[27] "Political Geography"/"On War of Words," 1.
[28] "Political Geography"/"On War of Words," 4.
[29] "Political Geography"/"On War of Words," 4.
[30] "Political Geography"/"On War of Words," 5.
[31] "Political Geography"/"On War of Words," 5.
[32] "Political Geography"/"On War of Words," 5. Original underlining.
[33] "Political Geography"/"On War of Words," 6.
[34] "Political Geography"/"On War of Words," 6.
[35] "Political Geography"/"On War of Words," 2.
[36] "Political Geography"/"On War of Words," 6.
[37] "Political Geography"/"On War of Words," 6.
[38] Rothberg, *Multidirectional Memory*, 121.
[39] Rothberg, *Multidirectional Memory*, 130.
[40] See "The Freeing of the Slaves," December 24, 1952, Sol Stein Papers, 1943-2004, MS 1437 Box 48 Folder 11 Series 3, Rare Book and Manuscript Library, Columbia University Library.
[41] Handwritten note attached to script "This is Our Answer to the Communist Purges," January 30, 1953, Sol Stein Papers, 1943-2004. MS 1437 Box 48 Folder 18 Series 3, Rare Book and Manuscript Library, Columbia University Library.
[42] Jonathan Herzog, *The Spiritual-Industrial Complex: America's Religious Battle against Communism in the Early Cold War* (New York: Oxford University Press, 2011), 129.
[43] Herzog, *The Spiritual-Industrial Complex*, 128.
[44] See Robert Griffith, *The Politics of Fear: Joseph R. McCarthy and the Senate*, 2nd ed. with a new introduction (1970; Amherst: University of Massachusetts Press, 1987).
[45] See endnote 16.

[46] "This is Our Answer to the Communist Purges," January 30, 1953, Sol Stein Papers, 1943-2004. MS 1437 Box 48 Folder 18 Series 3, Rare Book and Manuscript Library, Columbia University Library, 1.
[47] "This is Our Answer to the Communist Purges," 1.
[48] "This is Our Answer to the Communist Purges," 1-2.
[49] "This is Our Answer to the Communist Purges," 2.
[50] "This is Our Answer to the Communist Purges," 2.
[51] "This is Our Answer to the Communist Purges," 2.
[52] For a discussion of the overlap between colonial practices and Soviet power, see Maria Todorova, *Imagining the Balkans* (New York and Oxford: Oxford University Press, 1997). For a discussion of theoretical resistance to this correlation between colonialism and Soviet practices, see Bogdan Ştefănescu, "Reluctant Siblings: Methodological Musings on the Complicated Relationship between Postcolonialism and Postcommunism," *Word and Text. A Journal of Literary Studies and Linguistics* II.I (June 2012): 13-26.
[53] "This is Our Answer to the Communist Purges," 2-3.
[54] "This is Our Answer to the Communist Purges," 3.
[55] "This is Our Answer to the Communist Purges," 3.
[56] "This is Our Answer to the Communist Purges," 3.
[57] "This is Our Answer to the Communist Purges," 4.
[58] "This is Our Answer to the Communist Purges," 4.
[59] "This is Our Answer to the Communist Purges," 4.
[60] Mieke Bal, "Introduction," in *Acts of Memory. Cultural Recall in the Present*, eds. Mieke Bal, Jonathan Crewe and Leo Spitzer (Hanover, NH: Dartmouth College: University Press of New England, 1999), vii.
[61] Hirsch, *The Generation of Postmemory* 5.
[62] Hirsch, *The Generation of Postmemory*, 6.
[63] Hirsch, *The Generation of Postmemory*, 6.
[64] Hirsch, *The Generation of Postmemory*, 19.
[65] Hirsch, *The Generation of Postmemory,* 22.
[66] Hirsch, *The Generation of Postmemory*, 24.
[67] Jacques Derrida, *Archive Fever: A Freudian Impression*, trans. Eric Prenowitz (Chicago: University of Chicago Press, 1996), 1.
[68] Felman, *The Juridical Unconscious*, 18.
[69] Felman, *The Juridical Unconscious*, 4.
[70] Derrida, *Archive Fever*, 11.

CAST IN STONE: GENERATIONAL TRAUMA AND SELF-NARRATION IN ANNIE PROULX'S *THE SHIPPING NEWS*

ANNA SAJECKI

In American author Annie Proulx's *The Shipping News,* the novel's protagonist, Quoyle, a newspaper editor, crosses the United States/Canada border to return to his ancestral home Newfoundland. Proulx's novel, like Shakespeare's *The Tempest* and Daniel Defoe's *Robinson Crusoe*, presents a main character who finds himself on an island that encourages personal transformation. However, though *The Shipping News* is an island narrative, it is not an isolationist story. Written in 1993, Proulx's story of traumatic history and inheritance both echoes and engages with other traumatic narratives of the time, incorporating structurally Michael Rothberg's theory of multidirectional memory: his contention that memorializing certain traumatic histories—such as the Holocaust—does not preclude discussion of other traumatic pasts, but instead promotes deeper conversation about the different valences and histories of traumatic events.[1] For instance, Proulx's story of ancestral trauma and return invokes a number of Holocaust return narratives that started to appear in the 1990s, when Jewish writers journeyed to Europe to investigate the traumatic pasts of their parents and grandparents.[2] Moreover, *The Shipping News* was published one year after the 1992 L.A. Riots, an eruption rooted in years of traumatic racial prejudice; the novel registers these tensions via the black character Partridge, a friend of Quoyle's and fellow newspaper reporter, who transplants himself to L.A. and experiences first hand the violence of the event. The discussions over trauma that rose to the fore in both academic and media outlets in the early 1990s did not blanket other tragic histories—such as the African American slave trade—as some theorists contest,[3] but instead became a foundation encouraging alternate investigations into traumatic experience.

Proulx contributed to these investigations into alternative forms of trauma via her fictional work; I argue that for Proulx her discussions on trauma and working through hinge on understanding how definitions of space evolve and change. Trauma studies as a field is rooted in psychoanalysis; while some critics have evaluated the spatial topography in the work of psychoanalysts such as Sigmund Freud or Julia Kristeva,[4] most psychoanalytic theory does not thoroughly engage with theoretical comprehensions of space, even though a seminal tenet of psychoanalysis is that the interior world organizes one's experience of the exterior world. Conversely, prominent contemporary spatial theorists such as Henry Lefebvre, Edward Soja, and Michel De Certeau tend to shy away from psychoanalysis, writing on space mainly from a capitalist and/or Marxist framework, or—as with Doreen Massey—from a feminist paradigm.[5] Proulx's work in *The Shipping News* is distinctive, as it merges spatial theory with psychoanalysis and trauma studies, exploring critically not only landscape's potential impact on the psyche, but the relationship between space, trauma and the working through process.

Many critics emphasize Proulx's hyperreal depictions of the local and regional and fall into the trap of dismissing space as static;[6] this chapter registers a departure by emphasizing the dynamism of Proulx's spatial representation, and more explicitly space's potential to index and recast the autobiographical nuances of one's ancestral history and continuing choices—narratives crucial to the working through process. Proulx's particular depiction of generational trauma and working through suggests an intimate, evolving relationship between self and space that factors within traumatic experience; place not only impacts one's psychic makeup—the author links traumatic experience to survival amidst rugged rock and ocean—but is also an essential expression and record of ancestral pasts and personal narration. Place is a vital tool of narration that enables Quoyle to understand and work through ancestral tragedy while simultaneously communicating his ongoing self-narration. Thus, in *The Shipping News*, Proulx contributes to overarching discussions of trauma—and specifically intergenerational trauma—by exploring the capacity of space to generate and retain stories of upheaval and renewal.

At the outset of the novel, the protagonist, Quoyle, is an emotionally-void adult with zero confidence, "hive-spangled, gut roaring with gas and cramp, he survived childhood; at the state university, hand clapped over his chin, he camouflaged torment with smiles and silence. Stumbled through his twenties and into his thirties learning to separate his feelings from life, counting on nothing."[7] The narrator quickly reveals that Quoyle's state of mind is directly connected to his childhood, and specifically to a cruel and tormenting father who both pushes Quoyle too far and ridicules the boy when he fails. As time progresses, Quoyle's sense of failure manifests itself repeatedly in his studies, string of precarious jobs, and marriage. Born in Brooklyn, raised in a "shuffle of dreary upstate towns,"[8] Quoyle then settles in the fictional town of Mockingburg, New York where a friend helps him acquire a poor-paying and insecure job as a reporter for the *Mockingburg Record.* He manages to maintain his position at the paper amidst several firings and rehirings as his boss Ed Punch notices that, "Quoyle, who spoke little himself, inspired talkers. His only skill in the game of life."[9] While reporting on municipal affairs, Quoyle meets Petal Bear, who flippantly agrees to marry Quoyle and in between her multiple illicit affairs gives birth to two of his children. It is only when tragedy strikes—Quoyle's parents commit suicide, and Petal Bear dies in a car crash after an ill-fated ploy to escape the family—that the protagonist is introduced to his aunt Agnis Hamm, who convinces him to start anew in Newfoundland.

From his discussions with his aunt, it becomes apparent that Quoyle knows little of his familial history; that he only exists because his grandfather—a sealer in Newfoundland—incestuously had a child at 12 years old, just before dying by drowning under the ice. As Quoyle states, he "hated the thought of an incestuous, fit-prone, seal-killing child for a grandfather, but there was no choice. The mysteries of unknown family."[10] While the grandmother marries another brother, it quickly becomes apparent that both the latter, as well as her third husband, died young from drowning. Death from the harsh elements and a life on the ocean is the norm, not the exception; the survivors are haunted by the numerous tragedies. While earlier Quoyle reveals an inquisitiveness about his history, meaning that he "wondered about ancestors," his father is hesitant to talk about his past life in Newfoundland and prefers to focus instead on an immigrant narrative about how he had to work hard upon arriving in America, so as to provide opportunity for his children: "his father, self-hauled to the pinnacle of produce manager for a supermarket chain, preached a sermon illustrated with his *own* history."[11] Instead, Quoyle only has a few photographs to feed his curiosity,

> Foraging in a box of excursion momentoes, he found photographs of his father beside brothers and sisters at a ship's rail. A girl, somewhat apart from the others, looked toward the sea, eyes squinted, as though she could see the port of destination a thousand miles south. Quoyle recognized himself in their hair, their legs and arms. That sly-looking lump in the shrunken sweater, hand at his crotch, his father. On the back, scribbled in blue pencil, 'Leaving Home, 1946.'[12]

Marianne Hirsch calls the transmission of traumatic memory from one generation to the next "postmemory," and describes the family photo as a crucial artifact facilitating this transmission; when we look at photographic images from a lost past world, especially one that has been annihilated by force, we look not only for information or confirmation, but for an intimate connection that would transmit the affective quality of the events.[13] Because Quoyle has scarce access to family narratives regarding life in Newfoundland, the photograph becomes an overwhelming symbolic presence that hints at an ancestral past he barely understands.

Aside from the photograph, there are few conscious recognitions or artifacts of Quoyle's family history—though this does not negate the intensity of the transmitted trauma that imprisons Quoyle, "his earliest sense of self was as a distant figure: there in the foreground was his family; here, at the limit of the far view, was he."[14] Quoyle's transmission of trauma has mainly happened on a more unconscious, somatic level; he suffers from what Gabriele Schwab terms a "haunting legacy,"

> Children of a traumatized parental generation, I argue, become avid readers of silences and memory traces hidden in a face that is frozen in grief, a forced smile that does not feel quite right, an apparently unmotivated flare-up of rage, or chronic depression. Like photography, traumatized bodies reveal their own optical unconscious. It is this unconscious that second-generation children absorb. While being fully aware of it, they become skilled readers of the optical unconscious revealed in their parents' body language. I would add that, beyond the optical unconscious, children read their parents' unconscious more generally in the embodied language of affects. The second generation thus receives violent histories not only through the actual memories or stories of parents (postmemory) but also through the traces of affect, particularly affect that remains unintegrated and inassimilable.[15]

Schwab elaborates on the Freudian association of trauma with repeated nightmares and memories, suggesting that—because of the devastation of the traumatic event—violent histories, instead of being remembered, are repressed within "unreachable psychic recesses."[16] She relies on the critical work of psychoanalysts Nicolas Abraham and Maria Torok, who suggest that a progenitor carries his or her guarded secrets and trauma in the form of a repressed phantom—or crypt—which then passes from the parent's unconscious to the child's.[17] The crypt silences the phantom; however, entombment nevertheless preserves the trauma. Thus, a traumatic event can be affectively passed down across generations without specific narratives or memories accompanying the transmission.

This repressed transmission of trauma seems to qualitatively describe Quoyle's affective experience of his family's past, specifically his father's. Quoyle is traumatized by his father's early repeated attempts to make him swim—attempts undoubtedly shaped by generations of lives that came to an end in the ocean, "again and again the father had broken his clenched grip and thrown him into pools, brooks, lakes and surf."[18] The father's reaction soon becomes a regular fixture in the protagonist's life, "the father saw other failures multiply like an explosion of virulent cells—failure to speak clearly; failure to sit up straight; failure to get up in the morning; failure in attitude; failure in ambition and ability; indeed, in everything. His own failure."[19] However, this final three-word sentence presents an ambiguity, as the referent could either be the son *or* the father. This ambiguity between father and son is also emphasized by the protagonist's name: Quoyle is the *family*'s name, and is not particular to the protagonist. This confusion between generations emphasizes the impact of the intergenerational trauma that has been passed down; the conflation makes explicit not only what Schwab might term the affective perception of the child, but also the absorption of a parent's trauma to the point of confused identity.

Dominick LaCapra broadly defines trauma as both disorienting and dissociative, "a shattering experience that disrupts or even threatens to destroy experience in the sense of an integrated or at least viably articulated life. There is a sense in which trauma is an out-of-context experience that upsets expectations and unsettles one's very understanding of existing contexts."[20] One existing context to consider is space. While Walter Benjamin discusses the traumatic experience of urban space, and trauma theorists such as James Young critically consider the significance of the memorial site, there is still a gap to be filled in terms of critically understanding how traumatic experience shifts one's relationship with surrounding spaces both connected to, and unconnected with, the original trauma experienced. Proulx's writing, which lends considerable emphasis to the nuances of traumatic pasts and presents, and provides rich description of landscapes, becomes an excellent forum for the exploration of how places might be perceived differently within a traumatic context.

In *The Shipping News*, two forces of formation prevail and interact: the traumatizing influence of space on character formation, and secondly the potential for the individual to redefine place in conjunction with changes to his or her psyche. Proulx's conception of space aligns more with contemporary theories that diverge from the invention of space as absolute. While some critics have questioned her portrayal of Newfoundland, Proulx's emphasis on the intimate relation between person and landscape recasts space as subjective; her work is not to be read as an overarching static definition of place. Instead, Proulx's literary spaces are *produced* by social practices while simultaneously retaining the power to *shape* social practices, a concept central to the work of Henri Lefebvre consequently termed the "socio-spatial dialectic" by Edward Soja.[21] Moreover, "social space"—as Lefebvre terms it—has an infinite potential for definition, depending on different contexts, discourses, relationships, purposes etc.[22] Thus, one person's relationship with place has the ability to redefine how a space is understood, cognized or interpreted.

Quoyle's particular relationship with the town in which he lives, Mockinburg, is marked by a void. Regarding the representation of trauma, Benjamin proffers a distinction between *Erlebnis*, the condition of living through an event, and *Erfahrung*, the actual experience of an occurrence. The traumatized individual can recall and communicate the traumatic event mainly in accordance with *Erlebnis*, or in a detached, aloof manner.[23] What Proulx demonstrates is that the individual whose psyche is circumscribed by postgenerational trauma will continue to experience spatial surroundings in a manner closer to *Erlebnis*. Mockinburg, for Quoyle, is a town blunted of meaning, "Quoyle bought groceries at the A & B Grocery; got his gas at the D & G Convenience; took the car to the R & R Garage when it needed gas or new belts (…) lived in his rented trailer watching television."[24] For Jennifer Denise Ryan, Mockinburg is an "upstate town whose geography is so irrelevant to the lives of its residents that few of its attributes warrant mention at all."[25]

However, the geography of the town is compelling, specifically as a signifier of Quoyle's psychic state. Mockinburg is "a place in its third death … a long recession [had] emptied the downtown, killed the malls. Factories for sale. Slum streets, youths with guns in their pockets, political word-rattle of some litany, sore mouths and broken ideas."[26] In *The Shipping News*, there is a trope throughout that collapses the boundaries between death and sleep, where another person's death is cast as a sleep from which one cannot awaken. Quoyle's children confuse death and sleep, assuming that their mother, that the newspaper publisher Jack Buggit, that dead birds will eventually wake up. Thus, even in its "third death," Mockinburg seems an iteration of Quoyle, who sleepwalks through life because of his inherited traumatic experiences; Mockinburg as a dead town is the manifestation of Quoyle's own psychic condition. However, in the novel, Jack Buggit actually does wake up, and the dead bird disappears, opening the possibility for the reinvigoration of both individuals and space: for Quoyle, and even for Mockinburg, the potential for some form of vitalization is immanent.

After a series of tragic incidents, Quoyle's desire to work through his intergenerational trauma is marked by his desire for the north. When Quoyle agrees to move with his Aunt Agnis to Newfoundland, he is not seeking his family's history, but the empty, static space with which the north is traditionally associated. The artificial, misleading concept of empty space has long been associated with the European founding myths of the Americas, and even today somewhat persists as a false notion associated with Canada. Regarding static space, Doreen Massey writes that this longing for stasis has intensified with the rise of globalization and theories of postmodernism that promote an aesthetic of stabilized space.[27] Building off Lefebvre's conception of space, she critiques absolutist notions by insisting specifically on the centrality of interrelationships to evolving definitions of spaces, "the identities of place are inevitably unfixed. They are unfixed in part precisely because the social relations out of which they are constructed are themselves by their very nature dynamic and changing (…) moreover, that lack of fixity has always been so."[28] Proulx investigates relationships with space in *The Shipping News*, illuminating specifically the social milieu of traumatic community and how it affects definitions of space.

Proulx, engaging specifically with questions related to trauma studies, recasts Massey's contention in several ways: for one, Quoyle comes to realize quickly that Newfoundland is not an empty space, but a place marked by a particularly close-knit community united by complicated traumatic histories and social relations. Secondly, Proulx demonstrates that if social identities, and thus social relations, are strained by traumatic histories, then there must also inevitably be a strain on identifications of space as well. While Quoyle initially views Newfoundland as empty space, his Aunt Agnis sees the rock as striated and overflowing with traumatic stories, hence her detailed recollection on the ferry ride to the island,

> Spring starvation showed skully heads, knobbed joints beneath flesh. What desperate work to stay alive, to scrob and claw through hard times. The alchemist sea changed fisherman into wet bones, sent boats to drift among the cod, cast them on the landwash. She remembered the stories in old mouths: the father who shot his oldest children and himself that the rest might live on flour scrapings; sealers crouched on a floe awash from their weight until one leaped into the sea; storm journeys to fetch medicines—always the wrong thing and too late for the convulsing hangashore.
>
> She had not been in these waters since she was a young girl, but it rushed back (…).[29]

At the end of the ferry ride, Agnis wonders, "which had changed the most, place or self? It was a strong place. She shuddered. It would be better now. Leaned on the rail, looking into the dark Atlantic that snuffled at the slope of the past."[30] While this statement in part implies the strength of place over the self, as well as insinuating the potential of place to define and even override the self, it also elicits hope that a changed self might trump one's prior relationship with space. Different individuals leave their mark on how space comes to be defined, but the dynamism of space also surfaces as a palimpsest of sorts that evolves as individuals evolve; while Agnis still comprehends Newfoundland as etched with the trace of traumatic pasts, she tentatively hopes that the self can overwrite, or at least edit, that traumatic signature of the past.

Quoyle's changing perception of Newfoundland in the novel and space's palimpsestic qualities are reminiscent of the rhetoric Julia Kristeva uses to discuss the centrality of narration in the working through process;[31] though Kristeva connects space and narration only metaphorically, there is nevertheless the implication that space might retain stories that will help the working through process, an implication important for Proulx's work on trauma. According to Kristeva, the condition of one's psychic space influences how one experiences life; self-introspection and vocalization as reflexive processes illuminate how the psyche has been shaped—the creation of a personal narrative allows one to manifest an understanding of one's symptoms and neuroses allowing for an expanding and active definition of the self.[32] In *New Maladies of the Soul*, Kristeva urges the creation of "an 'inner zone'—a secret garden, an intimate quarter, or more simply and ambitiously, a psychic life."[33] She continues this spatial emphasis in *Intimate Revolt*, in which she proffers her conceptualization of the "return," seeking to re-establish in contemporary society the classical and later Christian connection between revolt and the concept of re-turn as a turning towards the self, towards an intimate knowledge.[34] This turn, in essence, marks the creation of a psychic space, where narration is the privileged mode of acquiring this space—by discovering the past through narrative, one begins to give a name to and identify one's psychic pathologies. In many regards, *The Shipping News* is an allegory of Kristevian return, although Quoyle's evolving definition of Newfoundland involves a more nuanced form of actual space that diverges from Kristeva's rhetorical, metaphorical references to space. Newfoundland as a literal space can be read to reveal the cause and history of trauma, and the island is an active text responsive to Quoyle's changing definition of self.

Indeed, in *The Shipping News* it is impossible to separate self-narration from land; for one, the spatial conditions of Newfoundland are the source of Quoyle's intergenerational trauma, a manifestation of postmemory that must be vocalized as part of the working through process. This sentiment is inherent in the speech and reflections of several characters. For instance, Agnis Hamm recalls her emigration as a journey "away from the outports, islands and hidden coves, rushing like water away from isolation, illiteracy, trousers made of worn upholstery fabric, no teeth, away from contorted thoughts and rough hands, from desperation."[35] The isolation is a factor in the perpetual sexual abuse that happens within families on the island—an abuse Agnis herself experienced, and which is more widely reported in the local weekly paper the *Gammy Bird.*

Beyond abuse and isolation, the ocean also perpetuates trauma. For Mrs. Buggit, the elements are responsible for taking away her son, who drowned like so many others. It only thus seems rational that a storm, exemplifying elemental power, would recall these traumatic events, "the aunt marked the beating of the sea, a pummeling sound that traveled up through the legs of the bed. Up the road Mrs. Buggit recognized the squealing gasps of a drowning son."[36] However, these spatially-prompted recollections are the building blocks of narration, if one allows oneself to face them. When trauma remains silenced in what Schwab terms the "crypt" form, then according to Schwab the individual remains in a state where they have incorporated the event, severing "the process of vital exchange between self and world and [foreclosing] transformation and emergence."[37] Narration, Schwab states, is a form of introjection whereby traumatic loss is transformed into something new, "a transformational process that furthers continual self-fashioning."[38] In the novel, when Jack Buggit starts his own story, he begins with his family history, "Great-great-grandfather had to go to cannibalism to stay alive. We settled Flour Sack Cove, right here, only a few families left now. Buggits fished these waters, sealed, shipped out, done everything to keep going."[39] By beginning with the past of his family, Buggit's familial history forms the foundation of his self-identification; however, his narration continues as a form of active self-fashioning and the arc of his storytelling explicitly suggests that life can continue beyond traumatic hauntings without precluding the expression of traumatic pasts.

While Buggit acknowledges his own traumatic past, his position as publisher of the *Gammy Bird* also enables him to help others face their tragic pasts. The paper may seem sensational, because it emphasizes sexual abuse cases, car crashes and other tragedies, but the flip side of this sensationalism is the process of narration, naming, and awareness. As Nutbeem, Quoyle's coworker, observes,

> 'Have you noticed Jack's uncanny sense about assignments? He gives you a beat that plays on your private inner fears. Look at you. Your wife was killed in an auto accident. What does Jack ask you to cover? Car wrecks, to get pictures while the upholstery is still on fire and the blood still hot. He gives Billy, who has never married for reasons unknown, the home news, the women's interest page, the details of home and hearth—must be exquisitely painful to the old man. And me. I get to cover the wretched sexual assaults. And with each one I relive my own childhood. (…) And what I don't know is if Jack understands what he's doing, if the pain is supposed to ease and dull through repetitive confrontation, or if it just persists, as fresh as on the day of the first personal event. I'd say it persists.'[40]

Here Buggit is prompting his reporters to process what is haunting their unconscious by returning to the space of their hauntings and writing articles that confront, thus beginning the process of mourning through narration. Nutbeem's response to the consequences of this personal narration and re-visitation belies his own traumatic condition. While LaCapra agrees that with trauma, there is an element of incomprehensibility and that the healing of the past is not a realistic goal, he does believe that the working through process can still take place to help mitigate the effects of trauma.[41] He believes it promotes the transition from *Erfahrung* to *Erlebnis*, or in Schwab's words, from incorporation to introjection. The trauma and the pain may not disappear, but facing the spaces that reflect trauma opens up the potential for Nutbeem to reconnect with the world, to define himself more broadly, and to feel more deeply.

For Quoyle, the first scene analogizes this intersection between reading and narrating the past, and the creation of a new personal psychic space. The scene is of the Quoyle family in a car, steering up "the west coast of the Great Northern Peninsula along a highway rutted by transport trucks"[42] headed towards the old family home on Quoyle's point. When the highway was built mid-century in Newfoundland, it was a symbol of modernization on an island where boating was the main form of transportation; before the 1950s, many outport towns were inaccessible by road. However, while the highway represents the potential of a "new path," the house harkens to the past—the coexistence of the two seemingly conjures an imprint of Quoyle's psyche, producing a space that is nuanced, complex, dynamic, a space that acts as a palimpsest open to potentiality as well as the past.

When the family finally arrives at Quoyle's point, they find the house still standing after 40 years of abandonment; steadied by cables and iron rings set in the rock, the anchored abode stubbornly resists change. Moreover, the "distinctive feature" of the house is "a window flanked by two smaller ones, as an adult might stand with protective arms around children's shoulders,"[43] thus becoming a spatial metaphor for generations and the passage of time and traumatic history. As Quoyle, his aunt, and his daughters Bunny and Sunshine, move towards the building, "the house threw their voices back at them, hollow and unfamiliar."[44] The echoing suggests the vocalization of the past, the initial surfacing of a familial history still largely unknown to Quoyle. The family house itself is a text that holds and presents this history.

To better illuminate the nuances of Proulx's depiction of space, I suggest linking Kristeva's emphasis on narration as part of the working through process with Michel de Certeau's notion of spatial stories. De Certeau differentiates between place and space, defining space as "practiced place"—place that has been acted upon and written upon by individuals.[45] Thus, de Certeau insists on the existence of spatial stories that can be read to reveal past manipulations of place that have resulted in the founding of spaces.[46] When there is a lack of stories attached to a landscape—such as in Quoyle's Mockinburg—there is a loss of space and reversion to place, "deprived of narrations (as one sees it happen in both the city and the countryside), the group or the individual regresses toward the disquieting, fatalistic experience of a formless, indistinct and nocturnal totality."[47] When positioned within the context of trauma studies and Kristevian psychoanalysis, reading spatial narratives from one's own history both enlivens space and delineates one's own psychic condition, encouraging the creation of a new psychic space remindful of Kristeva's metaphorical garden, as well as encouraging the spatial writing of new autobiographical stories. Combining Kristeva and de Certeau helps to more precisely envision and recast Proulx's own theory on trauma, space and the working through process as a theoretical framework.

Reading spatial stories containing familial traumatic pasts becomes integral to Quoyle's ability to work through his transgenerational trauma. When Billy Pretty—the protagonist's coworker at the *Gammy Bird*—takes the protagonist to the original site of the Quoyle family in Newfoundland, Quoyle learns the spatial narratives written generations ago by his family; by hearing these stories, Quoyle himself is able to attach narrative to his own inherited trauma. As they walk around the old family haunt, as Pretty takes Quoyle to the old family cemetery, stories of the original Quoyles surface. When Quoyle admits he doesn't know the old stories of his family, Pretty elaborates, "loonies. They was wild and inbred, half-wits and murderers. Half of them was low minded."[48] He tells Quoyle about Nolan Quoyle, the protagonist's only other remaining family member on the island aside from his aunt and children, describing him as "the old style of Quoyle": "they say there's a smell that comes off him like rot and cold clay. They say he slept with his wife when she was dead and you smell the desecration coming off him."[49] Also, Nolan lives a traditional fisherman's life among the rock and water and has made home a shack that is "more boat shed than house."[50] When the protagonist visits the family member, he sees in Nolan "the poverty of another century," and realizes that this "was what he had sprung from."[51] Not only is Quoyle's past spatialized via Nolan and his personal belongings, but also the story of harsh life in Newfoundland seems to be contained in a fishing line below Nolan's foot, "the snarl trodden into compacted detritus, a churn of splinters, sand, rain, sea wet, mud, weed, bits of wool, gnawed sheep ribs, spruce needles, fish scales and bones, burst air bladders, seal offal, squid cartilage, broken glass, torn cloth, dog hair, nail parings, bark and blood."[52] By ending the description with "blood," Proulx emphasizes the connection between space and bloodline; as Quoyle views Nolan and Nolan's house, he is also reading the materialized story of his own generational history.

Quoyle's generational history also persists in the names of certain Newfoundland locales, as he learns on his outing with Billy Pretty. While travelling about Gaze Island with Pretty, the protagonist learns of a defining traumatic point in the Quoyle family history, when in the late 1800s members of the family had to drag their house across the ice to another point, followed by "a wrangle-gangle mob of islanders behind them. For over the years others came and settled. Drove the Quoyles away."[53] The bay the family was specifically driven away from was named Omaloor Bay, which Pretty elaborates was named after the Quoyles, Omaloor meaning a simple-minded or stupid person.[54] The bay named after the family indexes the spatial narratives written over a century earlier by the family; in the name Omaloor Bay, space and narrative intersect. Moreover, Omaloor Bay is on Gaze Island, which stares across to Quoyle's Point, the current site of the family house. While Gaze does not specifically reference the family's past, the name still elicits the history of the Quoyle family—as a chronotope, the island stands as a reminder of the historic trauma of the Quoyle family; the space holds within its uncomfortable grasp even later generations like an unrelenting gaze. In its name, Gaze Island explains the potential of traumatic past to become powerfully inscribed onto space and later generations.

It is off the Gaze Island coast, as well, where Quoyle finds a suitcase with a severed head inside. Quoyle identifies the head as belonging to a man he interviewed for the shipping news column, who owned with his wife a pleasure yacht that once belonged to Hitler. When Quoyle first finds the suitcase, Pretty acknowledges that the protagonist is a "real Quoyle," "a wracker" whose plundering is remindful of the Quoyles's long history as pirates.[55] This conflation with the old Quoyles not only refracts Quoyle's quest to find trauma within the narration of his ancestral past, but also signifies the confusion of familial identity that follows the inheritance and transmission of trauma. Later, Quoyle finds the remaining body of the decapitated man near Quoyle's Point, by a specific rock referred to as the Ovens. The association of the dead man with both Hitler and with the Ovens elicits a tenuous connection with the Holocaust and the fate of the bodies belonging to the millions killed. Finding the body so close to the historical spots of his own family brings together two very different forms of historical trauma, presenting an embodied form of Rothberg's belief in multidirectional memory, whereby opening the discussion of one form of trauma also helps to surface and open conversation about other forms of trauma.[56] So too, does this subtle reference to the Holocaust function as a bridge, implying a connected community of radically different traumatic histories that contextualize Proulx's otherwise seemingly isolated example of generational trauma. It is no coincidence that the body parts are found so close to historical spaces associated with the Quoyles; the dead man is a visible manifestation of Quoyle's own perished ancestors: the body is thus a synecdoche that dramatizes the protagonist's own ability to face the tragic histories of his family.

Quoyle finds the headless body after spending a weekend alone at the family house, working on an article entitled "For God's Sake, Help Me."[57] The article departs from Quoyle's usual columns that focus mostly on tragedy and on pressing issues related to the shipping industry. The article instead historically maps the invention of the Plimsoll line on boats by Samuel Plimsoll; water covering up the line on a boat indicates that the cargo load is too heavy and thus more likely to capsize. The column is about someone who encountered tragic deaths within the shipping industry in 1868, and who instead of remaining passive created an interventionist safety mechanism that aimed to prevent future deaths. After starting the article, that night Quoyle has another terrific dream about his former wife Petal Bear, but admits that he is "getting used to nightmares."[58] Both the article and the comment about nightmares suggest transition, a state reified when Quoyle walks out to the end of Quoyle's Point, which he describes as a frontier, "a wild place that seemed poised on the lip of the abyss. No human sign, nothing, no ship, no plane, no animal, no bird, no bobbing trap marker no buoy."[59] The area is described as a place without signification on one hand, but somehow simultaneously beset with meaning, "haunted by lost ships, fishermen, explorers gurgled down into sea holes as black as a dog's throat…the Inuit in skin boats, breathing, breathing, rhythmic suck of frigid air, iced paddles dipping, spray freezing, sleek back rising, jostle, the boat torn, spiraling down."[60] Proulx's depiction of Quoyle's Point is dynamic; marked by the stories and trauma of the past, the space is poised to be written on again. Not only is Quoyle suspended on the edge of a point, but psychically he seems ready for a transition, wherein he can spatially narrate the creation of an identity that transcends the inherited trauma.

When Quoyle finds the body, the moment evokes the protagonist's direct confrontation with an embodied memory of unwitnessed trauma that is no longer hidden and elusive within a crypt, but now materialized and accessible. After he finds the body, Quoyle realizes boating is the fastest way to the police authorities. When his boat capsizes, however, Quoyle makes direct contact with the ocean. As a result, he learns to swim for the first time and manages to stay alive until he is rescued; he avoids drowning and, thus, the traumatic death of his grandfather, and forges a new fate. Throughout life, Quoyle had been ashamed of his body, his enormous girth, as well as his jutting chin, from "some anomalous gene [that] had fired up at the moment of his begetting."[61] The chin, similar to Nolan Quoyle's, is a mark of the family's, and Quoyle's shame is related to his father's repression of the family's past; however, after nearly drowning, Quoyle views his enormous body as powerful—it had kept him alive in the cold water. Quoyle's drowning is a pivotal moment that illuminates his psychic shift towards introjection.

The immersion in water is symbolic of Quoyle's relationship to his transgenerational trauma, and the novel gradually displays how Quoyle's own fear of water dissipates and his perception changes as he works through his family's past; in doing so, Proulx illuminates the extent of the variability of spatial perception and its close relationship to one's psychic health. In *Civilization and Its Discontents*, Freud refers to an "oceanic feeling," which he describes as "a feeling of something limitless, unbounded."[62] However, for Proulx, the ocean has a more aggregated meaning; it is a binding force inseparable from the inherited trauma that affected Quoyle in his early years, a memory trace of the failed swimming lessons from his father and Quoyle's inability to swim and the surfacing of a perceived failure. But, water—a materially fluid substance—also has a fluid definition for Quoyle; as he becomes stronger and cultivates his own individualism, the ocean begins to resonate with limitlessness, with renewal, with the forces of life that counteract the many drownings, deaths and traumatic bindings. Space is not tethered solely to the past—Proulx demonstrates that its potential for narration is just as alive as the self's potential for invigoration.

As Quoyle fosters his own life in Newfoundland, he must learn to face his fear of water and to redefine his relationship, if only for practicality, since given the geography and weather conditions, boating to work is a more reasonable option than driving. As Quoyle begins to express himself and to define himself, he spatially renegotiates his relationship with the ocean, carving and constructing his own path, "if he got in there with axe and saw, set some pressure-treated steps in the steepest pitches, built a bridge over the wet spots, gravel and moss—it would be a beauty of a walk down to the sea."[63] The protagonist views the path as a place he could call "his own."[64] Quoyle's renegotiation of life, narrated in his renegotiated relationship with water, is also embodied in his redefined understanding of marriage. When Quoyle marries Petal Bear, his devotion and attraction to her proffers an example of acting out or behavioral repetition; Petal Bear's abusive behavior towards him is simply an iteration of the emotional abuse he received from his father. When Quoyle marries Wavey however, the moment no longer signifies this behavioral repetition but emphasizes his own working through. Quoyle is consciously uniting with an individual named after water, herself a Newfoundlander who must coexist and cope with her own traumatic past. Both Wavey and Quoyle's lives will continue to be marked by the past, but their marriage also promises new directions. The word "wavey" denotes an oscillation, a continued movement between two poles, in this case the space of trauma and the space that transcends the trauma and thereby opens onto something broader. As Quoyle opens himself up to possibility, both surrounding relationships and spaces become imbued with a deeper, more multifarious meaning. Fiona Polack argues that water in *The Shipping News* represents the "maternal abject"[65]—however, the ocean is not bounded by a singular definition; indeed, by the end of the novel, water, "blue, after months of ice,"[66] comes to symbolize hope and transition.

Experiencing life does not entail overcoming and forgetting traumatic pasts, but living and facing tragic circumstances while simultaneously fostering a space for something more complex that also opens onto areas that transcend the trauma. On a berry picking outing with his aunt and his children, as well as Wavey and her handicapped son Herry, Quoyle experiences a vision,

> He pressed his groin against the barrens as if he were in union with the earth. His aroused senses imbued the far scene with enormous importance. The small figures against the vast rock with the sea beyond. All the

> complex wires of life were stripped out and he could see the structure of life. (…)
>
> The sharpness of his gaze pierced the past. He saw generations like migrating birds, the bay flecked with ghost sails, the deserted settlements vigorous again, and in the abyss nets spangled with scales. Saw the Quoyles rinsed of evil by the passage of time. He imagined the aunt buried and gone, himself old, Wavey stooped with age, his daughters in faraway lives, Herry still delighted by wooden dogs and colored threads (…).
>
> A sense of purity renewed, a sense of events in trembling balance flooded him.[67]

Space in Quoyle's vision is no longer simply haunted by the past, by the curse of unchanging generations. In his union with the earth, Quoyle experiences on a visceral level the possibility for the present to entwine with the past. Just as he envisions the "deserted settlements made vigorous again," no space, no story is unsusceptible to personal interpretation and manipulation. Instead, there is always the possibility of altered narration, a reading and writing of space as text that reconfigures Jacques Derrida's contention that there is "nothing outside the text."[68] For Christian Hummelsund Voie, nature in *The Shipping News* presents comfortable security, and Quoyle "comes to worship nature specifically as an 'other,' a reliable constant, a source of recourse that is unimpeachable and permanent."[69] While Quoyle does cultivate a special relationship with land, space blurs any confining lines between self and other, the internal and the external, and its dynamism occludes any absolutist notions. Though the past will always leave traces in the landscape, each generation also has its own potential to create something lasting; just as there is significance in the "generations like migrating birds," there is also significance in the "small figures against the vast rock."

If anything symbolizes the power of the past to haunt the present, it is the Quoyle family home, which had remained stubbornly shackled with cables to the ground, as "a bound prisoner straining to get free."[70] In the house, Quoyle feels like "a tethered animal, dumb but feeling."[71] However, Proulx disqualifies the notion that the past must remain permanently fixed in a singular form when at the end of the novel, the Quoyle home collapses after a storm. When Quoyle views the rubble of the old house, only the bolts and loops that fastened the cables into the stone remaining, he registers the significance: "even though his secret path was still there, [he] felt as if he'd (…) lost silence. (…) The Quoyles on the shift again."[72] The word "shift" resonates with the storytelling concept of emplotment, or spatially with a sense of mobility and progression. Shift does not recognize destruction, but movement from one point to another point: it entails the creation of a new space, while the old remains a trace and is remindful of the transition that accompanies the psychic working through process. Elements of the house still exist, such as the old bolts, as well as Quoyle's secret path—the conduit he created between the old house and the water, symbolizing the ongoing existence and remembered narration of his own transition from his traumatic past. However, with the collapse of the house, the bound prisoner has been set free, and Quoyle himself need no longer feel tethered, but has more liberty for self-definition. According to Schwab, traumatic postmemory in crypt form is a tragic secret that has been silenced. Quoyle's "lost silence" explicitly reveals his own process of narration and working through, the creation of a legacy that no longer chains the prisoner, but instead is a crucial building block that enables the registration of a more spacious, expansive psyche and self.

Lost silence, Proulx demonstrates, is of the utmost importance in the development of the self; this process is perhaps most apparent in Quoyle's work at the *Gammy Bird*. Quoyle's articles allow him to develop a voice by advancing his interaction with Newfoundland, and each article strengthens his own stance on and perception of the significance of living in relation to landscape and waterscape, thus altering the traumatic bind. His first opinion piece ruminates on the developing oil industry in Newfoundland and his emphatic support for the care and preservation of the local fishing industry and the local ecology. The issue of the oil industry is so contentious, however, that when Quoyle airs his critical views, his incensed managing editor changes the worded political stance of the article before publication. When Quoyle finds out about this alteration, for the first time he stands up for himself—he declares his disgust that the editor had made the column into "rotten cheap propaganda for the oil industry."[73] The original article, entitled "Nobody Hangs a Picture of an Oil Tanker" in part reads,

> Hundreds of people watched Monday morning as 14,000 metric tons of crude washed onshore from a ruptured tank of the *Golden Goose*. Thousands of seabirds and fish struggled in the oil, fishing boats and nets were fouled. 'This is the end of this place,' said Jack Eye, 87, of Little Despond, who as a young man, was a dory fisherman with the schooner fleet.[74]

Quoyle, no longer comfortable living in a place like Mockinburg, which is in its "third death," is now concerned with fighting for the continued vitality of space. Quoyle's fight to alter community perceptions of, and connections with, Newfoundland is a form of spatial story writing.

For de Certeau, writing spatial stories pertains more to the direct manipulation of place;[75] with the newspaper, Quoyle may not be physically moving through space, but he is nevertheless persuading the public to view Newfoundland in a particular light as his articles attempt to reorient and thus rewrite space. His experience at the *Gammy Bird* is ultimately Arendtian, since the paper serves not only as a public vehicle from which Quoyle can persuade opinion on space, but also a vehicle that enables Quoyle to experience a naissance as his newspaper articles promote the articulation and birth of his own identity and opinions.[76] Thus, while Kristeva encourages narrating the past as part of the working through process, as Proulx demonstrates, creating a new narration that frames one's connection with the land also positively impacts the birth of individual identity.

By the end of the novel, Quoyle has achieved the title of managing editor at the *Gammy Bird*. Just before a meeting with Jack Buggit about the following week's issue of the paper, Quoyle receives a call from his old friend and coworker Partridge in L.A., who lets him know that the office of the *Mockinburg Record* had been gunned down, "Bad, all right. Not only L.A. It's like the whole country got infected with some rage virus, going for their guns like it used to be you'd look at your watch."[77] The proximity of the trauma to Quoyle—the fact that it happened at his old workplace—is a reminder that traumatic existence can never be fully isolated, erased or left behind, even if one has engaged the working through process. Partridge, who is black, also recalls his own experience of the L.A. riots, of his partner Mercalia being shot at, "Show you how crazy the scene is, I made a joke about living in California, about L.A. style. Fucking bullet holes through her windshield. Missed her by inches."[78] While it might be easy to then contrast Newfoundland as a place of refuge, away from the chaos, Proulx promptly demonstrates that Newfoundland still has its own problems, though of a different nature. During his meeting with Jack, Quoyle reveals that a fishing factory is closing down. For Jack, the closing is a symptom of the continued local crisis at play,

> Jesus! You think it can't get worse, it gets worse! (…) They say 'too many local fishermen for not enough fish.' Well, where has the fish gone? To the Russians, the French, the Japs, West Germany, East Germany, Poland, Portugal, the UK, Spain, Romania, Bulgaria (…). 'How can the fish come inshore if the trawlers and draggers gets 'em all fifty, a hundred mile out? And the long-liners gets the rest twenty mile out? What's left for the inshore fishermen?'[79]

The crisis is thus tied to globalization, a reminder that the isolation of Newfoundland is illusory; these seemingly distant tragedies are, in fact, connected, whether through globalization and capitalism, or even through the shared tangible experience of trauma. Newfoundland is dependent on the fishing industry. While the dangers of the ocean and weather have always made the profession a difficult one, now the overall depletion of fish is foreboding and envisions that the locals' lives will be made increasingly complicated and unsustainable by an increasingly difficult trade.

Although trauma inevitably remains, it does not mean one's position and relationship to it cannot change. For Proulx, connection is crucial if one is to work through the experience of postmemory. Indeed, if there are to be any counterforces set up, if one is to cultivate a life that breathes beyond the space of trauma, then acknowledgements and connections made between the past and present, between communities, between self and space are crucial. The very notion of connection connotes a trace between two entities, an affective imprint that is shared and mutually reflective. Thus, in *The Shipping News*, Proulx offers a novel mode of reading intergenerational trauma through the individual's connection with space, simultaneously proffering the possibility that the spatial can influence and also record the working through process. It is this socio-spatial dialectic, the way each narrates the other, that opens up a new possibility for understanding the traumatized individual's place and potential within the world. Learning to live with postmemory, trauma, and uncertainty—reading their presence in the land—ultimately enables human possibility. The connections between self and space can never erase or prevent the encounter with trauma or violence; however—as Quoyle learns—these relations also encourage life to be experienced with magnified meaning, "If life was an arc of light that began in darkness, ended in darkness, the first part of his life had happened in ordinary glare. Here it was as though he had found a polarized lens that deepened and intensified all seen through it."[80] If one allows oneself to experience pain, to question that pain and to face the past, one transcends trauma's capacity to restrict and delimit the boundaries of the self, instead gaining the ability to feel and to experience vigorously—a shift that not only affects relationships, but one's connection with the world.

Bibliography

Abraham, Nicolas, and Maria Torok. *The Shell and the Kernel: Renewals of Psychoanalysis*. Translated by Nicholas T. Rand. Chicago: University of Chicago Press, 1994.

Arendt, Hannah. *The Human Condition*. Chicago: University of Chicago Press, 1958.

Benjamin, Walter. "On Some Motifs in Baudelaire." In *Illuminations*, 157-200. New York: Random House, 1968.

Butler, Judith. *The Psychic Life of Power: Theories in Subjection*. Stanford: Stanford University Press, 1997.

De Certeau, Michel. *Practice of Everyday Life*. Berkeley: University of California Press, 1984.

Defoe, Daniel. *Robinson Crusoe*. New York: Simon & Schuster, 2001.

Derrida, Jacques. *Of Grammatology*. Baltimore, MD: Johns Hopkins University Press, 1976.

Freud, Sigmund. *Beyond the Pleasure Principle*. Translated by James Strachey. Seattle, WA: Pacific Publishing, 2010.

—. *Civilization and Its Discontents*. Translated by David McLintock. London: Penguin Books, 2004.

Freud, Sigmund, and Josef Breuer. *Studies in Hysteria*. Trans. Nicola Luckhurst. London: Penguin Modern Classics, 2004.

Hirsch, Marianne. *The Generation of Postmemory: Writing and Visual Culture after the Holocaust*. New York: Columbia University Press, 2012.

Hirsch, Marianne, and Leo Spitzer. *Ghosts of Home: The Afterlife of Czernowitz in Jewish Memory*. Berkeley: University of California Press, 2010.

Hummelsund Voie, Christian. "Drinking the Elixir of Ownership: Pilgrims and Improvers in the Landscapes of Annie Proulx's *That Old Ace in the Hole* and *The Shipping News*." In *The Geographical Imagination of Annie Proulx: Rethinking Regionalism*, edited by Alex Hunt, 39-50. Lanham, MD: Lexington Books, 2009.

Hunt, Alex, ed. *The Geographical Imagination of Annie Proulx: Rethinking Regionalism*. Lanham, MD: Lexington Books, 2009.

Kirby, Kathleen M. *Indifferent Boundaries: Spatial Concepts of Human Subjectivity*. New York: The Guilford Press, 1996.

Kirwin, W.J., G.M. Story, and J.D.A. Widdowson. *Dictionary of Newfoundland English*. Toronto: University of Toronto Press, 1990.

Kristeva, Julia. *Intimate Revolt: The Powers and Limits of Psychoanalysis.* Translated by Jeanine Herman. New York: Columbia University Press, 2002.

—. *New Maladies of the Soul.* Translated by Ross Guberman. New York: Columbia University Press, 2002.

LaCapra, Dominick. *History in Transit: Experience, Identity, Critical Theory.* Ithaca, NY: Cornell University Press, 2004.

Lefebvre, Henri. *The Production of Space.* Translated by Donald Nicholson-Smith. Oxford: Blackwell, 1991.

Massey, Doreen. *Space, Place, and Gender.* Cambridge: Polity Press, 1994.

Polack, Fiona. "Taking the Waters: Abjection and Homecoming in *The Shipping News* and *Death of a River Guide.*" *Journal of Commonwealth Literature* 41.1 (2006): 93-109.

Proulx, E. Annie. *The Shipping News.* New York: Macmillan Publishing, 1993.

Rothberg, Michael. *Multidirectional Memory: Remembering the Holocaust in the Age of Decolonization.* Stanford: Stanford University Press, 2009.

Ryan, Jennifer Denise. "Landed Bodies: Geography and Disability in *The Shipping News.*" In *The Geographical Imagination of Annie Proulx: Rethinking Regionalism*, edited by Alex Hunt, 127-40. Lanham, MD: Lexington Books, 2009.

Scanlon, Julie. "Why Do We Still Want to Believe? The Case of Annie Proulx." *Journal of Narrative Theory* 38.1 (2008): 86-110.

Schwab, Gabriele. *Haunting Legacies: Violent Histories and Transgenerational Trauma.* New York: Columbia University Press, 2010.

Shakespeare, William. *The Tempest.* London: Longman UK, 2002.

Soja, Edward. "The Socio-Spatial Dialectic." *Annals of the Association of American Geographers* 70. 2 (1980): 207-25.

West-Pavlov, Russell. *Space in Theory: Kristeva, Foucault, Deleuze.* Amsterdam: Rodopi, 2009.

Young, James. *The Texture of Memory: Holocaust Memorials and Meaning.* New Haven, CT: Yale University Press, 1993.

Notes

[1] Michael Rothberg, *Multidirectional Memory: Remembering the Holocaust in the Age of Decolonization* (Stanford: Stanford University Press, 2009), 3.

[2] Marianne Hirsch and Leo Spitzer, *Ghosts of Home: The Afterlife of Czernowitz in Jewish Memory* (Berkeley: University of California Press, 2010), 10.

[3] Rothberg's work is a response to critics such as Walter Benn Michaels, who contrastingly "considers the seemingly incompatible legacies of slavery and the Nazi genocide in the United States." Rothberg, *Multidirectional Memory*, 1.
[4] For more details on spatial metaphors in psychoanalysis, see Kirby, as well as West-Pavlov.
[5] There are some exceptions. For instance, Judith Butler, working within queer theory, has addressed the intersection of space and psychoanalysis. Additionally Walter Benjamin, situated mainly in a Marxist paradigm, has produced important work on the intersection of urban space and the experience of shock.
[6] See, for instance, Julie Scanlon's work, or the essays in Alex Hunt, ed., *The Geographical Imagination of Annie Proulx: Rethinking Regionalism* (Lanham, MD: Lexington Books, 2009).
[7] Annie E. Proulx, *The Shipping News* (New York: Macmillan Publishing, 1993), 1.
[8] Proulx, *The Shipping News*, 1.
[9] Proulx, *The Shipping News*, 9.
[10] Proulx, *The Shipping News*, 25.
[11] Proulx, *The Shipping News*, 3, emphasis mine.
[12] Proulx, *The Shipping News*, 2-3.
[13] Marianne Hirsch, *The Generation of Postmemory: Writing and Visual Culture after the Holocaust* (New York: Columbia University Press, 2012), 38.
[14] Proulx, *The Shipping News*, 2.
[15] Gabriele Schwab, *Haunting Legacies: Violent Histories and Transgenerational Trauma* (New York: Columbia University Press, 2010), 14.
[16] Schwab, *Haunting Legacies*, 2.
[17] Nicolas Abraham and Maria Torok, *The Shell and the Kernel: Renewals of Psychoanalysis*, trans. Nicholas T. Rand (Chicago: University of Chicago Press, 1994), 173.
[18] Proulx, *The Shipping News*, 2.
[19] Proulx, *The Shipping News*, 2.
[20] Dominick LaCapra, *History in Transit: Experience, Identity, Critical Theory* (Ithaca, NY: Cornell University Press, 2004), 117.
[21] Writing from a Marxist perspective, Soja states, "The structure of organized space is not a separate structure with its own autonomous laws of construction and transformation, nor is it simply an expression of the class structure emerging from the social (i.e. aspatial) relations of production. It represents, instead, a dialectically defined component of the general relations of production, relations which are simultaneously social and spatial." Edward Soja, "The Socio-Spatial Dialectic," *Annals of the Association of American Geographers* 70.2 (1980): 207-25.
[22] Henri Lefebvre, *The Production of Space*, trans. Donald Nicholson-Smith (Oxford: Blackwell, 1991), 87-88.
[23] Walter Benjamin, "On Some Motifs in Baudelaire," in *Illuminations* (New York: Random House, 1968), 163.
[24] Proulx, *The Shipping News*, 11.

[25] Jennifer Denise Ryan, "Landed Bodies: Geography and Disability in *The Shipping News,*" in *The Geographical Imagination of Annie Proulx: Rethinking Regionalism*, ed. Alex Hunt (Lanham, MD: Lexington Books, 2009), 131.
[26] Proulx, *The Shipping News*, 11.
[27] Massey specifically points to Marxist spatial theorist David Harvey, who equates space with "being" when he discusses the contemporary longing for stability and coherence associated with "the local" (168).
[28] Doreen Massey, *Space, Place, and Gender* (Cambridge: Polity Press, 1994), 169.
[29] Proulx, *The Shipping News*, 33.
[30] Proulx, *The Shipping News*, 34.
[31] The centrality of narration to the working-through process has a long legacy within the psychoanalytic method and does not originate with Kristeva, cf. Sigmund Freud and Josef Breuer on the "talking cure" in *Studies on Hysteria.*
[32] Julia Kristeva, *New Maladies of the Soul*, trans. Ross Guberman (New York: Columbia University Press, 2002), 143.
[33] Kristeva, *New Maladies of the Soul*, 27.
[34] Julia Kristeva, *Intimate Revolt: The Powers and Limits of Psychoanalysis,* trans. Jeanine Herman (New York, Columbia University Press, 2002), 6.
[35] Proulx, *The Shipping News*, 33.
[36] Proulx, *The Shipping News*, 318.
[37] Schwab, *Haunting Legacies*, 56.
[38] Schwab, *Haunting Legacies*, 56.
[39] Proulx, *The Shipping News*, 64.
[40] Proulx, *The Shipping News*, 221.
[41] LaCapra, *History in Transit*, 207.
[42] Proulx, *The Shipping News*, 35.
[43] Proulx, *The Shipping News*, 42.
[44] Proulx, *The Shipping News*, 42.
[45] Michel de Certeau, *The Practice of Everyday Life* (Berkeley: University of California Press, 1984), 117.
[46] de Certeau's distinction between place and space runs counter to prominent definitions within spatial theory that associate "space" with the abstract and absolute, and "place" with the particular. For instance, Massey defines place as "formed out of the particular set of social relations which interact at a particular location." de Certeau, *The Practice of Everyday Life*, 168.
[47] de Certeau, *The Practice of Everyday Life*, 123.
[48] Proulx, *The Shipping News*, 162.
[49] Proulx, *The Shipping News*, 162.
[50] Proulx, *The Shipping News*, 264.
[51] Proulx, *The Shipping News*, 264.
[52] Proulx, *The Shipping News*, 265.
[53] Proulx, *The Shipping News*, 172.
[54] W.J. Kirwin, G.M. Story and J.D.A. Widdowson, *Dictionary of Newfoundland English* (Toronto: University of Toronto Press, 1990), 359.
[55] Proulx, *The Shipping News*, 174.

[56] Rothberg, *Multidirectional Memory*, 3.
[57] Proulx, *The Shipping News*, 207.
[58] Proulx, *The Shipping News*, 208.
[59] Proulx, *The Shipping News*, 209.
[60] Proulx, *The Shipping News*, 209.
[61] Proulx, *The Shipping News*, 2.
[62] Proulx, *The Shipping News*, 2.
[63] Proulx, *The Shipping News*, 105.
[64] Proulx, *The Shipping News*, 105.
[65] Fiona Polack, "Taking the Waters: Abjection and Homecoming in *The Shipping News* and *Death of a River Guide*," *Journal of Commonwealth Literature* 41 (1) (2006): 100.
[66] Proulx, *The Shipping News*, 294.
[67] Proulx, *The Shipping News*, 196.
[68] Jacques Derrida, *Of Grammatology* (Baltimore, MD: Johns Hopkins University Press, 1976), 158.
[69] Christian Hummelsund Voie, "Drinking the Elixir of Ownership: Pilgrims and Improvers in the Landscapes of Annie Proulx's *That Old Ace in the Hole* and *The Shipping News*," in *The Geographical Imagination of Annie Proulx: Rethinking Regionalism*, ed. Alex Hunt (Lanham, MD: Lexington Books, 2009), 43.
[70] Proulx, *The Shipping News*, 263.
[71] Proulx, *The Shipping News*, 263.
[72] Proulx, *The Shipping News*, 321.
[73] Proulx, *The Shipping News*, 203.
[74] Proulx, *The Shipping News*, 201.
[75] de Certeau, *The Practice of Everyday Life*, 117-18.
[76] According to Arendt, during the classical period the public forum was a place where individuals attempted to persuade others through words and actions, a method of politics that Arendt promotes because it allows for the proliferation of a multiplicity of opinions and identities. It is through this process of persuasion through words and action, that individuals form identities and weave themselves into the fabric of the community. As Arendt elaborates: "In acting and speaking, men show who they are, reveal actively their unique personal identities and thus make their appearance in the human world." Hannah Arendt, *The Human Condition* (Chicago: University of Chicago Press, 1958), 179.
[77] Proulx, *The Shipping News*, 290.
[78] Proulx, *The Shipping News*, 291.
[79] Proulx, *The Shipping News*, 292.
[80] Proulx, *The Shipping News*, 241.

Creating a Neo-Hoodoo Mythology: Past, Present, and Future in Ishmael Reed's Multidirectional Memory

Elisabeth Oyler

Ishmael Reed's oeuvre defies definition. Reed is a prolific writer, publishing numerous novels, poems, essays, and plays throughout his lengthy career. In these works, Reed challenges his readers with both the complexity of his ideas and the form these ideas take. His works often focus on the oppression minority cultures have historically faced in Western society. However, he does not discuss this oppression in simple, easy to follow narratives. Instead, he uses a sense of humor and sharp satire to critique American culture. Reed's works are often nonlinear, surreal, and outrageous (*Free-Lance Pallbearers*, for example, is set in a country called HARRY SAM, ruled by a former used car salesman Harry Sam from his toilet throne), which allows him to critique dominant Western and American society from all sides while still infusing his writing with humor. The surrealism of Reed's works enables him a narrative space to push boundaries and defy binaries, what he calls "synthesizing and synchronizing."[1]

Reed's synthesizing and synchronizing is most evident in the theory he uses to frame all of his writing, Neo-Hoodoo, a tradition which "takes its/ 'organization' from Haitian VooDoo,"[2] building upon the Americanized version of VooDoo, HooDoo. As Reed explains, the Haitian practice of VooDoo is the closest tie African Americans have to their African culture, and thus Neo-HooDoo "borrows from Haiti Africa and South/ America."[3] In Reed's work, African culture is embodied in Neo-HooDoo, and defined as a celebratory, evolving movement that is "sexual, sensual and digs the old 'heathen'/ good good loving."[4] Neo-HooDoo's rituals focus on "the drum the ankh and the Dance,"[5] typical of African-based traditions. However, Neo-HooDoo is also very different from VooDoo in that it is "building our own American 'pantheon'" of the "loa (Spirits)."[6]

I will discuss Neo-HooDoo in further detail in the context of Reed's novels, but Neo-HooDoo itself is important in that it is Reed's focus in many of his works, particularly during the 1960s and 1970s, as he develops Neo-HooDoo as a cultural practice. This focus on Neo-HooDoo influences not only the way Reed discusses the present, but also the way he looks to and conceptualizes both the historical and cultural past and future. Reed's work suggests that Western culture has historically silenced African culture in a struggle for domination, creating a tradition of traumatic memory for African Americans, who have been denied a cohesive cultural tradition. It is the reclaiming of a lost African historical remembrance and addressing of that tradition of traumatic memory that informs his development of Neo-HooDoo as African Americans' lost history is intertwined with and essential to the cultural future for African Americans.

However, Reed argues that the cultural future he envisions with Neo-HooDoo is not only available to African Americans. Reed reinterprets history by tracing the origins of all cultures, including Western traditions, to Ancient Egypt, theorizing that Ancient Egypt is the nodal point for all cultures, the common genesis for the cultures of the world. This view is an alternative to the traditional Western narrative of world history where Western traditions have dominated, subsumed, and oppressed minority cultures. According to Reed, Western culture refuses to acknowledge its common roots with the minorities of the world, instead insisting on its superiority. Because Western culture has oppressed and suppressed minority cultures, the dominant historical remembrance has been Western culture's version, characterizing minority cultures as Other. This devaluing of minority cultures has been traumatic, Reed suggests; he thus proposes Neo-HooDoo as a multicultural and inclusive practice that welcomes all cultures to (re)join, reclaiming a lost cultural history in an attempt to create an inclusive cultural future.

Throughout this chapter, I will show the way that Reed envisions Neo-HooDoo as a way to address the traumatic history of minorities and a path for an inclusive cultural future for America. To do so, establishing the historical remembrance Reed presents and develops within his Neo-HooDoo framework is essential. Further, it is important not only to look at the *past* that he presents, but also the future he envisions with a Neo-HooDoo mythology. I will do so by exploring two of his novels, *Mumbo Jumbo* and *Yellow Back Radio Broke-Down*. These works are essential to Reed's addressing a traumatic past and a Neo-HooDoo future. Each novel contributes to addressing African American trauma within a context characterized by the lack of historical remembrance, while also acting as a foundation for Neo-HooDoo to succeed in the future. In both novels, Reed's characters represent and develop aspects of Neo-HooDoo and the conflict between Neo-HooDoo and Western culture. Moreover, as I will show, although *Yellow Back Radio Broke-Down* (1969) was published before *Mumbo Jumbo* (1972), we can see how the latter novel works as an origin story for Neo-HooDoo, whereas *Yellow Back Radio Broke-Down* is an adventure episode for Neo-HooDoo. This combination of origin story and adventure episode creates a mythology for Neo-HooDoo that Reed sees as reclaiming a lost historical remembrance, addressing the current Western monoculture that dominates America and the tradition of traumatic memory that has plagued minorities. For Reed, these mythologies will help create a historical remembrance that will allow minority cultures to move forward, establishing a multicultural society that values multiplicity and hybridity in cultural heritages and historical remembrances.

Historical Remembrance and Multidirectional Memory

To understand Reed's presentation of history and memory in his works through Neo-HooDoo, I will use two frameworks. The first concerns the relationship between history and memory. One of the results of the recent emphasis on memory in scholarship is a reconsideration of how we conceptualize the terms *history* and *memory*, as well as the relationship between the two. While many theorists have described history and memory differently recently, most recognize that history is not an isolated and objective conception of the past, but is also related to, influenced by, and a part of personal and collective memory. Jay Winter labels this postmodern conception of history as *historical remembrance*, which he says "helps us avoid the pitfalls of referring to memory as some vague cloud which exists without agency, and to history as an objective story which exists outside of the people whose lives it describes."[7] Instead, historical remembrance acknowledges that history and memory are intertwined, and it is with both history and memory that we develop a "set of cultural practices."[8] The term historical remembrance, then, is a postmodern acknowledgement that discussions about either history or memory are not isolated but intertwined. It is within this context that I analyze Reed's own presentation of African Americans' traumatic history and memory; while we might debate the exact connection between history and memory, we must acknowledge that this connection, however messy and complex, does exist. Thus, Reed's presentation of history is not a simple rewriting of the past; it is also a reconfiguring and reestablishing of historical remembrance, of a past for the many cultures that have been overshadowed and silenced by dominating Western and Christian traditions. For Reed, this reconfiguring and reestablishing of historical remembrance is intertwined with and a part of his discussion of Neo-

HooDoo as he concurrently recounts the tradition of traumatic historical remembrance minority cultures have faced and looks to future possibilities of cultural equality.

Michael Rothberg's concept of multidirectional memory is another framework from memory studies that is useful in illuminating the ways Reed develops a new historical remembrance in Neo-HooDoo. Rothberg positions his term of multidirectional memory in contrast to collective memory, "What happens when different histories confront each other in the public sphere? Does the remembrance of one history erase others from view?"[9] Rothberg's answer to these questions is his model of multidirectional memory, a nuanced way of thinking about memory where collective memories can be discussed together in a positive, meaning-generating manner. This conversation is not a competitive "zero-sum game," but a collaborative effort for a better understanding of and new insights about history.[10] Multidirectional memory gives us insight into Reed's presentation of Neo-HooDoo and historical remembrance in the way his discussions of historical remembrance are creative, inclusive, conversation-generating, and revealing of new possibilities. Reed incorporates discussions of many traumatic historical remembrances throughout history to illuminate the pattern of oppression from Western society. By bringing these disparate traumatic historical remembrances together, Reed reveals a larger picture of oppression that highlights the need for a change in cultural practices. Thus, I will discuss multidirectional memory in the context of Reed's works, using this framework to illustrate how Reed works to reclaim lost African historical remembrance and argue for the establishment of Neo-HooDoo as a modern, multicultural tradition in America.

Traumatic Cultural Suppression and Denial

Historical remembrance has become increasingly important in our modern society. Anthony Smith explains that the modern world is constantly evolving and changing due to globalization, increased physical distance from immediate family, a greater rate of urban living, and rapid changes in technology. Technology in particular creates uncertainty, Andreas Huyssen suggests, because it causes an "instability of time"[11] in which everything works at a progressively faster pace. All of these modern changes generate a need for something to ground us. Smith suggests that the past does this grounding as people look to cultural traditions to make sense of our world. This look to the past helps us create the feeling that we are not isolated or alone, but part of something bigger than ourselves. As both of these authors note, a cultural history or historical remembrance is one way to create stability and connections, a sense of belonging and safety in an increasingly unstable and unconnected society.

While historical remembrance has become all the more important, African Americans' historical remembrances have been ignored, and they have been denied their cultural roots in many ways. Physical severing of ties occurred when slaves were taken from Africa itself. However, physical enslavement also led to a lack of stabilization in their culture. While Freddi Williams Evans recounts the way Congo Square in New Orleans was able to function as "the venue, the place and space, for Africans to engage in African-derived cultural practice,"[12] Carolyn Morrow Song attributes New Orleans' uniqueness as a place where HooDoo and VooDoo developed to "waves of immigration from Haiti, Cuba, Puerto/ Rico, and other Caribbean and South America countries."[13] New Orleans and its importance to Neo-HooDoo will be discussed later in this chapter, but it clearly was a unique space for African-based traditions, not the norm. Rod Davis explains that New Orleans was and still is a singular place where VooDoo and HooDoo developed and thrived; however, this was not the case in the rest of America. In his travels throughout the rural South, Davis reports that VooDoo and HooDoo practices virtually disappeared in everyday life. In the rest of the United States, for the most part, slaves were forced to convert to Christianity. *Debow's Review* (a contemporary pro-slavery newspaper) reported American slaves converting to Christianity at a rate five times higher than slaves in the Caribbean.[14] Slave masters limited slave communities' freedom to dance, sing, and gather, isolating slaves and inhibiting their participation in and continuation of their African-based traditions. While cultural and religious traditions have survived and adapted in America, slavery certainly disrupted African Americans' ability to practice their culture freely.

Even after slavery ended, this cultural suppression continued. Cultural traditions may have survived slavery in various forms, but Orlando Patterson explains, "slaves (…) were not allowed freely to integrate the experience of their ancestors into their lives, to inform their understanding of a social reality with the inherited meanings of their natural forebears, or to anchor the living present in any conscious community of memory."[15] The loss of historical remembrance for African Americans did not end with slaves or freed slaves, but permeated throughout generations. Patterson describes this social isolation for African Americans as "natal alienation," which refers to the loss of cultural history in both "ascending and descending generations."[16] The loss of a cultural heritage for African

American slaves affected the next generations, creating a traumatic loss of historical remembrance. The traumatic tradition for African American slaves was compounded when they were never allowed to participate in the dominant Western and White society of America, but neither able to practice African-based traditions. This lack of cultural freedom caused what Reed presents as an inability to create a true African-based historical remembrance.

This denial of individual or collective identity for African Americans as a group created a tradition of traumatic memory. Paul Gilroy theorizes that African Americans have been forced into a double consciousness that creates a "special stress" because they are forced to "face (at least) two ways [of being] at once."[17] This double consciousness continues into modernity as the trauma of slavery and the awareness that the oppression of African Americans' cultural freedom has been ignored. Trauma itself is characterized by a latency to be seen or arrive; in the case of slavery, national discourses have never fully confronted this trauma, continuing the effects of this trauma on successive African American generations.[18] Reed's works address these two issues at once: he confronts the trauma of slavery by addressing the cultural oppression of African Americans; at the same time, he also addresses African Americans' need for a historical narrative that incorporates their experience.

African Americans are not alone in the denial of their culture; one can say the same of many minorities, including Native Americans. Davis recounts the various ways European colonizers suppressed minority traditions. The genocide of Native American peoples effectively destroyed their cultural traditions, transforming Native Americans and their culture into what Davis describes as "another footnote in a history textbook."[19] Reed acknowledges this shared oppression in *Yellow Back Radio Broke-Down* when Chief Showcase rescues the Loop Garoo Kid, saying, "Indians and black people have been roaming the plains of America together for hundreds of years (…) And Seminole fought invasion after invasion against the Fiend to protect black fugitive slaves."[20] Although they might have been silenced in different ways, minorities in America all share the common struggle against an oppressive Western society that will not acknowledge their cultures as valid alternatives.

The need to reassert different cultures' viability and value is what Reed seeks to fulfill in his own works as he attempts to address their traumatic past and reclaim a multicultural, historical remembrance. Neo-HooDoo will be modern Americans' way of embracing and incorporating a "modernized" HooDoo, "a 'Lost American Church' updated," into their lives to reclaim a collective cultural heritage.[21] Western culture has been perpetrating a fraud; Reed works to correct the flawed Western narrative and to provide a necessary alternative mythology of Neo-HooDoo through *Mumbo Jumbo* and *Yellow Back Radio Broke-Down.*

Flattening History: Reed's Multidirectional Historical Remembrance

Historical remembrance is at the center of Reed's development of Neo-HooDoo. In both *Mumbo Jumbo* and *Yellow Back Radio Broke-Down*, Reed flattens history by literally placing histories in confrontation with one another through his characters, which I discuss shortly. A flattened and multidirectional historical remembrance becomes part of Neo-HooDoo. However, to understand Neo-HooDoo fully, we need to first understand the historical remembrance Reed presents through the lens of multidirectional memory.

Multidirectional memory allows us to "consider memory (…) as subject to ongoing negotiation, cross-referencing, and borrowing; as productive and not privative."[22] Rothberg's explanation of multidirectional memory echoes Reed's own discussions of Neo-HooDoo and historical remembrance as he further aims to create productive discussions of history while he searches to *create* opportunities for minority cultures and rediscover a lost historical remembrance. Multidirectional memory is also similar to Reed's methods in its syncretic nature as multidirectional memory is often used to bring seemingly disparate historical remembrances together in conversation.

The productive, cross-referencing, and borrowing nature of multidirectional memory is an alternative way of presenting history than that of most of the Black Arts Movement authors writing as Reed was first developing Neo-HooDoo. As a writer during the Black Arts Movement, Reed has often been associated with this movement's other authors, including Amiri Baraka (LeRoi Jones), Larry Neal, Ron Milner, Ethridge Knight, and Sonia Sanchez.[23] However, Reed's work differs from the Black Arts Movement because of his multicultural approach. Larry Neal suggests that the Black Arts Movement asks the central question, "Whose truth shall we express, that of the oppressed or of the oppressors?"[24] Amiri Baraka, the Black Arts Movement's "prime mover and chief designer" answers that *Black* culture and truth should be expressed.[25] For Baraka, the integration of Black and White cultures only empowers White men, "weakening" Black men by making them "somehow, less black."[26] This us-versus-them attitude influences much of the Black Arts Movement and presents a competitive view of memory. Etheridge Knight echoes Baraka's sentiments, stating that Black artists "must create a new history, new symbols, myths and legends (and purify old ones by fire)."[27] As these statements show, the idea that Black culture must overpower White culture can be seen in many parts of the Black Arts Movement. This view essentially flips the traditional power structure, positioning Black culture in a dominating and oppressing position over White culture. For many of the writers within the Black Arts Movement, then, the only solution to racial inequality is for Black culture to win the war on memory and culture.

As part of the Black Arts Movement, Reed's work also rejects the monoculture of Western society, but his focus is not on replacing the White monoculture with an Afrocentric monoculture. Afrocentric thought is a common theme within the Black Arts Movement, focusing on the competition between Western and African perspectives of history. For these authors, the way to overcome African Americans' past traumas has been to replace their oppressors with the oppressed. Instead, Reed "aims at reconnecting the African Diaspora in its complexity in order to create a space for cultural and spiritual pluralism."[28] Like many within the Black Arts Movement, Reed also sees White culture as flawed, limiting, and, in a sense, dead, centering around "the graveyard."[29] However, Reed does not see memory as a contest that must have winners and losers; he offers an alternative, a multidirectional view of history in which White and minority cultures have always been connected, but White culture has always limited what is acceptable to Western ideals. As Frank McConnell suggests, Reed's work focuses on letting historical "associations merge instantaneously one into another, while still retaining their individuality, their historical specificity."[30] Put differently, Reed is working to open the options of what we consider history, memory, and culture so that all cultural traditions can work together, creating pluralistic, syncretic, and inclusive cultural possibilities for all cultures and traditions.

Generating Productive Conversations in Neo-HooDoo

One of the clearest ways Reed creates conversations is in the physical embodiment of Western culture and African culture in his writing. In *Mumbo Jumbo*, Reed presents Papa Labas, who Pierre-Damien Mvuyekure interprets as a reconfiguration of the HooDoo figure Papa Legba,[31] embodying a developing Neo-HooDoo.[32] Papa Labas interacts with other characters representing other histories and traditions: Benoit Battraville (representing Haitian VooDoo); Hierophant 1, the leader of the Wallflower Order (Western society); and Hinckle Von Vampton, a Knights Templar (Christianity). Reed uses a similar technique in *Yellow*

Back Radio Broke-Down as he places the Loop Garoo Kid (Neo-HooDoo) in conversation with Drag Gibson (a commercialized Western society), along with the many other historical figures that make appearances in the novel. Reed literally and physically places these characters together into the mythology of Neo-HooDoo so that the histories and traditions they represent can interact with one another. While the representatives of African and Western culture clearly do not agree with each other in both of these works, Reed advocates for a conversation between them to gain a new understanding and perspective on the cultures themselves and their history.

This creation of new understanding and perspectives is another similarity between multidirectional memory and Neo-HooDoo; both focus on productive and positive interactions. It is important for both Reed and Rothberg that conversations between historical remembrances occur, but that these conversations do not result in one history dominating another. As Rothberg explains, "debates about collective memory and group identity are primarily struggles over injustices of recognition, over whose history and culture will be recognized (…) but the rethinking of the relation between memory and identity can contribute to a rethinking of cultural recognition beyond zero-sum logic."[33] A view of history as multidirectional allows for a Western and African historical remembrance to exist simultaneously. This means that, for Reed, everyone is welcome to participate in Neo-HooDoo, bringing their own cultural influences to help develop Neo-HooDoo further. One example of how Neo-HooDoo expands beyond the African American community occurs at the beginning of *Mumbo Jumbo*. Here, the reader is introduced to Jes Grew when the Major of New Orleans and 10,000 New Orleans citizens succumb to Jes Grew's "slipping dipping gliding."[34] It is not just New Orleans' African American population who is affected by the Neo-HooDoo "pandemic,"[35] but also many of the White citizens exemplifying Western society, including the elite (the Major, a doctor, and scientists). This equalizing characteristic of Neo-HooDoo connects with multidirectional memory's own goal to place historical remembrances on the same footing.

Reed's creation of productive conversation also becomes evident when he recounts the history of African culture in *Mumbo Jumbo*. Benoit Battraville traces African roots back to Egyptian mythology for Papa Lebas, who then explains this history for the reader and a public audience. According to their historical remembrance, the first incarnations of African-based traditions began with Osiris, "As Osiris danced he would experiment (…) and they caught-on."[36] Osiris's brother, Set, is described as the original oppressor of African culture and connected with Western culture. He is described in *Mumbo Jumbo* as "the stick crook and flail man" who "deal[s] firmly with enemies, holding them by the hair and chopping off their heads. Set wanted to use the death of their father as an excuse for invading foreign countries."[37] This description of Set evokes the sterile "antibiotic" Western society that is presented elsewhere in *Mumbo Jumbo*. Set's own oppressive and imperialistic tendencies precede the same characteristics of Western society, connecting this early Egyptian figure to modern inequalities. Reed continues by connecting the Christian figure of Moses to Set and showing how Christianity and Western culture have continued to suppress African culture throughout history. Reed characterizes Western society as oppressive, dominating other cultures, but also as hypocritical, refusing to acknowledge its shared cultural origins with other traditions. By revealing the true history of all cultures, Reed creates new meaning and a new understanding of African Americans' heritage. The reader is able to compare and contrast these historical remembrances, allowing us to see the world's history in a new way, as well as providing a new perspective on the current struggle between African and Western culture.

While multidirectional memory is a useful framework for reading *Mumbo Jumbo*, it becomes essential to understanding *Yellow Back Radio Broke-Down*, overpowering Reed's presentation of historical remembrance in this novel. The larger-than-life nature of this story allows Reed freedom to place different histories into conversation with one another in new and different ways. While *Mumbo Jumbo* focuses on establishing the history of African culture and the origin of Neo-HooDoo for the reader, *Yellow Back Radio Broke-Down* has a timeless quality. Although the reader can see that Yellow Back Radio, the city the novel centers on, is in the Western frontier (the novel satirizes the western cowboy genre), it is the Western frontier in a general sense, never associated with a specific place or time. The references to Lewis and Clark's expedition, Thomas Jefferson, the commercialism of suburban life in the 1960s, and laser-shooting helicopters evidence this timeless quality of *Yellow Back Radio Broke-Down*. Without the ability to place this novel in a specific time or place, the reader and Reed can easily compare different historical remembrances without reservation. Subsequently, Yellow Back Radio becomes a physical manifestation of this convergence of historical remembrances.

Another example of Reed's productive conversations in *Yellow Back Radio Broke-Down* occurs between the Loop Garoo Kid and Pope Innocent. Reed illustrates both the limits of Western culture and the possibilities of a collaborative Neo-HooDoo in this conversation. Loop and the Pope are larger-than-life figures who discuss their shared past. The

Pope and Loop talk about God as Loop's father, noting that Loop is "the eldest" and how "there were others (…) and he drove them all underground."[38] Here, Loop refers to the continued persecution of African-based traditions by Christianity. Loop is also described as older than Christianity, referencing Reed's belief that Christianity actually evolved out of Egypt and the African-based traditions it oppresses. Loop/Neo-HooDoo is one of many alternatives to Christianity that has been demonized and silenced. The Pope also refers to Loop's "uprising" in the Middle Ages, which Loop quickly explains, "was never an uprising (…) that was some of his propagandists (…) who came up with that idea."[39] Here, Loop first establishes Neo-HooDoo not as inherently opposed to Christianity. Instead, Loop wishes Neo-HooDoo to be recognized and allowed to exist alongside Christianity and Western culture. Loop views all cultures as equal; it is Western culture that began and has perpetuated conflict against minority cultures through their "propaganda."[40] This conflict is unnecessary because Western society's premise, that it is at inherent odds with minority cultures, is false. By placing Pope Innocent and Loop into conversation in the timeless *Yellow Back Radio*, Reed is able to make this point and reveal the hypocrisy of the Christian church.

In fact, throughout *Yellow Back Radio Broke-Down* Neo-HooDoo is portrayed as authentic when compared to a hypocritical Western culture comprised of deception and violence. The Loop Garoo Kid's reference to God's "propagandists" highlights how Western culture has covered up its past misdeeds. Loop accuses Pope Innocent of making him "the scapegoat of all history," saying "You and the crowd are the devils. The way you massacred the Gnostics, not to mention the Bogomils, Albigenses, and Waldenses."[41] While Christianity advocates for nonviolence and acceptance, it clearly has not practiced what it has preached. Loop reveals Christianity as deceitful and unaccepting and, instead, sets himself (and Neo-HooDoo) as the alternative to this deception, an alternative that frees people and allows them to live outside of the prescriptions of Western culture.

Invention and Creation in Neo-HooDoo

Again, we can see how Reed's focus on commonality and innovation echoes Rothberg's own work with memory. Multidirectional memory "is irreducibly transversal; it cuts across genres, national contexts, periods, and cultural traditions (...) the comparative critic must first constitute the archive by forging links between dispersed documents."[42] Rothberg envisions a multidirectional framework as being creative in finding commonalities rather than focusing on reductive fundamentalist and oppositional positions. For example, W. G. Sebald uses multidirectional memory in his novel to create conversations. Sebald references the Holocaust, but also Belgium's colonial history in the Congo and the current French government. Sebald's use of multidirectional memory in this way brings various historical remembrances together, illuminating each historical remembrance as they are compared to and discussed alongside each other.[43] Similarly, Charlotte Delbo's memoir of her time in a Nazi concentration camp, *Auschwitz and After,* speaks to her dissent with the French-Algerian War of the 1960s.[44] These works are similar to Reed's in that they flatten history, using multidirectional memory and creating productive, conversation-generating comparisons to reveal similarities between historical remembrances.

An important characteristic of Neo-HooDoo is its inventive and creative nature, which allows Reed to present it as an alternative to Christianity. Reed describes Neo-HooDoo as "multitudinous, individual-like" in *Mumbo Jumbo*,[45] and even in ancient Egypt "people would mimic [Osiris] and add their variations to fit their country and their clime."[46] Reed continues this tradition and asks that participants in Neo-HooDoo "bring your own creative ideas/ to Neo-HooDoo" as "an innovator and/ improviser."[47] The representative of Haitian VooDoo in *Mumbo Jumbo*, Benoit Battraville, compares VooDoo to Neo-HooDoo by saying, "We do not work the way you do. You improvise here a great deal."[48] According to Battraville, Neo-HooDoo has "synthesized the HooDoo and VooDoo. Its bleepblop essence," whereas Haitian VooDoo has a "long and tedious list of deities and rites" that Neo-HooDoo does not subscribe to, allowing for a more diverse tradition. Instead, Neo-HooDoo focuses on the "unknown factor."[49]

Reed's central point in developing Neo-HooDoo is that fundamentalism, whether fundamental VooDoo or Christianity, is destructive. It devalues other ways of being, which has significant implications for African Americans. Fundamentalism has contributed to the rupture of historical remembrance that slaves experienced when they were brought to America, as well as perpetuating this rupture, creating a repetition of slavery's trauma throughout American history.[50] Fundamentalism, Reed shows, limits culture in modern America; instead, his presentation of culture is characterized by multiplicity. Neo-HooDoo is a living and breathing tradition that itself has rejected the strict rules and rites of Haitian VooDoo in favor of its practitioners' ability to follow Neo-HooDoo how they see fit. Reed explains that Neo-HooDoo "believes that every man is an artist and every/ artist a priest,"[51] emphasizing the way individuals can mould and shape their Neo-HooDoo practice to suit their individual needs. This reclaiming of the past to create a culture of multiplicity is a shift away from fundamentalist attitudes that create and perpetuate trauma. Reed looks towards an inclusive historical remembrance that will begin to address traumatic historical remembrances and break the cycle of trauma.

Reed shows the detrimental effect of fundamentalism in the final scene of *Yellow Back Radio Broke-Down* where the Loop Garoo Kid joins Pope Innocent on "the Pope's ship which was heading back to its point of origin."[52] This ending of *Yellow Back Radio Broke-Down* complicates the dichotomy that could be set up between Neo-HooDoo and Christianity. Whether the "origin" Loop and the Pope are traveling to Ancient Egypt or some version of Heaven is not clear. Yet, Pierre-Damien Mvuyekure interprets this ending as a message from Reed that Neo-HooDoo is not in opposition to Western society. Their shared cultural roots and intertwined history ensure that they will also have a shared future; it is Reed's hope that this future includes a move towards pluralism and acceptance. As Reed notes, if "you scratch the Christian-Judaic culture, underneath you got a Pagan. And the thing that would unite all is the thing I call HooDoo,"[53] acknowledging all cultures' common roots. Reed would prefer that multiple traditions be available for everyone, in the form of Neo-HooDoo, as we focus on commonalities rather than differences.

Works that often include multidirectional views of memory are also creative in incorporating various genres to create a cross-referencing of history as part of the "irreducibly transversal" nature of multidirectional memory.[54] In *Austerlitz*, Sebald includes photographs of history and architecture to supplement or comment on the story being told. Sebald's work also crosses genre boundaries, causing John Zilcosky to ask, "Were these works facts or fictions?"[55] Delbo also crosses boundaries of genre as she incorporates fiction and nonfiction, poetry and short stories, and newspaper clippings in her memoir. This combining of genres allows these authors to create multidirectional memory in their works.

Reed's innovative combination of genres is another way that his writing is multidirectional. As Loop says in *Yellow Back Radio Broke-Down*, "No one says a novel has to be one thing. It can be anything it wants to be, a vaudeville show, the six o'clock news, the mumblings of wild men saddled by demons."[56] *Mumbo Jumbo* and *Yellow Back Radio Broke-Down* reflect Reed's unique approach to literature as he combines genres, mediums, and styles. He combines these forms in an attempt (arguably a successful one) to free his writing from "those decreative and self-reflexive fictive modes in which his White contemporaries seem imprisoned."[57]

Both of Reed's books are diverse, borrowing from many different traditions. In *Mumbo Jumbo,* he quotes historical figures (like Louis Armstrong), uses dictionary definitions, includes information from critical sources (and a bibliography), and integrates photographs. He also adopts the scientific field's practice of expressing all numbers in numeral form. In *Yellow Back Radio Broke-Down*, Reed draws from western dime novel stereotypes and oral traditions; as he explains, "it's an oral book, a talking book."[58] His combination of these non-fiction techniques in his fictional novel and use of various genres blurs the line between genres and allows him to compare and contrast various traditions and memories in his works. All of this comparison contributes to the multidirectional characteristic of Reed's writing, but also the multidirectionality of Neo-HooDoo.

Reed's writing and development of Neo-HooDoo are multidirectional in nature. His writing cannot be separated from how he develops Neo-HooDoo, just as his conceptualization of Neo-HooDoo influences his writing, and both rely heavily on their productive, inventive, and comparative natures as a shift away from the trauma fundamentalists have created. Using Rothberg's conceptualization of multidirectional memory illuminates how Reed develops Neo-HooDoo and a corresponding new, positive, historical remembrance, creating an inclusive, multicultural vision for America's cultural future. This new historical remembrance addresses the trauma African Americans have faced, revealing past traumas, but also paves a way forward.

The Development of Neo-HooDoo's Origin Story and Adventure Episode

Before Reed can move forward to create a viable Neo-HooDoo tradition in America, however, he first needs to recapture what he sees as a lost historical remembrance through a Neo-HooDoo mythology. Although *Mumbo Jumbo* was published after *Yellow Back Radio Broke-Down*, we can understand these works as working together by fulfilling different parts of the mythology, or Text, of Neo-HooDoo. This is a mythology that Reed believes he must create for Neo-HooDoo to have any lasting effect in America. In "Neo-HooDoo Manifesto," Reed states,

> Neo-HooDoo is a litany seeking its text
> Neo-HooDoo is a Dance and music closing in on its words
> Neo-HooDoo is a Church finding its lyrics

> Cecil Brown Al Young Calvin Hernton
> David Henderson Steve Cannon Quincy Troupe
> Ted Joans Victor Cruz N. H. Pritchard Ishmael Reed
> Lennox Raphael Sarah Fabio Ron Welburn are Neo-
> HooDoo's 'Manhattan Project' of writing…[59]

In this passage, Reed establishes that Neo-HooDoo is still developing, which includes "seeking its text." It already has the spirit—the "litany (…) Dance and music" and is "a Church"—but has yet to formalize itself in "its words." It is the many artists Reed lists, including himself, that have undertaken the project of establishing a Neo-HooDoo tradition. In contrast, Reed describes Christianity as "the successful law and order candidate/in the mythological relay of the 4th century A.D."[60] Reed attributes Christianity's success to its "formalized" mythology, which he implies helped to sustain and cement itself as a dominating ideology. Neo-HooDoo, however, has yet to establish an established narrative or mythology, like Christianity, that will concretely establish it in America. Thus, artists (including himself) are developing this text for Neo-HooDoo, a mythology that will be an alternative narrative to Christianity.

However, an important note must be made here; the essence of Neo-HooDoo is acceptance of cultural pluralism. The mythology that Reed creates for Neo-HooDoo is meant to be an alternative to Western society, another cultural option, but is not meant to completely erase or replace it. Reed illustrates the type of coexistence and cultural pluralism he advocates for throughout *Yellow Back Radio Broke-Down*. Near the beginning of the novel, the Loop Garoo Kid is attacked by a neo-social realist gang, which expresses many of the militant and Afro-centric views that Loop and Reed reject.[61] Just as the gang is about to torture Loop, however, Chief Showcase rescues him, defeating the neo-realist gang and taking Loop away from the desert. This scene is indicative of the kind of relationship Reed promotes in Neo-HooDoo; rather than promoting an Afro-centric and monocultural viewpoint, Reed aligns himself with other minorities (in this case Native Americans) to promote cultural pluralism. This coexistence of cultures extends to Western traditions as well, as seen in the ending of *Yellow Back Radio Broke-Down* when Reed returns with the Pope. These scenes are just a few of the instances where Reed shows his willingness to work with other traditions, creating an accepting Neo-HooDoo tradition.

Neo-HooDoo's Origin Story

In *Mumbo Jumbo,* the origin story of Neo-HooDoo is presented to readers. Loosely set within the United States just before the Great Depression and during the height of the Harlem Renaissance, the novel focuses on a plague called Jes Grew. Jes Grew, Reed's representation of Neo-HooDoo, spreads from New Orleans to New York City and across the country, fought by the Wallflower Order, representing Western culture and Christianity. This battle between Jes Grew and the Wallflower Order becomes the origin story for Neo-HooDoo. *Mumbo Jumbo*'s inclusion of the Wallflower Order, the enemy of Neo-HooDoo, gives Reed the opportunity to trace this conflict throughout history, what he sees as an essential backstory for Neo-HooDoo. To emphasize that this conflict is not a modern invention, Reed presents African Americans' cultural origins to Egyptian mythology, explaining how African culture was oppressed from its inception. From this novel, the reader not only understands that the conflict between African and Western cultures has a long history, but can connect this long history to Reed's Neo-HooDoo movement.

One of the focuses within *Mumbo Jumbo* is the Text that Jes Grew is searching for. The Text, in fact, becomes a character in *Mumbo Jumbo* as Reed anthropomorphizes it, "Jes Grew needed its words to tell its carriers what it was up to. Jes Grew was an influence which sought its text, and whenever it thought it knew the location of its words and Labanotations it headed in that direction."[62] For Jes Grew, the Text is not static like the Christian Bible and ideology; instead, it evolves, changes, and, literally, moves from city to city. Even the description of the Text moving towards its "Labanotations" is significant, referring to the way dancers use symbols to record their movements. Reed's word choice emphasizes the inherent movement that is embedded within Neo-HooDoo. In this way, *Mumbo Jumbo*'s characterization of the Text contributes to the origin story for Neo-HooDoo by establishing certain characteristics of this movement.

A Neo-HooDoo Adventure

Yellow Back Radio Broke-Down recounts one of the adventures of Neo-HooDoo, embodied in the character the Loop Garoo Kid. The Loop Garoo Kid is larger than life, the action figure that Neo-HooDoo needs to fight its battles against Western culture. Just as Christianity can tell myths of Saints and their good deeds, Neo-HooDoo needs a central figure to fight its battles in this new mythology. Similar to the battle between Neo-HooDoo and Western culture in *Mumbo Jumbo*, Loop fights a representative of Western culture in the form of Drag Gibson. Drag Gibson's goal is to take over an oasis in the middle of the American west, Yellow Back Radio. However, Loop consistently thwarts him through VooDoo practices and guerilla-type warfare. The absurdity of *Yellow Back Radio Broke-Down,* where historical figures like Pope Innocent, Meriwether Lewis, William Clark, and John Wesley Hardin make appearances, underlines the larger-than-life quality of this work. While *Mumbo Jumbo* has some sort of narrative structure and realism (even if they are not consistent), *Yellow Back Radio Broke-Down* is firmly planted in satire where anything can happen and anyone can appear in this adventure episode of Neo-HooDoo. This adventure episode is a necessary component in Reed's Neo-HooDoo mythology as he builds on the foundations of Neo-HooDoo to show the possibilities of an active Neo-HooDoo.

Unlike *Mumbo Jumbo*, *Yellow Back Radio Broke-Down* does not describe Neo-HooDoo's history or Text in depth. Instead, Reed looks forward to the future of Neo-HooDoo. At one point, Loop is talking to Pope Innocent and says, "Hoo-doo, which in America flowered in New Orleans, was an unorganized religion without ego-games or death worship," continuing to explain, "I just wanted to show the world what they [Christianity] were really up to."[63] While Loop is working within a Neo-HooDoo framework, he reveals the hypocrisy of Western culture, the focus of *Yellow Back Radio Broke-Down.* Loop refers to the entire situation in Yellow Back Radio as a "horse opera."[64] Similar to the western dime novels Reed satires in *Yellow Back Radio Broke-Down*, horse operas confirmed the dominant Western narrative of history, the history of the oppressors.[65] Loop's disruption of Yellow Back Radio's horse opera is what Reed imagines Neo-HooDoo accomplishing in American culture. Reed aims to free Americans, offering an accepting, pluralistic cultural tradition very different from the limited fundamentalist approach of Western culture.

It is essential to create novels that bring forth a Neo-HooDoo mythology: one to act as the origin story and one to act as the fulfillment of that origin, the adventure episode. As Reed consistently explains, the origins of minority cultures have been lost and oppressed, creating a void, an absence that results in a cycle of traumatic historical remembrance for these cultures. Moreover, although HooDoo exists in parts of American culture, it has been "underground" and unable to translate successfully into modern urban America. Reed explains, "Neo-HooDoo is the Now Locomotive swinging/ up the Tracks of the American Soul."[66] Reed not only needs to establish the history of Neo-HooDoo to reestablish the lost historical remembrance of minority cultures, he also needs to establish

Neo-HooDoo as a viable and important component of American culture in today's society. And, the way he can achieve this is by establishing a Text or mythology for Neo-HooDoo since "if it could not find its Text then it would be mistaken for entertainment."[67] If Neo-HooDoo does not find this Text, it will be dismissed and disregarded. A Neo-HooDoo mythology helps fill the void, creating a historical remembrance, as well as establishing a future for Neo-HooDoo, a way for it to exist and thrive today,

> Almost 100 years ago HooDoo was forced to say
> Goodbye to America. Now HooDoo is
> back as Neo-HooDoo
> *You can't keep a good church down!*[68]

Centrality of Urban Spaces to Traumatic Historical Remembrances and Neo-HooDoo

Discussions of multidirectional memory often center on urban spaces as cities can be conceptualized as the physical locations of historical remembrances. Cities are where cultures develop as people congregate and are the centers of government and commerce, and thus cities are the physical locations of society's historical remembrances. Cities have become an important space for African Americans, particularly after the Civil War as freed slaves migrated in droves; Sarah-Jane Mathieu reports that during three phases, more than six million African Americans moved from the rural south to the urban west and north after the Civil War,[69] often to New York, Chicago, Detroit, and Los Angeles.[70] This migration changed the demographics of the cities where African Americans moved, creating a dramatic shift in the cultures of many neighborhoods where migrants settled. Many Whites moved to the suburbs as African Americans came into the city,[71] and entire neighborhoods like Harlem became predominantly African American. Harlem in particular would eventually be central to the Harlem Renaissance and the Black Arts Movement.

For the Black Arts Movement, urban centers were important to their work. James Smethurst explains that the Black Arts Movement was "rooted in the landscape of the urban ghetto" as a way to take advantage of the large concentrations of African Americans in small geographical areas.[72] Smethurst connects the Black Arts Movement focus on urban centers to James Boggs, a political activist, who thought African Americans could (and should) gain political and economic power in the cities where they were the majority. The Black Arts Movement was a movement influenced and sustained by its urban artists and audience because of the city's importance in cultural development and historical remembrances.

Following the importance the Black Arts Movement placed on urban spaces, Reed stresses the importance of urban spaces as the physical manifestation of cultural development in his presentation of Neo-HooDoo. While HooDoo is often associated with New Orleans, Reed also describes it as "driven underground where to this day it flourishes in the Black ghettos throughout the country."[73] HooDoo, even in its oppressed form, continued in the ghettos of America's cities even as it was persecuted. Reed also acknowledges that it is in urban spaces that culture develops and cultural wars are waged, which is why he connects the development of Neo-HooDoo to these urban centers.

While theorists, the Black Arts Movement, and Reed have acknowledged the importance of cities as places of cultural development, it is in cities that African Americans' trauma is most clearly seen. As the physical manifestation of cultural development and an important location in the development of historical remembrances, cities' museums and memorials are central to acknowledging past traumas, addressing and confronting traumatic historical remembrances. But, these memorials and museums do not treat all historical remembrances equally; some historical remembrances are privileged over others. In this way urban spaces reflect both reflecting *and* forgetting.[74] Derek H. Alderman suggests that African Americans are more often reflected in the forgetting within urban places than the remembering as "Southern and American public history have been narrated in white-centric ways, marginalizing if not altogether ignoring the memories, contributions and struggles of African Americans."[75] Alderman specifically traces this process of forgetting chronologically by one Southern woman's struggle to erect a statue memorializing the slave trade in Savannah, Georgia. The city, in the absence of historical remembrances, perpetuates African American trauma, continuing to deny African Americans a cohesive historical remembrance.

It is because African Americans have been forgotten in cities that Reed presents the urban as central to Neo-HooDoo. In "Neo-HooDoo Manifesto," Reed mentions the battles of this war occurring in cities such as New York, and specifically in Harlem, Chicago, New Orleans, and San Francisco; these are "examples of underground centers [of Neo-HooDoo] found in ghettos throughout America."[76] Reed notes that "Neo-HooDoo targets are TV the/ museums they symphony halls and churches art music and/ literature departments in Christianizing (...)/universities,"[77] all of the "metropolitan urbanity" that Huyssen describes. Thus, it is in these urban spaces that he centers his discussion of Neo-HooDoo.

New Orleans, as an urban space, has specific significance for Reed and African Americans. *Mumbo Jumbo* begins in New Orleans because it is here that VooDoo and HooDoo first grew and continued secretly. Davis argues that VooDoo only survived in New Orleans because of its connections to Haiti and the Caribbean, where "syncretization" was allowed between VooDoo and Christianity, effectively masking VooDoo in the more acceptable religious tradition.[78] In the rural south, however, VooDoo disappeared—it was effectively stamped out—except for hints of HooDoo. VooDoo is often associated with the "Voodoo Queen of New Orleans", Marie Laveau, who was sought out for her conjuring abilities in the 1800s.[79] Reed recognizes this, acknowledging the importance of New Orleans as the place where slaves were allowed to practice VooDoo and HooDoo. It is in New Orleans that Jes Grew initially rears its head in *Mumbo Jumbo* and is launched in cities across America. New Orleans becomes a natural location for the origins of Neo-HooDoo as a "psychic epidemic" that is in danger of spreading, becoming a "pandemic."[80]

We can also see Reed's focus on other cities in *Mumbo Jumbo* and *Yellow Back Radio Broke-Down*. It is the movement of Jes Grew from city to city that disturbs Western society. Additionally, most of *Mumbo Jumbo*'s action occurs in New York City, the cultural center of a consumer-driven America. Reed portrays the consumerism of modern cities as destructive; Papa Labas drives a Town Coupe Locomobile that is "designed to accommodate the philosophy 'small numbers make for distinction, quantity destroys'."[81] Rather than embracing American consumerism, Reed places his novels in cities because urban spaces are where Neo-HooDoo will have the most effect to address African Americans' traumatic historical remembrance and counter traditional Western and American culture. In *Yellow Back Radio Broke-Down*, the action centers on the city of Yellow Back Radio. Yellow Back Radio is unique because it is not identifiable with a real city. It is an oasis in the middle of the western landscape. Thus, possibly even more so than *Mumbo Jumbo*, *Yellow Back Radio Broke-Down*'s action centers on a city that literally contains a disseminator of culture, a radio station. Radio stations are mass transmitters of culture (usually Western culture), and so in *Yellow Back Radio Broke-Down* we see a clear connection between the city and culture. It is in these cities, in both of Reed's novels, that the struggle to reestablish African culture will take place, addressing the traumatic African American historical remembrance and working to create a positive future historical remembrance. The ability to engage with

Western society is precisely why Reed centers his development of Neo-HooDoo in cities. It is only here that Reed can fully engage with and fight Western culture, establishing a cultural future of Neo-HooDoo. It is in these urban spaces that Reed sees this new cultural practice and mythology succeeding.

Past, Present, and Future via a Multidirectional Neo-HooDoo

The framework of multidirectional memory reveals the way in which Reed creates a new historical remembrance that emphasizes the multicultural and common roots minority cultures have with Western cultures. He does so to address the inequalities and traumas that oppression has created, both for African Americans through slavery and for other minorities through colonialism. By reimagining the world's historical remembrance, Reed confronts the silence the trauma of slavery has created around African American cultural history. But, Reed's development of Neo-HooDoo does not end with a reimagining of the past. Reed critiques the current American culture in light of the past while creating the possibility of a new cultural future. The mythology Reed creates with *Mumbo Jumbo* and *Yellow Back Radio Broke-Down* is the foundation for this cultural future that is an alternative to Western traditions. As Reed explains, "Jes Grew needs its words and steps, or else it becomes merely a flair-up. Without substance it never fully catches on."[82] Part of this substance Neo-HooDoo requires is an audience, one that Reed finds in urban America as he targets cities as the places where this cultural revolution will take root and succeed.

Ultimately, what Reed offers is a nuanced way of viewing cultural traditions. Neo-HooDoo is a cultural tradition for everyone, a tradition we can all take and use in our own way. As Reed says, "Why do I call it 'The Neo-HooDoo Aesthetic'?/ *The proportions of ingredients used depend upon the cook!*"[83] This individualism that Reed identifies as a central characteristic of Neo-HooDoo is also Reed's central message. By recovering the lost historical remembrance of the world's cultures, Reed envisions an inclusive and accepting cultural future that "knows no class no race no consciousness."[84]

Bibliography

Alderman, Derek. "Surrogation and the Politics of Remembering Slavery in Savannah, Georgia (US)." *Journal of Historical Geography* 36 (2010): 90-101.

Apter, Andrew. "Herskovits's Heritage: Rethinking Syncretism in the African Diaspora." *Diaspora: A Journal of Transnational Studies* 1.3 (1991): 235-60.

Davis, Rod. *American Voudou: Journey into a Hidden World*. Denton: University of North Texas Press, 1999.

Delbo, Charlotte. *Auschwitz and After*. Trans. Rosette C. Lamont. New Haven: Yale University Press, 1995.

Dick, Bruce, and Amritjit Singh, eds. *Conversations with Ishmael Reed*. Jackson: University Press of Mississippi, 1995.

Evans, Freddi Williams. *Congo Square: African Roots in New Orleans*. Lafayette: University of Louisiana at Lafayette Press, 2011.

Gilroy, Paul. *The Black Atlantic: Modernity and Double Consciousness*. Cambridge: Harvard University Press, 1993.

Gover, Robert. "An Interview with Ishmael Reed." *Black American Literature Forum* 12 (1978): 12-19.

Huyssen, Andreas. "Present Pasts: Media, Politics, Amnesia." *Public Culture* 12 (2000): 21-38.

Jones, LeRoi [Amiri Baraka]. "American Sexual Reference: Black Male." In *Home: Social Essays,* 243-62. New York: William Morrow & Co., 1968.

Mathieu, Sarah-Jane. "The African American Great Migration Reconsidered." *OAH Magazine of History* 23.4 (2009): 19-23.

McConnell, Frank. "Ishmael Reed's Fiction: DaHoodoo is Put on America." In *Black Fiction: New Studies in the Afro-American Novel Since 1945*, edited by A. Robert Lee, 136-48. London: Vision Press, 1980.

McKinney, Louise. *New Orleans: A Cultural History*. New York: Oxford University Press, 2006.

Morrow Song, Carolyn. *Spiritual Merchants: Religion, Magic & Commerce*. Knoxville: University of Tennessee Press, 2001.

Mvuyekure, Pierre-Damien. *The "Dark Heathenism" of the American Novelist Ishmael Reed: African Voodoo as American Literary HooDoo*. Lewiston, NY: Edwin Mellen Press, 2007.

Neal, Larry. "The Black Arts Movement." In *Visions of a Liberated Future: Black Arts Movement Writings,* edited by Michael Schwartz, 62-78. New York: Thunder Mouth's Press, 1989.

Patterson, Orlando. *Slavery and Social Death: A Comparative Study*. Cambridge: Harvard University Press, 1982.

Reed, Ishmael. *Mumbo Jumbo*. New York: Simon & Schuster, 1972.

—. "Neo-HooDoo Manifesto." In *New and Collected Poems 1964-2007*, 25-33. New York: Thunder's Mouth Press, 2006.

—. "The Neo-HooDoo Aesthetic." In *New and Collected Poems 1964-2007,* 34. New York: Thunder's Mouth Press, 2006.

—. *Yellow Back Radio Broke-Down*. Champaign: Dalkey Archive Press, 1969.

Rothberg, Michael. *Multidirectional Memory: Remembering the Holocaust in the Age of Decolonization*. Stanford: Stanford University Press, 2009.

Scharnhorst, Gary. "'All Hat and No Cattle': Romance, Realism, and Late Nineteenth-Century Western American Fiction." In *A Companion to the Literature and Culture of the American West* (2011). Accessed November 27, 2013. http://www.blackwellreference.com/subscriber/tocnode.html?id=g9781405187336_chunk_g978140518733618.

Schmitz, Neil. "Neo-HooDoo: The Experimental Fiction of Ishmael Reed." *Twentieth Century Literature* 20.2 (1974): 126-40.

Sebald, W. G. *Austerlitz*. New York: The Modern Library, 2001.

Smethurst, James. *Black Arts Movement: Literary Nationalism in the 1960s and 1970s*. Chapel Hill: University of North Carolina Press, 2005.

Tuhkanen, Mikko. "'Out of Joint': Passing, Haunting, and the Time of Slavery in *Hagar's Daughter*." *American Literature* 79.2 (2007): 335-61.

Winter, Jay. *Remembering War: The Great War between Memory and History in the Twentieth Century*. New Haven: Yale University Press, 2006.

Zilcosky, John. "Lost and Found: Disorientation, Nostalgia, and Holocaust Melodrama in Sebald's *Austerlitz*." *MLN* 121.3 (2006): 679-98.

Notes

[1] Bruce Dick and Amritjit Singh, eds. *Conversations with Ishmael Reed* (Jackson: University Press of Mississippi, 1995), 53.

[2] Ishmael Reed, "Neo-HooDoo Manifesto," in *New and Collected Poems 1964-2007* (New York: Thunder's Mouth Press, 2006), ll 60-61.

[3] Reed, "Neo-HooDoo Manifesto," ll 89-90.

[4] Reed, "Neo-HooDoo Manifesto," ll 41-42.

[5] Reed, "Neo-HooDoo Manifesto," ll 80.

[6] Reed, "Neo-HooDoo Manifesto," ll 139, 138.

[7] Jay Winter, *Remembering War: The Great War between Memory and History in the Twentieth Century* (New Haven: Yale University Press, 2006), 427.
[8] Winter, *Remembering War*, 427.
[9] Michael Rothberg, *Multidirectional Memory: Remembering the Holocaust in the Age of Decolonization* (Stanford: Stanford University Press, 2009), 2.
[10] Rothberg, *Multidirectional Memory*, 10.
[11] Andreas Huyssen, "Present Pasts: Media, Politics, Amnesia," *Public Culture* 12 (2000): 21-38.
[12] Freddi Williams Evans, *Congo Square: African Roots in New Orleans* (Lafayette: University of Louisiana at Lafayette Press, 2011), 2.
[13] Carolyn Morrow Song, *Spiritual Merchants: Religion, Magic & Commerce* (Knoxville: University of Tennessee Press, 2001), 29-30.
[14] Rod Davis, *American Voudou: Journey into a Hidden World* (Denton: University of North Texas Press, 1999), 133.
[15] Orlando Patterson, *Slavery and Social Death: A Comparative Study* (Cambridge: Harvard University Press, 1982), 5.
[16] Patterson, *Slavery and Social Death*, 281.
[17] Patterson, *Slavery and Social Death*, 3.
[18] Mikko Tuhkanen, "'Out of Joint': Passing, Haunting, and the Time of Slavery in *Hagar's Daughter*," *American Literature* 79.2 (2007): 335.
[19] Davis, *American Voudou*, 11.
[20] Ishmael Reed, *Yellow Back Radio Broke-Down* (Champaign: Dalkey Archive Press, 1969), 42.
[21] Reed, "Neo-HooDoo Manifesto," ll 1.
[22] Rothberg, *Multidirectional Memory*, 3.
[23] James Smethurst, *Black Arts Movement: Literary Nationalism in the 1960s and 1970s* (Chapel Hill: University of North Carolina Press, 2005).
[24] Larry Neal, "The Black Arts Movement," in *Visions of a Liberated Future: Black Arts Movement Writings,* ed. Michael Schwartz (New York: Thunder Mouth's Press, 1989), 64.
[25] Neal, "The Black Arts Movement," 68.
[26] LeRoi James, "American Sexual Reference: Black Male," in *Home: Social Essays* (New York: William Morrow & Co., 1968), 223.
[27] Neal, "The Black Arts Movement," 64.
[28] Pierre-Damien Mvuyekure, *The "Dark Heathenism" of the American Novelist Ishmael Reed: African Voodoo as American Literary HooDoo* (Lewiston, NY: Edwin Mellen Press, 2007), 115.
[29] Reed, "Neo-HooDoo Manifesto," ll 78.
[30] Frank McConnell, "Ishmael Reed's Fiction: DaHoodoo is Put on America," in *Black Fiction: New Studies in the Afro-American Novel Since 1945*, ed. A. Robert Lee (London: Vision Press, 1980), 139.
[31] Lileth Dorsey explains that, in Haitian VooDoo, Papa Legba is the paternal creation deity, an intermediary between the spiritual world and the earth, and as such begins many of the VooDoo rituals (see also Pierre-Damien Mvuyekure). Thus, Papa Labas acts as an intermediary between differing cultural traditions in Reed's writing, as well as an intermediary between the Harlem Renaissance of the

1920s and the Black Arts Movement of the 1960s, as shown at the end of *Mumbo* Jumbo.
[32] Mvuyekure, *The "Dark Heathenism,"* 117.
[33] Rothberg, *Multidirectional Memory*, 20.
[34] Ishmael Reed, *Mumbo Jumbo* (New York: Simon & Schuster, 1972), 6.
[35] Reed, *Mumbo Jumbo,* 4.
[36] Reed, *Mumbo Jumbo,* 162.
[37] Reed, *Mumbo Jumbo,* 162.
[38] Reed, *Yellow Back Radio Broke-Down*, 164.
[39] Reed, *Yellow Back Radio Broke-Down*, 165.
[40] Reed, *Yellow Back Radio Broke-Down*, 153.
[41] Reed, *Yellow Back Radio Broke-Down*, 165.
[42] Rothberg, *Multidirectional Memory*, 18.
[43] W. G. Sebald, *Austerlitz* (New York: The Modern Library, 2001).
[44] For example, Delbo quotes a news report about the execution of Algerian patriot Abderahmane Laklifi from *L'Express* in Charlotte Delbo, *Auschwitz and After*, trans. Rosette C. Lamont (New Haven: Yale University Press, 1995), 132-33. This inclusion of newspaper clippings (she also includes a clipping that references the Vietnam war elsewhere in the memoir) previews her later work, *Les belles lettres,* which discusses the French-Algerian war in the context of Nazi atrocities.
[45] Reed, *Mumbo Jumbo,* 204.
[46] Reed, *Mumbo Jumbo,* 165.
[47] Reed, "Neo-HooDoo Manifesto," ll 69-70, 71-72.
[48] Reed, *Mumbo Jumbo*, 134.
[49] Reed, *Mumbo Jumbo*, 134.
[50] Tuhkanen, "'Out of Joint.'"
[51] Reed, "Neo-HooDoo Manifesto," ll 68-69.
[52] Reed, *Yellow Back Radio Broke-Down,* 177.
[53] Robert Gover, "An Interview with Ishmael Reed," *Black American Literature Forum* 12 (1978): 15.
[54] Rothberg, *Multidirectional Memory,* 18.
[55] John Zilcosky, "Lost and Found: Disorientation, Nostalgia, and Holocaust Melodrama in Sebald's *Austerlitz*," *MLN* 121.3 (2006): 679.
[56] Reed, *Yellow Back Radio Broke-Down,* 36.
[57] Neil Schmitz, "Neo-HooDoo: The Experimental Fiction of Ishmael Reed," *Twentieth Century Literature* 20.2 (1974): 127.
[58] Dick and Singh, *Conversations with Ishmael Reed,* 63.
[59] Reed, "Neo-HooDoo Manifesto," ll 194-201.
[60] Reed, "Neo-HooDoo Manifesto," ll 169-170.
[61] Reed, *Yellow Back Radio Broke-Down,* 36.
[62] Reed, *Mumbo Jumbo,* 211.
[63] Reed, *Yellow Back Radio Broke-Down,* 164-165.
[64] Reed, *Yellow Back Radio Broke-Down,* 163.
[65] Gary Scharnhorst, "'All Hat and No Cattle': Romance, Realism, and Late Nineteenth-Century Western American Fiction," in *A Companion to the Literature and Culture of the American West* (2011), accessed November 27, 2013,

http://www.blackwellreference.com/subscriber/tocnode.html?id=g9781405187336_chunk_g978140518733618. para. 8.
[66] Reed, "Neo-HooDoo Manifesto," ll 207-208.
[67] Reed, *Mumbo Jumbo,* 211.
[68] Reed, "Neo-HooDoo Manifesto," ll 209-212.
[69] Sarah-Jane Mathieu, "The African American Great Migration Reconsidered," *OAH Magazine of History* 23.4 (2009): 20.
[70] Andrew Apter, "Herskovits's Heritage: Rethinking Syncretism in the African Diaspora," *Diaspora: A Journal of Transnational Studies* 1.3 (1991): 240-41.
[71] Apter, "Herskovits's Heritage," 240-41
[72] Smethurst, *Black Arts Movement*, 80.
[73] Reed, "Neo-HooDoo Manifesto," 25.
[74] Derek Alderman, "Surrogation and the Politics of Remembering Slavery in Savannah, Georgia (US)," *Journal of Historical Geography* 36 (2010): 91.
[75] Alderman, "Surrogation and the Politics of Remembering Slavery," 91.
[76] Reed, "Neo-HooDoo Manifesto," 28.
[77] Reed, "Neo-HooDoo Manifesto," ll 184-187.
[78] Davis, *American Voudou.*
[79] Louise McKiney, *New Orleans: A Cultural History* (New York: Oxford University Press, 2006).
[80] Reed, *Mumbo Jumbo,* 4-5.
[81] Reed, *Mumbo Jumbo,* 48.
[82] Reed, *Mumbo Jumbo,* 213.
[83] Reed, "The Neo-HooDoo Aesthetic," ll 10-11.
[84] Reed, *Mumbo Jumbo,* 5.

PART TWO:

TRAUMA, LINEAGE, AND TRANSMISSION IN AUTOBIOGRAPHY

FROM "ANGEL OF MERCY" TO "RADICAL MUSLIM": ZEITOUN'S STORY TRAVELS

KATE PARKER HORIGAN

Since the mid-20th century, the collective dynamics of memory have fascinated many scholars, but most have focused on memory as a performance or a product, rather than studying the processes by which memories take shape, circulate, and gain force in social contexts. In this chapter, I discuss the autobiographical narrative of Hurricane Katrina survivor Abdulrahman Zeitoun, in order to make the case for studying not just the "what" of collective memory but the "how." In other words, by analyzing the transformations Zeitoun's story takes as it moves from personal narrative to public discourse, I trace the micro-level dynamics that determine which stories come to dominate the formations of collective or social memory.

Abdulrahman Zeitoun's story has found commercial success through its adaptation in *Zeitoun*, Dave Eggers' nonfiction bestseller. I identify textual shifts in this adaptation, revealing readers' desires for a simplified understanding of traumatic experience: one that distorts popular understanding of disastrous events and shapes public memory of those events for generations to come. First published as a blog authored by Mr. Zeitoun, then collected by Lola Vollen for the interview collection *Voices from the Storm* (2006), and finally recounted by Dave Eggers in his 2009 book, Zeitoun's story reaches the peak of its circulation when it is told by someone else. Eggers is an authority figure, vouching for the story and promising readers an authentic, compelling, real-life protagonist. However, the changes in Zeitoun's story from blog to book reflect a transition from an urgent first person account, with a narrator who expresses ambiguity, to a lyrical drama that offers clear resolution. Ultimately, Eggers presents Zeitoun as an uncomplicated hero battling natural forces, rescuing helpless women, and facing down anti-Muslim sentiment and the prison-industrial complex. Liberally minded audiences are especially eager to embrace this heroic figure, as he comes to represent a hardworking immigrant at whose treatment they can feel self-righteously outraged. Meanwhile, Zeitoun's own involvement in the narration is erased. I illustrate how these shifts happen in the analysis below, with the aim of demonstrating the dynamic relationship between individual narrative and collective memory.

In his book *Remembering the Year of the French: Irish Folk History and Social Memory*, historian Guy Beiner synthesizes major developments in memory studies in the 20th century. He begins, "The founding father of the concept of collective memory was the French sociologist Maurice Halbwachs, who furthered ideas raised by his illustrious mentor Émile Durkheim to argue against the validity of individual psychology and to claim that memory is fundamentally a collective function."[1] Beiner goes on to explain how, "Halbwachs even insisted that all memory is collective, insofar as individual recollections are structured by group identities and conditioned by social consciousness, so that 'no memory is possible outside frameworks used by people living in society to determine and retrieve their recollections.'"[2] As others have done, I object to Halbwachs' statement above by contending that memory is social but not determined by society.

In *Narrating Our Pasts*, Elizabeth Tonkin addresses this objection more fully. Tonkin writes that, "[m]emory for [Halbwachs] mediates between the social world and the mind, but only so as to reproduce society."[3] She points out how this suggests a static view of memory, one wherein people are passive recipients. This model fails to account, then, for the capacity of individuals to modify memory, leading to action and change. Tonkin's contribution to a collective memory model does take these interactions into consideration; she proposes, "[t]he missing term in Halbwachs' account is socialisation, which I would define as the ways and means by which we internalise the external world."[4] To return to Guy Beiner, he finds Tonkin's theoretical shift from collective memory to social memory effective in "acknowledging the role of socializing processes."[5] Beiner makes his own addition by distinguishing between what constitutes memory as opposed to the actions of remembering. As he puts it, he "prefers the term *social memory* when referring to representations of traditional bodies of knowledge, and *social remembering* (or simply *remembrance*) in reference to dynamic processes of reproduction."[6]

Beiner's distinction is largely in line with one I make as well, between memory as product and memory as process. I differentiate my own understanding from his in that I focus my attention on a different point in the process. He asserts, "[a]lthough it may be unfeasible to pinpoint social memory as referring to a single clearly defined subject, nonetheless it is possible to positively identify expressions of social memory and moments of social remembering in action."[7] I agree with this view, and I add that it is possible and worthwhile not only to identify active "expressions" of memory, but also memory's processes of formation. This goal informs my attention to personal narratives, an integral piece in a comprehensive model of social memory. I ask how narratives circulate, accumulate social power, and become part of social memory, taking up the challenge that Guy Beiner identifies, "explaining why certain information was remembered and other information forgotten."[8]

Memory and forgetting happen at many levels, sometimes taking the shape of institutional emphasis and exclusion, or of public acceptance and rejection. To account for these complex interactions, my discussion below draws on the interdisciplinary approach of critical discourse analysis.[9] I incorporate close readings of textual features, investigate processes of production, distribution, and consumption, and consider the sociocultural contexts that Zeitoun's story evokes. On a textual level, I analyze variable claims to credibility by the authors, editors, and publishers. The shifts among versions indicate generic expectations, so my analysis points to demands in the literary marketplace. Finally, I highlight where dominant narratives are engaged, disputed, and reinforced: in the blog, Zeitoun counteracts stereotypes about immigrants; in the interview collection, the editors negotiate anxieties about the believability of eyewitness accounts; and in the book, Eggers writes against a narrative of Islamophobia—but in his very doing, he shores that narrative up so that it is readily available for the re-characterization of Zeitoun in his present legal predicament. As Zeitoun faces charges of domestic violence and attempted murder, his personal narrative is subject yet again to changing public interpretation. This chapter offers the tools to understand that interpretation and its consequences, as well as other personal accounts publicized, received, and remembered as individual representations of collective trauma.

Zeitoun's Beginnings

Abdulrahman Zeitoun is a Syrian American contractor who has spent most of his adult life in New Orleans with his family. The story of his experiences during and after Hurricane Katrina is in some ways extraordinary and in other ways representative. Like many New Orleanians, Zeitoun remained in the city in order to protect his property. There were other reasons, which resonate for locals, such as reluctance to deal with the hassles of evacuation, belief that predictions of danger were overstated, and curiosity and desire for adventure. For people with fewer resources than Zeitoun, these reasons were compounded by financial and logistical obstacles to evacuation. In Zeitoun's case, however, staying is a choice, and it is one that results in a nightmare scenario: flooding of his home and neighborhood, abandonment of those awaiting rescue, and ultimately, his wrongful incarceration. Zeitoun is snatched without explanation from his own property, informally accused of terrorism then formally accused of looting, held for three and a half weeks in various jails, strip searched, robbed, interrogated, and denied basic rights including a phone call to his family, who meanwhile presume him dead. He is eventually released on bail, and continues to deal with the legal and personal repercussions of his incarceration—a terrible mistake forged in the fires of panic, Islamophobia, and crippled bureaucracy. Audiences are outraged and sympathetic when reading the account of this ordeal as told in Eggers' 2009 book *Zeitoun*. Before *Zeitoun*, the human rights organization Voice of Witness, of which Eggers is co-founder, included excerpts of interviews with Zeitoun in their 2008 publication *Voices from the Storm*. Before that book hit the shelves, a first-person blog chronicling Zeitoun's experiences appeared on the Nola.com website, parts of which were handed over to local survivors in the months following the hurricane as a forum to share information and stories. The blog entry was published online in November of 2005, only two months after Zeitoun's release from the Hunt Correctional Center.

This chapter examines Zeitoun's narrative as it morphs in each version, and considers the external elements that influenced these changes, including contexts of production, expectations attached to genre, and relevant dominant narratives. A comparative analysis reveals at least four features of Zeitoun's story that emerge as both significant and variable: the strategies used to affirm credibility; the management of emotional content, particularly in figurative language; the use of reported speech; and finally, what William Labov calls narrative evaluation, or the point of the story according to its narrator.[10] Identifying the trajectory of these qualities ultimately reveals that when Zeitoun's account travels, it becomes what its genres demand and what its various audiences want to hear: the honest tale of a hardworking immigrant, then the broken voice of an emotional eyewitness to trauma, and finally, the exotic foreigner who is transformed—temporarily—into an all-American hero.

To compare Zeitoun's experiences as they appear in blog, interview, and non-fiction bestseller, my analysis focuses on a significant moment that emerges in all three narrative contexts. Each text includes a visually striking recollection where Zeitoun enters a house to rescue an elderly woman who is literally hanging on for her life, holding herself up by the rafters of her flooded home, surrounded by her billowing dress. This moment lends itself to retelling for a number of reasons. First of all, its imagery is vivid and memorable. As Ulf Palmenfelt describes in his study of World War II narratives, one of the most often-repeated stories is one where a child uses his family's cherished ration book to purchase milk, and then drops the jar of milk on the way back home. The story centers on the heart-wrenching image of the white milk spreading out over a cobblestone street.[11] In stories like these, the repeated visual element takes on the qualities of an icon—instantly recognizable, both symbolic and indexical in its representation of suffering. Like the spilled milk, the floating woman appears in multiple renditions of this story, almost unchanged, and is a narrative moment that reviewers and readers often discuss.[12]

The encounter with the elderly woman is the first and perhaps most crucial depiction of Zeitoun as the hero of this story. As Zeitoun paddles around flooded streets in his canoe, he and his friend hear the woman call out for help. Zeitoun goes to great lengths to rescue this woman, swimming up to her home, kicking down the swollen door, going to find more help because the woman is heavy and nearly immobile, and finally maneuvering her into a waiting boat. Given her age, gender, and frailty, she fits the quintessential description of a helpless victim, and Zeitoun's rescue efforts in this scenario serve as a dramatic counterpoint to his later categorization as a criminal. This heroic moment makes his wrongful arrest and imprisonment even more ludicrous. To varying degrees in each narrative, Zeitoun reflects on the sense of purpose he feels after saving this woman, which lends a motive to his actions and adds to the tragic irony of his incarceration. In the context of Zeitoun's narrative, seeing him as a hero on a mission enables the audience to fully sympathize with the obstacles he later faces. Thus, this pivotal moment serves as a focal point for analyzing the differences in each narrative as it emerges first in the context of his blog, then in his interview, and finally in *Zeitoun*.

The Blog: "I found this old lady"

Under the title "Rescue efforts lead to arrest nightmare for N.O. businessman," Zeitoun's story appeared on a blog on NOLA.com on November 24, 2005. NOLA.com is the website associated with the New Orleans daily newspaper the *Times Picayune*, although the site's contents are often more geared toward tourism and entertainment than headline news.[13] The blog originally bore the name "Bourbon Street Journal: Tales from the Quirky Side of the French Quarter," and although many of the entries in the months immediately following Katrina still have contributing editor Jon Donley's name in the byline, their content is provided entirely by other contributors. Many of the blogs associated with the *Times Picayune* and NOLA.com were transformed into emergency communication or other community forums in the wake of the storm. For example, Zeitoun's blog entry follows an open letter to FEMA from an angry resident, and it precedes a nostalgic entry from a local writer who relocated to Texas. Other items on the news website from November 24, 2005, include stories about Thanksgiving meals served to volunteers and homeless survivors, the installation of temporary mail trailers, and photos of the dark skyline of the still power-less city. In other words, the website in general is almost entirely focused on post-Katrina developments, and the blog in particular is dedicated to personal accounts of survival and recovery.

Zeitoun's entry is extensive, about twelve pages in length, and its first half is segmented into discrete days in the style of a journal. After the description of his arrest, the account is no longer organized into days, and time stretches out indefinitely as it must have for the jailed man himself. Zeitoun begins by explaining that he is a local businessman, assuring readers that he has "a very good reputation through out the city of New Orleans" and that he is "listed with the Better Business Bureau."[14] This introduction offers credentials before he launches into his story. In addition to the common tendency for narrators to make claims to credibility, Zeitoun's awareness of the outrageous treatment he endured dictates added necessity for proof of his trustworthiness. As William Labov suggests, Zeitoun's story defies believability because of the events that transpire within it, ironically the very events that make it a story worth sharing.[15] He has also been through an ordeal in which his reputation was disregarded, so he is reaffirming that measure of his identity. To invoke authority, he refers to official organizations and emphasizes hard work as his defining characteristic. He writes, "I started my life from scratch, and worked my way up to where I am now."[16] This claim also places him in a narrative framework recognizable to his (primarily local and American) audience, that of the hardworking immigrant whose bootstrap mentality has paid off in a successful business. This relatively positive stereotype of hardworking immigrant may be conjured to counteract an alternative stereotype that plagued Zeitoun post-Katrina, when he was suspected of terrorism because he is a Muslim man of Middle Eastern descent. In subsequent iterations of Zeitoun's story, efforts to establish credibility continue, although the measures taken to do so change with the storytelling genre.

Other shifting features of storytelling also mark the description of the rescue scene in which Zeitoun and his friend encounter the elderly survivor. Reading this scene across genres, readers encounter fluctuation in explicit emotional content, changing patterns in the inclusion of reported speech, and a variable evaluation. This scene emerges during the fifth segment of Zeitoun's Nola.com blog entry, which recounts the events of Wednesday, August 31. It is Zeitoun's first trip out in his canoe since the levee failure on the previous day, and he sets out with the intention to check on his rental properties and "even help people if they needed help."[17] At the point where he and his friend encounter the elderly woman, he writes, "[W]e heard this muffled scream coming from somewhere. We couldn't find where it was coming from. I think the only reason we heard it was because the streets were so quiet. We yelled out to it. Asking 'Where are you?' The muffled voice was found coming from a house on Nashville Ave."[18] The description of the woman's voice changes slightly throughout the transformation of this narrative; here, it is a "muffled scream." Zeitoun's observation about why they were able to hear the muffled scream at all ("because the streets were so quiet") also repeats later on with slight variation.

Following their realization of where the cries are coming from, Zeitoun describes his rescue efforts, "I hopped out the canoe and swam to the door. I tried to open it, but it was stuck. The lady inside kept yelling 'Please help me! Please help me!' I kicked her door and finally got it open. I found this old lady in a one-story house, floating on her back, holding on to a piece of furniture calling for help. I told her I came to help her."[19] The dramatic discovery of an elderly woman floating helplessly inside her own home repeats as this story travels to subsequent audiences, but important aspects of it change. This version is matter of fact; it moves bluntly from problem to solution with little added emotional content. This is not to say the narrative is not a moving one, but rather to point out its simplicity, its focus on action, and the relative absence of the emotionally laden imagery that emerges later.

Finally, Zeitoun narrates his levelheaded response to the crisis in which he finds the elderly woman,

> She said she can't swim. I grabbed hold of her and tried to pull her out of the house. She was a heavyset woman, so it was very hard. When I got her out of her house, I told her to hang on to her porch railing. She said 'Please don't leave me, please don't leave me.' I told her, 'I can't put you in the canoe, it might flip.' I promised her that we would be back with help. She yelled 'I can't hold on very long. Please hurry, please hurry!' I got back in my canoe and we continued up Nashville to look for help. As much as I

> was happy to have this little canoe, was as much as I hated that it was so small.[20]

In this manner, Zeitoun sums up his first attempt to rescue the woman, his realization that he and his friend could not do it alone, and his decision to seek out more help. After this, he goes on to recount how they finally found a larger boat with helpful civilians aboard—though they were passed up by several official first responders[21]—and together the men managed to get the woman onto the larger boat and take her to safety. Quoted speech in this version portrays Zeitoun as straightforward and forceful, and the woman appears nearly hysterical; he describes her as "yelling," and in his quoted language, she repeats everything twice. Finally, Zeitoun's evaluation, his suggestion of the point of this story, can be found in his poignant remark that "as much as I was happy to have this little canoe, was as much as I hated that it was so small." In other words, he feels good about being able to help but simultaneously unable to do enough. As the arena for storytelling changes in subsequent versions, so does the form this narration takes.

The Interview: "I see one old lady, remind me like my grandma"

Voices from the Storm is one in a series of books edited by Dave Eggers and Lola Vollen and published by Voice of Witness and McSweeney's Books. The aim of the series, as stated in each of their publications as well as their website, is, "Using oral history as a foundation, the series illustrates human rights crises through the stories of the men and women who experience them"; this serves the dual purposes of "allow[ing] those most affected by contemporary social injustice to speak for themselves" and simultaneously educating readers who are "interested in a reality-based understanding of ongoing injustices." The series includes nine books; in addition to narratives from Katrina, the topics include narratives from wrongfully convicted Americans, undocumented immigrants in America, "the abducted and displaced people of Sudan," Zimbabweans, "survivors of Burma's military regime," "narratives of post-9/11 injustice," and "narratives from women's prisons."[22] This series and its editors are clearly dedicated to the premise that circulating narratives of human rights abuses has the potential to bring attention to and presumably ameliorate those abuses. Identifying the books as texts that address "human rights crises" already frames the events and narrators in certain ways, creating expectations associated with popular discourses of human rights. For example, a reader of such a text will most likely expect to be moved and outraged by the stories, although perhaps not to identify with the narrators. The stories might carefully balance exoticization with familiarization in order to engender empathy without creating too much discomfort.[23] Before even encountering "those most affected" who are "speaking for themselves," readers are being instructed about how to listen, encouraged to feel enlightened by this access to authentic voices, and to bestow sympathy from the privileged distance that consuming these texts provides.

Voices from the Storm is based on interviews with thirteen narrators who lived in New Orleans and survived the hurricane. The interviewees comprise a wide range of ethnic backgrounds and professions, and in terms of socioeconomic background they tend toward the working class. There are five women and eight men among those represented. The interview excerpts are arranged chronologically, first offering snippets from each narrator's life prior to Katrina, then interweaving daily accounts from August 27 to September 4, continuing with excerpts describing the week after the hurricane (September 5 to 11), then more broadly "weeks after," then finally segments of interviews where narrators are "looking back" on their experiences. After the interview-based portion, the book continues with a brief note about methodology followed by an extensive section of appendices.[24]

Between each chronologically arranged section there are editorial inserts, including sketches of each narrator accompanied by mini-bios, maps, and a bulleted list of what the editors viewed as key context. For instance, the introductory page for Monday, August 29 explains that, "At 8:14 a.m., the National Weather Service warns of a breach in the Industrial Canal."[25] These notes, in addition to the several appendices, presumably serve as guideposts for the reader, who may encounter conflicting memories from narrators, or who may doubt the veracity of these accounts without the authoritative framework that bolsters them. As in Zeitoun's citation of the Better Business Bureau, references like the one to the National Weather Service validate stories that seem incredible. In contrast to Zeitoun's invocation, however, these "truth-frames" erode narrators' authority rather than adding to it. Whereas Zeitoun makes himself more credible by referring to his good reputation, these inserts imply a lessened credibility of narrators by insisting on the need to substantiate their accounts with facts and figures. In other words, the inclusion of these materials suggests that, from the editors' perspective, the narrators are incapable of establishing credibility on their own. This is not to say the narrators *are* less credible, but rather to argue that the authority asserted by the volume's framing devices in fact undermines its contents.

This may be reason enough to question the imposition of outside authority onto the narrators' stories, but the editorial inserts are problematic for other reasons as well. The September 4 page, for instance, reports, "New Orleans police kill at least five New Orleans residents on the Danziger Bridge *after those residents opened fire* on government contractors hired to repair the 17th Street Canal."[26] Subsequent investigations and trial proceedings revealed that the residents were only suspected of opening fire, and that in fact, police shot six unarmed civilians, killing a man with mental disabilities and a teenager.[27] The report offered by *Voices from the Storm* may have been the only information available to the editors about those events at the time of publication. This discrepancy is not meant to imply carelessness in research, but rather to illustrate that the "facts" framing the interviews are equally as subject to reconsideration and revision as a personal account might be, and the use of such framing devices creates a false sense of superiority when it comes to outsider, official knowledge as opposed to insider, informally recounted experience.

In an excerpt from Zeitoun's interview in *Voices from the Storm*, he describes the same dramatic moment discussed above, when he rescues a neighborhood woman from inside her home. He begins, "We hear this quiet noise and we stop to hear, to see where the noise come from, and we start following the voice and we got to very small house, few houses before Claiborne, one-story house, and have like green awning, I remember."[28] In this version of their discovery of the woman, the woman signals her presence with a "quiet noise" as opposed to the "muffled scream" of the blog entry. Zeitoun continues, "To go closer, I have to jump from my canoe, jump to the water, and I open a screen door, go to the porch and I get to the house. Inside, I see one old lady, remind me like my grandma. Her dress full like a big balloon, floating in the water, and she's on her back holding to her furniture."[29] Zeitoun's narrative is both more elaborate and more subdued in this context. In contrast to the short, violent phrases of his blog (he kicks the door, she yells repeatedly), in this version Zeitoun enters the house with ease and the woman barely makes a sound. In fact, he does not quote the woman at all in this section of the story. Whereas reported speech disappears from this version, the emotionally laden content that was absent from the blog makes an appearance here. The metaphorical language Zeitoun uses to describe her helplessness—her dress floating around her "like a balloon"—juxtaposes the fragility and innocence of that childhood toy with the desperation of the woman hanging from her ceiling. It also evokes a sense of the bizarre, in that a balloon is a strange and unexpected object in a story of a flood; this has the effect of conveying the inexplicable nature of some things encountered by survivors.[30] Even more explicitly in terms of emotional impact, Zeitoun tells his audience that this woman "remind me like my grandma." This statement not only confirms the woman's age and perhaps her weakness, but also the sense of obligation Zeitoun felt to help her.

Finally, in addition to credibility claims, use of reported speech, and emotional content, Zeitoun's evaluation of the narrative's point changes with this version of his story as well. He wraps up this vignette, "I drag her by her shoulder, and brought her outside through the door. No way to put her in the canoe. To save her would be to drown her if I tried put her in the canoe, because it would flip no question. And I take her to the porch to try to go get some help."[31] Whereas in the first account he used the small size of his canoe to represent both his feeling of pride in helping and his limited capacity to do so, here he emphasizes his frustration even more in his starkly poetic narrative evaluation, "to save her would be to drown her."

The Book: "like a great floating flower"

Dave Eggers' *Zeitoun* is a compelling work of literary non-fiction, which adapts the story of Zeitoun into another generic category. In this version, instead of first-person blog or minimally edited interview, readers encounter a third-person narrative, a tale artfully crafted by a well-known writer, but one which sticks—according to its author—to the true story of Zeitoun's life and experiences. *Zeitoun* begins with Abdulrahman's childhood in Syria, and includes his world travels as a Merchant Marine, his marriage to Kathy and her conversion to Islam, and the growth of their family and their contracting business in New Orleans. The narrative centers on Zeitoun's decision to stay in New Orleans during Katrina, as well as the actions he took to save his properties and help stranded neighbors, and climaxes with his wrongful arrest and imprisonment. This story gives far more background and depth than either of the other two, as the events of the storm are incorporated into the narrative context of an entire life. Nonetheless, this version also shares elements, especially in terms of its implicit and explicit claims to truthfulness and in its representation of the rescue scene.

In much the same way that *Voices from the Storm* gathers facts and statistics between its covers in an effort to validate its first-person accounts, the narrative of *Zeitoun* is surrounded by affirmations of credibility as well as promises of fidelity to its subject's original story. The truth claims that frame the story of Zeitoun in this literary text go beyond those in *Voices from the Storm*. Whereas those framing devices undermined narrators' credibility by indicating a necessity for external evidence, Eggers' book makes this same move but then attempts to counter it by insisting its story is told "through [Zeitoun's] eyes."[32] These claims produce the illusion of autobiographical credibility, but in fact what Eggers does is create a credible character of Zeitoun, who is portrayed in this literary work. The problem inherent in this kind of storytelling is that Zeitoun transforms from narrator to narrator *in absentia*, and Eggers' efforts to redeem his disappearance result in a characterization that becomes a character type.

Zeitoun becomes the silent, long-suffering immigrant whose heroic actions are righteous in the face of his treatment by xenophobic Americans. As Gillian Whitlock has noted in her book *Soft Weapons*, life narratives, especially about lives foreign to Western audiences, are often accompanied by "endorsements and authorizations in the form of introductions, prefaces, appendixes, and blurbs that guide the reception of the text," and as "public intellectuals confer authority on the narrator; they both encourage and instruct the reader to read the text properly."[33] Whitlock's study is of autobiographical texts from or about Muslim cultures, whereas *Zeitoun* is an American-written biographical account of a Muslim American. However, her theorization of how and why such accounts circulate in the Western literary marketplace is accurate and useful in understanding *Zeitoun*'s strengths and weaknesses. Whitlock notes, "Ethnic autobiography is highly valued for its exotic appeal and educational value, for the status it confers on the consumer as an enlightened, sympathetic, and politically correct individual, and for that comforting narcissistic recognition that denies difference across cultures."[34] Eggers' authoritative framing of Zeitoun's story does the problematic work of conferring this status, and the harder Eggers works at making the character of Zeitoun appeal to readers, the more the book serves "that comforting narcissistic recognition."

Zeitoun's characterization as a particular type continues beyond the story's paratextual framing to the narrative itself. In the section of this book describing Zeitoun's rescue of his elderly neighbor, the narrative management of reported speech, emotional content, and evaluative commentary shift yet again. The story begins, "As they were paddling (…) they heard a faint female voice. It was a kind of moan, weak and tremulous….It was coming from a one-story house on Nashville. They coasted toward the front door and heard the voice again: 'Help me.'"[35] In this iteration, the woman's voice has transformed from the blog's "muffled scream," to the interview's "quiet noise," to a "weak and tremulous" moan. Not only has the sound become increasingly meek and pleading, but it has also acquired a gender: before, it was introduced as a scream from an unidentified source; now, it is heard initially as a "faint female voice." The difference may seem insignificant; however, the dramatic necessity of Zeitoun's heroism is dependent on the dire circumstances of his quest—in Eggers' rendering of this tale, readers can instantly read this as a damsel (albeit an elderly one) in distress. The fact that she is actually an older woman might add to the appeal of this story for readers; Zeitoun poses no threat to popular conceptions of Western masculinity, as he might if he were rescuing a beautiful young (white) maiden from the flood.

The story continues, describing Zeitoun's entrance into the house and his first sight of the woman,

> Zeitoun dropped his paddle and jumped into the water. He held his breath and swam to the porch… 'Hello?' the voice said, now hopeful. He tried the front door. It was stuck. Zeitoun kicked the door. It wouldn't move. He kicked again. No movement. With the water now to his chest, he ran his body against the door. He did it again. And again. Finally it gave.[36]

This description of Zeitoun's attempts to get into the house are reminiscent of his blog entry, bearing more in common with that forceful language than with the toned down interview account. Even the woman's voice has re-surfaced in the form of reported speech, but just barely, with her pleading "hello?" In this case, however, Zeitoun's continued bursts of activity ("He kicked again") are interspersed with the inactivity of the door itself ("No movement"). Thus, while the language echoes Zeitoun's previous action-oriented statements, the narration also incorporates a new element of dramatic suspense. The drama continues, "Inside he found a woman hovering above him. She was in her seventies, a large woman, over two hundred pounds. Her patterned dress was spread out on the surface of the water like a great floating flower. Her legs dangled below. She was holding on to a bookshelf. 'Help me,' she said."[37] In this case, the language echoes the interview version of the story, with its memorable image of the dress. Whereas Zeitoun described a balloon, however, Eggers uses the simile of "a great floating flower." This continues to capture the vulnerability of the woman evoked by the balloon comparison, but it loses its bizarre quality: in many ways, a flower is not surprising at all—what more clichéd image is there to describe a woman awaiting a man's arrival? The woman being rescued and her rescuer both become generalized to some extent, in part because of the recognizable narrative tropes and metaphorical language, but also because Eggers leaves out the most personal appeal to emotion that Zeitoun included in his earlier story: in this tale, there is no reference to the woman reminding him of his grandmother.

As this segment of narrative nears its conclusion in Eggers' book, Zeitoun's evaluation does not emerge as it does in the other narrative contexts. At the comparable point in the story, where Zeitoun and his friend decide they need more help and a bigger boat to get the woman to safety, what previously served as evaluation serves here as a conflict to be resolved. Eggers writes, "No one knew what to do next. It would be very difficult to fit a woman of her size into the canoe....The canoe would certainly capsize....They had no choice but to leave her and find help....She was unhappy to be left alone again, but there was no choice."[38] The narration goes on to describe their search for help, their success in getting the woman to safety, and before the story cuts over to Baton Rouge to describe Kathy Zeitoun's simultaneous experiences, the reader leaves Abdulrahman "alone in the canoe...soaked and exhausted."[39] Zeitoun's quandary is perhaps implied in the statement, "there was no choice," but this evaluative statement obscures the conflicting emotions Zeitoun endured. Nowhere does this mini-narrative grasp with the same concision the combination of utility and despair that Zeitoun expresses in previous narratives, "as much as I was happy to have this little canoe, was as much as I hated that it was so small," in his blog; and in his interview, "to save her would be to drown her."

The overall patterns of change from one narrative to the next are not a clear-cut movement from more personal to more archetypal. Rather, each text relies on different rhetorical strategies to convey meaning and engage an audience. In the blog, Zeitoun appeals to external validations of his individual credibility, and draws on generalized conceptions of immigrants in America. He characterizes his rescue efforts matter-of-factly, portrays the woman he rescues as agitated and even somewhat difficult, and expresses ambiguity about his ability to help those in need. In his interview with the editors of the human rights compilation, Zeitoun's story is framed by external assurances that, by implicitly deferring to discourses of "fact-checking," diminish the value of the interviews, or at the least treat them as secondary evidence for a story being told with more authority by others. In this context, Zeitoun emphasizes the personal relationship he felt to the woman he rescued, and he downplays both her aggressiveness and his own. He introduces new elements of metaphorical language with more explicit emotional content, and he emphasizes his feelings of futility. The strategies used to convey credibility, meaning, and emotional impact evolve based on where the anticipated audience might locate authority. In Eggers' case, he has the luxury of already possessing credibility as a narrator, so he is free to take more liberties with the management of Zeitoun's credibility. Rather than having to focus solely on external validation of factuality and a narrative evaluation that conveys this story's purpose, Eggers' challenge is to fit this story into a framework that readers accustomed to literary genres will recognize and read correctly. Thus, where Zeitoun is concerned with expressing authority, urgency, and finally ambiguity, Eggers is concerned with creating a believable character type, a suspenseful buildup, and finally, a clear resolution. The impact of these changes in Zeitoun's narrative becomes clearer with an expanded study of the narrative's publication. In other words, once the story is distributed, which parts of it are received well by audiences and critics? Which parts are remembered, repeated, and passed on as important? Two instances of *Zeitoun*'s reception, first in an NPR interview and then in a *New York Times* book review, help illuminate both the potential motivations for the changes described above as well as their possible implications.

"He was needed": Zeitoun's Reception

Shortly after *Zeitoun*'s release, NPR aired an episode of *All Things Considered*, titled "War On Terror, Katrina Intersect In *Zeitoun*." The episode uses the same rescue scene discussed throughout this chapter to illustrate the dramatic appeal of the book. The show transitions from Eggers' interview responses to Zeitoun's, with the two voices edited into a continuous narrative by the show's host. The effect is a hybrid of their two storytelling styles, with Zeitoun's urgency and ambivalence and Eggers' clear sense of purpose. Eggers begins, "he hears a faint voice, coming from a home, and…he was with a friend at that point, and they paddled up to the house and…."[40] The recording cuts to Zeitoun's voice, distinguishable by its relatively accented English: "and we start slowly follow the noise."[41] In case the transition of speakers is not clear for listeners, the host interjects, "Zeitoun picks up the story from here."[42] Zeitoun continues,

> I jump to the water, swim to her house, and got the door. I try force the door to open; I kick it to open. As soon I open I see the lady—she have one story house. And middle her living room, she have furniture all over covered with water. She holding to her dining room table and like she's—the water up to her shoulders. And her dress floating 'round her like—like flower or like umbrella, however you going to say it. And she said 'please, take me out of here.' I mean when I saw her, I—first thing I see, like, my

> grandmother. I mean full of so sadness, and so happy at the same time I discover her.[43]

This rendition bears familiar elements from Zeitoun's second account, in *Voices from the Storm*, with its reference to his grandmother. He also reiterates the ambivalent evaluation at the anecdote's end, with this conclusion that he was "full of so sadness, and so happy at the same time I discover her."

In relating the image that has become the iconic kernel of this narrative, Zeitoun describes the woman's "dress floating 'round her like—like flower or like umbrella, however you going to say it." He nods to Eggers' word choice, "flower," but he returns to a less vulnerable and feminine metaphor of his own—"or like umbrella"—which also evokes a similar unexpectedness as his earlier simile, in which her dress looked like a balloon. Finally, in an equivocating move, Zeitoun concludes, "however you going to say it." This appears to acknowledge Zeitoun's awareness of the differences in representation between his version of the story and Eggers', but it also gestures toward dismissing either choice. Though this may undercut Zeitoun's description, it has the simultaneous consequence of undermining Eggers. In keeping with the ambiguity expressed elsewhere in Zeitoun's account, he seems unwilling to endorse Eggers' consistency in portraying him as a hero with a definite purpose.

Again with the host's explanation, the audience turns "back now to author Dave Eggers," who adds his own narrative evaluation to the story Zeitoun has just told, "Because the canoe was so quiet, he was able to hear things that others weren't. And others going around in motorboats and fan-boats that are so incredibly loud, he was in this quiet canoe and was able to sort of help animals and people and see things and hear things that others weren't able to."[44] By offering this explanation, Eggers paints Zeitoun's presence as somewhat mysterious, or even predestined. He is singled out from other survivors and rescuers, a patient figure moving calmly through the chaos. This image resonates with readers and reviewers, who tend to tune out the ambiguity suggested in Zeitoun's version and zero in on those qualities that form a familiar narrative of heroism.

For example, in an August 2009 review of *Zeitoun* for the *New York Times*, Timothy Egan echoes Eggers' heroic tune. Egan writes, "Zeitoun paddles around New Orleans in his canoe for a week, an angel of mercy."[45] He continues, focusing once more on the rescue scene,

> Zeitoun saves elderly and dehydrated residents trapped in rotting, collapsing homes: 'Help me,' comes the voice of an old woman. 'Her patterned dress was spread out on the surface of the water like a great

> floating flower. Her legs dangled below. She was holding on to a bookshelf.' In his first day in the canoe, Zeitoun assists in the rescue of five residents. 'He had never felt such urgency and purpose,' Eggers writes. 'He was needed.'[46]

Not only is this review noteworthy for its choice to quote the very same lines as *All Things Considered*, with the scene that resurfaces time after time in retellings of this tale, it is also interesting in its condensing of Eggers' language. In the book, the quote Egan selects about Zeitoun's "urgency and purpose" appears three pages after the description of the woman in the floating dress. In between, the story cuts to the actions of Kathy Zeitoun, who has evacuated to Baton Rouge with the couple's young children. In the book's reception, then, what gets emphasized and crystallized are the helplessness of the woman being rescued and the unequivocal purpose of her rescuer, combining to forge a familiar heroic tale that audiences recognize and embrace.

Conclusion

In an ironic and sad turn of events, the public "character" of Abdulrahman Zeitoun has transformed from valiant to evil. In fact, I argue, the demand for unambiguous heroism finds its inverse in Zeitoun's most recent publicity, wherein allegations of domestic abuse against him have been received with eagerness to cast him as a villain. As many news outlets reported in early August 2012, Zeitoun was arrested twice for assaulting his wife Kathy. After the first incident, the two were divorced. While in jail as a result of the second assault, Zeitoun allegedly hired another man to murder his former wife; Zeitoun was then jailed again for solicited murder. As the *New York Times* sums up the events, "[t]he couple divorced last year after he was convicted of assaulting her. And on Wednesday, the New Orleans police charged him with plotting to have Kathy Zeitoun, her son and another man murdered."[47] The article also explains, "Ms. Zeitoun said the book [*Zeitoun*] had accurately portrayed their relationship at the time. But she said her ex-husband had since grown angrier and more violent and his Islamic views had become more 'radical.'"[48]

Although many of the vitriolic comments regarding Zeitoun's Muslim faith have since been removed from the various articles which reported this crime, a representative response in this vein reads,

> He comes from a culture/religion of violence and hate, where, after a divorce—the woman gets NOTHING, and where beating women you

> own—is an accepted practice, as evidenced by the lack of negative reaction (and indeed the support) of the local muslim/arabic populace in New Orleans. I don't see where there is anything to be shocked, or surprised about, here.[49]

This commenter equates Zeitoun's abuse of Kathy with his Muslim religion, based on prevalent American stereotypes associated with Muslim men and women, and admonishes other readers for being astonished after Eggers' hero turned out to be a violent criminal.

In their book examining "the roots of Islamophobia," Gottschalk and Greenberg ask, "how, in the minds of so many Americans, has Islam become synonymous with the Middle East, Muslim men with violence, and Muslim women with oppression?"[50] They describe the extent to which these misconceptions are entrenched in American discourse,

> Despite more than a half-century of both economic dependence on Middle Eastern oil and political involvement in Middle Eastern affairs, American images and understandings of Middle Eastern cultures remain largely unchanged. From the package for Camel cigarettes to the décor of the Trump Taj Mahal Casino in Atlantic City, pyramids, men in kaffiyehs, exotic women, and onion-domed mosques remain as central components of a stereotypical scene. This usually implies latent or actual violence directed outward at 'unbelievers' or inward toward women.[51]

Thus, a ready-made story exists to explain Zeitoun's crime, that of the violent Muslim man who is abusive towards his oppressed wife.

Just as Zeitoun's post-Katrina exploits were fitted to a dominant narrative of American heroism, his recent actions are aligned with a different dominant narrative of Islamic masculinity. Zeitoun has become no more complex or dynamic a character, he is just starring in a different role. What I find remarkable about this transition is the ease with which it occurs. Dave Eggers went to extraordinary measures to cast Zeitoun as a hero, countering the discursive contexts of his arrest and imprisonment that cast him as at best, suspect, and at worst, a violent proponent of Islamic fundamentalism. It is not merely ironic that this worst-case narrative ends up describing Zeitoun in another context. In part, Eggers' departure from Zeitoun's ambiguity, in his efforts to create a fixed oppositional narrative, ultimately lent authority to the discourse he tried to discredit. Tracking the seemingly minor variations of Zeitoun's story as it moves from personal experience to public discourse reveals precisely what Guy Beiner identifies as the mystery of social memory and the task of those who would study it, "why certain information was remembered and other information forgotten." The nuances of Zeitoun's character slowly but surely fall away as his story travels, whereas the traits that fit the mold of dominant narratives are heightened. In this and in other cases of personal narratives made public, those stories most likely to interrupt dominant discourse are those that opt for complexity over fixity. Unfortunately, though, what becomes "fixed" as public memory is not the complex story; instead, it is the one that sounds most familiar.

Bibliography

Albert F. Comment on Schwiegershausen, Erica. "Protagonist of Dave Eggers's 'Zeitoun' Arrested Again." *The New York Observer*. August 7, 2012. Accessed August 15, 2012, comments since removed. http://observer.com/2012/08/protagonist-of-dave-eggerss-zeitoun-arrested-again/.

Beiner, Guy. *Remembering the Year of the French: Irish Folk History and Social Memory.* Madison, WI: University of Wisconsin Press, 2007.

Brown, Robbie. "Katrina Hero Facing Charges in New Orleans." *New York Times*, August 9, 2012. http://www.nytimes.com/2012/08/10/us/celebrated-hero-in-zeitoun-book-faces-murder-charges-in-new-orleans.html.

Egan, Timothy. "After the Deluge." Review of *Zeitoun*, by Dave Eggers. *New York Times*, August 16, 2009. *Sunday Book Review*. http://www.nytimes.com/2009/08/16/books/review/Egan-t.html?pagewanted=all&_r=0.

Eggers, Dave. *Zeitoun.* San Francisco: McSweeney's Books, 2009.

Fairclough, Norman. *Critical Discourse Analysis: The Critical Study of Language*. Essex: Longman Group, 1995.

Gottschalk, Peter, and Gabriel Greenberg. *Islamophobia: Making Muslims the Enemy*. Lanham, MD: Rowman & Littlefield, 2008.

Halbwachs, Maurice. *On Collective Memory*. Translated by Lewis A. Coser. Chicago: University of Chicago Press, 1992.

Labov, William, and Joshua Waletzky. "Narrative Analysis: Oral Versions of Personal Experience." In *Essays on the Verbal and Visual Arts: Proceedings of the 1966 Annual Spring Meeting of the American Ethnological Society*, edited by June Helm, 12-44. Seattle: University of Washington Press, 1966.

Lindahl, Carl. "Legends of Hurricane Katrina: The Right to Be Wrong, Survivor-to-Survivor Storytelling, and Healing." *Journal of American Folklore* 125 (2012): 139-76.

McCarthy, Brendan. "Judge imposes stiff sentences on 5 NOPD officers convicted in Danziger shootings." *The Times-Picayune*, April 4, 2012.

http://www.nola.com/crime/index.ssf/2012/04/judge_imposes_sentences_on_5_n.html.

Ochs, Elinor, and Lisa Capps. "Narrative Authenticity." *Journal of Narrative and Life History* 7.1-4 (1997): 83-89.

Palmenfelt, Ulf. "The Celestial Attraction of the Invisible Grand Narratives." Lecture given at Ohio State University, Columbus, OH, October 17, 2011.

Schaffer, Kay, and Sidonie Smith. *Human Rights and Narrated Lives: The Ethics of Recognition*. New York: Palgrave Macmillan, 2004.

Shuman, Amy. *Other People's Stories: Entitlement Claims and the Critique of Empathy*. Champaign, IL: University of Illinois Press, 2005.

Tonkin, Elizabeth. *Narrating Our Pasts: The Social Construction of Oral History*. Cambridge: Cambridge University Press, 1992.

Vollen, Lola, and Chris Ying, eds. *Voices from the Storm*. San Francisco: McSweeney's Books, 2008.

"War On Terror, Katrina Intersect in *Zeitoun*." Interview of Dave Eggers by Guy Raz. *All Things Considered*. NPR. July 25, 2009. http://www.npr.org/2009/07/25/107009266/war-on-terror-katrina-intersect-in-zeitoun.

Whitlock Gillian. *Soft Weapons: Autobiography in Transit*. Chicago: University of Chicago Press, 2007.

"Voice of Witness." Voice of Witness, 2009. http://voiceofwitness.org.

Zeitoun, Abdulrahman. "Rescue efforts lead to arrest nightmare for N.O. businessman." *The Times-Picayune*, November 24, 2005. http://blog.nola.com/bourbon/2005/11/rescue_efforts_lead_to_arrest.html.

Notes

[1] Guy Beiner, *Remembering the Year of the French: Irish Folk History and Social Memory* (Madison, WI: University of Wisconsin Press, 2007), 25.

[2] Beiner, *Remembering the Year of the French*, 25.

[3] Elizabeth Tonkin, *Narrating Our Pasts: The Social Construction of Oral History* (Cambridge: Cambridge University Press, 1992), 105.

[4] Tonkin, *Narrating Our Pasts*, 105.

[5] Beiner, *Remembering the Year of the French*, 26. Beiner also cites James Fentress and Chris Wickham's use of the term social memory, and points out the added benefits of that term's distance, as opposed to Halbwachs' "collective memory," from Carl Jung's notion of a collective unconscious.

[6] Beiner, *Remembering the Year of the French*, 28.

[7] Beiner, *Remembering the Year of the French*, 28.

[8] Beiner, *Remembering the Year of the French*, 32.

[9] See especially Norman Fairclough, *Critical Discourse Analysis: The Critical Study of Language* (Essex: Longman Group, 1995).

[10] William Labov and Joshua Waletzky, "Narrative Analysis: Oral Versions of Personal Experience," in *Essays on the Verbal and Visual Arts: Proceedings of the 1966 Annual Spring Meeting of the American Ethnological Society*, ed. June Helm (Seattle: University of Washington Press, 1966), 33.

[11] Ulf Palmenfelt, "The Celestial Attraction of the Invisible Grand Narratives" (lecture, Ohio State University, Columbus, OH, October 17, 2011).

[12] Although as my colleague Brian McAllister pointed out on reading a draft of this work, Palmenfelt's image of milk appears in a variety of stories told by different narrators, whereas the image of the floating woman appears in multiple versions of the same story.

[13] This accurately describes the site and the newspaper at the time of Zeitoun's blog; however, the website has shifted toward headline news since the *Times Picayune* reduced its daily print distribution in 2012 to three times per week.

[14] Abdulrahman Zeitoun, "Rescue efforts lead to arrest nightmare for N.O. businessman," *NOLA.com* (blog), *The Times-Picayune*, November 24, 2005, http://blog.nola.com/bourbon/ 2005/11/rescue_efforts_lead_to_arrest.html.

[15] Labov writes, "[r]eportable events are almost by definition unusual. They are therefore less credible than nonreportable events. In fact, we might say that the more reportable an event is, the less credible it is. Yet credibility is as essential as reportability for the success of a narrative," Elinor Ochs and Lisa Capps, "Narrative Authenticity," *Journal of Narrative and Life History* 7.1-4 (1997): 83.

[16] Abdulrahman Zeitoun, "Rescue efforts lead to arrest nightmare for N.O. businessman," *The Times-Picayune*, November 24, 2005, http://blog.nola.com/bourbon/2005/11/ rescue_efforts_lead_to_arrest.html.

[17] Zeitoun, "Rescue efforts."

[18] Zeitoun, "Rescue efforts."

[19] Zeitoun, "Rescue efforts."

[20] Zeitoun, "Rescue efforts."

[21] Many Katrina survivors' personal narratives convey frustration that official first responders, such as the National Guard, were absent or unhelpful in the flood's immediate aftermath.

[22] "Voice of Witness," 2009, www.voiceofwitness.org.

[23] See, for examples and analysis of these patterns, Kay Schaffer and Sidonie Smith, *Human Rights and Narrated Lives: The Ethics of Recognition* (New York: Palgrave MacMillan, 2004).

[24] The appendices comprise information such as maps, demographics, National Weather Service warnings, government agency reports, and meeting transcripts.

[25] Lola Vollen and Chris Ying, eds., *Voices from the Storm* (San Francisco: McSweeney's Books, 2008), 73.

[26] Vollen and Ying, *Voices from the Storm*, 171 (emphasis added).

[27] Brendan McCarthy, "Judge imposes stiff sentences on 5 NOPD officers convicted in Danziger shootings," *The Times-Picayune*, April 4, 2012, http://www.nola.com/crime/index.ssf/2012/04/judge_imposes_sentences_on_5_n.html.

[28] Vollen and Ying, *Voices from the Storm*, 120.

[29] Vollen and Ying, *Voices from the Storm*, 120.
[30] For more on strange occurrences and their implications in survivor narratives, see Carl Lindahl, "Legends of Hurricane Katrina: The Right to Be Wrong, Survivor-to-Survivor Storytelling, and Healing," *Journal of American Folklore* 125 (2012): 139-76.
[31] Vollen and Ying, *Voices from the Storm*, 120.
[32] Dave Eggers, *Zeitoun* (San Francisco: McSweeney's Books, 2009), 345.
[33] Gillian Whitlock, *Soft Weapons: Autobiography in Transit* (Chicago: University of Chicago Press, 2007), 20.
[34] Whitlock, *Soft Weapons*, 15.
[35] Eggers, *Zeitoun*, 109.
[36] Eggers, *Zeitoun*, 109.
[37] Eggers, *Zeitoun*, 110.
[38] Eggers, *Zeitoun*, 110.
[39] Eggers, *Zeitoun*, 114.
[40] "War On Terror, Katrina Intersect in *Zeitoun*," interview of Dave Eggers by Guy Raz, *All Things Considered*, NPR, July 25, 2009, http://www.npr.org/2009/07/25/107009266/war-on-terror-katrina-intersect-in-zeitoun.
[41] "War On Terror."
[42] "War On Terror."
[43] "War On Terror."
[44] "War On Terror."
[45] Timothy Egan, "After the Deluge," review of *Zeitoun*, by Dave Eggers, *New York Times*, August 16, 2009, Sunday Book Review, http://www.nytimes.com/2009/08/16/books/review/Egan-t.html?pagewanted =all&_r=0.
[46] Egan, "After the Deluge."
[47] Robbie Brown, "Katrina Hero Facing Charges in New Orleans," *New York Times*, August 9, 2012, http://www.nytimes.com/2012/08/10/us/celebrated-hero-in-zeitoun-book-faces-murder-charges-in-new-orleans.html.
[48] Brown, "Katrina Hero."
[49] Albert_F, comment on Erica Schwiegershausen, "Protagonist of Dave Eggers's 'Zeitoun' Arrested Again," *The New York Observer*, August 7, 2012, http://observer.com/2012/08/ protagonist-of-dave-eggerss-zeitoun-arrested-again/.
[50] Peter Gottschalk and Gabriel Greenberg, *Islamophobia: Making Muslims the Enemy* (Lanham, MD: Rowman & Littlefield, 2008), 4.
[51] Gottschalk and Greenberg, *Islamophobia*, 4.

Personal and Collective Traumas of Mutilation and James Ellroy's Los Angeles

Sostene M. Zangari

In the morning of June 22, 1958, the dead body of Geneva "Jean" Hilliker Ellroy was found beside the playing field of Arroyo High School in El Monte, a community in Los Angeles' San Gabriel Valley. The woman had been choked to death; around her neck a cotton cord and a nylon stocking were found. To this day, the murder has remained unsolved. For her only child, future crime novelist James Ellroy, this event would prove to be the most significant in his life. Motherless at a premature age, given in custody to a negligent father who survived on temporary and precarious jobs, the writer-to-be went through a turbulent adolescence and young adulthood that involved theft, burglaries, drugs, alcoholism, Nazi sympathies, multiple arrests and convictions,[1] a veritable "descent into hell" which he managed to escape only when a serious illness threatened to kill him in his late twenties. The mother's murder also became the symbolic center of Ellroy's poetics, affecting the emergence of a narrative style and vision whose features, this chapter will maintain, conform to a politics of mutilation.

Investigations on the relationships between trauma and literature have yielded a vast body of research that shows how events of shocking horror generate peculiar reactions on the psyche, affecting the way the experience is, or is not, retold. Research on Holocaust narratives has set the paradigm, emphasizing how the horror of concentration camp experiences reset the psychic processes of the survivors, functioning as a violent blow that overwhelms the very functioning of the psyche.[2] The victim fails to process the brutal event, which lingers in the subconscious and resurfaces later. This description, however, is also useful to understand the response to a vast range of traumatic events of less historical magnitude, such as rape, violence and murder. To a certain extent, the general public has become desensitized to such crimes, and the few occurrences that make it into history books are granted the honor less for any specific features of the murder itself than because they have come to represent the anxieties of a particular time and environment. Nevertheless, they are likely to leave a deep mark on victims and their families. In the case of Ellroy, the trauma set off a complex web of reactions, shaped by the contrasting impulses towards destruction and re-unification that would find an outlet in his narrative style.

Starting from Ellroy's own self-scrutiny in *My Dark Places*, the 1996 autobiographical book where the writer reconstructs the intricate relationship with his mother and his own problematic life after the murder, this chapter will proceed to analyze the *Los Angeles Quartet* in light of the worldview engendered by Jean's death and Ellroy's subsequent efforts to cope with the event. More specifically, I will point out how the violated corpse of his mother, seen as one in a long line of female victims of "male desire"—i.e. men's compulsion to relate to women as objects of pleasure—will inspire the construction of a narrative world around the paradigm of man-perpetrated mutilation: the fragmentation of the narrative into multiple sub-plots and viewpoints, the fixation on troubled characters, a recurrent indictment of patriarchy, as well as a vision of the metropolis as atomized space—crossed by racial, social and gender fault lines—, coalesce into a worldview that reflects the shattered psyche of a child brutally deprived of his mother. Although *My Dark Places* records how the young James felt a sense of liberation when he learned about Jean's horrible death, the event created an interpretative void that persisted throughout Ellroy's development, both as a man and as a writer, and was the trigger for his hyper-sensitivity toward rifts and gaps that mar the unity of people and places.

"Ashamed and horrified of what I had inside of me": Ellroy's Confession in *My Dark Places*

My Dark Places is a unique and invaluable item in James Ellroy's bibliography, offering the reader a crude and somewhat merciless account of how the writer reacted to the traumatic experience of having his mother violently raped and murdered when he was still a child. The corpse showed bruises on the face, the tongue was protruding from the open mouth, and a nylon stocking and a cotton cord were tightly knotted around her neck—testifying to a violence that a nine-year-old boy was not equipped to understand and codify. It took Ellroy almost 40 years to find the chutzpah to go back to the episode, to look at the pictures of the corpse, and read through police files containing abominable details of the abuse perpetrated by the killer and the dissection carried out during autopsy.

The journey back in time, however, was not part of Ellroy's writing plans. In January 1994 he received a call from Frank Girardot, a journalist friend, who informed him of his intention to write about five still unsolved murders that had occurred in the San Gabriel Valley, including that of Jean Ellroy. Girardot explained that, as part of his research, he would have to go through police files and also gain access to pictures of Jane's corpse. As Ellroy himself records in *My Dark Places*, it was then that he felt an immediate urge to see those files and pictures himself. Although this urge is motivated by the possible sale of an article about that experience to *GQ* magazine—a piece that, in turn, would "stir up publicity for my next novel"[3] —it is clear there was a deeper reason to act on Ellroy's part. In particular, the fact that a stranger was about to access a part of his mother that he had refused to confront until then conveyed the notion of personal possession that would be violated—a symbolic re-enactment of the rape of almost 40 years before.

The investigation files, as well as the pictures, produced a version of Jane that clashed with what Ellroy recalled. Pushed by a gender bias that he inherited from his father Armand, and which would be later nurtured by the misogynist attitudes that constituted the standard fare in the cheap crime novels[4] he swallowed as a young boy and teenager, Ellroy had always considered his mother a libertine whose promiscuity eventually, and maybe even deservedly, led to her demise.

Young Ellroy's closeness to his father was due to a peculiar reversal of traditional gender roles in their family. Having lost a permanent job in 1952, Armand spent more time at home than his wife did, and had the opportunity to create the stronger bond with the boy and influence him. Jean, instead, was the main breadwinner and figure of order. Thus, when the couple divorced in 1954, and Jean was granted custody of their only child, the writer began to share the man's grudge against the ex-wife, "I hated her. (…) Some unknown killer just brought me a brand-new beautiful life. (…) I cared for her solely in conjunction with my father. When she broke the marriage, she made me his son exclusively."[5] Such resentment in both Armand and James betrays anxiety towards a woman that did not fit in the traditional categories of domesticity. Their reaction, which also materialized in a vision of Jean as libertine, mirrors the way Hollywood has responded to the contemporary empowerment of women—a legacy of the crucial role the movie industry played in the US economy during World War II—with the ascent of the *femme fatale*: according to Jack Boozer, the greedy over-sexualized woman reflects a "postwar readjustment in society" whereby man's dominant position was increasingly threatened by female independence.[6] Armand was a victim of the same mechanism of thinking, and he heaped on James his bitterness toward a wife that could support herself without his help. "My father"—Ellroy confesses—"began to systematically poison my mind against my mother,"[7] feeding his son with presumably made-up anecdotes about her promiscuous behavior.[8] In 1994, what James gathered from investigation accounts, and from a picture taken a few months before his mother's death, in which the woman looked as though she had aged prematurely, was an altogether different message. It was a reversal of perspective that must have taken into account Ellroy's own inner growth, as well as an expanded capacity to sympathize with women: what the son perceived after so many years was the tragedy of a woman who was giving a last shot at romantic love, and possibly fell victim to a man she would have wished to draw into a solid relationship.

In the late 1950s, however, Armand's accusations found a receptive audience in his son, mainly because his antics mirrored a more widespread suspicion of society towards women who defied traditional roles. About a year after Jean's death, the writer got acquainted with the Black Dahlia murder by reading *The Badge*, a selection of LAPD's most well-known cases compiled by actor and screenwriter Jack Webb, famous for his role in the TV show *Dragnet*. The murder of Elizabeth Short, a young woman whose mutilated body was found on a vacant lot in January 1947, and whose predilection for dark clothes prompted tabloids to nickname her "Black Dahlia," was one of the most famous postwar cases in Los Angeles, one followed with morbid curiosity by the whole population.[9] It exerted a morbid curiosity on Ellroy too, not only because of the similarities between the Dahlia case and Jean's murder, but also because of the sheer violence perpetrated on the woman's body, which was cut in two at the waist. With the passing of the years, this mutilation came to symbolize the destructive effect of the patriarchal order, a deadly "collision with male desire,"[10] the violent clash with a society that forces women into predetermined and subordinate roles.

According to Ellroy, Webb's account of the murder epitomized the ethos of the time, whereby "Femme fatales die hard and are complicit in attracting death by vivisection."[11] With the benefit of hindsight, Ellroy understood that tagging Elizabeth Short under the "Black Dahlia" moniker, "nullified her and vilified her and turned her into a sainted lost daughter and a slut."[12] In his young impressionable mind—a "cultural sponge"[13]—what the newspapers reported about Short's dissolute lifestyle applied to Jean as well. Fatally, Webb's narrative was the only one available to young Ellroy to make sense of the murder of his mother, and he accepted it.[14] Also, this categorization fitted with what Freud considers a standard reaction in male children during puberty, namely the discovery that, "the difference between his mother and a whore is not after all so very great, since basically they do the same thing."[15] The Dahlia, therefore, became a "symbiotic stand-in for Geneva Hilliker Ellroy."[16] Yet, its main function was to provide a narrative to screen out the painful memory of Jean's loss, a defense mechanism towards which the writer's guilt and longings could be safely directed.

The narrative was also a convenient strategy to camouflage a deeper grudge: James blamed Jean for having allowed other men into her life and thus destroying the exclusive, although turbulent, relationship between mother and child.[17] The longing for Jean's love becomes more apparent as the reader proceeds with *My Dark Places*, when Ellroy describes how the woman unexpectedly intruded upon his sexual fantasies,

> I was in the tub. I was jacking off to a cavalcade of older women's faces. I saw my mother naked, fought the image and lost. I jerry-rigged a story straight off.
>
> It was '58. My mother didn't die in El Monte. She wasn't a drunk. She loved me woman to man. We made love. I smelled her perfume and cigarette breath. Her amputated nipple thrilled me. I brushed her hair out of her eyes and told her I loved her. My tenderness made her cry. It was the most impassioned and loving story I'd ever perpetrated. It left me ashamed and horrified of what I had inside me.[18]

Until that moment, Elizabeth Short had been the sole protagonist of Ellroy's daydreaming and nightmares, while Jean was rarely given any attention at all. For years, the writer-to-be's favorite pastime was to contrive plots where he "rescued Betty Short and became her lover (…) saved her from a life of promiscuity. (…) tracked down her killer and executed him."[19] Both versions, the salvation tale and the revenge fantasy—again, standard reactions reflecting Oedipal desire[20]—are also attempts to moralize an uncomfortable reality and betray a feeling of guilt towards his mother, albeit on a subconscious level, as well as the urgent desire to prove his love to her.

The doubling of the female figure, the mutilated body, and the love/hate relationship form a pattern of division that finds echo in Ellroy's own representation of his adolescent life as "living in two worlds."[21] This inner rift will nourish Ellroy's narrative fantasies, an imaginary space where the impossible task of restoring the unity of the Dahlia body was to be attempted. It is also the space where gaps can be bridged and lost unities reconstructed. By uncovering the power structures in postwar Los Angeles, with the links between crime and politics, the *Quartet* in fact deconstructs the society responsible for the brutal death of Elizabeth Short, and of several other women that shared her fate, Jean included. It is only in a fictional space liberated from the power structures which oppress women that attempts to recover the genuine identities of women can be performed. By providing Elizabeth Short with a personal story that complicates tabloid reports and Webb's description,[22] and by giving life to a gallery of women who unwillingly adapt to the social order, the *Quartet* sees Ellroy rewriting his relationship to his mother. Although the writer's self-examination in *My Dark Places* appeared only a couple of years after the completion of the tetralogy, stylistic choices, subject matter, individual profiles, a gendered division of narrative labor—whereby males represent destructive forces while women symbolize redemption—and an obsessive propensity to focus on geographical details betray Ellroy's attempt to re-appropriate his mother by expiating his guilt and exposing his poisonous father.

Prodigal Sons in Search of Redemption: Mutilated Selves and Vision in Ellroy's *L.A. Quartet*

It is no accident that James Ellroy chose noir as narrative language. After Jean's murder, he started reading crime novels and watching gangster movies, partly in the hope they might help him to understand what had happened to his mother. Therefore, as he himself acknowledges, the writer started to see the world through the lens of crime. But noir fit into Ellroy's mindset also because the genre combined contrasting drives toward fragmentation and reconciliation. The dissection of the urban landscape into separate social pockets and the detective's struggle to move through the different strata of society in order to solve the crime provided equal fascination to a writer conflicted between an obsession for mutilated bodies and an innermost desire to restore the original unity. Moreover, according to William Marling, the basic formula of the noir novel reinscribes the parable of the prodigal son, a very flexible narrative pattern that moves "from decision to dissolution to well being and restoration,"[23] and involves "division," "a dangerous journey" that proves transformative, and a return home.[24] When applied to the detective's quest, this pattern fits with the overt symbolic role played by the investigation, where the solution of a case restores the order threatened by a murder or, to a lesser extent, a theft. Whereas this movement from dissolution to restoration works well for both the "classic" and the hardboiled detective story, it is the remark about the "transformative journey" that underlines the affinity between the latter and the biblical parable; for the hardboiled hero must find his way, both metaphorically and literally, through a dangerous territory where he might get killed and where it is easy to get lost. Needless to say, the prominence of the prodigal son archetype in the noir tale could not but appeal to a young boy who subconsciously felt he had been unfair to his mother and craved for an impossible re-unification.

Ellroy's career itself can be seen as a re-enactment of the parable, a return home after a tumultuous journey involving homelessness, drug and alcohol abuse, multiple convictions that almost led to self-destruction. As chronicled in *My Dark Places*, Ellroy's bibliography configures a progressive confrontation with Elizabeth Short and his mother. The first book, *Brown's Requiem* (1981), was developed starting from an alcoholic hero who "nursed a lifelong obsession with the Black Dahlia case."[25] In the novel, however, Elizabeth Short gets only a passing reference. The murder involves a male caddie, Fat Dog Baker, who nurtures an unsound obsession towards his sister, Jane.[26] It was only in the following novel, *Clandestine* (1983), that Ellroy decided to have a "first confrontational swipe at Jean Ellroy"[27]: set in Los Angeles in the 1950s, the book features a female character modeled on his mother or, rather, his own interpretation of her, "a tortured drunk with hyperbolically tortured past in Hicktown Wisconsin."[28] The writer also gave the woman a nine year-old son and an abusive ex-husband. The tribute to Jean, however, was only superficial. What the book was really about, Ellroy states, is himself, an ambitious young man at 32 concealed under the shape of a cop, Fred Underhill. It took another six years and four novels for him to take a further step and devote a whole book to the case involving Elizabeth Short and to recreating the Los Angeles of his childhood, i.e. the four volumes comprising the *L.A. Quartet*: *The Black Dahlia* (1987), *The Big Nowhere* (1988), *L.A. Confidential* (1990), *White Jazz* (1992). Only when this massive effort was over was Ellroy ready to turn to his mother and write *My Dark Places* (1996).

As suggested by Mike Davis, Ellroy's *Los Angeles Quartet*, "depending on one's viewpoint, is either the culmination of the genre [noir], or its *reductio ad absurdum*."[29] In fact, Ellroy's style features a baroque gusto for excess and complication. His plots drift into endless meanders, and the apparent journeys toward conclusion and resolution frequently result in dead ends, adding layer upon narrative layer. Ellroy himself has often made use of pictorial analogies to discuss his work, stating his penchant for "the big canvas"[30]; the visual effect of his style could be likened to "action painting," as Peter Wolfe has fittingly suggested.[31]

A further complication, running against the established convention of the detective as the one and only hero of the noir, originates from the writer's need to split narrative into different streams, a narratological mutilation of the text that re-enacts the violence on the body of Elizabeth Short. In so doing, Ellroy experiments with different possibilities. In *The Black Dahlia* there is a traditional first-person narrator, Bucky Bleichert, whose storytelling is complicated by the presence of an alter ego, Lee Blanchard. To a certain extent, their relationship is reminiscent of F.S. Fitzgerald's *The Great Gatsby*: much like Nick Carraway, Bleichert's perspective is limited by the many things about Blanchard he doesn't know, and will only discover as the plot unfolds. *The Big Nowhere* and *L.A. Confidential* feature three distinct heroes (or rather *anti-heroes*), each one haunted by different disturbing thoughts and obsessions; as Jonathan Walker aptly notes, they are "characters on the brink of moral and psychological collapse."[32] *The Big Nowhere* trio of cops consists of Danny Upshaw, Mal Considine, and "Buzz" Meeks. Upshaw is a repressed homosexual, uncomfortable in the milieu of the LAPD constructed on the performance of brutal masculinity; similarly, Considine is averse to violence and,thus, his wife, Celeste, a Czech Buchenwald survivor, takes advantage of his weakness to get a divorce and the custody of their son; finally, Meeks regards police work as a cover up for his illicit dealings with movie producer Howard Hughes and gangster Mickey Cohen. *L.A. Confidential* replicates the same pattern, with the three cops Jack Vincennes, Ed Exley, and Bud White. The first is in league with the tabloid *Hush Hush* to implicate movie stars in sensationalistic scoops, while his self-imposed sobriety is a way of expiating the accidental killing of an elderly couple. Exley is an ambitious officer whose determination to climb the career ladder is a way to show his over-demanding father he is worth his dead brother, once the most promising young recruit of the LAPD. Instinctive and quick-tempered, White is a self-appointed defender of female victims of male violence. *L.A. Confidential* also makes room for an additional protagonist, the press: in the book, newspaper excerpts from *Hush Hush*, the *Examiner* and the *Times* project alternative versions of events that differ from what is related throughout the narrative. For instance, Exley is constantly referred to in the papers as a war hero and a brilliant officer, while the narrator undermines this impeccable picture by revealing the obscure circumstances of the heroic feat in Guadalcanal that earned him a Medal of Valor, as well as stressing how his opportunism affects his police work.

Although broken down into different threads, the narrative projects a unitary universe joined together by guilt and indictment of patriarchy—in Ellroy's fiction, fathers are held accountable for the deviant behavior of their children, who become "damaged sons wreaking revenge, seeking atonement and trying to demonstrate that they are tough enough."[33] Personal histories of several characters trace back their obsession to childhood trauma: White's father, for instance, handcuffed his son to the bed and made him watch his mother beaten to death. Instead, Considine's father was a Puritan minister, and punished his son with whipping or submitting him to dinners of pine tap soap and castor oil.[34]

The Big Nowhere possibly presents the most extreme example of the destructive influence that fathers exert on their male progeny. Reynolds Loftis, a Hollywood actor and communist sympathizer, gets to know his son Coleman when the latter is grown up. Struck by Coleman's resemblance with himself as a young man, Loftis presses him to undergo plastic surgery in order to make him into a twin image of his former self. The two also start an incestuous relationship, re-enacting the Ancient Greek myth of Narcissus. This inordinate instance of self-love will be terminated only when Loftis, in order to keep up appearances in a homophobic Hollywood, decides to marry the millionaire Claire DeHaven. Coleman reacts by implicating the father in a series of murders he commits by using a grey wig in order to pass for him. In this instance, the male obsession to dominate through violence is seen as an egoistic act of self-gratification at the expense of others. Coleman's revenge provides a blueprint for Ellroy's own: both act not through direct confrontation, but by spoiling the reputation of their parent. The storyline is a way of settling scores: the rehabilitation of Jean implies the condemnation of Armand, a representative as well as an agent of a patriarchal order based on inhuman brutality and violence.

The other major force of Ellroy's moral landscape is guilt, and in several cases women are seen as agents of redemption—the facilitators of that "transformational journey" of the prodigal son archetype that, according to the scheme, should lead the character home. Through women, males attempt to achieve reconciliation with an imagined uncorrupted former self. In *The Black Dahlia*, for instance, Blanchard rescues Kay Lake from the hands of Bob De Witt, a sadistic drug dealer—he provides for her and pays her college fees. Although they live together, what motivates Blanchard is neither love nor lust, but the need to seek forgiveness for having failed to protect his young and promising sister from a kidnapping that turned into rape and murder. Another example is the relationship between Exley and Inez Soto, a Mexican girl who was raped and brutalized by a group of African Americans, in *L.A. Confidential*. The officer is hurt when the woman accuses him of being interested in her case not out of concern or sympathy, but because of possible career advancement. She tells him he is not a hero, while agent White is, because the latter has killed one of her assailants to restore her honor. Exley feels the urge to start a competition to show Inez—and himself—that he too is capable of disinterested heroic feats, and he really cares for the girl and wants to save her. He becomes Inez's lover, provides for her, finds her a home and a job, but is routinely met by the girl's remark about White's superior commitment to her.[35] Both attempts, then, are doomed to fail, and Lee and Exley cannot achieve complete purification. The way they look at women is affected by a personal disorder, they do not accept them as they are: once again, this male gaze that turns females into agents of redemption is an act of symbolic brutality, whereby women are made to conform to male desire in order to expiate.

White Jazz, the last installment of the tetralogy, carries Ellroy's experimentalism even further. This time, the writer gives up the articulation of multiple viewpoints, and the story is told from the perspective of inspector David Klein, and with the use of the stream of consciousness technique.[36] The reduction of polyphony to a monologist discourse, in narrative, is usually interpreted as an attempt to control, to keep the multiple fragments of a sparse universe in check. Thus, should we see *White Jazz* as restoring order, healing the wounds in the psyche of the writer, reconnecting the body of Elizabeth Short?

My answer is negative. As Franco Moretti shows in *Modern Epic*, the advent of monologism in the novel, around the mid-19th century, was soon undermined by the hopeless battle against the plurality of experience. The Italian scholar rightly asks, can the reader distinguish the source of each utterance when the prose is stuffed with "resumes, simplifications, mnemonic endeavours, semi-disputes, attempts at compromise"[37]? The character of David Klein that Ellroy himself characterizes as "paranoid, jagged, enervated" is the average cop whose grasp on reality is mediated through violence and crime, a grown-up version of the author as a child. He is aware of a reality where different voices—his own, and those of the gossip newspapers, the police bureau, the criminals, the politicians—compete for control. The choice of stream of consciousness, a technique that allows the everyday to enter the individual conscience, preserves the plurality of voices. Thus, *White Jazz* preserves the fragmented pattern of Ellroy's universe. In fact, the stream of consciousness brings fragmentation even further because, on the one hand, it dissects and deconstructs the external world, while, on the other, it exposes the fragmentary self of the narrator. By using chopped sentences that avoid unnecessary grammar units, Ellroy reinforces the sense of a mutilated individual unable to keep reality under control. Therefore, he belongs wholly in the fraternity of those prodigal sons who share Ellroy's fate, namely living with their mutilation and with the impossibility to conclude the "transformative journey" home.

This drama of frustrated attempts at reconciliation is played out in an urban milieu crossed by fault lines that mirror the internal mutilation of the individual. The following section will show how Ellroy exploits Los Angeles' geographical dispersion, architectural diversity, and class as well as ethnic divisions to produce a fragmented spatiality which his multiple heroes can register but are ultimately unable to counteract. I will also show how Ellroy's deviant gaze transfigures lines of social, territorial and historical separation into scars that cut through the Southern Californian metropolis, making it a physical projection of Betty Short's mutilated body.

Fragments in Search of a City: Ellroy's Los Angeles

Conventionally, the origins of American detective fiction are traced back to the publication of "Murders in the Rue Morgue," the 1842 short story by Edgar Allan Poe. The timing was not incidental as a growing process of urbanization in the 1840s was making obsolete the image of America as a prelapsarian Eden. In the following decades, city growth engendered a marked differentiation of the urban space into business districts, residential and industrial areas, leisure centers, working class slums, and so forth. Class divisions meant no single citizen could be familiar with all the different sections, and increasingly the once paradoxical possibility of feeling a stranger in one's own city became reality.[38] Detective fiction was one of the cultural answers to this feeling of displacement; the private eye and the police inspector became a 20th century version of Natty Bumppo. Like James Fenimore Cooper's hero, the detective is a liminal figure who is able to explore and read the different fragments of the urban space. Since investigations put him in contact with the underworld as well as with the moneyed elite, the detective is able to accumulate knowledge that is inaccessible to the majority of city dwellers.

Los Angeles, of all places, was—and still is—one of the most extreme examples of urban dispersion. Still a slumbering small town in 1880, Los Angeles started to grow into a metropolis in consequence of a deliberate project: dispersion, racial homogeneity, and the warm climate were marketed to well-to-do Easterners as an alternative to the cold, congested, and multiethnic metropolis of the Atlantic seabed, stimulating a constant flow of migrants with money to spend. To accommodate an increasing number of newcomers who prized the independence of the single-family home, urban planning had to privilege horizontal over vertical expansion. The appearance of the automobile intensified this outward trend, allowing the more distant valleys to be colonized.[39]

Thus, the fragmentary image of the urban space that the reader gets from Ellroy's novels is not only in tune with the stylistic features typical of the genre, but with the very topographic peculiarity of Southern California that Carey McWilliams defined as "a collection of suburbs in search of a city."[40] There is a specific Ellrovian quality in this penchant for the fragmented space of Los Angeles; according to Frederic Sounac, Ellroy's work "rests on a meticulous and obsessive survey of the neighborhoods of Los Angeles, a merciless observation of the city's sociology and history, a love-hate relationship with its architecture."[41] Nevertheless, the way the writer constructs the urban map, by juxtaposing neighborhoods that are seldom reached after a continuous ride, but seem to suddenly emerge out of the narrative action, points to a preference for showing how these areas lack any connection to the urban fabric. Here, again, Ellroy's recurrent attraction for mutilation is clear. Each neighborhood appears as a self-contained world, where each insulated community carries on specific customs, language, and habits—as though no connecting tissue exists between them. This mapping is concerned with a "codified social subgroup (…) to such an extent that the 'squarejohn citizens' (...) are barely represented."[42]

Mapping is carried out through a peculiar pictorial technique involving the use of a few strong juxtaposed brushes—a strategy that further stresses the insularity of each urban section. In *The Black Dahlia*, for instance, the reader is acquainted with "skid row," along "East 5th Street from Main to Stanford", "Blood banks, liquor stores selling half pints and short dogs exclusively, fifty-cent-a-night flophouses and derelict missions."[43] Newton Street Division was "95 percent slums, 95 percent Negroes, all trouble. There were bottle gangs and crap games on every corner; liquor stores, hair-straightening parlors and poolrooms on every block."[44] The area around Hoover and Vermont, instead, "was an invitation to boredom: Mixed white and Negro, small factories and tidy houses."[45] In *The Big Nowhere*, among others, the reader finds mention to "Hancock Park, pheasant under glass acres, old LA money,"[46] and the "Broadway Department Store on Hollywood and Vine," which "had a fourth-floor men's room known as 'Cocksucker's Paradise.'"[47] In *LA Confidential*, North Havenhurst is classified as "a longtime call-house block."[48]

The construction of the city through a panoply of isolated exotic communities exemplified above transforms the urban landscape into a curio-shop; in fact, this is connected to the display function played by architecture in Southern California, which function is linked to an attempt to make legible a city that is homogeneous flatland. The tendency is to dissect surfaces in the panoramic views of single streets, such as Allegro Street, "A narrow residential road, half Spanish bungalow courts, half building sites fronted by signs promising DELUXE LIVING in the Tudor, French Provincial and Streamline Modern styles."[49] Or better yet, when confronting an area devoted to a specific activity, the narrator is interested in outlining differences. This is the case, for instance, of the jazz clubs in South Central, "Bido Lito's was shaped like a miniature Taj Mahal, only purple; Malloy's Nest was a bamboo hut fronted by phony Hawaiian palms strung with Christmas-Tree lights. Zebra stripes comprised the paint job on Tommy Tucker's Playroom."[50]

The same kaleidoscopic pattern is repeated in Ventura Boulevard, the place where most of the lesbian bars are located,

> The Swank Spot had a log cabin façade and double swinging doors like the saloons in western movies. (…) The Dutchess was (…) all in an old English

> motif. (…) La Verne's Hideway (…) was dark inside, baby spots affixed to ceiling beams casting shadowy light on walls covered with cheap palm tree paper.[51]

Such dissimilarities, again according to McWilliams, result from a tendency towards an "onomatopoeic architecture,"[52] which advertises the essence of an establishment in a place where high mobility, the constant flow of immigrants, and territorial dispersion have always meant that no shared and long-lasting knowledge can be accumulated. Again, Ellroy's gaze highlights the discontinuities which fracture the external environment and make it to conform to his own shattered inner self.

What makes Ellroy's sociological effort exceptional, however, is the fact that the writer carries the metaphor of subdivision even further, as he engages the racial and class lines that are quite often silenced, although recognizable, in crime fiction. His sensibility toward mutilation and grudge against the patriarchal order drive Ellroy to include in his mapping of Los Angeles those marginal groups that are seen as a threat to established authority. In so doing, the writer identifies his own self with the city, and his personal distress becomes part of a deeper historical trauma, both signaled by the perpetration of a violent act. In fact, the starting-point for Ellroy's tetralogy is the Zoot Suit Riots, a civil disturbance that exploded in June 1943, when US marines and civilians hunted for Mexican Americans wearing zoot suits and massacred them. It is during these riots that the narrator of *The Black Dahlia*, Dwight "Bucky" Bleichert, first meets his alter ego, Lee Blanchard. The discovery of Elizabeth Short's mutilated body, in compliance with actual chronology, occurs later in the book, but the two events are placed in a dialogue and create a pattern whereby crackdowns on racial and political minorities are seen as brutal murders, with the male principle of authority putting an end to the female principle of minority that defies the established order. All throughout the *Quartet* there appear other major historical events that expose the racial and class rifts in Southern California: the 1942 Sleepy Lagoon trial, where seventeen Mexican Americans were convicted and sentenced for murder in contravention of normal judicial procedures, the Hollywood witch hunt, with the coalition between FBI, studio moguls and the underworld working to fight communist activism in the studios, and the demolition of low-income housing in Chez Ravine, a Mexican community, to make room for Dodgers Stadium. In this sense, then, the Zoot Suit riots mark the beginning of the postwar era: pitting white people versus black, an act of division that, in the book, is fittingly followed by the discovery of Elizabeth Short's "divided" body. The Black Dahlia murder, as well as the several homicides that are portrayed in the tetralogy, are therefore "symptoms, expression of and intimately connected to the wider culture."[53]

As D. S. Neff points out in Deleuzian-Guattarian parlance, the 1940s in Los Angeles were "a period in history marked by extreme territorialization and reterritorialization,"[54] an apt commentary for a moment in which society was in extreme flux, with the massive incorporation of women into the workforce due to the war effort and a lingering left-wing social activism as potential destabilizers of the traditional order. Another scholar, Maureen Sunderland, justly sees continuities between this period and the Frontier era: both World War II and the conquest of the West, in fact, associated a rhetoric of liberty with the use of violence. Similarly, what happens in post-World War II Los Angeles, in Ellroy's books, is the attempt by the traditional (male) leadership to re-conquer an urban space that the war effort had left as a wilderness that challenges the traditional order, since "in the postwar landscape, the rise of apparently subversive and anti-American groups is presented as producing a national paranoia."[55] Ellroy's detectives submit to this plan with no idealism but as the foot soldiers of the re-conquest and re-establishment of the pre-war system. Like pioneers or infantrymen, they sweep the land and eradicate all those elements who threaten the hegemony of the city fathers. Or, at least, they attempt to achieve Captain Dudley Smith's version of the Truman doctrine, "to contain crime, to keep it south of Jefferson with the dark element."[56] In other words, their aim is to keep anti-Americans into small pockets where they can thrive but cannot threaten the system. Perhaps, this says something about what had happened with Ellroy himself, with all his obsessions safely contained in his books, no longer representing a threat to his emotional stability.

Conclusion: The Return of the Vanishing Mother

In *The Return of the Vanishing American*, Leslie Fiedler argues that American literature is haunted by the ghost of the Native American, which has infiltrated several texts and myths, a force that has been crucial in shaping that peculiar strand of whiteness that is American culture. A similar case can be made for the work of James Ellroy, where the native force is clearly represented by his mother—whom the writer had fought and negated but who eventually came back to haunt his son and lead him on a new path to self-knowledge.

Jean's murder engendered a worldview where violence is the driving force of historical progress, and the foundation of a patriarchal order that has poisoned Southern California. It is no accident that, besides being blamed for the obsessions that castrate their children, in the *L.A. Quartet* fathers are also associated with wounds inflicted on the city itself: Emmett Sprague, for instance, the man who "built half of Hollywood and Long Beach,"[57] is tainted by the collapse of several houses that were made with the cheapest possible material, and of all the people who lived inside them. Another city father, Preston Exley, runs a construction company that built the freeway system and a Disneyland-like amusement park, but his fortune rests on an illegal agreement that saved the reputation of movie director Raymond Dieterling. The fortunes begotten from these criminal acts testify to a disease that taints the American system, as its driving forces, individualism and the search for profit have released the mighty forces of male brutality whose effects are exposed in Ellroy's oeuvre. The fall of the "LAND" part of the HOLLYWOODLAND sign, related in the last part of *The Black Dahlia*, as pointed out by Sounac, metaphorically deprives the locality of its attachment to the soil. It creates a void that leaves the city, a living organism, lacking a center, with all its components discarded and disconnected—a graphic representation of the shattered psyche of a nine-year-old deprived of the balancing force of order personified by his mother.

Bibliography

Boozer, Jack. "The Lethal Femme Fatale in the Noir Tradition." *Journal of Film and Video* 51.3-4 (1999): 20-35.

Breu, Christopher. *Hard-Boiled Masculinities*. Minneapolis: University of Minnesota Press, 2005.

Caruth, Cathy. *Unclaimed Experience: Trauma, Narrative, and History*. Baltimore: Johns Hopkins University Press, 1996.

Cash, William. "Mean Streets and Dark Hearts." *Telegraph Magazine*, January 14, 1995: 30-35.

Davis, Mike. *City of Quartz. Excavating the Future in Los Angeles*. London: Verso, 1990.

de Beauvoir, Simone. *America Day by Day*. Duckworth: London, 1952.

Ellroy, James. *L.A. Confidential*. London: Random House, 1990. 2012.

—. *My Dark Places*. London: Random House, 1996. 2011.

—. *The Big Nowhere*. London: Random House, 1988. 2011.

—. *The Black Dahlia*. London: Arrow, 1987. 1993.

—. *White Jazz*. New York. Fawcett Gold Medal, 1992.

Felman, Shoshana. *The Juridical Unconscious: Trials and Traumas in the Twentieth Century*. Cambridge: Harvard University Press, 2002.

Fogelson, Robert M. *The Fragmented Metropolis: Los Angeles, 1850-1930*. Berkeley: University of California Press, 1993.

Forter, Greg. *Murdering Masculinities: Fantasies of Gender and Violence in the American Crime Novel*. New York: New York University Press, 2000.

Freud, Sigmund. "A Special Type of Choice of Object made by Men (Contributions to the Psychology of Love I)." In *The Standard Edition of the Complete Psychological Works of Sigmund Freud* 11 (1910), 165-75. London: Hogarth Press, 1957.

Hamm, Theodore. "Fragments of Postwar Los Angeles: The Black Dahlia In Fact And Fiction." *Antipode* 28.1 (1996): 24-41.

Horsley, Lee. "Founding Fathers: 'Genealogies of Violence' in James Ellroy's *L.A. Quartet*." *Clues* 19.2 (1998): 136-61.

LaCapra, Dominick. *Representing the Holocaust: History, Theory, Trauma*. Ithaca: Cornell University Press, 1994.

—. *Writing History, Writing Trauma*. Baltimore: Johns Hopkins University Press, 2001.

Marling, William. *The American Roman Noir: Hammett, Cain, and Chandler*. Athens: University of Georgia Press, 1998.

McWilliams, Carey. *Southern California. An Island on the Land*. Layton: Gibbs Smith, Publisher, 1973.

Meyer, Joshua. "Haunted Subjects: Fragments of the 'Sexual Mosaic' in James Ellroy's Los Angeles." *Philament* 13 (2008): 57-79.

Moretti, Franco. *Modern Epic*. London: Verso, 1998.

Neff, D.S. "Anoedipal Fiction: Schizoanalysis and *The Black Dahlia*." *Poetics Today* 18.3 (1997): 301-42.

Rich, Nathaniel. "James Ellroy, The Art of Fiction No. 201." *Paris Review*, Fall 2009. Accessed November 13, 2013. http://www.theparisreview.org/interviews/5948/the-art-of-fiction-no-201-james-ellroy.

Sounac, Frédéric. "Regard noir sur la Cité des Anges: James Ellroy." *E-rea. Revue électronique d'études sur le monde anglophone* 7.2 (2010). Accessed November 13, 2013. http://erea.revues.org/1252.

Sunderland, Maureen. "Revisiting Paranoia: The 'Witch Hunts' in James Ellroy's *The Big Nowhere* and Walter Mosley's *A Red Death*." In *The Millennial Detective: Essays on Trends in Crime Fiction, Film and Television, 1990-2010*, edited by Malcah Effron, 142-56. Jefferson, NC: McFarland, 2011.

Teaford, Jon C. *The Twentieth-Century American City: Problem, Promise, and Reality*. Baltimore; London: Johns Hopkins University Press, 1986.

Walker, Jonathan. "James Ellroy as Historical Novelist." *History Workshop Journal* 53.1 (2002): 181-204.

Wolfe, Peter. *Like Hot Knives to the Brain: James Ellroy's Search for Himself*. Lanham, MD: Lexington Books, 2006.

Notes

[1] This "picaresque" phase of Ellroy's life is chronicled in *My Dark Places.*

[2] Cathy Caruth's *Unclaimed Experience: Trauma, Narrative, and History* (Baltimore: Johns Hopkins Univ. Press, 1996) and Shoshana Felman's *The Juridical Unconscious: Trials and Traumas in the Twentieth Century* (Cambridge: Harvard University Press, 2002) are the main reference points for scholarship that highlight the destructive and de-structuring effect trauma has on the human psyche, and consequently on the narrative representation of trauma itself, which appear to be irreducible to traditional fictional modes. Other scholars, such as Dominick LaCapra in *Representing the Holocaust: History, Theory, Trauma* (Ithaca: Cornell University Press, 1994) and *Writing History, Writing Trauma* (Baltimore: Johns Hopkins University Press, 2001) have been critical of the apocalyptic rhetoric emphasizing the *aporia* between trauma and representation, and have suggested specific strategies for bridging the gap.

[3] James Ellroy, *My Dark Places* (London: Random House, 2011), 221.

[4] See, for instance, Christopher Breu, *Hard-Boiled Masculinities* (Minneapolis: University of Minnesota Press, 2005) and Greg Forter, *Murdering Masculinities: Fantasies of Gender and Violence in the American Crime Novel* (New York: New York University Press, 2000).

[5] Ellroy, *My Dark Places*, xliv.

[6] Jack Boozer, "The Lethal *Femme Fatale* in the Noir Tradition," *Journal of Film and Video* 51.3-4 (1999): 20-21.

[7] Ellroy, *My Dark Places*, xlviii.

[8] In *My Dark Places*, Ellroy recalls his father telling him that Jean was going to bed with a lawyer in order to be granted custody.

[9] Ellroy notes this in his own work, as follows, "Elizabeth Short's death inspired a minor hysteria. Postwar L.A. coalesced around the body of a dead woman. Hordes of people fell sway to the Dahlia" (Ellroy, *My Dark Places*, 113). Additionally, Simone de Beauvoir, who happened to visit Los Angeles at the time of the murder, recorded the collective hysteria in her travelogue *America Day by Day* (Duckworth: London, 1952).

[10] Ellroy, *My Dark Places*, 112.

[11] Ellroy, *My Dark Places*, 110.

[12] Ellroy, *My Dark Places*, 110.

[13] Ellroy, *My Dark Places*, 123.

[14] For examples of the language used by the major Los Angeles papers (such as *Times, Herald-Express*, *Daily News)* to describe Elizabeth Short's lifestyle, see Theodore Hamm, "Fragments of Postwar Los Angeles: The Black Dahlia In Fact And Fiction," *Antipode* 28.1 (1996): 24-41.

[15] Sigmund Freud, "A Special Type of Choice of Object made by Men (Contributions to the Psychology of Love I)," in *The Standard Edition of the Complete Psychological Works of Sigmund Freud* 11 (London: Hogarth Press, 1957), 171. I would like to thank Alessandra Diazzi for drawing my attention to this text.

[16] Ellroy, *My Dark Places*, 110.

[17] Jean did not have a stable relationship, but she had seen some men in the two years between her divorce and death.
[18] Ellroy, *My Dark Places*, 154.
[19] Ellroy, *My Dark Places*, 111.
[20] See "in the rescue-phantasy he [the male child] is completely identifying himself with his father" in Freud, "A Special Type," 173.
[21] Ellroy, *My Dark Places*, 118.
[22] Ellroy creates for Elizabeth Short an alternative past that connects her active sexual life to the trauma of having discovered as a young girl that she couldn't have children—this is a plot twist that testifies to the writer's need of rescuing Short's reputation.
[23] William Marling, *The American Roman Noir: Hammett, Cain, and Chandler* (Athens: University of Georgia Press, 1998), 15.
[24] Marling, *The American Roman Noir*, 19.
[25] Ellroy, *My Dark Places*, 163.
[26] Of course, the choice of giving to the novel's main female character a name resembling that of his own mother is quite revealing.
[27] Ellroy, *My Dark Places*, 163.
[28] Ellroy, *My Dark Places*, 163.
[29] Mike Davis, *City of Quartz. Excavating the Future in Los Angeles* (London: Verso, 1990), 45.
[30] See "I like the idea of a big canvas, which is why I write books in series. I am drawn to a complex panoply of events" quoted in William Cash, "Mean Streets and Dark Hearts," *Telegraph Magazine*, January 14, 1995, 35.
[31] Peter Wolfe, *Like Hot Knives to the Brain: James Ellroy's Search for Himself* (Lanham, MD: Lexington Books, 2006), 134.
[32] Jonathan Walker, "James Ellroy as Historical Novelist," *History Workshop Journal* 53 (2002): 185.
[33] Lee Horsley, "Founding Fathers: 'Genealogies of Violence' in James Ellroy's *L.A. Quartet*," *Clues* 19.2 (1998): 140.
[34] Ellroy, *The Big Nowhere* (London: Random House, 2011), 256.
[35] Ellroy, *L.A. Confidential* (London: Random House, 2012), 184.
[36] The decision to use a different technique may have something to do with editorial concerns about Ellroy's sprawling manuscripts. In fact, *L.A. Confidential* had to be cut down by more than a hundred pages, and Ellroy complied by leaving out all the unnecessary words—the result was a telegraphic style that became his signature thereafter. Later on, when he started to plan the follow-up, Ellroy might have thought of a way to limit himself. See Nathaniel Rich, "James Ellroy, The Art of Fiction No. 201", *Paris Review* 190 (2009).
[37] Franco Moretti, *Modern Epic* (London: Verso, 1998), 71.
[38] Jon C. Teaford, *The Twentieth-Century American City: Problem, Promise, and Reality* (Baltimore, London: John Hopkins University Press, 1986).
[39] Robert M. Fogelson, *The Fragmented Metropolis: Los Angeles, 1850-1930* (Berkeley: University of California, 1993).
[40] Carey McWilliams, *Southern California. An Island on the Land* (Layton: Gibbs Smith, Publisher, 1973), 235.

[41] This is my translation of Frédéric Sounac, "Regard noir sur la Cité des Anges: James Ellroy," *E-rea. Revue électronique d'études sur le monde anglophone* 7.2 (2010): [l'oeuvre d'Ellroy] "repose sur un arpentage minutieux et obsessionnel des quartiers de Los Angeles, une observation cruelle de sa sociologie et de son histoire, un rapport de haine-amour avec son architecture."
[42] Joshua Meyer, "Haunted Subjects: Fragments of the 'Sexual Mosaic' in James Ellroy's Los Angeles," *Philament* 13 (2008): 57.
[43] Ellroy, *The Black Dahlia* (London: Arrow, 1993), 235.
[44] Ellroy, *The Black Dahlia*, 299.
[45] Ellroy, *The Black Dahlia*, 302.
[46] Ellroy, *The Big Nowhere*, 197.
[47] Ellroy, *The Big Nowhere*, 217.
[48] Ellroy, *L.A. Confidential*, 137.
[49] Ellroy, *The Big Nowhere*, 3.
[50] Ellroy, *The Big Nowhere*, 44.
[51] Ellroy, *The Black Dahlia*, 133-35.
[52] McWilliams, *Southern California*, 229.
[53] Walker, "Historical Novelist," 183.
[54] D.S. Neff, "Anoedipal Fiction: Schizoanalysis and *The Black Dahlia*," *Poetics Today* 18.3 (1997): 317.
[55] Maureen Sunderland, "Revisiting Paranoia: The 'Witch Hunts' in James Ellroy's *The Big Nowhere* and Walter Mosley's *A Red Death*," in *The Millennial Detective: Essays on Trends in Crime Fiction, Film and Television, 1990-2010*, ed. Malcah Effron (Jefferson, NC: McFarland), 142.
[56] Ellroy, *L.A. Confidential*, 71.
[57] Ellroy, *The Black Dahlia*, 180.

The After-Life of Images: Archives and Intergenerational Trauma in Autographic Comics

Golnar Nabizadeh

This chapter explores how the transmission of memories and intergenerational trauma takes place via archival registers in works by Alison Bechdel (*Fun Home*, 2006) and Art Spiegelman (*MetaMaus,* 2011 and *In the Shadow of No Towers*, 2004). These works offer useful interventions in debates around trauma and visual representation, particularly because of the way in which the graphic narrative or comic form "calls a reader's attention visually and spatially to the act, process, and duration of interpretation."[1] I suggest that the demand of comics for readers to look and then look again, along with the static, sequential structure of the comics form means that this kind of visual narrative offers important possibilities for exploring trauma, memory, and representations of subjectivity. Concomitantly, I will focus on the role of intimate archives such as diaries, letters, recordings, and interviews in the representation of intergenerational trauma in non-fictional "autographic" narratives. I have selected the three creative works by Bechdel and Spiegelman because they each represent archives at work in different ways. In *Fun Home*, Bechdel literally re-produces archival materials such as diaries and photographs within the body of her narrative. In *MetaMaus*, Spiegelman and editor Hillary Chute arrange a vast range of archival materials including photographs, Spiegelman's sketches for *Maus*, drawings, book and magazine covers, editor's letters, and other sources, to trace the intensive processes that the creation and delivery of *Maus* involved. On the other hand, Spiegelman compiled an appendix of comics and cartoons from the turn of the 20th century in *In the Shadow of No Towers*, to demonstrate their continued relevance and refuge that they offered him after the collapse of the World Trade Center Towers on September 11, 2001. Spiegelman also imitates the visual conventions and styles of these strips within the text proper to achieve a vibrant and hypermediated representational mode that attests to his own hysteria after 9/11. Across the three texts, one can see the varied ways in which the authors have made use of archival materials to mediate their narration of traumatic events. Both Bechdel and Spiegelman are highly self-conscious artists and this is reflected in the multiple layers of narrative meaning that emerges from their play with archival resources, representations of subjectivity and consideration of intergenerational trauma.

In the last decade, a fine body of critical scholarship has emerged in the area of comics and visual literacies. I adopt the term "autographics" to delineate the scope of analysis in relation to these texts. Gillian Whitlock coined this neologism in her article "Autographics: The Seeing 'I' of the Comics" as a way of drawing attention to "the specific conjunctions of visual and verbal text in this genre of autobiography, and also to the subject positions that narrators negotiate in and through comics (…)."[2] The definition of autographics was later expanded upon by Whitlock and co-editor Anna Poletti; the authors present the neologism as a dictionary entry, complete with phonetic pronunciation: "*Autographics, n. Áwtográffiks. 2007: Life narrative fabricated in and through drawing and design using various technologies, modes, and materials. A practice of reading the signs, symbols and techniques of visual arts in life narrative. See also autobiography, biography, testimony, autobiographics, comics, self-portrait, avatar* (…)."[3] Along with the elements offered in this definition, the term "autographics" or "self-writing/drawing," is also useful in the present discussion because the texts under examination are hand drawn by their respective authors. While *MetaMaus* is not a comic, I consider it a useful literary adjunct to exploring the function of the archive, given the status of *Maus* itself as an autographic text *par excellence*. The autobiographical content of these texts raises important questions about how life narratives are rendered in comics and graphic novels, particularly when sensitive stories are involved. So for example, in relation to *Fun Home*, I suggest that Bechdel's use of her family's and her personal archives represents an important move towards rendering visible that which is invisible—the death of her father, her relationship with him, and exploring her own autobiographic subjectivity. The works by Spiegelman to which this chapter attends also make extensive use of personal and public archives, and offer important insights into how personal traumas can be imagined and negotiated.

Archival Explorations

What is meant by the term "archive" or "archives"? The *Oxford English Dictionary* defines the term "archive" as both noun and verb. As a noun, "archive" refers to both a place in which "public records or other important historic documents are kept," as well as the historical "records or documents so preserved."[4] In relation to memory, then, archival material might be regarded as contents that attest to the history of the past. Just how this content is constituted is, of course, subject to the material circumstances surrounding its production and whether it survives in time. In itself, the archive can be perhaps understood as bearing a nostalgic or melancholic relation with its own history. Its status then, bears the mark of that history, and the survival of archival material becomes particularly poignant when its creators are no longer present. For example, in *MetaMaus*, Spiegelman refers to drawings he saw that were made by inmates at the Auschwitz concentration camps who may or may not have survived their internments. Spiegelman describes how,

> [t]hose drawings were a return to drawing not for its possibilities of imposing the self, of finding a new role for art and drawing after the invention of the camera, but rather a return to the earlier function that drawing served before the camera—a kind of commemorating, witnessing, and recording of information—what Goya referred to when he says, 'This, I saw.'[5]

The statement by Goya to which Spiegelman refers can be understood in relation to Goya's own work in *The Disasters of War* (1810-20), a series of etched plates on Spain's war of independence against Napoleon between 1808 and 1814. The sequential nature of the etchings locates them in time, and Goya called plate 44, *Yo lo vi*, or, "I saw this." Curiously, in this scene a mother scrambles to collect her children from a terror that remains unseen. Only the direction of one child's head to the left and his or her terrified expression (validated by the equally terrorized countenances of the men in the foreground of the image) alerts the viewer to the presence of the horrific. In contrast to the clear declaration of the title, as viewers we are left wondering exactly what was seen by the inhabitants of the scene and by Goya, who bears the "I" of the title.[6] This reading responds to Ernst van Alphen's suggestion that traumata often constitute "failed experiences."[7] Specifically, van Alphen argues that trauma is characterized by "the impossibility of experiencing, and subsequently memorizing, an event,"[8] and in a phenomenological sense, remains outside the domain of assimilable knowledge. At this juncture, it is tempting to locate the narration at the level of the archive, as though the archival can itself testify to what can otherwise not be narrated. Yet while archival content can certainly illuminate certain facets of history, I suggest it is often at the fissures in narrative construction and representation that stories of trauma are highly valuable. In relation to Goya's etching, it is as though the horrors of war could, at least in this etching, be referred to only obliquely, rather than through direct representation, and this illuminates one aspect of the tension between the role of the witness and the work of representation.

Nonetheless, in Goya's work, as well as in the drawings of Auschwitz, there is a kind of commemoration taking place not only in terms of what is depicted, but also in the way that the hand-drawn illustrations bear the indexical traces of their creators. This is also true of the meticulous drawings in *Fun Home, MetaMaus*, and *In the Shadow of No Towers*. In this way, drawings can be doubly encoded as archives of time past as well as creative acts that bear witness to their own production. The archival materials that the three texts utilize include photographs, diaries, interviews, maps as well as institutional archival contents, such as the papers of Spiegelman's parents from The Auschwitz Museum in Poland,[9] or Bruce Bechdel's prison record for allegedly buying beer for a minor. While the archival tradition is not new—indeed, the practice of record-keeping stretches back to the second or third millennium BC, I suggest that, in a postmodern age, personal or intimate archives present an important antidote to the digital proliferation of information because they stage the potential for inter-generational learning and commemoration. By delving into historical, literary, and personal archives, Bechdel and Spiegelman explore inter-generational trauma through the re-shaping of archival materials, and, in doing so, illuminate the intersections between private and public networks. As Spiegelman has commented in relation to *Maus*, he considers it more a story about a father and son "trying to understand each other" rather than the Holocaust itself.[10] As Marianne Hirsch has written, "[p]erhaps it is *only* in subsequent generations that trauma can be witnessed and worked through, by those who were not there to live it but who received its effects, belatedly, through the narratives, actions and symptoms of the previous generation."[11] While Hirsch's statement was written in response to the postmemorial witnessing in *Maus*, how trauma is witnessed inter-generationally is of critical relevance to all three texts under examination here.

Ways of Seeing

In "An Archival Impulse," Hal Foster suggests that "archival artists seek to make historical information, often lost or displaced, physically present."[12] I take up this suggestion in relation to comics and graphic narratives to consider how the urgency of traumata is tended to within the visual-verbal nexus that constitutes graphic narratives. Before doing so, I would like to take a brief detour to elucidate a working definition of trauma. Whilst "trauma" is derived from the Greek word for a physical wound, with the advent of psychoanalysis in the late 19th century, it has come to include psychical wounds. In the late 19th century, Freud and Breuer developed a theory of traumatic hysteria, which found physical ailments in their patients, such as speech impediments, and other hysteric symptoms of the body, to have been caused by purely psychical "shocks" or wounds.[13] This discovery was one of the first steps taken in the theory of psychoanalysis and has been retained ever since.

In response to the devastating impact of World War I, Freud refined his theory of trauma. *Beyond the Pleasure Principle* (1922) arose in response to the overwhelming evidence stemming from "shell-shocked" soldiers returning from battlefronts. Freud found that shocks of this kind were also apparent in non-military sufferers who had survived accidents that posed a sudden "risk to life."[14] In this work, he identified psychic trauma as a mechanism that disturbs the individual's relation to time. Commenting on Freud's formulation of trauma, Cathy Caruth explains that, "[w]hat causes trauma, then, is a shock that appears to work very much like a threat to the body's spatial integrity, but is in fact a break in the mind's experience of time."[15] Breaks in linear temporality, then, are one hallmark of traumatized time and the texts by Bechdel and Spiegelman evoke—by different means—this conception of traumatized, fissured time, where the past and present bear painfully upon each other.[16] The breakages in time are evident in the text as breakages in narrative, and it is often found that the narrative is in some way thwarted. Judith Butler similarly describes trauma as a radical "interruption" to the life narrative that sustains our being-in-the-world:

> If a life is constituted through a fundamental interruption, even interrupted prior to the possibility of any continuity, then narrative reconstruction will also have to be subject to an interruption if it is to approximate the life it means to convey. Of course, learning to construct a narrative is a crucial practice, especially when discontinuous bits of experience remain dissociated from one another by virtue of traumatic conditions.[17]

If trauma means to be "possessed" by an image, as Caruth suggests, then possession could manifest itself in different ways. In the instance of Goya's etching (Plate 44), the force of possession could mean that the traces of the scene of the crimes in the other witness's horrified expressions register the overwhelming nature of the event. As a counterpart to van Alphen's characterization of trauma as a non-experiential phenomenon, Susan Brison locates the particular phenomenological imprint of trauma within the somatic symptoms of the body. She suggests that traumatic memories are embodied in physical responses that call upon or are triggered by remembrance of a traumatic event.[18] The texts under examination offer their own images of how the aftermath of trauma reveals itself within and without representation. Some of these images accord with well-known definitions of trauma such as that from Cathy Caruth's *Unclaimed Experience*, in which trauma "describes an overwhelming experience of sudden or catastrophic events in which the response to the event occurs in the often delayed, uncontrolled repetitive appearance of hallucinations and other intrusive phenomena."[19] Caruth characterizes these invasive repetitions as a double-edged form of haunting where the victim attempts to realize "not only the reality of the violent event, but also the reality of the way that its violence has not yet been fully known."[20] The field of autographic comics offers a rich vein within which the limits of traumatic representation can be explored. In this respect, Gillian Whitlock has previously suggested that, "[c]learly we live in times when attending to the relation between visual cultures and the transmission of memories of trauma and violence is both urgent and necessary (…)."[21] At a time when the circulation of images via the internet and mass media occurs at high frequency and at immense volumes, comics retain a critical role in providing a space that evades censorship, and through their structural content allow their creators and readers to envision different ways of seeing the world. This is particularly useful when it comes to memory and trauma studies, areas that rely on re-reading the past to enable new kinds of understanding.

Drawing the Self, Constructing the Subject in *Fun Home*

In an interview from 2006, Alison Bechdel explains that she relied on a wealth of archival material to construct her "autographic" narrative, *Fun Home: A Family Tragicomic*, published in the same year.[22] This archival material included family photo albums, letters, and perhaps most critically, Bechdel's personal diaries which she had started keeping from the age of ten. Bechdel wryly addresses her extensive collection of diaries, stating, "I've always had this archiving impulse … I'm the most anal-retentive person I've ever met."[23] Bechdel goes on to explain that, "[i]n many ways photographs really generated [*Fun Home*],"[24] specifically referring to a photograph of her family's babysitter, taken by her father, Bruce Bechdel, when Alison was eight years old. As she notes, the re-production of this photograph forms the "centerfold" of the work, an apt description not only because of its double-page spread across the middle pages of the text, but also because of the way the spread replicates the desiring gaze with which the photograph was initially taken, what Bechdel describes as her father's "illicit awe."[25] The re-presentation of this photograph acts as the visual keystone in Bechdel's narrative, the lynchpin around which Bechdel explores her father's mostly repressed homosexuality and suicide. In brief, the non-fictional narrative traces Alison's childhood and early adulthood as the narrator Bechdel, reflects on her family life and particularly her relationship with her parents.

Bechdel's story, then, tells the reader about the frequently contrapuntal relationship between Alison and her father, where the formation of her autographic subjectivity and coming out as a lesbian takes place alongside her discovery of some awkward "home truths." As the *récitatif* notes, Bechdel constructs herself in opposition to her father, and describes herself as "Spartan," "modern," and "butch" compared to her father's "Athenian," "Victorian," "nelly" persona.[26]

Met with critical and popular success, *Fun Home* attests to how comics produce multi-layered stories using a wealth of visual cues and clues. Alison's father Bruce ran the local funeral home, from which the title is derived—and in the dedication to her mother and siblings, Bechdel states, "we did have a lot of fun, despite everything."[27] Bechdel's analysis of both her mother and father is largely constituted through literary references and Bechdel relies not only on the references but also on her parents' reading and acting practices to make sense of their, and by extension her own, motivations and desires. In this way, references to Oscar Wilde, Henry James, Albert Camus, James Joyce, Marcel Proust, and Lev Tolstoy among others, entwine these texts and Bechdel's story in an intimate arrangement that maps the past onto the present. As Bechdel has commented, each of the seven chapters of the book focus on her father's favorite authors. Indeed, the narrative demonstrates the way in which the past is reiterated into the visual present. For example, in one panel, Bechdel reproduces a passage from her father's copy of Camus' *The Myth of Sisyphus*, along with the sentence that he had underlined on the relationship between suicide and the absurd.[28] Immediately underneath this extract is a black and white reproduction of a photo, with a man sitting in a sports car. Whether this figure is Bruce or Camus is not clear, and the *récitatif* further supports this ambiguity, "A snapshot of him [Bruce] in a frat brother's sports car reminds me of Cartier-Bresson's photos of Camus."[29] The ambivalence between text and image about the subject in this image draws attention to the way in which archival sources, far from presenting an unproblematic and unmediated history, are constructed to a degree. As with any text, the archival contents can literally speak volumes about not only the memories therein, but also the nature of memory itself and its occlusion. Indeed, the gap between word and image in the structure of comics mimics the ontological uncertainties and slippages between language and meaning. The rendition of such relations in a visual-verbal realm activates exciting junctures for debates on witnessing, commemoration and trauma, and allows theories of the latter to be tested in this narrative modality.

In *Fun Home*, Alison Bechdel relies on a variety of different archival forms around which she structures her story. Returning to her comment that a photograph of a babysitter generated the "whole story" of *Fun Home*, the reader can immediately discern the discursive power of the photograph not only for its evidentiary content, but for the questions that it generated within a broader network of relations between Alison, her father, Roy (the babysitter in the photograph) and her family. Importantly, what the reader encounters within the pages of the text is not a facsimile of the photograph but rather Bechdel's drawing of the image. This transposition of the photograph into a hand drawn form, I suggest, involves the author in an intimate restaging of her family's history as the archive is produced afresh. Hilary Chute has similarly observed that "[t]he narration of … [*Fun Home*]… is rooted in *acts of looking at archives*,"[30] and this is evident in the depiction of Roy's photograph.

Reproduced in a larger-than-life format, the reader encounters not only the fuzzy details of the image, but also what is presumably Bechdel's hand holding the photograph up for inspection. The exaggerated dimensions of the photo seem appropriate for the discovery of this outsized event. In fact, Bechdel found the photograph one year after her father's death, and as she explained in an interview, "I felt this sort of posthumous bond with my father, like I shared this thing with him, like we were comrades. I didn't start working on [*Fun Home*] then, but over the years that picture persisted in my memory."[31] Later in the story, Alison learns from her mother that her father had had an affair with Roy at the time he snapped the photograph. Around this narrative epicenter, Bechdel's thoughts are arranged in an almost random order—the flow of the captions disrupted by the questions that this photograph throws up. Unlike the rest of the pages, this centerfold does not contain page numbers, which further emphasizes its dislocating power in Bechdel's narrative. An accidental discovery among a box of family photographs, Alison recognizes the subject as Roy, a childhood babysitter, but in this frame he is cast in a different light, marked by what Bechdel describes as her father's "illicit awe." Despite its illicit contents, Bechdel wonders why the subject witnessing the photograph (Alison as a seventeen-year-old) is "not properly outraged" by the photo, but rather finds it beautiful. The next caption ponders whether Alison might identify all too well with the taboo desire that she locates within this image. The double spread also mimics the *Esquire* advertisement that Bechdel draws on the previous page, where she notes her and her father's shared "appreciation for masculine beauty," albeit desired for markedly different reasons. This nexus of homosexual desire seems to refract her father's photographic gaze against Alison's own to provide a surprising moment of unity within the disruptive force of her discovery.

The discovery of the photograph also raises questions about its uncertain archival status. For example, the year "69" in the photograph's border is blotted out, but not the month. Bechdel as narrator notes this "ineffectual attempt at censorship," and asks, "Why cross out the year and not the month?" and "Why, for that matter, leave the photo in the envelope at all?" These questions seem to attest to Derrida's suggestion in *Archive Fever* that contradictory desires govern the creation of an archive: on the one hand, the drive to conserve memories, and on the other, the destructive drive (or in Freud's terms, the death drive) to forget.[32] This suggestion seems a particularly fertile source of anxiety in relation to family secrets, and one that finds literal and figurative expression in Alison's "curvy circumflex" that at times overwhelms her own archival drive in keeping a diary. In *Fun Home* Bechdel painstakingly reproduced several diary entries, and much like the photographic reproductions, the archival significance of her records is galvanized through its copy. As the *récitatif* notes, Alison's response to her father's deceptively simple suggestion, "Just write down what's happening," for the purposes of keeping a diary, carried the hallmarks of an "epistemological crisis"; "How did I know that the things I was writing there were absolutely, objectively true?" The query concludes on a grim note, "My simple, declarative sentences began to strike me as hubristic at best, utter lies at worst."[33] In a household characterized by an "arctic climate," the narrative insecurity represented in an equally intimate setting—the diary—is perhaps not surprising.

What we can see here is the way in which the circumflex symbolically bears the burden of Bechdel's unknowingness in her early family life. Indeed, the upward curve of the circumflex looks a little like a crutch. The steep bell curve of the symbol also seems to attest to the hope and confusion in the statement "I think," where the inability to know is marked by both the attempt to think and its covering over, represented in the rise and dip of the shape. The transition between one kind of sign ("I think") to another (circumflex) is significant because it draws attention to the fluidity of meaning and the biocularity of visual-verbal signs. The attention Bechdel draws to the work of the curvy circumflex is reinforced by her transcription of her personal archives within the pages of *Fun Home*. The reinscription of her diary maintains the past *as past*, yet enlivens its pages as they are drawn anew for the narrative present. In this way, the text is literally productive in its re-presentation of the past, as the reader accesses Bechdel's reproduction of her diary. The circumflex, then, seems to offer two functions as a shield against and a representation of the epistemological crisis in Alison's confusion between appearances and reality. Bechdel has explained that part of the narrative of *Fun Home* details her father's obsession with restoring the family's Victorian home and her father's eye for detail, including the use of color. Bechdel notes that she became a cartoonist partially because it meant that she could construct worlds in black and white and not "think about color."[34] Notwithstanding her father's legacy, Bechdel ultimately chose to render her work in a dichromatic scheme, coloring her story in cool hues of an elegiac green. This productive melancholy is enhanced by the muted grey-green that colors the pages of *Fun Home*, which suggests at once a narrative somehow worn down by time, and yet one whose green hue still presents a possibility for regeneration.

Returning to photography, Bechdel used polaroid photographs in which she posed herself for the drawings of her father and the other characters that populate *Fun Home*. I suggest that Bechdel's use of herself in these photographs permits a further entwining of history upon the body, or more explicitly, allows her to cast her past literally against the contours and outlines of her own body. Bechdel also uses the representation of bodies, or more accurately, black silhouettes to present a kind of radical otherness. Early in the narrative, she draws a parallel between her father and Daedalus, the "clever worker" whom her father resembles in several capacities—artful, committed, and at times, cruel. In one panel, the *récitatif* recounts Daedalus' creation of a Labyrinth in which to hide the Minotaur, and refers to the latter as "a half-bull, half-man monster."[35] Below this description, Alison gingerly replaces the top of a crystal decanter as she cowers below her father's silhouette which consumes at least half the panel. Reading the verbal and visual together in this scene, Alison's terror of her father—who at this point resembles more the Minotaur than Daedalus—is palpable. And yet, her father is also depicted as radically other when he is unexpectedly loving and tender, such as when he bursts into song as he puts Alison to bed. In this panel, which arises not long after the reference to Daedalus, Bruce's form also consumes much of the space, and his silhouette is dark against the hallway light as he sings to Alison. This time the *récitatif* states, "[h]is bursts of kindness were as incandescent as his tantrums were dark,"[36] and this description eloquently conveys the visual force that accompanies such moments. The contrast between his silhouette and the term "incandescent," which Bechdel uses to describe her father's kindness, instils an affective complexity in this scene. On each occasion the black form hints not only at the unknown component or facets in Alison's perception of her father, but also at the strong emotional charge that this unknown amalgam presents.

This technique acquires even greater force some time later, when Bechdel depicts her realization in the university campus bookstore that she is a lesbian. In this scene, she stands before a bookshelf holding *Word Is Out*, a landmark work that includes interviews with 26 gay men and lesbians speaking about their experiences with sexuality. The panel itself depicts a moment as Alison looks up from the book, with a large exclamation sign standing in for the significance of her own sexuality. Of particular interest here, however, is the profile of the figure that stands to the back of the bookshelf—again in black silhouette. The profile seems remarkably like that of Roy—whose significance has already been illustrated in the book's centerpiece—with curly hair and a button nose. This silhouette is also evident much earlier in the book, in Bechdel's first iteration of this scene.[37] Only a few pages after its second iteration, Alison pays her maiden voyage to her university's "Gay union" and upon entering the reader can discern the figure of a young woman who may also fit the profile of the silhouette in the campus bookstore.[38] Again, Bechdel's visual economy creates ambivalence about the shadowy presence in the bookstore. It seems to at once beckon to Alison's past (in the form of Roy) and future (her visit to the Gay union), and in this way, the figure seems to abridge different moments in time to elevate the importance of Alison's discovery about her sexuality. It is as though Roy's image haunts this memoir as a fraudulent presence—appearing in different guises throughout the story, where the shape-shifting testifies to the complex position which Roy occupies in relation to how Alison perceives her family, but also the construction of her own identity. The silhouette then is perhaps colored in by virtue of the memories and emotions that constitute its blackness and draws attention to the way in which past and present are continually brought to abut against one another in *Fun Home* as in the other texts under examination.

Affective Inconveniences

A quality shared by Bechdel's work and *In the Shadow of No Towers* by Art Spiegelman is the way in which the respective authors capture the rupturing of the everyday by the uncomfortable emotions that surface after traumatic events. For example, Bechdel recalls crying only once after finding out about her father's death, and that her anger, annoyance and feelings of emptiness did not fit within conventional mourning rituals. Instead, an angry jerk of her elbow from a funeral director's "reassuring" hand provides a measure of reassurance that she is somehow "still there." Similarly, Spiegelman depicts his hysteria after the events of September 11, 2001 and the way in which his fear, anger and paranoia, among other emotions, circle outside of the patriotic fervor that he encounters in New York. It appears that the emotive power of these texts resides in their expression of discontent and in the heterodox nature of grief that cannot be neatly categorized. In both works, the visual content of the narrative frequently spills out of the panels, and yet while Bechdel's work is colored in melancholic shades of grey-green, Spiegelman's hysteria or troubled mourning is supported by the use of bright colors including clanging yellows, oranges, and reds that seem to yell out against other, more muted tones.

Written between September 2001 and August 2003, Spiegelman's "album" (as he refers to the book in the documentary, *The Art of Spiegelman* (2009)), is notable for its large dimensions and "baby-book" cardboard pages, as though the dislocating effect of the collapse of the World Trade Towers necessitated a text that was easier to grasp. The date of each double-page spread is inscribed at the bottom of the page, thus carving out pockets of time in which Spiegelman created each broadsheet. He clarifies in the introduction (aptly titled "The Sky Is Falling") that "the idea of working in single page units corresponded to my existential conviction that I might not live long enough to see them published."[39] Thus, while the ten episodes are arranged chronologically, they do not follow one another in terms of content, but are rather characterized by narrative loops in which the vivid burning skeletons of the twin towers are repeatedly recalled against different reflections. Aside from this image, the rest of the episodes reference an archive of cartooning styles contained in an appendix to the work. Introduced by Spiegelman, the supplement includes comics such as Richard Outcault's *Hogan's Alley*, Rudolph Dirks' *Katzenjammer Kids*, Frederick Burr Opper's *Happy Hooligan* and Lyonel Feininger's *Kinder Kids*, among others. As Spiegelman explains, "[t]he only cultural artifacts that could get past my defenses to flood my eyes and brain with something other than images of burning towers were old comic strips; vital, unpretentious ephemera from the optimistic dawn of the 20th century." Indeed, it seems that the pulpy nature of these daily strips or "ephemera" in Spiegelman's words offered some relief from a world in which all that was solid had indeed melted into air. Here, Spiegelman recalls his own childhood via the early comics form, and it seems that this relationship offers a space for solace and reparation through which the devastation of September 11 can be mediated. In other words, Spiegelman triangulates the present of the narrative through the past by folding in representational modes from these archived comic strips. This perspective is achieved by reference to visual conventions and narrative cues.

For example, in the spread dated "April 29-May 27 2003," Spiegelman parodies George McManus's *Bringing Up Father*, making fun of his relentless attachment to consuming media reports and conspiracies about 9/11. In the original *Bringing Up Father* strip, Jiggs the Irishman visits Italy and dreams about the leaning tower of Pisa falling over, after which he is shown placing wooden planks around the base of the tower and then returning contentedly to sleep. Imagining himself as Jiggs and his wife,

Françoise Mouly as the harridan Maggie, Spiegelman paints a brief scenario in which Françoise drags Art off to bed where he proceeds to watch CNN reports on the attacks on the World Trade Towers after already having spent most of the night reading conspiracy theories on the internet. The sketch, entitled "Marriage Blitz," continues into the next morning, where Spiegelman-Jiggs jumps awake as his wife turns on the radio in the bathroom to a new bulletin about Ground Zero. In the final panel of this episode, Art clings to bedroom ceiling light and yells "Turn off that damn radio, ya terrorist!"[40] as Françoise, sporting an Osama bin Laden like beard, enters the room to admonish his hysterical exclamation. By adopting the larger-than-life persona of the Irishman Jiggs, and infusing the sense of the ridiculous that pervades the original *Bringing Up Father* strips into his own narrative, Spiegelman vitalizes this sketch. The comedic style and shrill interaction between the couple (for example, Art explains to Françoise, "But dontcha get it? This **proves** the Pentagon was in on the attack!"[41]) creates a narrative that poignantly attests to the trauma created not only by the events of September 11, but the post-traumatic tension of its aftermath.

Spiegelman's turn to archives by way of form and content provides a literary space for exploration and experimentation and offers one way of negotiating trauma by turning to the past both as a refuge from the present and as a way of understanding it. As an autographic text, *In the Shadow of No Towers* also allows its author to supplant his shattered perception of the world by playing with different monikers with which to imagine himself and the world around him. This form of play seems to suggest that the archive provides a partial sanctuary precisely because of scrappiness and fragility of early comics, against which their survival is pitted. I suggest that this point of vulnerability offers a different vantage point from which to consider trauma, where the physical vulnerability of the early comics reflects the psychic vulnerability of Spiegelman and his narrative. It is useful to note that the episodes offer little, if any closure; on one occasion they detail extreme relief, for example after Art and Françoise find their daughter Nadja at her school, located at the foot of the twin towers. Here, the *récitatif* is constructed alternatively through third-person narration (which bookends the episode) with a first-person voice used to link the single-cell panels that seem to mimic falling window panes in their fragmented structure. These panels are drawn in a more naturalistic form with watercolor and ink used to depict glimpses into Spiegelman's memories of rushing to find Nadja. The oscillation between past and present is supported by the structure of the comic itself.

Spiegelman has previously stated that comics are the perfect medium for representing memory because of the sequential arrangement of the panels and the way that the eye flickers between the different panels to create "a map of time itself" (*The Art of Spiegelman*). Tellingly, the opening caption of this episode states, "He remembers that morning yet again…"[42], which draws attention to the repeated recollection of September 11. The idea of repetition is already foregrounded in the title page of the book, where the reader encounters a reproduction of the front page of *The World* newspaper from September 11, 1901. The headline of this issue is located immediately above the title of Spiegelman's text, and reads "President's wound reopened; slight change for worse," which refers to the assassination attempt on William McKinley, the twenty-fifth President of the USA. To the left and immediately below this headline, a sub-heading also provides more clues regarding the politicized origins of this event. The article on the left hand side of the page refers to Emma Goldman, a leading anarcho-feminist and her defense against her alleged involvement in a plot to kill President McKinley. As noted earlier, the terms "trauma" and "wound" are semantically linked, and the headline in the title page alerts the reader to the fact that wounds can be reopened. In this instance, McKinley did not recover from the assassination attempt, and again, the loss that this event heralds seems to reverberate within the pages of the comic, where the narrative does not try to recoup the losses it describes, but more productively, leaves the events of 9/11 open to question. The final episode ends with three images of the familiar glowing bones of the tower within an increasingly muted and distant perspective. Against these images the *récitatif* states, "[t]he towers have come to loom far larger than life…but they seem to get smaller every day…Happy Anniversary."[43] In these final moments, the apparition of the tower is ironically confirmed as it fades from view, and more disturbingly, from memory, the final panel confirming that this repeated image has been preserved in the artist's memory.

Spiegelman's more recent work, *MetaMaus* is an archival work *par excellence*, and traces the history and development of his ground-breaking comic *Maus*. Diligently compiled from a broad range of archival materials, including sketches and plans for *Maus*, research materials and images, the book is accompanied by a CD-ROM which includes recordings of Spiegelman's interviews with his father Vladek, as well as Spiegelman's own thoughts on the creative and critical processes behind *Maus*. More than the other texts discussed, *MetaMaus* draws attention to its own status as compilation of archival contents, and the ways in which archives complicate the lines between fact, history, memory, and fiction. Far from being problematic, this narrative complication seems to corroborate with the difficulties bound up in acts of witnessing and testimony. For example, Spiegelman asks his father whether prisoners in Auschwitz were marched past an inmate orchestra, to which his father replies, "I remember only marching … how could it be there an orchestra?"[44] Spiegelman describes the importance of testimony and it appears that it is critical to pay attention to testimony precisely where it differs from what might be expected, such as Vladek agreeing or confirming that there was indeed an orchestra that played in Auschwitz. Spiegelman states that,"[i]t's very possible that for him the orchestras didn't exist, and I don't want to deny that."[45] In an equally poignant example, Dori Laub has previously documented how one of his patients, also an Auschwitz survivor, came to believe that she saw four chimneys blow up in Auschwitz. In this regard, Laub writes,

> She was testifying not simply to historical facts, but to the very secret of survival and of resistance to extermination . . . she saw, in other words, the unimaginable taking place right in front of her own eyes. And she came to testify to the unbelievability, precisely, of what she had eye-witnessed—this bursting open of the very frame of Auschwitz.[46]

I suggest that both of these examples are critical because they delineate the instances where archives must fail (such as a photograph of an inmate orchestra included in *MetaMaus*) to enable other narratives to be understood. In both cases, the listener became sensitized to the exigencies and conditions which meant that the individual providing testimony believed in the truth of their statement. This is significant because the archive and archival contents are not in themselves true or false, but are perhaps most useful in blurring the lines between history and memory. This seems of vital importance in relation to how frames of understanding might burst open, to use Laub's terms, or fall apart under the impact of trauma.

In an interview for *Critical Inquiry*, Bechdel explains that she is fascinated by the way in which internal realities are externalized, and then suggests that she suspects that she decathects her relationship with different object and, by extension, the past via the act of drawing. It seems that the hand-drawn nature of both Bechdel and Spiegelman's work allows them to recreate the past literally in the images they draw but also figuratively—to flesh out emotional relations, and introduce different ways of understanding to bear upon the difficult and painful themes they choose to examine. As Hillary Chute and Marianne DeKoven argue, the "mark of handwriting is an important part of the rich extra-semantic information a reader receives,"[47] and Chute has elsewhere suggested that the "subjective mark of the body is rendered directly onto the page and constitutes how we view the page."[48] The indexical presence of the "authorial," then, provides critical clues about not only the contents of the narrative, but how its formation constructs the reader's visual access to the story therein. The perspectives, line method, framing, color and narrative choices within each graphic narrative creates a complex network within which the personal impacts of trauma and its transmission can be imagined and reconfigured. In different ways, Bechdel and Spiegelman create living archives by incorporating archival materials into their work. In *Fun Home*, Bechdel traces the contours of the past through her penwork, whereas in *In the Shadow of No Towers*, Spiegelman partially incorporates past and present through his creative reinvention, or remediation, of early comic strips.

Astrid Erll and Ann Rigney suggest that in the same way that cultural memory is constructed via mediation, but also that "there is no mediation without remediation."[49] What is of particular interest here is the way that technologies of re/mediation reference the past as part of their representative function. To follow Erll and Rigney's suggestion, remediation "reminds the viewer of the presence of a medium and thus generates an 'experience of the medium.'"[50] In Spiegelman's work, the reader encounters specific early comic strips alongside the author's reinterpretation of those strips in the body of the text to convey his narrative. If reading a comic strip enacts a particular perspective or modality of looking, then it seems that Spiegelman is directing the reader to understand the present through explicit reference to past ways of constructing a vision of the world. One can perhaps suggest, then, that it is precisely by recycling the vision of early comic strips by Richard Outcault, Rudolph Dirks, Frederick Burr Opper, and Lyonel Feininger, for example, that Spiegelman locates an alternative lens through which to explore his troubled memories of a more recent past. In this instance, a deliberate mode of "distanced viewing" provides a reassuring antidote to illusions of certainty post-9/11, and it is this remediated vision of the present via the past that constructs much of the poignancy and yearning in Spiegelman's work.

In *Fun Home* and *In the Shadow of No Towers*, the respective authors attempt to envisage the trauma of a father's suicide, or September 11 by remediating visual and intimate archives. The act of remediation instantiates a movement between "now" and "then," which in turn brings both states to bear on each other in productive and important ways. Significant visual and theoretical research has informed the development and production of both texts, as well as of course, in *MetaMaus*. In *Fun Home*, Bechdel's perusal of intimate family archives produced an unexpected document—Roy's photograph—which sparked further investigations, whereas in *In the Shadow of No Towers*, Spiegelman's retreat into comics archives enabled him to produce a vision of his troubled *milieu* that is mindful of its fragile perspective, much like the delicate constitution of the early comics themselves. In both cases, the authors' use of visual archives productively troubles neat distinctions between remembering and forgetting the past and the present. By remediating images from the past into the narrative present—

be it through re-production of photographs and other archives in the case of Bechdel, or re-imagining early comic strips in Spiegelman's work—the losses of the past are literally drawn into the present, wherein they offer new ways of seeing.

Bibliography

Bal, Mieke, Jonathan Crewe, and Leo Spitzer, eds. *Acts of Memory: Cultural Recall in the Present.* Hannover: University Press of New England, 1999.

Bechdel, Alison. *Fun Home: A Family Tragicomic.* New York: Houghton Miffler, 2006.

—. "An Interview with Alison Bechdel." By Hillary Chute. *MFS Modern Fiction Studies* 52.4 (2006): 1004-13.

—. "Hillary Chute interviews Alison Bechdel." By Hillary Chute. *Critical Inquiry*, August, 2011. Accessed September 1, 2013. http://criticalinquiry.uchicago.edu/hillary_chute_interviews_alison_bechdel.

Boime, Albert. *Art in an Age of Bonapartism, 1800-1815.* Chicago: University of Chicago Press, 1990.

Brison, Susan J. "Trauma Narratives and the Remaking of the Self." In *Acts of Memory: Cultural Recall in the Present*, edited by Mieke Bal, Jonathan Crewe and Leo Spitzer, 39-54. Hannover: University Press of New England, 1999.

Butler, Judith. "Giving an Account of Oneself." *Diacritics* 31.4 (2001): 22-40.

Caruth, Cathy. *Unclaimed Experience: Trauma, Narrative, and History.* Baltimore: The Johns Hopkins University Press, 1996.

—. "Violence and Time: Traumatic Survivals." *Assemblage* 20 (1993): 24-25.

Chute, Hillary. *Graphic Women: Life Narrative and Contemporary Comics.* New York: Columbia University Press, 2010.

DeKoven, Marianne, and Hilary Chute. "Introduction: Graphic Narrative." *Modern Fiction Studies* 52.4 (2006): 767-82.

Derrida, Jacques. *Archive Fever: A Freudian Impression.* Translated by Eric Prenowitz. Chicago: University of Chicago Press, 1996.

Erll, Astrid, and Anne Rigney, eds. *Mediation, Remediation, and the Dynamics of Cultural Memory.* Berlin: Walter de Gruyter, 2009.

Foster Hal. "An Archival Impulse." *October* 110 (2004): 3-22.

Freud, Sigmund. *Beyond the Pleasure Principle. The Standard Edition of the Complete Psychological Works of Sigmund Freud.* Translated and edited by James Strachey. Vol.19. London: Hogarth, 1961.

Freud, Sigmund, and Josef Breuer. *Studies in Hysteria*. Translated by Nicola Luckhurst. London: Penguin, 2004.

Grove, Laurence. *Comics in French: The European Bande Dessinée in Context*. New York: Berghahn Books, 2010.

Hirsch, Marianne. "Surviving Images: Holocaust Photographs and the Work of Postmemory." *The Yale Journal of Criticism* 14.1 (2001): 5-37.

—. "Editor's Column: Collateral Damage." *PMLA* 119.5 (2004): 1209-15.

Hirsch, Marianne, and Leo Spitzer. "Testimonial Objects: Memory, Gender and Transmission." *Poetics Today* 27.2 (2006): 353-83.

Huyssen, Andreas. "Of Mice and Mimesis: Reading Spiegelman with Adorno." *New German Critique* 81 (2000): 65-82.

Laub, Dori, and Shoshana Felman. *Testimony: Crises of Witnessing in Literature, Psychoanalysis, and History*. New York: Routledge, 1992.

Leys, Ruth. *Trauma: A Genealogy*. Chicago: Chicago University Press, 2000.

McKinney, Mark, ed. *History and Politics in French-Language Comics and Graphic Novels*. Jackson: University Press of Mississippi, 2008.

Oxford English Dictionary Online. Oxford: Oxford University Press, 2013. Accessed January 20, 2014. www.oed.com.

Rose, Gillian. *Visual Methodologies: An Introduction to the Interpretation of Visual Materials*, 2nd ed. London: Sage, 2007.

Spiegelman, Art. *In the Shadow of No Towers*. New York: Pantheon, 2004.

—. *MetaMaus*. London: Penguin, 2011.

The Art of Spiegelman. Directed by Clara Kuperberg and Joelle Oosterlinck. Paris: ARTE, 2009.

van Alphen, Ernst. "Symptoms of Discursivity: Experience, Memory and Trauma." In *Acts of Memory: Cultural Recall in the Present*, edited by Mieke Bal, Jonathan Crewe and Leo Spitzer, 24-38. Hannover: University Press of New England, 1999.

Whitlock, Gillian. "Autographics: The Seeing 'I' of the Comics." *Modern Fiction Studies* 52.4 (2006): 965-79.

—. "Bookends: AutoGraphics." In *Soft Weapons: Autobiography in Transit*, by Gillian Whitlock, 187-201. Chicago: The University of Chicago Press, 2007.

Whitlock, Gillian, and Anna Poletti. "Self-Regarding Art." *Biography* 31.1 (2008): iv-xxiii.

Notes

[1] Marianne DeKoven and Hilary Chute, "Introduction: Graphic Narrative," *Modern Fiction Studies* 52.4 (2006): 767-82. See also Gillian Rose, *Visual Methodologies: An Introduction to the Interpretation of Visual Materials*, 2nd ed. (London: Sage, 2007); Marianne Hirsch, "Editor's Column: Collateral Damage," *PMLA* 119.5 (2004): 1209-15; Marianne Hirsch and Leo Spitzer, "Testimonial Objects: Memory, Gender and Transmission," *Poetics Today* 27.2 (2006): 353-83; Andreas Huyssen, "Of Mice and Mimesis: Reading Spiegelman with Adorno," *New German Critique* 81 (2000): 65-82; Mark McKinney, ed., *History and Politics in French-Language Comics and Graphic Novels* (Jackson: University of Mississippi Press, 2008); Gillian Whitlock, "Bookends: AutoGraphics," in *Soft Weapons: Autobiography in Transit* (Chicago: The University of Chicago Press, 2007), 187-201, and also "Autographics: The Seeing 'I' of the Comics," *Modern Fiction Studies* 52.4 (2006): 965-79.

[2] Gillian Whitlock, "Autographics: The Seeing 'I' of the Comics," *Modern Fiction Studies* 52.4 (2006): 966.

[3] Gillian Whitlock and Anna Poletti, "Self-Regarding Art," *Biography* 31.1 (2008): v, italics in the original.

[4] *Oxford English Dictionary Online*, s.v. "Archive." (Oxford: Oxford University Press, 2013).

[5] Art Spiegelman, *MetaMaus* (London: Penguin, 2011), 49.

[6] Albert Boime, *Art in an Age of Bonapartism, 1800-1815* (Chicago: University of Chicago Press, 1990), 307-8.

[7] Ernst van Alphen, "Symptoms of Discursivity: Experience, Memory and Trauma," in *Acts of Memory: Cultural Recall in the Present*, eds. Mieke Bal, Jonathan Crewe and Leo Spitzer (Hannover: University Press of New England, 1999), 25.

[8] van Alphen, "Symptoms of Discursivity," 26.

[9] Spiegelman, *MetaMaus*, 63.

[10] *The Art of Spiegelman*, directed by Clara Kuperberg and Joelle Oosterlinck (2009; Paris: ARTE, 2009), DVD.

[11] Marianne Hirsch, "Surviving Images: Holocaust Photographs and the Work of Postmemory," *The Yale Journal of Criticism* 14.1 (2001): 12.

[12] Hal Foster, "An Archival Impulse," *October* 110 (2004): 4.

[13] Sigmund Freud and Josef Breuer, *Studies in Hysteria*, trans. Nicola Luckhurst (London: Penguin, 2004).

[14] Sigmund Freud, *Beyond the Pleasure Principle. The Standard Edition of the Complete Psychological Works of Sigmund Freud*, Vol.19, trans. and ed. James Strachey (London: Hogarth, 1961), 12.

[15] Cathy Caruth, "Violence and Time: Traumatic Survivals," *Assemblage* 20 (1993): 25.

[16] In her work, *Trauma: A Genealogy* (Chicago: Chicago University Press, 2000), Ruth Leys launches a vigorous criticism of Caruth's reading (in her book, *Unclaimed Experience: Trauma, Narrative, and History* (Baltimore: The Johns Hopkins University Press, 1996)) of Freud's account of Tasso's poem, "Gerusalemme Liberata," wherein Tancred "twice-kills" his beloved, Clorinda. Leys argues that Caruth problematically characterizes Tancred as a traumatized "victim," a status

that Leys suggests would be more properly ascribed to Clorinda, who is murdered unintentionally by Tancred. While a comprehensive discussion of this criticism is outside the scope of my work, in brief, one can suggest that Caruth's focus on Tancred's trauma is not to deny Clorinda's murder, but rather to illustrate the repetitive wounding that Caruth offers as the founding economy of the missed experience that characterizes traumata.

[17] Judith Butler, "Giving an Account of Oneself," *Diacritics* 31.4 (2001): 32.

[18] Susan Brison, "Trauma Narratives and the Remaking of the Self," in *Acts of Memory: Cultural Recall in the Present*, eds. Mieke Bal, Jonathan Crewe and Leo Spitzer (Hannover: University Press of New England, 1999), 42.

[19] Caruth, *Unclaimed Experience,* 11.

[20] Caruth, *Unclaimed Experience*, 4.

[21] Whitlock, "Autographics," 966.

[22] In this chapter I use the name "Alison" to refer to the author's autobiographical avatar in *Fun Home*, whereas I use Bechdel to refer to the author figure of the text. I also use the term "*récitatif*" to refer to the extra-diegetic narrative voice throughout the text. The use of "*récitatif*" is consistent with French scholarship on comics or *bandes dessinées*; as Laurence Grove, in *Comics in French: The European Bande Dessinée in Context* (New York: Berghahn Books, 2010), 32, explains, the use of this term introduces, "many of the ambiguities of textual narrative discourse, ambiguities which may be confirmed or contradicted by our visual approach to the images."

[23] Alison Bechdel, "An Interview with Alison Bechdel," interview by Hillary Chute, *MFS Modern Fiction Studies* 52.4 (2006): 1007.

[24] Bechdel, "An Interview with Alison Bechdel," interview by Hillary Chute, 1007.

[25] Bechdel, *Fun Home*, 101.

[26] Bechdel, *Fun Home*, 15.

[27] Bechdel, *Fun Home*, n.p.

[28] Bechdel, *Fun Home*, 47.

[29] Bechdel, *Fun Home*, 47.

[30] Hillary Chute, *Graphic Women: Life Narrative and Contemporary Comics* (New York: Columbia University Press, 2010), 182.

[31] Bechdel, "An Interview with Alison Bechdel," interview by Hillary Chute, 1005.

[32] Jacques Derrida, *Archive Fever: A Freudian Impression*, trans. Eric Prenowitz. (Chicago: University of Chicago Press, 1996).

[33] Bechdel, *Fun Home*, 141.

[34] Bechdel, "An Interview with Alison Bechdel," interview by Hillary Chute, 1011.

[35] Bechdel, *Fun Home*, 12.

[36] Bechdel, *Fun Home*, 21.

[37] Bechdel, *Fun Home*, 74.

[38] Bechdel, *Fun Home*, 210.

[39] Spiegelman, *In the Shadow of No Towers*, n.p.

[40] Spiegelman, *In the Shadow of No Towers*, 8.

[41] Spiegelman, *In the Shadow of No Towers*, 8, emphasis in the original.

[42] Spiegelman, *In the Shadow of No Towers*, 4.

[43] Spiegelman, *In the Shadow of No Towers*, 7.

[44] Spiegelman, *MetaMaus*, 30.

[45] Spiegelman, *MetaMaus*, 30.
[46] Dori Laub and Shoshana Felman, *Testimony: Crises of Witnessing in Literature, Psychoanalysis, and History* (New York: Routledge, 1992), 62.
[47] DeKoven and Chute, "Introduction: Graphic Narrative," 767.
[48] Hillary Chute, *Graphic Women: Life Narrative and Contemporary Comics* (New York: Columbia University Press, 2010), 11.
[49] Astrid Erll and Anne Rigney, eds., *Mediation, Remediation and the Dynamics of Cultural Memory* (Berlin: Walter de Gruyter, 2009), 4.
[50] Erll and Rigney, *Mediation, Remediation and the Dynamics of Cultural Memory*, 4.

THE TRANSGRESSIVE MOURNER IN JOAN DIDION'S *THE YEAR OF MAGICAL THINKING* (2005) AND *BLUE NIGHTS* (2011), AND JOYCE CAROL OATES'S *A WIDOW'S STORY* (2011)

MIHAELA PRECUP

In a recent review of *The Inevitable: Contemporary Writers Confront Death* (2011), edited by David Shields and Bradford Morrow, Colin Dickey notes that in present-day United States, mourners are "people who do not want to be seen mourning."[1] He also takes issue with the unconvincing translation of grief in the short pieces included in *The Inevitable*, some of which are penned by contemporary authors—such as Mark Doty, Joyce Carol Oates or Jonathan Safran Foer—well-known for expressing themselves on loss and mourning,

> If these writers weep, they simultaneously try to hide it from us, as though it would be unseemly (…). There's an artfulness here that's impressive, though it seems to work as a defense against any risk or feeling, and the polish of these pieces echoes the polish on a granite monument, as if desperate to hide the real fact of death buried somewhere far below. The essays here are eloquent reflections on grief, but they are not grief itself.[2]

What the reviewer finds upsetting is not the suspected absence of grief, but rather these authors' reluctance to show the full extent of private grief in their rather "polished" public writings. He thus gestures at two important social expectations, i.e. the invisibility of the dead and the creative transformation of raw private grief into a palatable public version of itself. The fact that the mourner has internalized the obligation of avoiding manifestations of grief that are too visible is not actually a new feature of contemporary mourning in America, nor is Dickey the first to articulate it, but it seems that it is starting to become central to what appears to be a new public debate about mourning that has been shaping up during the past two decades, following the surge of autobiographical writings about trauma in the 1990s. I am starting this chapter from Dickey's observations because I believe they do signal a significant lack of patience with current expectations of private and public mourning, among which a few stand out: the paradoxical expectation that professional writers should not be too "eloquent" when it comes to grief, the proposal that no expression of grief should be acceptable if it does not mimic the rawness of fresh (not past or lingering) grief, and finally the expectation that these authors are responsible for adequately expressing and preferably amending the whole white Western culture of mourning.

In what follows, I am going to examine these and other negotiations with normative ways of mourning performed in three recent best-selling American memoirs: Joan Didion's *The Year of Magical Thinking* (2005) and *Blue Nights* (2011), and Joyce Carol Oates's *A Widow's Story* (2011). All of these accounts are constructed by their authors as works of mourning for recently departed family members, and they all have at some point or another become part of heated public debates on the adequacy of the performances of mourning expressed therein. Joan Didion writes about the sudden death of her husband, writer John Dunne, followed almost two years later by the death of their adoptive daughter, Quintana, after a series of illnesses. Joyce Carol Oates mourns the unexpected death of her husband, publisher Ray Smith, in a work that sometimes reads like a manual and at other times, like a draft or a scrapbook, and also contains diary excerpts and e-mails exchanged by the author and her acquaintances around her husband's death.

I begin by attempting to briefly circumscribe the social "limits of mourning"[3] these authors negotiate; I argue that these are complicated by their peculiar autobiographical position as professional authors performing personal grief publicly while struggling to remain outside the feared but loosely defined state of pathological mourning. In the second part of the chapter, I am looking at the public response to these three books as it can be read in online reviews and "comments" sections of very popular reader-oriented websites of both widely-read publications such as *The New York Times* and *The Guardian*, and niche websites focused on addiction and loss (such www.thefix.com) but mainly the very rich "comments" section on www.amazon.com. In the last part of my chapter I examine how these memoirs amend contemporary norms of mourning, more specifically their proposal that it is necessary to identify and cultivate a specific post-traumatic way of looking where the invisibility of the dead may be combated and where mourning does not have to be a process with a certain number of prescribed stages and a compulsory end-point in sight. My purpose is to both test the theory that mourning-related grief has been sanitized and included in a model of hygienic mourning, and to see if these memoirs manage to contribute to the construction of a new and usable model of mourning. In doing so, I will be in conversation with contemporary trauma and autobiography theorists such as Cathy Caruth and Leigh Gilmore, practicing psychoanalysts who rely on their experience working with mourners, like Ilany Kogan and Darian Leader,[4] but also researchers interested in the way mourning practices are shifting in the Western world and across cultures, like Philippe Ariès.

The Limits of Mourning

Any cursory examination of the staple psychoanalytical literature on mourning (which in the Western world is inevitably in conversation with Freud's "On Murder, Mourning, and Melancholia") will show that mourners are expected to perform their grief privately, on the one hand, but also inscribe that loss within the paradigm of public mourning their culture prescribes. While definitions of mourning may vary, many of them seem to thus converge around the fact that mourning is a period of public and private performances of grief following significant loss, and that public manifestations will cease after a socially sanctioned time period has passed. The cessation of public grief should be a fairly adequate translation of the end of private grief, a process that must take place should the subject not wish to fall prey to melancholia/depression/pathological mourning. What is not at all clear in the literature is how one may identify and label the official end of mourning; the consensus is that it has to either end or become pathological. However, as I will be showing at some length in the second part of my chapter, should mourning end earlier than scheduled, the mourner may be suspected of lacking either some poorly defined universal measure of "humanity" or genuine affection for the dead.

The question of healing is specifically relevant in the field of practicing psychiatry. In his 2008 study of mourning that contains many examples from his own practice, *The New Black. Mourning, Melancholia, and Depression*, Darien Leader bemoans the shortage of literature on mourning and melancholia and justifies it through the popularity of the relatively new term "depression," a favorite with both the public and the pharmaceutical companies, whom Leader openly accuses of contributing to creating and feeding the fuel of this particular ailment. Leader thus convincingly expresses the frustration of a large number of patients in an over-medicalized psychiatric system. While he is against the well-worn five-stage process of mourning,[5] Leader's work is also prescriptive, as he proposes four necessary steps of the work of mourning that can enable the subject to stave off melancholia. Leader identifies four processes that indicate that the subject is engaged in the process of mourning, a process that does not follow automatically and may sometimes not even take place, leaving the subject forever susceptible to melancholia. These four elements are: "the introduction of a frame to work out a symbolic, artificial space, the necessity of killing the dead, the constitution of the object – involving the separation of the image of the loved one and the place they occupied for us – and the giving up of the image of who we were for them."[6] Even though he starts by claiming that it is wrong to expect the "working-through" to be a close-ended process, then he quotes psychoanalyst Margaret Little's pronouncement, "Mourning is for life,"[7] and even notes Freud's hesitations on the subject, Leader does finally prescribe a symbolic killing of the dead in order for the mourner to be able to successfully complete the process. This is his solution to the mourner's difficult positioning between, on the one hand, the prescriptions of the medical profession that tell them that depression must be staved off with a pill, and the instruments of a "vast industry of remembering"[8] that encourage people in the Western world to keep the dead close.[9] His book displays an understandable hesitation between the attempt to demonstrate that mourning need not be a regimen of pills and psychological work-out that finally results in a healthy mind and body, and the necessity of providing a working frame of reference for fellow psychiatrists and their patients.

Although practicing psychiatrists are interested in drawing a line between mourning and melancholia, and encourage a reading of mourning as a process that ends, it may be tempting for theoreticians and political activists to contemplate and perhaps even excitedly applaud the mimicking of trauma in writing,[10] the fragmentation of discourse, the debris on the page that lies there as proof that language can only reveal how insufficient it has always been in the face of trauma. Also, even if it is difficult to gauge the productivity of the imperative that mourning should end with specific results and after a standard time period,[11] it is equally problematic to embrace a rhetoric that idealizes melancholy or endless mourning. For instance, in an article about the specific idealization of melancholy in Scott Fitzgerald's *The Great Gatsby*, Greg Forter draws attention to the dangers of the proposition that phenomena such as the AIDS crisis should generate endless mourning, so that the dead may not be forgotten and any similar future crises may be averted. Forter refers to writings by Michael Moon, Philip Novak, and José Muñoz,[12] and suggests that,

> those analyses are strangely out of touch with the *affect* of melancholia. Freud is interested in this condition *because it is characterized by numbed disconnection and a self-loathing whose logical conclusion is suicide*. To make this condition a basis for political solidarity is to substitute elegant theorizing for actual, lived experience in a way that encourages a collective self-hatred whose progressive implications are far from clear.[13]

Forter thus draws attention to the fragile relationship between traumatic personal experience and theory, as well as the subsequent replication of the social mechanisms of exclusion and invisibility of the same marginalized groups the theory was supposed to support.

Closely connected to the issue of post-traumatic healing is the manifestation of a certain anxiety of sincerity felt by the survivor and stemming not only from the sentiment that by the mere fact of surviving one has abandoned the dead, but also from the truth-telling conventions of autobiography. In *The Limits of Autobiography. Trauma and Testimony*, Leigh Gilmore notes that it may be more productive to write about personal trauma by testing the "limits" of autobiography, particularly if one is to achieve a successful "working through." The reason for this lies in the strictness of the rules of autobiographical writing, particularly "its almost legalistic definition of truth-telling, its anxiety about invention, and its preference for the literal and verifiable."[14] These strictures and expectations created by autobiographical writing may impose "silencing or shaming effects,"[15] as well as legal consequences. Gilmore's observation is particularly valuable in the case of the memoirs I am looking at here, even if, in this case, the danger of being sued for one's comments is practically null; there are other conventions of truth-telling that police these narratives, and they are as solid as a notarized contract.[16]

The Transgressive Mourner

Joan Didon's *The Year of Magical Thinking* (2006) and Joyce Carol Oates's *A Widow's Story* (2011) have been discussed together previously both in widely-read and well-respected publications such as *The New York Times*, *Slate* and *The New Yorker*, as well as in lesser known online journals. *Blue Nights* appeared the same year as *A Widow's Story*, but reviewers did not generally connect the two; rather, *Blue Nights* was constantly set against Didion's previous memoir. The two authors are also clearly not unaware of the other's published works of mourning, and Oates even states in an interview with Deborah Solomon for *The New York Times*, on her collection of short stories, *Dear Husband* (2009), that it was at the time her intention to write a book very different from Didion's "beautiful and elegiac" *Year of Magical Thinking*.[17] Rather—she claims, in what reads like a peevish remark directed at Didion—that she would rather produce a volume "filled with all sorts of slapstick, demeaning and humiliating things."[18] Oates says that she thinks Didion "took it on a very high plane" and that "she [Didion] does have assistants and maybe a maid," which is why Didion's book does not convey the fact that mourning is "a very hardscrabble experience."[19] In this comment,

Oates displays a competitiveness of suffering that appears to be the source of much of the criticism she herself receives from her amazon.com reviewers, who also similarly compare their own traumas to the author's.

In what follows, I will be looking mainly at the online "comments" section of the previously mentioned newspapers and magazines, as well as the very productive review section of amazon.com in order to set some of the norms of mourning discussed in the first part of this chapter against actual readers' responses. I believe that these generally carefully worded online reviews provide invaluable and immediate insight into what expectations this segment of the public has of this particular autobiographical sub-genre, and what public performance of mourning it deems adequate. Based on their online aliases and brief self-descriptions, I would identify the majority of these readers as part of a college-educated middle-class, many of them already familiar with or even fans of the work of authors like Oates and Didion. Apart from the obvious number of people who say they bought the books randomly, it is also possible to identify an important sub-category that includes mourners who were perhaps not familiar with the previous work of these writers and who claim they bought the books either because they were recommended to them by their therapists or because they were themselves actively looking for texts that would confirm their own expressions of grief and/or teach them how to move past the initial stages of mourning.[20]

All the three books I am discussing here—although generally positively reviewed—also receive substantial negative feedback that is, quite tellingly, considering the apparent difference, both in subject and in style, sometimes identically worded, and finally coalesces as a complicated list of common transgressions. These—for the purpose of this chapter—can be placed in several broad categories: a) the transgression against the conventions of autobiographical **truth-telling** through the omission of important facts that the readers discovered on their own; b) the related transgression against the conventions that predicate **sincerity of feeling** for the dead both during and after life; c) the transgression against the appropriate **duration** of said feelings; and d) the transgression against the implied promise that the memoir will provide a usable **model of grief**. In what follows, I shall briefly examine all these transgressions against the text of the memoirs.

The quite heated online debate on truth-telling in Oates and Didion's memoirs gained momentum with Janet Maslin and Julian Barnes's respective reviews of Joyce Carol Oates's *A Widow's Story*. Published in 2011, the book is composed primarily of diary excerpts from February-August 2008; in February, Ray Smith, Oates's husband of forty-seven years, had died suddenly from a hospital-acquired infection following a bout of pneumonia. In a book that chooses to document only the first six months of mourning,

Oates also includes a few retrospective sections on their meeting, marriage, and life together, as well as "how to" sections for the general use of widows, alongside reproductions of e-mails and letters. However, she fails to mention that she had met another man six months after her husband's death, and that she remarried within a year.[21] Janet Maslin pulls no punches as she savagely criticizes Oates, claiming that the book dissembles, "while masquerading as a work of raw courage and honesty,"[22] while Julian Barnes, though perhaps more moderate in tone, still implies that the author should have mentioned her new marriage more openly, as well as discussed the difficult matter of the betrayal of the dead.[23]

In her response to Barnes, Oates shows substantial knowledge of the norms of mourning and autobiography she is accused to have broken. She says that, while hoping she will not be deemed "disingenuous,"[24] she did not think her "personal history in the aftermath of early widowhood was so relevant to the subject."[25] She also brings up her decision of mixing several genres in the book as an argument in favor of her omission when she claims that the book "is perhaps 98 per cent journal entries with only two or three conventionally composed chapters, to provide marital background," and that, "it was not meant to be an autobiographical work, which would include many, many developments in the memoirist's life subsequent to the early experience of widowhood."[26] However, she also concedes that it would probably have been a good idea if she had included some mention of her second marriage, to placate reviewers whom she accuses of resenting "that the memoirist is less miserable at the time of the writing."[27] This is a quick stab at Barnes and other reviewers who more or less openly accused her of holding back facts, she implies, not because they genuinely wanted her to abide by the truth-telling rules of autobiography but because they themselves adhered to a model of endless mourning, taking her to task for having survived grief. It is quite an efficient strategy, which shows Oates is well aware of mainstream expectations of widowhood and how she may negotiate them in her favor. However, her various musings from *A Widow's Story* about the pact of truth-telling in autobiography contradict the assumption that she is confined to the conventional temporal limits of the diary, "In writing this [a few words about Ray's relationship with his father], I feel that I am betraying Ray. Yet in not writing it I am not being altogether honest. There is no purpose to a memoir, if it isn't honest."[28] It is perhaps this sort of comment that gives readers license to see Oates's book as straying from its own purported honesty.

Oates pits the supposedly restrictive limits of the term "autobiographical work" (used here too generally) against what she claims are the even narrower limits of the "diary."[29] In spite of this, most readers' responses show that Oates's attempt at separating between the diary and the memoir cannot work for them mainly because the public often reads them both as "equally" autobiographical texts, with the same implied promise of disclosure. Rather, the readers' reviews that touch on this subject confirm Leigh Gilmore's comments on the limits of autobiography that leave the author exposed to accusations stemming from their understanding of the genre as a genre that allows readers to hold the writer accountable, as Barnes puts it, "for breach of narrative promise."[30]

Thus, most readers' comments[31] on Oates's omission tend to agree that she should have mentioned her new marriage in a direct manner, and not, as she did, by slipping in an oblique reference to someone new sitting next to her at a party near the end of the book. Within this more general common point, there are variations that show the specifics of various groups' expectations. For instance, "AlsoaWidow" comments on Janet Todd's review from *The Guardian* by questioning the advisability of current norms of swift healing, "I know 'moving on' is the vogue word, but after just six months? (…) How can it be that someone who professes to have suffered such a loss, can let it go after six months? I became a widow over three years ago, but for me it's as if it were last week…" A response to the previous comment simply states that people grieve differently ("edieinberlin"), or that Oates is in her seventies, and so she could not be expected to have waited longer than she did ("Ursa"), while others label Oates as "facilely prolix" ("EFW48") and even question the sincerity of the emotions expressed in the book. Perhaps the most fascinating response to this particular discussion topic takes Janet Todd to task for having divulged—albeit good-humoredly—the fact that Oates had remarried the mystery man fleetingly mentioned in one of the last pages of the book, thus spoiling the surprise, "Plot may not be the central element of memoirs, but the selective chronology of significant events allows the writer to underline their significance (…). I don't know why you found it necessary to spoil her odyssey for the rest of us by spilling this very telling detail of its conclusion?" ("tiggyt"). This comment shows that Oates's second marriage was not so widely advertised outside academic and literary circles as to enter public consciousness—in fact, many other online reviewers claimed they were quite surprised by the fact that Oates had remarried. What is interesting here is that Janet Todd is blamed for what is in fact Oates's omission, the implication being that perhaps it was poetic license, something any author is entitled to, even in a memoir.

Joan Didion is not taken to task, however, for a similarly important omission, i.e. failing to mention her daughter Quintana's death in the book dedicated to her examination of the year following her husband's own death. *The Year of Magical Thinking* is largely criticized for other reasons, with only a minority of readers objecting to not having been given more information about John Dunne's age and medical history, as well as Quintana's adoption. Instead, the large majority of the commentators are people who begin by recounting their own losses, and refer to a stage in their own process of mourning they identify as "magical thinking," during which they waited for the return of their loved ones, much as Didion notes she did when her husband died. Few take issue with the fact that by the end of the book she does not mention Quintana's death, possibly because they had not yet found out about it and because *Blue Nights* is seen as a book that addresses that specific omission. Julian Barnes also notes this other "strange parallel" between *The Year of Magical Thinking* and *A Widow's Story*,

> In Didion's case, the death of her daughter Quintana (which the author deals with in a subsequent edition); in Oates's, her remarriage to a neuroscientist, whose existence is hinted at rather coyly on the last page. You could argue that those writing about grief make their own literary terms more than most; but even so, in Oates's case there is something unhappy in the omission.[32]

It thus appears that treating the death of a spouse and the death of a child in two separate works of mourning is more socially acceptable than neatly separating between the death of a spouse and a remarriage. In a sense, Oates's omission is perceived as relevant for the readers who constantly attempt to measure—however imprecisely—the sincerity of the author's suffering. Didion's *The Year of Magical Thinking* is perhaps just as problematic for readers in terms of the quality of the sentiment of grief she is attempting to convey. That the authorial voice is "cold"/"distant"/"detached" comes first on the list of problems readers have had with the book; that it is a "boring" volume full of unnecessary data on grief and mourning is the second one; that it is a "self-involved" account full of snobbish name- and place-dropping, the third. All this contributes towards a construction, by people who gave the book one, two, and even three stars on Amazon, of the image of an inadequate mourner who either does not feel appropriately sad or has failed to convey the veracity of her feelings. The negative comments (on both Oates and Didion) voice an expectation that the narrator be a functional, articulate, but inconsolable mourner whose "redemption narrative" (as Leigh Gilmore calls this genre)[33] ends after an appropriate period of distraction, and who builds a comprehensive portrait of her dead while at the same time omitting matters that the dead person was keeping secret. In this respect, both Oates and Didion are chastised for not building comprehensive portraits of Ray Smith, John Dunne, and Quintana, respectively. It is true that Didion devotes much more time to Quintana's behavior as a child, detailing her favorite sayings and quirks, but chooses not to show readers who she had become as a young woman. Similarly, Oates's portrait of Ray Smith does little to acquaint the reader with him, so that by the end of the book his figure has dissolved behind Oates's much more comprehensively and frequently described bouts of "derangement," as she puts it.

However, the Joan Didion omission commentators focus on in their defense of the dead and (implied or open) accusation of indifference directed at the survivors is that the author did not more directly address Quintana's health problems—more specifically, her apparent alcoholism. In other words, Didion is accused of not having taken the social dimension of her book more seriously, and choosing instead to keep her memoir confined to personal suffering. In an article entitled "Did Alcoholism Kill Joan Didion's Daughter?," Jenna Sauers claims that one can understand that Didion may be "in denial" about how alcoholism caused the acute pancreatitis that killed Quintana after multiple hospitalizations that started with the flu (that Didion, according to Sauers, claimed was bird flu). At the same time, Sauers takes Didion to task not "as a mother," but "as an author" for failing to see or point out her daughter's alcoholism. She also refers to a previous article from thefix.com, a website on "addiction and recovery," where blogger Jennifer Matesa says that it is possible Quintana's "borderline personality disorder" and other mental problems were in fact caused by excessive drinking and not the other way round,[34] as Didion claims in *Blue Nights*, when she refers to "self-medication" through drinking as a valid solution to anxiety,

> She was depressed. She was anxious. Because she was depressed and because she was anxious she drank too much. This was called medicating herself. Alcohol has its own well-known defects as a medication for depression but no one has ever suggested—ask any doctor—that it is not the most effective anti-anxiety agent yet known.[35]

That alcohol helps people suffering from anxiety is, granted, a problematic statement, as well as an inaccurate theory, as Matesa herself points out. However, what Didion is really taken to task for here is, in fact, her untruthfulness, as well as her adequacy as a parent.[36]

Another sensitive matter Didion does address but is still accused of omitting—as she is perceived not to have devoted enough time to it—is Quintana's difficult position as an adopted child who displays signs of stress and fear of abandonment and who, later in life, as was indeed her case, may have to deal with the consequences of her birth parents seeking her out. Again, many readers' comments suggest that their main complaint is that Didion does not address the matter enough, or that she does not take her daughter's early manifestations of anxiety seriously enough. Thus, Didion's customarily straightforward recapitulation of what mistakes she may have made as a mother seems to have struck a nerve with some and she was promptly labeled a bad mother who only wanted "a child as an accessory and refused to deal with her issues because they were both an inconvenience and intellectually uninteresting to her" ("Sara Cotellese" in a comment on the Van Meter interview). Moreover, several commentators take issue with the word "perfect," used repeatedly by Didion in reference to their newly adopted baby,

> (…) I mention Saigon at all only by way of suggesting the extent of my misconceptions about what having a child, let alone adopting one, might actually entail.
>
> How could I not have had misconceptions?
>
> I had been handed this perfect baby, out of the blue, at St. John's Hospital in Santa Monica. She could not have been more exactly the baby I wanted. In the first place she was beautiful. *Hermosa, chula*. Strangers stopped me on the street to tell me so. 'I have a beautiful baby girl at St. John's,' Blake Watson had said, and he did.[37]

While the tone in the passage above is not disappointed or accusatory, as the commentators imply (in the sense that Quintana, the "perfect baby" ended up disappointing her parents through her illness), Didion unfortunately falls into a difficult cliché scenario here, one she could perhaps have been more wary of, as it can be easily read by some as the privileged position of a rich white lady whose doctor friend finds her an unbroken baby that ends up malfunctioning in the end.

When it comes to the appropriate duration of mourning, Didion's standard one-year of "magical thinking" for her husband satisfies the social expectations of all readers. Also, no readers seem keen on critiquing Didion's apparent decision to mourn indefinitely for Quintana, and nobody worries about the possibility that she might slip into the pathological and/or become melancholy. However, Oates's six months of mourning for Ray Smith, after which she meets someone else, are deemed insufficient by those who address this matter. It thus appears that, based on the data provided by Amazon readers, memoirs of mourning are expected to either abide by the one-year deadline common to many Western cultures or transgress against it by prolonging, rather than shortening it.

Underlying these various criticisms for autobiographical *faux pas* is the implication that they all contribute to the memoir not working as an efficient self-help book in the reader's hour of need. Thus, another consequence of Oates's peculiar authorial position and decision to insert a manual for widows in her book is that she thus spells out and draws attention to the old paradox of autobiography, i.e. that it both testifies to private experience and may propose it as a model. Offering a "handbook" to the widow means that every now and then Oates refers to herself as "the wife" and Raymond Smith as "the husband," a conceit that is randomly applied and has the unfortunate effect of muddling the readers' expectations, some of which contradict one another. Within the confines of a difficult genre where one does not attempt to dictate norms of mourning unless at least a sufficient number of studies have been performed, Oates seems to imply that it is possible to universalize her own specific experience, something that insults those who feel their own suffering is unique and frustrates those who were hoping for more autobiographical detail about the late Ray Smith and their marriage. What makes matters worse is that apparently Smith is attempting to universalize an experience which is that of a woman who was involved in a very traditional marriage, where as a bride younger than her husband she never dared ask him personal questions, and where she felt that, because her husband had read almost nothing of her fiction, there were significant parts of her to which he had no access.

Joan Didion, on the other hand, upsets readers by attempting to define and organize the experience, although she never goes so far as to say that she is proposing a model of mourning. A minor example is that, apart from quoting from C. S. Lewis, Philippe Ariès, and Emily Post, at some point she differentiates between grief and mourning, "Grief was passive. Grief happened. Mourning, the act of dealing with grief, required attention."[38] This effort of documentation and classification has made many readers complain that the book is "contrived"/"artificial"/"dull"/"elitist," although "boring" is actually the most frequent adjective readers use. While Didion's effort seems to be part of the already defeated attempt to assign meaning to trauma, she does not claim to speak for all widows, like Oates.

Conclusions

The memoirs of mourning I have been discussing here are generally disconnected from both complicated legal situations and wider political struggles, written as they are by white affluent women who are well-respected in the literary community. Their narratives of suffering are embedded in personal narratives of professional and financial success, instead of, say, a specific political struggle such as the AIDS crisis. From this perspective, they come closer to—although they cannot be included in—what Leigh Gilmore identifies as "the neoconfessional memoir" in America, a category that, through its sellable narrative of non-political oppression and redemption, obfuscates autobiographical discourses about social inequalities and instead promotes "an increasingly non-specific and generic self."[39] Thus, when *New York Times* reviewer Janet Maslin matter-of-factly—or perhaps some would say cynically—identified an "increasingly lucrative loss-of-spouse market,"[40] she might as well have widened the circle to include a more general growing market of "memoirs of mourning" penned by a certain segment of the white wealthy college-educated American population. However, the matter becomes more complicated here because the books I am examining are written by already widely-read public persons, thus contributing to the formation and/or consolidation of how mourning is read by communities outside the narrow segment to which their authors belong. Still, these samples of suffering uncomplicated by social marginalization and discrimination do not seem to enable their authors to dictate norms of mourning, but rather render them vulnerable to a wide array of criticisms, as well as a certain measure of trivialization of the grief expressed therein.

I believe it is quite telling that several important episodes in Didion's and Oates's books do not seem to upset any of the many readers who took the time to leave their feedback on amazon.com or the websites of the other publications I mentioned before. I am referring to those moments when Oates and Didion actively seek a solution for an impossible conundrum—how to bring back the dead. One would have expected stronger reactions on the part of readers to the fact that these three books seem to suggest (in bits and pieces, fleeting moments, sometimes regretted later) that it is possible or even advisable to discover a new regime of visuality wherein the presence of the dead becomes possible again. This type of logic—which has Didion apologetically keep her husband's shoes, for instance, because he would need them when he came back—is not sanctioned by the psychoanalytic narrative of healing that sees healthy mourning as a process with a beginning and an end. It is inside this type of logic of impossible return that the separation between the living and the dead becomes smaller. The audience is quite lenient on this score, perhaps also because this type of "magical thinking," as Didion puts it, is also attributed by both authors to the distraction brought about by grief.

In his 1974 *Western Attitudes toward Death*, Philippe Ariès claimed that, in the US, excessive mourning had become shameful. However, the rise of "popular trauma culture"[41] during the past three decades points to a new development. Based on the corpus of readers' responses I have looked at in this chapter, the public expectations of contemporary mourning are focused on the expression of a satisfactory level of suffering and disclosure, both included in a temporal framework that is long enough to provide a narrative of suffering and redemption. I find it significant that readers do not even signal Didion's and Oates's scattered proposals in favor of the cultivation of a state of ongoing mourning, a performative process that relies on the detective gaze of the mourner, a creative line of defense against pathological grief, and the introduction of new—and private—rituals of mourning.[42] This omission on the part of otherwise keenly critical readers—who are instead quick to judge the premature end of mourning—also shows that recent developments in mourning cultures in the US suggest that the separation between the dead and the living is no longer regarded as non-negotiable. Instead, it is seen as something that can be fought—with little risk of social stigmatization—through the work of memory, imagination, and private rituals of mourning.

Author's Note

A version of this chapter was first presented at the 2012 annual BAAS conference, organized by The University of Manchester. Research for this chapter was made possible by a PN-II-RU-TE-2011-3-0149 grant for the research project Cross-*Cultural Encounters in American Trauma Narratives: A Comparative Approach to Personal and Collective Memories*; project coordinator: Assoc. Prof. Roxana Elena Oltean; funded by the National University Research Council of Romania (NURC).

Bibliography

Ariès, Philippe. *Western Attitudes toward Death: From the Middle Ages to the Present*. London: Marion Boyars, 1976.

Barnes, Julian. "'For Sorrow There Is No Remedy.'" Review of *A Widow's Story*, by Joyce Carol Oates. *The New York Review of Books*, April 7, 2011. Accessed July 10, 2012. http://www.nybooks.com/articles/archives/2011/apr/07/sorrow-there-no-remedy/.

Caruth, Cathy. *Unclaimed Experience: Trauma, Narrative, and History*. Baltimore: Johns Hopkins University Press, 1996.

Dickey, Colin. "Grief and Solemnity. On the American Way of Death." Review of *The Inevitable: Contemporary Writers Confront Death*, edited by David Shields and Bradford Morrow. *Los Angeles Review of Books*, November 27, 2012. http://lareviewofbooks.org/post/13399515766/grief-and-solemnity.

Didion, Joan. *The Year of Magical Thinking*. New York: A.A. Knopf, 2005.

—. "Joan Didion on Losing Husband John Dunne and Daughter Quintana Roo." By Jonathan Van Meter. *New York Magazine*, October 2, 2005. Accessed September 5, 2012. http://nymag.com/nymetro/arts/books/14633/.

—. *Blue Nights*. New York: Alfred A. Knopf, 2011.

Forter, Greg. "Against Melancholia: Contemporary Mourning Theory, Fitzgerald's *The Great Gatsby*, and the Politics of Unfinished Grief." *Differences: A Journal of Feminist Cultural Studies* 14.2 (Summer 2003): 134-70.

Freud, Sigmund. "On Murder, Mourning, and Melancholia." In *On Murder, Mourning, and Melancholia*, 201-18. London: Penguin, 2005.

Gilmore, Leigh. *The Limits of Autobiography: Trauma and Testimony*. Ithaca, NY: Cornell University Press, 2001.

—. "American Neoconfessional: Memoir, Self-Help, and Redemption on Oprah's Couch." *Biography* 33.4 (Fall 2010): 657-79.

Kogan, Ilany. *The Struggle against Mourning*. Lanham: Jason Aronson, 2007.

Leader, Darian. *The New Black: Mourning, Melancholia, and Depression*. Minneapolis, MN: Graywolf, 2009.

Maslin, Janet. "The Shock of Losing a Spouse." Review of *A Widow's Story*, by Joyce Carol Oates. *The New York Times*, February 13, 2011. http://www.nytimes.com/2011/02/14/books/14book.html.

Matesa, Jennifer. "Is Joan Didion in Denial about Her Daughter's Alcoholism?" *The Fix,* August 12, 2011. Accessed September 5, 2012. http://www.thefix.com/content/Joan-didion-quintana-roo-blue%20nights-pancreatitis7033.

Moon, Michael. "Memorial Rags." In *Professions of Desire: Lesbian and Gay Studies in Literature*, edited by George E. Haggerty and Bonnie Zimmerman, 233-40. New York: Modern Language Association of America. 1995.

Muñoz, José Esteban. "Photographies of Mourning: Melancholia and Ambivalence in Van Der Zee, Mapplethorpe, and Looking for Langston." In *Race and the Subject of Masculinities*, edited by Harry Stecopoulos and Michael Uebel, 337-58. Durham: Duke University Press, 1997.

Novak, Philip. "'Circles and Circles of Sorrow': In the Wake of Morrison's *Sula*." *PMLA* 114 (1999): 184–93.

Oates, Joyce Carol. *A Widow's Story: A Memoir*. New York: Ecco, 2011.

—. "QUESTIONS FOR JOYCE CAROL OATES; A Woman's Work." By Deborah Solomon. *The New York Times*, April 12, 2009. http://www.nytimes.com/2009/04/12/magazine/12wwln-q4-t.html.

—. "'A Widow's Story' In Response To: 'For Sorrow There Is No Remedy' from the April 7, 2011 Issue." *The New York Review of Books*, May 26, 2011. Accessed January 18, 2014. http://www.nybooks.com/articles/archives/2011/may/26/widows-story/.

Rothe, Anne. *Popular Trauma Culture: Selling the Pain of Others in the Mass Media*. New Brunswick, NJ: Rutgers University Press, 2011.

Sauers, Jenna. "Did Alcoholism Kill Joan Didion's Daughter?." *Jezebel*, December 13, 2011. Accessed September 5, 2012. http://jezebel.com/5867725/did-alcoholism-killed-joan-didions-daughter.
Shields, David, and Bradford Morrow, eds. *The Inevitable: Contemporary Writers Confront Death*. New York: W. W. Norton & Company, 2011.
Todd, Janet. "*A Widow's Story*: A Memoir by Joyce Carol Oates." Review of *A Widow's Story*, by Joyce Carol Oates. *The Guardian*, March 18, 2011. Accessed September 5, 2012. http://www.theguardian.com/books/2011/mar/19/widows-story-joyce-carol-oates-review.
Whitehead, Anne. *Trauma Fiction*. Edinburgh: Edinburgh University Press, 2004.

Notes

[1] Dickey, Colin, "Grief and Solemnity. On the American Way of Death." Review of *The Inevitable: Contemporary Writers Confront Death*, eds. David Shields and Bradford Morrow. *Los Angeles Review of Books*, November 27, 2012, http://lareviewofbooks.org/post/13399515766/grief-and-solemnity.

[2] Dickey, "Grief and Solemnity. On the American Way of Death."

[3] This is a reference to Leigh Gilmore, *The Limits of Autobiography: Trauma and Testimony* (Ithaca, NY: Cornell University Press, 2001). I will be using Gilmore's comments on truth-telling and autobiography later in this chapter.

[4] I am particularly interested in including in my conversation the opinion of psychoanalysts like Kogan and Leader because I believe it may be the case that sometimes theoreticians who do not have to tackle the same problems as practicing psychoanalysts are less interested in the role memoirs of mourning play in the preservation of the quality of life of the mourner, and more excited by post-traumatic manifestations that may be interesting to analyze but are still deeply troubling for the subject who is the recipient and bearer of grief.

[5] The five stages of mourning, made popular through frequent quotations in the media (denial, anger, bargaining, depression and acceptance), are detailed in Elisabeth Kübler-Ross's *On Death and Dying*, first published in 1970.

[6] Darian Leader, *The New Black: Mourning, Melancholia, and Depression* (Minneapolis, MN: Graywolf, 2009), 168.

[7] Leader, *The New Black: Mourning, Melancholia, and Depression*, 98.

[8] Leader, *The New Black: Mourning, Melancholia, and Depression*, 118.

[9] Leader, *The New Black: Mourning, Melancholia, and Depression*, 142.

[10] Indeed, in her work on "trauma fiction," Anne Whitehead also observes that novelists working in this category (Benjamin Wilkomirski, Toni Morrison and W.G. Sebald, among others) have found it productive to mimic the symptoms of post-traumatic expression, mirroring the inadequacy of language that often results in repetition and indirect reference to events whose chronology is jumbled and missing various pieces.

[11] In some cultures, the staple period is one year, as also reflected in, for instance, the title of Joan Didion's *The Year of Magical Thinking*.
[12] Forter is here referencing three articles, Michael Moon's "Memorial Rags," Philip Novak's "Circles and Circles of Sorrow" and José E. Muñoz's "Photographies of Mourning: Melancholia and Ambivalence in Van Der Zee, Mapplethorpe, and *Looking for Langston*."
[13] Greg Forter, "Against Melancholia: Contemporary Mourning Theory, Fitzgerald's *The Great Gatsby*, and the Politics of Unfinished Grief," *Differences: A Journal of Feminist Cultural Studies* Summer 14.2 (2003): 139.
[14] Leigh Gilmore, *The Limits of Autobiography: Trauma and Testimony* (Ithaca, NY: Cornell University Press, 2001), 129.
[15] Gilmore, *The Limits of Autobiography: Trauma and Testimony*, 129.
[16] See Leigh Gilmore, "American Neoconfessional: Memoir, Self-Help, and Redemption on Oprah's Couch," *Biography* 33.4 (2010): 661. There, she notes that, "Compounding the confessional compact between reader and writer, and in fact reinforcing its confessional core, is the theoretical claim that the writer may be so bound and judged precisely because she or he has already assented to this quasi-juridical relation via the choice of genre (autobiography), and is now bound as if by contractual agreement. Legal contract and ethical relation reinforce each other within the confessional compact."
[17] Joyce Carol Oates, "QUESTIONS FOR JOYCE CAROL OATES; A Woman's Work," by Deborah Solomon, *The New York Times*, April 12, 2009, http://www.nytimes.com/2009/04/12/magazine/12wwln-q4-t.html.
[18] Oates, "QUESTIONS FOR JOYCE CAROL OATES; A Woman's Work," by Deborah Solomon.
[19] Oates, "QUESTIONS FOR JOYCE CAROL OATES; A Woman's Work," by Deborah Solomon.
[20] All the reviews are taken from amazon.com, where on the 31st of August 2012, *The Year of Magical Thinking* [paperback] had a total of 636 reviews (with an overall score of 3.8 out of 5), *Blue Nights* [paperback] had 108 reviews (with a score of 3.8 out of 5), and *A Widow's Story* [hardback] had 96 reviews (with a score of 4.1 out of 5).
[21] And this is perhaps the reason why Oates only includes an account of the first six months of mourning, although the social convention—confirmed by Didion's book about the death of her husband—would have dictated that she write about a whole year.
[22] Janet Maslin, "The Shock of Losing a Spouse," review of *A Widow's Story*, by Joyce Carol Oates, *The New York Times*, February 13, 2011, http://www.nytimes.com/2011/02/14/books/14book.html.
[23] Julian Barnes, "For Sorrow There Is No Remedy," review of *A Widow's Story. A Memoir*, by Joyce Carol Oates, *The New York Review of Books*, April 7, 2011, "'For Sorrow There Is No Remedy.'" *The New York Review of Books*. http://www.nybooks.com/articles/archives/2011/apr/07/sorrow-there-no-remedy/.
[24] Joyce Carol Oates, "'A Widow's Story' In Response To: 'For Sorrow There Is No Remedy' from the April 7, 2011 Issue," *The New York Review of Books*, May 26,

2011, accessed January 18, 2014, http://www.nybooks.com/articles/archives/2011/may/ 26/widows-story/.
[25] Oates, "'A Widow's Story' In Response To: 'For Sorrow There Is No Remedy' from the April 7, 2011 Issue."
[26] Oates, "'A Widow's Story' In Response To: 'For Sorrow There Is No Remedy' from the April 7, 2011 Issue."
[27] Oates, "'A Widow's Story' In Response To: 'For Sorrow There Is No Remedy' from the April 7, 2011 Issue."
[28] Oates, *A Widow's Story: A Memoir* (New York: Ecco, 2011), 365.
[29] She thus attempts to use the notoriously difficult generic classification of autobiographical texts to both insert letters, e-mails etc. in her "diary entries" and to justify the editorial decision of leaving out a specific element that would have only found its place in a text that would have examined the author's entire life, and not only the six months since her husband's death. It appears that Oates seems to be using the notoriously difficult positioning of autobiography within a specific genre to create a generic hodge-podge from behind whose shifting buttresses she defends her decision to remarry and not tell her audience.
[30] Barnes, "'For Sorrow There Is No Remedy.'"
[31] I have not made any changes to either the spelling or punctuations of the online comments I am quoting here.
[32] Barnes, "'For Sorrow There Is No Remedy.'"
[33] Gilmore, "American Neoconfessional: Memoir, Self-Help, and Redemption on Oprah's Couch."
[34] Jennifer Matesa, "Is Joan Didion in Denial about Her Daughter's Alcoholism?," *The Fix,* August 12, 2011, accessed September 5, 2012, http://www.thefix.com/content/Joan-didion-quintana-roo-blue%20nights-pancreatitis7033.
[35] Joan Didion, *Blue Nights* (New York: Alfred A. Knopf, 2011), 53.
[36] There were a lot of responses to Jenna Sauers's article, and most of them are classifiable into one of the following categories: a) the matter of Quintana's alcoholism is an important public, not private matter, since it appeared in a published document that was centered around her death; b) Didion does not owe the readers all the facts; c) this is a memoir, not journalism; d) it doesn't really matter, may Quintana rest in peace. Both Sauers and Matesa speak from a position where Didion's book on Quintana is inscribable—because of the nature of Quintana's illnesses—within a wider debate on mental illness and addiction that the author should have addressed. Matesa even suggests that it is possible Didion may have chosen to believe that her daughter's main problem was mental illness in order to avoid the more troubling social stigma of addiction.
[37] Didion, *Blue Nights*, 77.
[38] Joan Didion, *The Year of Magical Thinking* (New York: A.A. Knopf, 2005), 143.
[39] Leigh Gilmore, "American Neoconfessional: Memoir, Self-Help, and Redemption on Oprah's Couch," *Biography* 33.4 (2010): 658.
[40] Maslin, "The Shock of Losing a Spouse."
[41] See Anne Rothe, *Popular Trauma Culture: Selling the Pain of Others in the Mass Media* (New Brunswick, NJ: Rutgers University Press, 2011).

[42] While Darian Leader does mention creativity as an important premise for creating a community of grief where the members might be encouraged to express themselves by proxy (and even briefly discusses Didion's *The Year of Magical Thinking* as a useful example), he does not devote much time to how mourners themselves might become directly involved in creative activities that could protect them against melancholia. On the other hand, in the sixth chapter from her book *The Struggle against Mourning* (Lanham: Jason Aronson, 2007), psychoanalyst Ilany Kogan not only lists creativity among the defenses of the psyche against the potential destructiveness of mourning, but she sees it as a necessary developmental stage and a means of externalizing trauma. In this context, it is easier to read the disappointment of the readers discussed above, and whose experience of loss and grief was—in the absence of their own creative efforts—inadequately expressed by the creative energies of writers from whom they feel separated by social and financial status.

PART THREE:

COMMEMORATING TRAUMA, SHIFTING NATIONAL ICONS: MARGINAL AND MAINSTREAM PATHS OF REMEMBRANCE

Contemporary War Memorials and the Urban Landscape: The Memorialization of Marginalized Groups in Washington, D.C.

Emma Login

Recent attempts at a more inclusive approach to American history have resulted in greater emphasis on traumatic pasts which are perceived to have been marginalized or excluded, particularly in relation to conflicts. Increasingly, groups who believe that their conflict experiences have been marginalized or suppressed have spoken out against this exclusion. This chapter seeks to understand the ways in which these marginalized groups exert their claim on past conflict narratives through the urban environment, specifically through processes of war memorialization. It explores these memorial processes within the context of changing relationships with the past and examines the ways in which the processes of memorializing traumas experienced during conflict serve not only to commemorate the event itself but also as a method of defining and reinforcing each group in the present. It explores the multifaceted nature of the trauma experienced by such groups, which, although originating in conflict, is compounded by the trauma of subordination. Themes discussed below include how the memorials from these groups can be viewed as a response to existing memorials in Washington, D.C. and the ways in which internal group trauma is negotiated through the form of the memorial. The chapter seeks to demonstrate that it is in fact the *process* of memorialization, which itself allows for internal discussions within the group, that is of primary importance rather than the finished monument which can be continually interpreted and reinterpreted amongst group members.

These issues are discussed in relation to three contemporary memorials in Washington, D.C.: the African American Civil War Memorial, the Japanese American Memorial to Patriotism during World War II, and the American Indian Memorial Initiative. The African American Civil War Memorial, unveiled in 1997 on the corner of Vermont Avenue, commemorates the service of over 200,000 African American soldiers and sailors who fought for Union forces during the Civil War (Fig. 1). The Japanese American Memorial to Patriotism during World War II was unveiled in 2000 on the corner of Louisiana Avenue and D Street Northwest and has a dual purpose (Fig. 2). Whilst the memorial was originally intended to commemorate only the 800 Japanese American soldiers killed whilst fighting in the American military during World War II, refusal by the National Capital Memorial Commission to accept a military memorial which commemorated a single ethnic group necessitated a revision in the memorial's design and purpose. The memorial's goal was subsequently amended to encompass the entire Japanese American experience during World War II; including the internment of approximately 120,000 Japanese Americans, two-thirds of whom were full American citizens. Similarly, the American Indian Memorial Initiative originally began as a campaign to include a figure of an American Indian soldier on the Vietnam Veterans Memorial sculpture. Yet, as the campaign progressed it became clear that this would not be possible, and subsequently the proposal evolved into a separate memorial to incorporate the entire experience of American Indians in the US military, beginning with the Revolutionary Wars.

Fig. 1. African American Civil War Memorial (1997), Vermont Avenue, Washington, D.C., image courtesy of Hari Jones.

Fig. 2. National Japanese American Memorial to Patriotism during World War II (1997), image by Emma Login.

Increased Memorialization within the American Landscape

Historically the United States has had an uncomfortable relationship with the monument as memorial.[1] Despite this, recent memorialization has risen so dramatically that it has been described by some as "memorial mania."[2] Owing perhaps to the increased militarization of society and the greater importance given to the role of conflict in the history of the United States,[3] and triggered perhaps by the Vietnam Veterans Memorial (1982), greater emphasis is now being placed on historic experiences of conflict and their resulting traumas. Indeed, this "memorial mania" has been in no way restricted to the commemoration of conflicts within living memory; instead, the memory of conflicts dating back to the Revolutionary Wars has been re-evaluated and memorialized accordingly. Much of this memorialization has focused upon the nation's capital and, as a result, an increasing number of interest groups have campaigned to have their physical representation at the heart of the nation.[4] Yet, the memorials discussed in this chapter are not merely a reflection of a growing trend of memorialization, but should be seen as a response to changing relationships with the past.

Developments in historiography have resulted in greater account being taken of the ways in which the retelling of past events has involved the silencing of certain actions and actors.[5] No longer is a biased, insular view of the past, as dictated by a single dominant group perceived as either appropriate or acceptable. Increasingly, communities with a "stake in what is remembered, debate, challenge and contest which version of the past will be remembered."[6] Research has suggested that such marginalized groups are becoming ever more proficient at using the memory of past events to "challenge their own subordination."[7] In Washington, D.C., groups are increasingly willing to fight for representation within the national landscape. The past two decades have witnessed growing numbers of museums and heritage sites being dedicated to groups who feel that their experiences have, in the past, been deliberately marginalized from the national narrative. These include, for example, the Women in Military Service for America Memorial (1997), the National Museum of the American Indian (2004), the Martin Luther King, Jr. National Memorial (2011), and the forthcoming National Museum of African American History and Culture, in addition to the examples discussed in this chapter. By making their past more visible within the landscape of the nation's capital, these monuments and museums serve to physically embed a more diverse view of the past within the national narrative, counteracting each group's previous marginalization.

Increasingly, more holistic attitudes are taken towards historical, archaeological, and heritage approaches to the past.[8] Whilst heritage professionals have in the past been accused of the trivialization or appropriation of the concerns of minority scholars, activists and communities,[9] archaeology increasingly adopts a more inclusive approach both to the types of history being investigated, and also to the archaeological process itself.[10] Communities and descendants are increasingly involved in the planning of archaeological projects and have had significant input into their research designs, resulting in greater contributions towards the writing of their own histories.[11] Anna Agbe-Davies demonstrates the importance of this process, for both practitioners and the community, in her examination of concepts of community relating to inclusive archaeology. Agbe-Davies argues that "our ideas about *past* communities inform our interactions with people in the *present* day" and that this is especially so "when we conceive of these people as having some kind of link (historical, genealogical, cultural, geographic) with a past 'community.'"[12] Thus, perceptions of a group in the present can be based upon historical understandings of past contributions or *lack* of contributions to a particular event in the past, understandings which have been compounded by a selective historical process. Negative perceptions or misunderstandings of a particular group in the past can be detrimental to the understanding of that group in the present both by those outside the group and perhaps more importantly by its own members.

Misunderstandings of past experiences within the marginalized group can have a negative impact on the present-day identity of members of that group. Whilst the concept of identity has been disputed,[13] it is clear that many individuals do feel a connection to a distinct past, and as Pierre Nora suggests, for many minority groups "rehabilitating their past is part and parcel of reaffirming their identity."[14] There is, as a result, the perceived need to reinforce the identity of the group in the present, a process which is more frequently being carried out through the commemoration of the actions of that group in the past. Increasingly, groups are choosing to construct memorials to the past conflict experiences of this group in order to challenge negative perceptions of that group by both its own members and a wider audience. Yet, this process is problematic, as it must be carried out in a way which simultaneously reaffirms each group's distinct identity whilst also maintaining its inclusion within the wider narrative.

The incorporation of previously marginalized groups such as African Americans, Asian Americans, Irish Americans, American Indians, and women into the dominant white male conflict narrative is not at all an easy task, as their distinct identity is often seen as being at odds with a unified narrative. A jointly remembered past is often viewed as crucial for group cohesion on a national level.[15] Frequently, the original exclusion of the distinct identity of these groups represents a conscious decision to reframe the past in a way that is seen as beneficial in the present by reinforcing cohesive national narratives.[16] As Laurajane Smith and Emma Waterton discuss in their work on heritage, communities and archaeology, concepts of self-image and identification are often viewed as threats against this cohesion, as they do not fit with the image of a unified nation state.[17] This is particularly difficult when dealing with the incorporation of the memory of traumatic events experienced during conflict. As the memorialization process for the Vietnam Veterans Memorial demonstrated, attempts to collectively remember a shared past often create tensions between those directly affected by the trauma and defenders of a unified nation state.[18] This process is made even more complex by the added marginalization of groups; often, integrating their specific experience into the wider conflict narrative becomes problematic for both the dominant and the marginalized group.

The Complex Nature of Trauma

Before undertaking any discussion of the processes of memorialization carried out by these groups, it is necessary to briefly examine the nature of the traumatic experiences which they sought to commemorate. The varied nature of trauma experienced by each marginalized group and the difficulties of integrating these within a wider conflict narrative makes for a very problematic memorialization process. Michael Rothberg proposes that "one of the most agonizing problems of multicultural societies [is] how to think about the relationship between different social groups' histories of victimization."[19] African Americans, Japanese Americans and American Indians have all experienced victimization by European Americans resulting in a very specific experience during conflict, which will be discussed in more detail below. Discussion of these traumatic experiences is made difficult by the lack of discourse available for the particular conflict experiences of marginalized groups. As Stef Craps describes in his study of postcolonialism, trauma definitions have been constructed almost exclusively from the perspective of the dominant group which is predominately made up of "white, young, able-bodied, educated, middle-class, Christian men."[20] This has resulted in a lack of discussion of the very specific conflict traumas experienced by members of a marginalized group, and in a lack of public commemoration of these traumas.

Central to the difficulties encountered in the memorialization of marginalized groups is that the nature of trauma experienced by these groups actually takes two very different, although related, forms: 1. the experience of the conflict as an active participant in the US military, for example African American troops fighting for the Union during the Civil War or American Indian soldiers during Vietnam; 2. the experience of the conflict as a victim, such as African Americans enslaved by the Confederacy during the Civil War and Japanese Americans interned by the US government during World War II. Any commemoration or memorialization which seeks to engage both of these experiences will be necessarily difficult since, although related, the experiences can easily form dichotomic narratives which are difficult to reconcile. Commemoration of the active role of members of the marginalized group within the US military can be viewed as an attempt to show the contribution of that group towards the wider national narrative. By highlighting their shared experience with other, predominately white male combatants, each group can be viewed as integrating itself within the wider conflict narrative. Yet, commemorating the experience of the marginalized group as a victim necessarily defines that group as "other," separating it from the dominant group responsible for their persecution in order to secure that group's status as victim. Thus, a memorial which seeks to engage with the conflict experience of marginalized groups must overcome these dichotomic narratives.

This dichotomic division is, in some cases, potentially even more problematic as it can reflect conscious decisions undertaken at the time of the conflict. In particular, adult male members of the marginalized group were often required to decide between serving in the US military in order to demonstrate their loyalty to the nation, or to resist fighting on grounds of their persecution by the nation.[21] Amongst Japanese Americans for example, divisions within the community arose regarding responses to Executive Order 9066 and the resulting internment. Many went willingly to internment camps and many young males voluntarily joined the US military to demonstrate their loyalty. Others, however, viewed the internment as a great injustice, denying them their rights as citizens and undermining the constitution, and they sought ways to actively resist the process. Indeed, hundreds of third-generation Japanese American citizens resisted the draft on constitutional grounds, and were put in prison as a consequence. This resulted in a divide in the community between those who wished to demonstrate loyalty and integrate themselves within the United States, despite continued persecution on racial grounds, and those who sought to fight this persecution. This division, although originating at the time of the conflict, has been perpetuated to the present day, and continues to cause a divide. Whilst this type of divide is perhaps most pronounced in the American Indian community,[22] it is common to all groups discussed in this chapter and results in added difficulties for the processes of memorialization.

Yet, it is not just the historical legacy of the conflict trauma that must be addressed through the memorialization process, but each group's conflict trauma is amplified by their historic and continued experience of persecution based on racial grounds. I would suggest that continued racism, resulting in the exclusion of marginalized groups from broader commemorations of the conflict adds to the traumatic legacy of the conflict itself. As Stef Craps suggests, greater attention must be paid to the effects of "the kind of long term, cumulative trauma suffered by victims of racism or other forms of structural oppression."[23] The trauma of the original experience (either as active combatant or persecuted victim) is perpetuated by a lack of official recognition for that trauma. In his exploration of cinematic depictions of World War II, John Bodnar cites the 1949 film *Home of the Brave* in which the emotional distress of the central character is created not only by the combat itself but by the brutal racism experienced during both his military and civilian life. Bodnar describes the end of the film which sees the protagonist opening a bar with his friend and hints that, "the success of a postwar future will depend not only on putting the trauma behind us but on resolving racial inequality and prejudice as well.[24] I would suggest that greater account needs to be taken of the effects of such racism and subordination when examining the memory of the conflict experience of marginalized groups, both in terms of the group itself and in relation to the wider community.

Frequently, attempts at "resolving racial inequality" begin with calls for apologies for injustices carried out in the past.[25] In her support of historical apologies, Eleanor Fleming suggests that an apology for slavery is necessary as the legacy of slavery should be viewed as damaging to both African and European Americans as it was "a crime against humanity that violated the dignity of African slaves, and made a farce of America's experiment with democracy."[26] Whilst I agree that historical apologies do serve an important role in the present, I would argue that the processes of memorialization which are carried out by marginalized groups are less concerned with apologies from historic persecutors and that they engage instead with the internal dynamics of the group. After all, in the case of Japanese Americans, apologies and reparations have been made.[27] Yet this did not prevent the need for a tangible memorial to be created by the community itself. In fact, in all three memorials discussed here, it was of primary importance that the memorial was financed and designed by members of that community, and not by those outside as an act of apology.

Attempts have already been made to make the National Mall a space which represents all Americans. This has resulted in the inclusion of non-white American figures in the Vietnam Veterans Memorial Three Servicemen Statue, the Korean Veterans Memorial, and the National World War II Memorial. Yet this has not halted the progress of construction of memorials and museums to individual groups. Rothberg, in his examination of the memory of the Holocaust, questions what happens when different histories confront each other in the public sphere in this way and asks, "does the remembrance of one history erase others from view?"[28] I agree with Rothberg's suggestion that, in fact, this does not happen and that memory should not be seen as *competitive* but as *multidirectional* in that growing consciousness of the experience of one group can help to articulate discussions regarding other groups.[29] However, I would also suggest that whilst the remembrance of one history does not necessarily erase others from view, the memorialization of one particular group does serve to make the omission of the tangible representation of other groups more visible. And, in some cases it is this increased awareness of the continuing exclusion that acts as a catalyst for the memorialization of an individual group. For example, Robert Holden, director of the National Congress of American Indians commented on the lack of American Indian representation on the Mall with reference to existing depictions of varied groups, specifically the Vietnam Veterans Memorial Statue. Whilst discussing the campaign for the American

Indian Veterans Memorial, he argued that, "while the Three Servicemen Statue at the Vietnam Veterans Memorial represents Caucasian, African American and Hispanic service members, it excludes Native Americans, and does not fully depict their contributions."[30] Thus, the omission of American Indians from the Mall had been made more visible by the inclusion of other marginalized groups.

It is clear, therefore, that the memorialization of the conflict experiences of marginalized groups evinces difficulties which are specific to those groups. The dual nature of the conflict experience resulted in some members of the group experiencing combat trauma as active participants in the US military, whilst others suffered as victims of the American nation. Attempts to memorialize the contribution of these groups to the wider "dominant" narrative will, perhaps inevitably, cause a divide between those members who view commemoration as a positive step forward and those who believe that actively remembering these contributions denies proper recognition of the persecution experienced by the group. Yet, for a successful memorial process, these problems must be overcome. In her feminist critique of Holocaust memorialization, Janet Jacobs describes the ways in which women prisoners' discriminatory behavior towards one another is deliberately silenced in the presentation of this narrative.[31] I would argue that the silencing of the internal divisions of any marginalized group in this way is in fact necessary, as any presentation of this memory would undermine their status as victim and prevent a successful process of memorialization. But I would also suggest that the construction of a memorial facilitates the creation of an arena in which these issues can be discussed by members of the group, and that the construction of a memorial specifically to a conflict which also involved the dominant group is ideal for both preserving the individuality of that group whilst also incorporating it into wider national narratives.

The Suitability of the Memorial Form

Processes of memorialization are ideal for debating the shared history of these groups as they create a suitable platform for discussion within each group, and allow negotiations to take place regarding the divisions created during past conflicts. The construction of a memorial facilitates the resolution of these divisions through the provision of images and symbolism that allow for multiple interpretations of the same element.[32] The last two decades have seen increasing awareness of the divergent ways in which the past can be understood. There has been a greater understanding that the meaning of historical images is neither universal nor intrinsic, but that it "changes as audiences actively reinterpret what they see or hear by placing it in alternative contexts derived from their diverse social backgrounds."[33] It is, therefore, no longer expected that each visitor to a site of memory should have the same experience or that a singular narrative should be presented at the site itself. As Edward Linenthal observed, "museum exhibits, memorials and historic sites are increasingly vibrant arenas for debates over issues of national identity," no longer is the past thought of as "a store house of facts, as a fixed resource, with a single message to be retrieved by the historian."[34] Instead it is anticipated that memorials and museums should have multiple interpretations and allowances are made for this, making the memorial the ideal form to introduce a new group into a wider historical narrative since it has the potential to negotiate between the marginalized group and the wider community.

The war memorial form is particularly suitable for this aim, owing to the meanings associated with this particular form of monument. Implicit meanings of a war memorial have developed over time and I suggest that, as a result, memorials are no longer reliant upon the names of the "heroes" inscribed upon them to make the object sacred, but that the use of the memorial form itself now serves to sanctify the names. The names and the memorial have, therefore, become mutually reliant upon one another. When a new memorial is constructed, the names become sacrosanct through their physical presence on the memorial. Thus, by creating a tangible reminder of their wartime experience and situating their narrative within the war memorial form, previously excluded groups such as Asian Americans, African Americans, and American Indians can be seen to be producing an easily recognizable and legitimate form of monument in order to incorporate its particular past within the wider national narrative. As Kirk Savage discusses in relation to Civil War memorials, "public monuments exercise[d] a curious power to erase their own political origins and become sacrosanct."[35] This is particularly relevant to the memorialization of groups who are considered marginalized and have historically not had a comfortable relationship with the dominant group. The construction of these memorials presents the opportunity to incorporate alternative perceptions of the past within the historical narrative, and in particular to the narrative that is presented through existing memorials in Washington, D.C.

The memorialization process which takes place following a conflict frequently involves the conscious selection of memory to present a unified national narrative. By carefully selecting who and what is memorialized after a conflict, those constructing memorials can manipulate the narrative of the conflict and silence the actions of certain agents. The degree to which memorials can subvert the narrative of the conflict they commemorate is demonstrated through the memorials which contributed to the original marginalization of these groups. In the United States, widespread memorialization of all those who suffered as a result of conflict began following the Civil War. These monuments emerged as a result of a new relationship with soldiers and the bodies of the dead, and a growing expectation that they should be recorded and remembered.[36] Yet, this memorialization did more than simply commemorate those who had lost their lives; it served as a tool to further the memory of the Civil War as a war fought only amongst white men.[37] Most Civil War memorials were constructed when the nation was "dominated by the racism of Jim Crow laws and engaged in imperialist exploits like the Spanish-American War."[38] As a result, these memorials almost exclusively presented the war as a conflict over state rights. In this way those responsible for memorial construction were able to effectively write out narratives of slavery and the contribution of African American soldiers from the history of conflict.[39] The detrimental effect of this rewriting of the war, for both African Americans and the wider society was recognized at the time.[40] Yet, it did not outweigh attempts at national cohesion and throughout the late 19th and 20th centuries memorials continued to be constructed which commemorated the conflict as a war of honor fought only between white men. Memorialization of conflicts with American Indian Nations followed a similar development. After the Battle of Wounded Knee, the memory of the battle was taken over by the dominant white narrative in order to dehumanize the Lakota and justify the subsequent conquest.[41] Similarly, initial memorialization at the Little Bighorn Battlefield commemorated only Custer and his men, once again framing American Indians as uncivilized savages.[42] The understanding that war memorials have the symbolic power not only to rewrite the history of the conflict but to influence perceptions of groups in the present can be seen as well established and well understood.

By using this legitimate and well understood memorial form for their own means, previously marginalized groups are able to counteract their former subordination. Yet, it is not only the physical form of these monuments which is of importance. War memorials are also understood to have accompanying ritual ceremonies. These ceremonies serve not only as a method of perpetuating the memory of those who lost their lives during past conflicts but also facilitate the creation and reinforcement of groups around the memorial. These rituals depend on "self-renewal among the players to validate the ritual scene,"[43] and the expectation that the ritual will be regularly repeated makes them ideal for the reinforcement of social groups. The accepted traditions of remembrance ceremonies which accompany memorials provide the opportunity for new groups to develop, as it is not only those with a direct link to the people and events commemorated by the memorial that attend such ceremonies. Groups coming together to communally remember the past help to reinforce community ties in the present whilst also anchoring this remembrance within wider national themes. The use of the memorial form allows each group to celebrate their past simultaneously with other American anniversaries such as Memorial Day and Veterans Day. The positioning of the Japanese American and African American memorials away from the Mall allows the contribution of such groups to be commemorated simultaneously with and yet separate from other remembrance ceremonies.

The need to incorporate this narrative physically into the urban landscape is important in providing a tangible and lasting representation of the memory of each group. This is particularly important within the context of Washington, D.C.'s memorial landscape. Existing figurative representations in Washington, D.C are overwhelmingly representative of the white male, and other groups were often consciously omitted. For example, African American figures are noticeably absent both as a result of racist concepts of the aesthetic ideal and in order to create the illusion of a more cohesive national narrative.[44] Even when attempts were made to represent African American individuals, their role would often be marginalized through the design of the memorial.[45] In Washington, D.C. particularly, the representation of marginalized groups has often served to perpetuate their subordination or to demonstrate their passivity.

In the nation's capital, many 19th and early 20th century representations of African American individuals, for example, present a negative depiction, the most notorious being those of the Emancipation Memorial in Lincoln Park and the Confederate Memorial in Arlington National Cemetery. The Emancipation Memorial, erected in 1876, was funded entirely by freed slaves. Despite this, the memorial depicts a clothed Lincoln towering above a partially clothed African American kneeling in an inferior position.[46] Thus, the image of the African American as subordinate is immortalized in perpetuity through its inclusion in this prominent public memorial. Similarly, the Confederate Civil War Memorial presents the African American as slave, loyally caring for her master's children as he goes to fight in the conflict. In her study of memorialization throughout America, Doss questions the role of such depictions in the public memorial landscape and asks if "their abiding presence speak[s] to a national faith in freedom of expression" or if, in fact, it "legitimate[s] racism's ignoble presence throughout American history."[47] Similarly, depictions of American Indian individuals in the capital are equally negative and almost unanimously connected to the narrative of Columbus. This has been highly criticized amongst many American Indian groups, particularly those who view Columbus Day as the start of the genocide against the native populations.[48] Many view statues celebrating the arrival of Columbus and images depicting American Indians helping the first settlers as highly offensive, as demonstrated by continued vandalism carried out against such images.[49] The creation of memorials to marginalized groups by these groups themselves can be viewed as an effective way to counteract these negative images and change the way in which that particular group is thought about in relation to past conflicts.

A negative perception of a group's role in the past can be particularly damaging amongst the younger members of the group itself. Often, the full contributions of marginalized groups in the past have yet to be entirely examined. For example, whilst important steps have been taken to produce a more holistic view of American history in relation to slavery,[50] the contribution of African Americans in the Civil War and in particular their role in relation to emancipation has been less fully explored. The African American Civil War Memorial offers an alternative vision to black history in comparison to those which focus on slavery, demonstrating a more positive role model for younger members of that group. War memorials traditionally present the males they represent as strong and heroic and have connotations of acts of bravery. Thus the presentation of these groups in the war memorial form is the ideal form of monument for countering any interpretation as passive observer displayed in existing memorials.

The perception that the negative representation of a group in the past can affect perceptions of that group in a negative way in the present, particularly amongst members of the group itself, is a strong motivation behind increasing memorial construction amongst previously marginalized groups. Hari Jones from the African American Civil War Museum describes the concern over the impact that the lack of understanding of the African American contribution to the Civil War was having on the contemporary African American community,

> I was a marine officer at the Naval academy in the mid-90s and I was really concerned about the lack of understanding of our history as it pertained to the Civil War and the contributions of these Americans and I thought this was doing damage to us in the contemporary, we don't really understand ourselves. To me history is about understanding oneself and for me to do whatever it takes to get them excited about seeking understanding, about seeing the light, if you will, so I think that's very important I think that's how we deal with situations today, like when people talk about race relations.[51]

He saw this lack of understanding of the active part that African Americans played in their own emancipation as having a detrimental effect on this group in the present, and added, "I didn't suffer from a lack of self-esteem which I found most of my African American peers did and they did not know this narrative."[52] In Jones' opinion, the lack of understanding of active contributions in the past can be seen to contribute towards a lack of self-esteem in the present. Highly visible memorials such as the African American Civil War memorial, help to promote a new understanding of that group's past amongst members of the group itself. In this example, it was important that the group be portrayed as active participants in their own history. The strong sculptural centerpiece, created by artist Ed Hamilton, presents individuals actively fighting for their own emancipation, counteracting narratives of passive observation (Fig. 1).

Similarly, American Indian representations have been dominated by the tendency to present the group as a victim, which has in the past proved to be controversial. Doss discusses the contentious depiction of an American Indian individual in Glenna Goodacre's sculpture *He Is, They Are* from Rapid City, South Dakota. Here the figure of a dejected American Indian stands with his hands tied and head bowed. As Doss observes, today "tropes of Native American victimization, and notions of an Indian subjectivity defined in terms of pains, suffering, loss, and defeat are perceived as insults, especially among Indians and especially when pitted against tropes of national authority and masculine influence."[53] This has resulted in the overwhelming preference of the "warrior" image amongst American Indian groups. Thus, the introduction of a war memorial demonstrating the strength of this group when engaged in combat with the American military serves as a method of counteracting their negative images as victims who had been subjugated and forcibly removed from their lands. Yet, as previously discussed, it is this tension between fighting both for and against the dominant group that causes most problems within the memorialization process and can cause issues with group cohesion. How internal tensions regarding the role of American Indian soldiers within the US military will be dealt with by the American Indian Veterans Memorial Initiative is yet to be discovered.[54] But, as Anna Bohlin demonstrates in her study of the South African fishing village of Kalk Bay, there is scope for suppression and omission even amongst the marginalized group itself.[55]

I would argue that this memorialization process provides the ideal environment for the discussion of these issues as it enables the discussion and presentation of each group's history by the community itself, away from the influence of the dominant group. It facilitates the creation of a platform in which groups can formalize their own historical narratives and discuss how they themselves want to be presented, perhaps in ways in which other forms of representation such as the creation of museums, the interpretation of existing heritage sites and the creation of archaeological projects could not.

Such memorial initiatives represent the opportunity for groups to interpret their own role in the past and control their presentation in the present. To those within the community, the physical memorial represents not only an event in the past but also a process of negotiation and discussion regarding the presentation of their own history. Yet, whilst to those outside the community the completed memorial may be seen to present a coherent group narrative, to those within the group it can be symbolic of this internal discussion, and in some cases of division and increased marginalization.

Within some memorial processes, this took place in a relatively straightforward manner. For example, in the case of the African American Civil War Memorial, the original design was criticized for not representing African Americans who served in the Navy during the Civil War. Hari Jones describes descendants of sailors coming forward and saying "well what about us? We were there?"[56] The importance of all members of the group being represented is a significant factor in the war memorial process, something which is further highlighted by the presence of women and children on the back of the memorial (Fig. 3). Following decades of exclusion from the dominant narrative, that any part of that group should be subsequently omitted from the narrative is, as a result, deemed unacceptable.

Yet, for others, the process of omission and inclusion became much more complex. In the processes of memorialization to commemorate Japanese American Patriotism, tensions developed over whose history should be presented on the memorial. Many within the memorial panel called for greater salience to be given to acts of resistance carried out by Japanese American citizens against the internment process, including the many citizens who resisted the draft and were imprisoned as a consequence. This resulted in the re-emergence of suppressed tensions within the group between those who believed loyalty to America should be expressed at all costs and those who believed that government actions were unconstitutional and should be resisted. These tensions were consolidated around the inclusion of one quote praising America from Governor Mike Masaoka, and the controversy surrounding his inclusion came to symbolize the entire debate.

Masaoka had served the wartime Japanese American Citizens League (JACL), acting as its Executive Secretary. He left the institution in 1943 when he volunteered for the army. After the War, he returned to the JACL as its Washington lobbyist and is usually admired for his work supporting legislation that removed features in laws that discriminated against the Japanese in America. However, some members of the Japanese American community drew attention to the fact that no such consensus concerning his leadership in the JACL existed during World War II.[57] He was highly criticized by some members of the community for encouraging compliance with the government's requests for internment in order to demonstrate loyalty to the American government. The controversy of his actions was something which was recognized by Masaoka himself, and despite being part of the original memorial committee he resigned upon realizing that his presence would cause disunity within the group. However, following his death in 1991, the decision was taken by some members of the memorial committee that his name and a quote relating to the internment should be included on the memorial.

Fig. 3. Ed Hamilton, *Spirit of Freedom*, African American Civil War Memorial, Vermont Avenue, Washington D.C., view of sculptural reverse, image courtesy of Hari Jones.

As discussions surrounding Masaoka's inclusion developed, previously suppressed internal tensions grew regarding how the internment should have been dealt with and, most importantly, how it should be remembered. Many members of the memorial board voiced protests regarding his inclusion on the memorial in any form. The debate became so intense that a group calling itself the Japanese American Voice established a website and invited dissidents to sign a petition protesting his inclusion, which was submitted to the National Park Service with some one thousand signatures.[58] Yet Masaoka was retained in the memorial design and his quote was inscribed upon the finished memorial.[59] As a result, in November 2000, as the memorial was being dedicated, two members of the memorial board published and distributed a booklet titled "Japanese Americans Disunited" and created a website which they hoped would be "an alternative voice—one silenced by those who now control the content of the memorial—so that the scope of our understanding, the legacy of our forebears, and the lessons of our past will be articulated in full not only to future generations of Japanese Americans, but to Americans of all backgrounds."[60] It is clear, therefore, that those involved in the memorial process see the control of the memorial as control of the historic narrative of the Japanese American experience and that to certain members of the community the memorial will be viewed as symbolic of the internal divisions within the group, particularly as this debate remains hidden from those outside the Japanese American community.

Making Place within the Urban Landscape

In addition to its production of a physical object, the creation of a memorial by marginalized groups should be viewed as an important step towards the creation of place within the urban landscape. Growing urban multiculturalism has resulted in rising concerns over its inhabitants' shared narratives and the ways in which these are presented in the urban landscape. Issues surrounding exactly whose memory is preserved within the urban landscape are becoming increasingly important within the fields of archaeology and heritage management. In her examination of social sustainability, Setha Low questions "what happens when your places are not marked, or your personal or cultural history is erased."[61] Low goes on to describe the negative impact this can have on those who find themselves inhabiting a locale in which their histories and memories have no physical trace. The omission of certain groups through the selective preservation of the urban environment is currently being addressed through heritage agendas which give greater salience to, and privilege the preservation of, locations associated with previously marginalized groups.[62]

The establishment of places of memory has taken on great meaning and value for social actors and groups in establishing the legitimacy of their public identities and histories.[63] This is particularly pertinent in a multicultural urban environment such as Washington, D.C., where differing interest groups seek representation within the urban landscape. Space in a landscape can only become place when it is invested with meanings and these meanings must remain relevant if the place is to continue to be considered important. By choosing to construct a memorial, each group is making the conscious decision to create a place which is relevant to the memory of that group. Yet the choice of the precise space in which to create this memory place is not an arbitrary one, but reflects discussion within the group itself.

The Memorial to Japanese American Patriotism during World War II is unique amongst memorials to marginalized groups in that it references both active participation *and* victimization. It commemorates both the contribution of Japanese Americans to the United States military and the trauma which the community suffered at the hands of the United States. It is the trauma of the internment which takes the prime position in the memorial. As we have seen, the task of commemorating the internment by the community was not easy, although it should perhaps be viewed as less problematic than any attempt by the US government. As Kenneth Foote points out in his study of trauma in the American landscape, "reflective self-criticism does not fit easily into traditions that celebrate America's past, [t]here is no ready way to commemorate mistakes, to inscribe memorials with the message that a great injustice took place, one that should be forever remembered and never be repeated."[64] Yet, this was precisely what the Japanese American community chose to do through the inclusion of the quote from the Civil Liberties Act of 1988 on the memorial structure.[65]

The creation of this particular memorial right at the heart of the nation's capital was particularly important in the context of the Japanese American community. Their experience during World War II had been purposely marginalized spatially as the internment camps were deliberately located in remote "non" places.[66] This had largely prevented the use of the sites themselves as meaningful sites of memory, particularly by anyone outside of the community. As a result, it was seen as vitally important to locate this narrative in a space which is both accessible to large numbers of the community itself, but which also presents the narrative to the wider community. In her demonstration of the importance of involving affected African American communities in controversial archaeological sites, Cheryl LaRoche highlights the significance of discussing such issues within multicultural urban environments. LaRoche states that, whilst slavery was present in both northern and southern states, archaeologists had chosen to focus early excavations of African American sites on plantations and in relation to New York and despite historians being aware of the city's slaveholding past, "that understanding remained a buried part of the city's modern historical consciousness."[67] I would argue, therefore, that in the context of the establishment of memorials in an urban environment, the location becomes important for re-establishing these links to historic traumas and forcing the viewing public to acknowledge these events. No longer can events such as the Japanese American internment or the perpetuation of slavery be conveniently transferred to "other" places; instead, the memorial's presence re-establishes the role of urban environments in these crimes and acts as a reminder of the compliancy of their inhabitants.[68] In the case of the Japanese American community, by bringing the narrative of internment to Washington, D.C. and re-establishing the connection between the issuing of Executive Order 9066 (which ordered the internment), the memorial can be seen as fighting the marginalization of the experience and forcing other Americans to confront this act.

Yet, increased visibility amongst a wider public is not sufficient to make the memorial successful. In addition to this, there was a need to make the memorial spatially relevant to the trauma of the internment and the resulting campaigns for justice. Franklin Odo, a representative from the National Japanese American Memorial Foundation, described how this was achieved through its physical proximity to the United States Capitol building.[69] He explained that this location was considered important by members of the group, as this was where the official apology for the internment was declared. Yet the significance of the Capitol building location is not alluded to within the memorial itself. This narrative would only be understood by members of the Japanese American community with pre-existing knowledge of their history and not by every visitor to the memorial. Perpetuation of knowledge regarding the importance of the site is reliant upon transmission of this knowledge by members of the group responsible for the memorial. It is clear, therefore, that a hidden layer of meaning is contained within the memorial's location; a meaning which would only be understood by members of the group, or those chosen by the group. Community ties are thus reinforced through the selective transmission of this knowledge.

The African American Civil War memorial was similarly constructed in a location which had hidden relevance to the group's cause and whose justification was registered only internally within the African American community. No attempt was made to locate the memorial where it might interact with existing Civil War memorials in the national capitol and therefore influence a revision of that narrative within the wider public.[70] Instead its location next to U-Street Metro Station provides a primarily African American audience for the memorial. This site was chosen because it marked the location of a former "contraband camp."[71] The camp, known as Camp Barker, was set up in 1862 for refugees during the Civil War and had by the end of 1863 processed over 5,000 individuals.[72] Yet, this information is unlikely to be known outside of the African American community living in that area. Such inherent understandings of the monument, which can only be interpreted by those with a detailed knowledge of the memory associated with the site, serve to reinforce group cohesiveness.

However, not all groups approached this concept of space and place in the same way. The American Indian Veterans Memorial Initiative members are more determined to have their memorial on the Mall, at the very heart of the national narrative. It was initially suggested that any American Indian memorial should be located within the National Museum of the American Indian. But, campaigners for the memorial refused to accept such a peripheral location. When offered a space within the entrance to the National Museum of the American Indian many veterans were offended by the suggestion. They saw the construction of a memorial in this underground space as symbolically forcing their issues underground. A representative from the American Indian Veterans Memorial campaign described his experiences with the veterans and their desire to have prominent position for their memorial, "just like the other monuments that are on the National Mall."[73] This determination to have a more central location clearly demonstrates that there is no universal memorial process and that each memorial must be seen to reflect the individual needs of that group.

As previously discussed, once the memorial sites have been established in a public environment, they are open to multiple interpretations. As Paul Shakel posits in his discussion of the Robert Gould Shaw and the 54th Massachusetts Memorial, a memorial can be "read in various ways and different people will ascribe diverse meanings to it, depending upon the memory they have associated with the events."[74] David Glassberg suggests, "public historical representations such as an exhibit, war memorial or commemorative ceremony are often deliberately ambiguous to satisfy competing factions."[75] This space for multiple understandings of the same monument allows for a negotiation between the group members as to how it wished to present itself. Symbolism which can only be interpreted by the group itself allows an added layer of meaning to develop. This added meaning serves to reinforce group identity amongst its members through their ability to interpret these signs. Yet, even within the group the continual reinterpretation of these signs allowed for a multiplicity of meanings which could serve to heal the divisions within the group.

This capacity for multiple interpretations is most clearly demonstrated by the Japanese American Memorial to Patriotism during World War II, which

Fig. 4. Nina Akamu, *Golden Cranes,* National Japanese American Memorial to Patriotism during World War II, view of crane sculpture, image by Emma Login.

underwent many revisions within the community after it had been unveiled. Unlike memorials constructed at the place where the trauma was experienced, this memorial could not rely upon the indexical nature of the site itself in order to be understood.[76] Thus, new ways of representing the trauma had to be found. As a result, the trauma of internment was symbolized by two cranes entwined in barbed wire created by sculptor Nina Akamu (Fig. 4). Although the physical design of this element did not itself change throughout the memorialization process, it was continually reinterpreted by members of the community as the discussions progressed regarding how the internment experience should be remembered. Initially, those within the Japanese American community saw the cranes not only as symbolic of that which had happened in the past but of the continuing trauma of the internment, which was felt by the community in the present.

Those within the memorial board described the cranes as "emerging from a pedestal, wings reaching high in to the sky for freedom as they seek release from entangling barbed wire. The action symbolizes the Japanese American experience of freeing themselves from a deeply painful time."[77] Yet, as discussions regarding the memorial continued, the crane sculpture was reinterpreted amongst the context of growing discontent within the Japanese American community itself.

After the memorial had been unveiled and it became clear that there were deep internal divisions within the community the cranes were instead described as "nestled side-by-side with their free wings pressed against each other, symbolizing *both* individual effort *and* communal support, emphasizing interdependency."[78] This suggests the importance of the Japanese American community working together as a coherent unit if it is to fight such injustices as internment and emphasizes the need for mutual support. Similarly, the inclusion of five large rocks within the reflecting pool was originally intended to symbolize the five islands of Japan, thus providing a direct link to the home country within the American urban landscape (Fig. 5).[79] However, a representative from the memorial describes the ways in which, as the memorial evolved, these symbols were reinterpreted within the Japanese American community to represent the five generations of Japanese who had lived in the United States at the time of the memorial's construction.[80] Instead of providing a tangible symbol of Japanese ancestry, this part of the memorial now demonstrates the ways in which those of Japanese heritage have remained loyal to America and have literally become embedded within the American nation. This demonstrates that a memorial remains open to reinterpretation after it has been completed and that its meaning is in no way static, but rather it continues to be re-appropriated with new meanings depending upon the circumstances in which it is being viewed. Yet, this reinterpretation took place solely within the community which was responsible for the memorial and would not be understood by those outside of that distinct community. This suggests that the primary importance of these memorials is their role in defining the function of that group within the community itself, not in promoting recognition of that particular group within the wider community.

Fig. 5. National Japanese American Memorial to Patriotism during World War II, view of the reflecting pool and 5 rocks, image by Emma Login.

Conclusion

As American history becomes increasingly militaristic, and more emphasis is placed on the importance of conflict narratives within this history, more and more groups seek to define their own place within these narratives. War memorials constructed in Washington, D.C. by groups who feel that their conflict experience has been marginalized or excluded from the dominant narrative present a desire to incorporate their experience into the national narrative. Whilst important steps have been taken towards a more inclusive approach to the past, much of this discussion has taken place within the context of the wider public and has not been led by the groups themselves. The process of memorialization allows for the discussion of these issues by large numbers of the group itself, separate from the influence of the dominant group.

Yet, this process is highly problematic, not least because the trauma which these groups seek to memorialize is multifaceted and highly complex. Whilst the initial trauma is based upon the conflict experience itself, it is amplified through the divisions it creates within the group itself, resulting in the breakdown of a coherent group identity. This traumatic experience is further increased by the prejudiced attitudes of the dominant group, and perpetuated by a lack of official recognition for each group's conflict experience by the dominant group, often as a result of these prejudiced attitudes. The process of memorialization is important in its ability to simultaneously address each level of trauma. This creation of a tangible memorial is ideal for introducing the narrative of a previously excluded group into the wider historical narrative as the memorial form is well established and serves to legitimize the cause which it commemorates. In addition, the creation of physical memorials within the urban setting of Washington, D.C. serves to permanently embed this narrative into the national landscape, providing an alternative image to the negative representations of each group found on existing monuments.

Yet, whilst the physical memorial is important for presenting the contribution of a particular group to a wider audience and counteracting the trauma caused by lack of recognition, it is the discussion process which takes place as the memorial is constructed which should be viewed as central to its importance. The lack of commemoration of each group's particular contribution resulted in a lack of opportunity for the open discussion of these issues. As a result, divisions within the groups caused by their war time experiences were perpetuated. Memorialization offers the opportunity to heal these divisions, and yet this process is not easy as it brings to the surface previously suppressed internal tensions. The heated discussions and passionate campaigns instigated by these groups demonstrate that in no way should temporal distance be considered as an indication of lower emotive responses to the events. The construction of a memorial therefore facilitates the creation of a platform in which to discuss these previously suppressed tensions. These tensions can be openly negotiated through debates relating to the form and location of the memorial and it is this that is central to its significance, rather than the finished memorial which is continually interpreted and reinterpreted amongst the group as the discussion develops.

Whilst those outside of the group may perceive the monument to be static and un-changing, it is continually reinterpreted and re-defined by the group itself and it is the transmission of this knowledge which allows members of the group to make these interpretations, defining who is a member of the group and who is outside. Thus, memorials such as the African American Civil War Memorial, The Memorial to Japanese American Patriotism during World War II, and the proposed American Indian Veteran's Memorial provide important public opportunities for group cohesion and definition which may not otherwise be possible.

Bibliography

Agbe-Davies, Anna. "Concepts of Community in the Pursuit of an Inclusive Archaeology." *International Journal of Heritage Studies* 16.6 (2010): 373-89.

Anderson, Benedict. *Imagined Communities: Reflections on the Origin and Spread of Nationalism.* Brooklyn, NY: Verso, 2006.

Blight, David W. "'For Something Beyond the Battlefield': Frederick Douglass and the Struggle for the Memory of the Civil War." *The Journal of American History* 75 (1989): 1156-78.

—. *Race and Reunion: The Civil War in American Memory*. Cambridge, MASS: Harvard University Press, 2002.

Bodnar, John. *Remaking America: Public Memory, Commemoration, and Patriotism in the Twentieth Century*. Princeton: Princeton University Press, 1992.

—. "Saving Private Ryan and Postwar Memory in America." *The American Historical Review* 106.3 (2001): 805-17.

Bohlin, Anna. "Places of Longing and Belonging: Memories of the Group Area Proclamation of a South African Fishing Village." In *Contested Landscapes: Movement, Exile and Place*, edited by Barber Bender and Marot Winer, 273-87. New York: Berg, 2001.

Boyle, Katherine. "Native American Veteran's Memorial Gets Legislative Push." *The Washington Post*, May 23 2013. Accessed July 31, 2013. http://articles.washingtonpost.com/2013-05-23/lifestyle/39472647_1_american-indians-native-americans-fitting-memorial.

Brown, Gail. "Wounded Knee: The Conflict of Interpretation." In *Myth, Memory, and the American Landscape*, edited by Paul Shackel, 103-18. Florida: University Press of Florida, 2001.

Craps, Stef. *Postcolonial Witnessing: Trauma Out of Bounds.* Houndmills: Palgrave Macmillan, 2013.

Doss, Erica. *Memorial Mania: Public Feeling in America.* Chicago: Chicago University Press, 2010.

Echo-Hawk, Roger C. "Ancient History in the New World: Integrating Oral Traditions and the Archaeological Record in Deep Time." *American Antiquity* 65.2 (2000): 267-90.

Epperson, Terrence W. "Critical Race Theory and the Archaeology of the African Diaspora." *Historical Archaeology* 38.1 (2004): 101-108.

Faust, Drew G. "'Numbers of Top of Numbers': Counting the Civil War Dead." *The Journal of Military History* 70.4 (2006): 995-1009.

Finkle, Lee. "The Conservative Aims of Militant Rhetoric: Black Protest during World War II." *The Journal of American History* 60.3 (1973): 692-713.

Fleming, Eleanor B. "When Sorry Is Enough: The Possibility of a National Apology for Slavery." In *The Age of Apology: Facing up to the Past*, edited by Mark Gibney, Rhoda E. Howard, Jean-Marc Coicaud, and Niklaus Steiner, 95-108. Philadelphia: University of Pennsylvania Press, 2008.

Foote, Kenneth E. *Shadowed Ground: America's Landscapes of Violence*. Austin: University of Texas Press, 2003.

Gallicchio, Marc, ed. *The Unpredictability of the Past: Memories of the Asia-Pacific War in the U.S.-East Asian Relations*. Durham: Duke University Press, 2007.

Giroux, Henry A. "War on Terror: The Militarising of Public Space and Culture in the United States." *Third Text* 18.4 (2004): 211-21.

Glassberg, David. "Public History and the Study of Memory." *The Public Historian* 18.2 (1996): 7-23.

Guelzo, Allen C. *Lincoln's Emancipation Proclamation: The End of Slavery in America*. New York: Simon & Schuster, 2006.

Handler, Richard. "Is 'Identity' a Useful Concept?." In *Commemorations: The Politics of National Identity*, edited by John R. Gillis, 27-40. Princeton: Princeton University Press, 1994.

Hatamiya, Leslie T. *Righting a Wrong: Japanese Americans and the Passage of the Civil Liberties Act of 1988*. Stanford: Stanford University Press, 1993.

Hayden, Dolores. *The Power of Place: Urban Landscapes as Public History*. Cambridge, MASS: MIT Press, 1995.

Hoelscher, Steven, and Derek H. Alderman. "Memory and Place: Geographies of a Critical Relationship." *Social and Cultural Geography* 5.3 (2004): 347-55.

Jacobs, Janet L. *Memorializing the Holocaust: Gender, Genocide and Collective Memory*. London: IB Tauris & Company Limited, 2010.

LaRoche, Cheryl J. "Archaeology the Activist Community, and the Redistribution of Power in New York City." *Archaeologies: Journal of the World Archaeological Congress* 7.3 (2011): 619-34.

Linenthal, Edward T. Foreword to *Myth, Memory, and the Making of the American Landscape*, edited by Paul A. Shackel, xi-xii. Florida: University Press Florida, 2001.

Low, Setha M. "Social Sustainability: People, History, and Values." In *The Heritage Reader*, edited by Graham Faiclough, Rodney Harrison, John H. Jameson Jr, and John Schofield, 392-404. London: Routeldge, 2008.

Masur, Kate. "'A Rare Phenomenon of Philological Vegetation': The Word 'Contraband' and the Meanings of Emancipation in the United States." *The Journal of American History* 93.4 (2007): 1050-84.

Matthews, Christopher, Carol N. McDavid, and Patrice L. Jeppson. "Dynamics of Inclusion in Public Archaeology: An Introduction." *Archaeologies: Journal of the World Archaeological Congress* 7.3 (2011): 482-89.

Mayo, James M. "War Memorials as Political Memory." *Geographical Review* 78.1 (1988): 62-75.

McDavid, Carol. "Archaeologies that Hurt; Descendants that Matter: A Pragmatic Approach to Collaboration in the Public Interpretation of African-American Archaeology." *World Archaeology* 34.2 (2002): 303-14.

National Japanese American Memorial Foundation. *Patriotism, Perseverance, Posterity: The Story of the National Japanese American Memorial.* Rockville: NJAMF, 2001.

National Japanese American Memorial Foundation. "Visit the Memorial." Accessed November 22, 2013. http://njamf.com/page18/page18.html.

Nora, Pierre. "Reasons for the Current Upsurge in Memory." *Transit-Europäische Revue* 22 (2002): 1-14.

Piehler, G Kurt. *Remembering War the American Way.* Washington: Smithsonian Institution Press, 1995.

Rose-Redwood, Reuben, Derek Alderman, and Maoz Azaryahu. "Collective Memory and the Politics of Urban Space: an Introduction." *GeoJournal* 73.3 (2008): 161-64.

Rosenzweig, Roy, and David Thelen. *The Presence of the Past: Popular uses of History in American Life.* New York: Columbia University Press, 1998.

Rothberg, Michael. *Multidirectional Memory: Remembering the Holocaust in the Age of Decolonization.* Stanford: Stanford University Press, 2009.

Savage, Kirk. *Monument Wars: Washington, D.C., the National Mall, and the Transformation of the Memorial Landscape*. Berkeley: University of California Press, 2009.

—. *Standing Soldiers, Kneeling Slaves: Race, War, and Monument in Nineteenth-Century America*. Princeton: Princeton University Press, 1997.

Schuman, Howard, and Jacqueline Scott. "Generations and Collective Memories." *American Sociological Review* 54.3 (1989): 359-81.

Shackel, Paul A. "Public Memory and the Search for Power in American Historical Archaeology." *American Anthropologist* 103.3 (2001): 655-70.

—. "'Where we need to go': Comment on 'Decennial Reflections on A Geography of Heritage.'" *International Journal of Heritage Studies* 19.4 (2013): 384-87.

Smith, Laurajane, and Emma Waterton. *Heritage, Communities and Archaeology*. London: Duckworth, 2009.

Sogi, Francis, and Yeichi Kuwayama. "Japanese American Voice: Making Our Voices Heard." Last modified, February 15, 2001, http://www.javoice.com/.

Trouillot, Michel-Rolph. "Abortive Rituals: Historical Apologies in the Global Era." *International Journal of Postcolonial Studies* 2.2 (2000): 171-86.

Trouillot, Michel-Rolph. *Silencing the Past: Power and Production of History*. Boston: Beacon, 1995.

Violi, Patrizia. "Trauma Site Museums and Politics of Memory: Tuol Sleng, Villa Grimaldi and the Bologna Ustica Museum." *Theory Culture Society* 29.1 (2012): 36-75.

Young, James E. *The Texture of Memory: Holocaust Memorials and Meaning*. New Haven: Yale University Press, 1993.

Notes

[1] Kirk Savage, *Monument Wars: Washington, D.C., the National Mall, and the Transformation of the Memorial Landscape* (Berkeley: University of California Press, 2009), 1-4.

[2] Erica Doss, *Memorial Mania: Public Feeling in America* (Chicago: Chicago University Press, 2010), 2.

[3] For increased militarization in a post 9/11 context, see, for example, Henry A. Giroux, "War on Terror: The Militarising of Public Space and Culture in the United States," *Third Text* 18.4 (2004): 211.

[4] For an overview, see Kirk Savage, *Monument Wars: Washington, D.C., the National Mall, and the Transformation of the Memorial Landscape* (Berkeley: University of California Press, 2009).

[5] Michel-Rolph Trouillot, for example, examines the ways in which certain events and individuals become silenced within the historical narrative. He successfully demonstrates that it is not an absence of facts that results in this silencing but the appropriation of narratives by various interest groups. Of particular relevance here are his explorations of the ways in which, at certain times, "collectivities experience the need to impose a test of credibility on certain events and narratives because it matters to them whether these events are true or false, whether these stories are fact or fiction." Michel-Rolph Trouillot, *Silencing the Past: Power and Production of History* (Boston: Beacon, 1995), 11.

[6] Marc Gallicchio, ed., *The Unpredictability of the Past: Memories of the Asia-Pacific War in the U.S.-East Asian Relations* (Durham: Duke University Press, 2007), 5.

[7] Steven Hoelscher and Derek H. Alderman, "Memory and Place: Geographies of a Critical Relationship," *Social and Cultural Geography* 5.3 (2004): 349.
[8] As illustrated, for example, by the Dynamics of Inclusion in Public Archaeology workshop held September 17-18, 2010 at the African Burial Ground National Monument in New York City. This workshop brought together both academic and non-academic professionals to explore public participation in archaeological projects at both the planning and execution stages. It challenged assumptions about the inherent value of the past and called on professionals to "accept that their interests in material culture, history and the making of place are no more or less valid than, nor even radically distinct from, those in other communities." Christopher Matthews, Carol N. McDavid, and Patrice L. Jeppson, "Dynamics of Inclusion in Public Archaeology: An Introduction," *Archaeologies: Journal of the World Archaeological Congress* 7.3 (2011): 483.
[9]Terrence W. Epperson, "Critical Race Theory and the Archaeology of the African Diaspora," *Historical Archaeology* 38.1 (2004): 101.
[10]See, for example, Roger C. Echo-Hawk's discussion of the integration of oral records and the archaeological record in scholarship relating to American Indians, Roger C. Echo-Hawk, "Ancient History in the New World: Integrating Oral Traditions and the Archaeological Record in Deep Time," *American Antiquity* 65.2 (2000): 267-90.
[11] Paul Shackel, "'Where we need to go': Comment on 'Decennial Reflections on A Geography of Heritage," *International Journal of Heritage Studies* 19.4 (2013): 386.
[12]Anna S. Agbe-Davies, "Concepts of Community on the Pursuit of an Inclusive Archaeology," *International Journal of Heritage Studies* 16.6 (2010): 374.
[13] Richard Handler, for example, warns that we should be as suspicious of "identity" as we have learned to be of "culture," "tradition," and "ethnic group," but, accepts that in some cases it is appropriate within a Western context. Richard Handler, "Is 'Identity' a Useful Concept?," in *Commemorations the Politics of National Identity*, ed. John R. Gillis (Princeton: Princeton University Press, 1994), 27.
[14]Pierre Nora, "Reasons for the Current Upsurge in Memory," *Transit- Europäische Revue* 22 (2002): 8.
[15] David, Glassberg, "Public History and the Study of Memory," *The Public Historian* 18.2 (1996): 13.
[16] Benedict Anderson, for example, describes the way in which the indigenous population in Peru were decreed not Indians or natives but "Peruvians" in an attempt to create a cohesive and continuous national narrative from that point on. Benedict Anderson, Imagined *Communities: Reflections on the Origin and Spread of Nationalism* (Brooklyn: Verso, 2006), 193.
[17] Laurajane Smith and Emma Waterton, *Heritage, Communities and Archaeology* (London: Duckworth, 2009), 77.
[18] John Bodnar, prologue to *Remaking America: Public Memory, Commemoration, and Patriotism in the Twentieth Century*, by John Bodnar (Princeton: Princeton University Press, 1992) 3-9.
[19] Michael Rothberg, *Multidirectional Memory: Remembering the Holocaust in the Age of Decolonization* (Stanford: Stanford University Press, 2009), 2.

[20] Laura S. Brown, "Not Outside the Range: One Feminist Perspective on Psychic Trauma," *American Imago* 48.1 (1991): 119-33, qtd. in Stef Craps, *Postcolonial Witnessing: Trauma Out of Bounds* (Houndmills: Palgrave Macmillan, 2013), 20.
[21] That is not to say that only male members of the group had opinions regarding the right course of action towards loyalty to the US nation, but merely that they were in a position to actively demonstrate that loyalty in a more overt way through military service.
[22] This is the case particularly among those who chose to stay on reservations and those who relocated to an urban environment. For more on this matter, see Roy Rosenzweig and David Thelen, *The Presence of the Past: Popular Uses of History in American Life* (New York: Columbia University Press, 1998), 147-76.
[23] Craps, *Postcolonial Witnessing: Trauma Out of Bounds*, 4.
[24] John Bodnar, "*Saving Private Ryan* and Postwar Memory in America," *The American Historical Review* 106.3 (2001): 814. For a discussion of African American acknowledgement of this and of attempts to combat racism during World War II, see Lee Finkle, "The Conservative Aims of Militant Rhetoric: Black Protest during World War II," *The Journal of American History* 6.3 (1973): 692-713.
[25] See, for example, Michael-Rolph Trouillot, "Abortive Rituals: Historical Apologies in the Global Era," *International Journal of Postcolonial Studies* 2.2 (2000): 171-86.
[26] Eleanor B. Fleming, "When Sorry is Enough: The Possibility of a National Apology for Slavery," in *The Age of Apology: Facing up to the Past*, eds. Mark Gibney et. al. (Philadelphia: University of Pennsylvania Press, 2008), 96.
[27] In 1987 the Smithsonian Institution's National Museum of American History mounted an exhibition which detailed the internment of the Japanese American community and their contributions during World War II, followed in 1988 by the signing of the Civil Liberties Act which denounced the internment as unjust and ordered reparations of $20000 to be paid to each surviving victim. For discussion of the interment and the campaign for reparations, see Leslie T. Hatamiya, *Righting a Wrong: Japanese Americans and the Passage of the Civil Liberties Act of 1988* (Stanford: Stanford University Press, 1993).
[28] Rothberg, *Multidirectional Memory*, 2.
[29] Rothberg, *Multidirectional Memory,* 3.
[30] Robert Holden, quoted in an article by Katherine Boyle, "Native American Veteran's Memorial Gets Legislative Push," *The Washington Post*, May 23, 2013, accessed July 31, 2013, http://articles.washingtonpost.com/2013-05-23/lifestyle/39472647_1_american-indians-native-americans-fitting-memorial.
[31] Janet Jacobs, *Memorializing the Holocaust: Gender, Genocide and Collective Memory* (London: IB Tauris & Company Limited, 2010), 61-62.
[32] James Young, for example, describes the ways in which the multiple interpretations available for the Los Angeles Holocaust Memorial were used to overcome divisions within the local community. James E. Young, *The Texture of Memory: Holocaust Memorials and Meaning* (New Haven: Yale University Press, 1993), 303.
[33] Glassberg, "Public History," 10.
[34]Edward T. Linenthal, foreword to *Myth, Memory, and the Making of the American Landscape*, ed. Paul A. Shackel (Florida: University Press Florida, 2001), xi.

[35] Kirk Savage, *Standing Soldiers, Kneeling Slaves: Race, War, and Monument in Nineteenth-Century America* (Princeton: Princeton University Press, 1997), 7. However, arguably the most salient example of this is provided by the Vietnam Veterans Memorial, Washington, D.C. This memorial proved highly controversial during the planning stages but since its construction it has become one of the most visited memorials in the United States.
[36] Drew G. Faust, "'Numbers of Top of Numbers': Counting the Civil War Dead," *The Journal of Military History* 70.4 (2006): 996.
[37] For a broad reading of the memory of the Civil War in American culture, see David W. Blight, *Race and Reunion: The Civil War in American Memory* (Cambridge, MASS: Harvard University Press, 2001).
[38] Doss, *Memorial Mania*, 212-213.
[39] Paul Shackel, for example, demonstrates the ways in which Civil War memorials were used to establish the memory of that conflict, legitimizing a patriotic white-male narrative whilst excluding all other forms of experience and reinforcing racist attitudes in the decades that followed the conflict. See Paul A. Shackel, "Public Memory and the Search for Power in American Historical Archaeology," *American Anthropologist* 103.3 (2001): 655-70.
[40] For an overview of attempts by Frederick Douglass to stop the formation of a legacy of the Civil War which silenced the emancipation and focused only on white male heroism on both sides, and which had no political or moral meaning, see David W. Blight, "'For Something Beyond the Battlefield': Frederick Douglass and the Struggle for the Memory of the Civil War," *The Journal of American History* 75 (1989): 1156-78.
[41] For a discussion of this and the subsequent American Indian reclamation of the battlefield through processes of memorialization, see Gail Brown, "Wounded Knee: The Conflict of Interpretation," in *Myth, Memory, and the Making of American Landscape*, ed. Paul A. Shackel (Florida: University Press of Florida, 2001), 103-18.
[42] Doss, *Memorial Mania*, 328-38.
[43] James M. Mayo, "War Memorials as Political Memory," *Geographical Review* 78.1 (1988): 71.
[44] Savage, *Monument Wars,* 171.
[45] Kurt G. Piehler, *Remembering War the American Way* (Washington: Smithsonian Institution Press, 1995), 69.
[46] Savage, *Standing Soldiers,* 114-19.
[47] Doss, *Memorial Mania,* 11.
[48] Rosenzweig and Thelen, *The Presence of the Past,* 167.
[49] Doss, *Memorial Mania,* 324.
[50] See, for example, Carol McDavid's discussion of archaeological excavations at the Levi Jordan Plantation, Brazoria, Texas and her examination of the use of an online site to allow for discussions between both African American and European American descendants of the original residents of the plantation in order to produce a more inclusive history of the site. Carol McDavid, "Archaeologies that Hurt; Descendants that Matter: A Pragmatic Approach to Collaboration in the Public Interpretation of African-American Archaeology," *World Archaeology* 34.2 (2002): 303-14; Cheryl J. LaRoche, "Archaeology the Activist Community, and the Redistribution of Power in

New York City," *Archaeologies: Journal of the World Archaeological Congress* 7.3 (2011): 619-34.
[51] Hari Jones in discussion with the author, November 19, 2012.
[52] Hari Jones in discussion with the author, November 19, 2012.
[53] Doss, *Memorial Mania,* 342.
[54]These difficulties were overcome in the National Museum of the American Indian through the presentation of all American Indian groups as united, silencing the narrative of conflicts between tribes and instead championing the narrative of Indians persecuted by white Americans.
[55] Anna Bohlin, "Places of Longing and Belonging: Memories of the Group Area Proclamation of a South African Fishing Village," in *Contested Landscapes: Movement, Exile and Place*, eds. Barber Bender and Marot Winer (New York: Berg, 2001), 274.
[56] Hari Jones in discussion with the author, November 19, 2012.
[57] Francis Sogi and Yeichi Kuwayama, "Japanese American Voice: Making Our Voices Heard," last modified February 15, 2001, http://www.javoice.com/.
[58]Sogi and Kuwayama, "Japanese American Voice."
[59] This is the text of the quote: "I am proud that I am an American of Japanese ancestry. I believe in this nation's institutions and traditions. I glory in her heritage. I boast of her history. I trust in her future."
[60]Sogi and Kuwayama, "Japanese American Voice."
[61] Setha M. Low, "Social Sustainability: People, History, and Values," in *The Heritage Reader*, eds. Graham Faiclough et. al. (London: Routledge, 2008), 392.
[62] See, for example, Dolores Hayden, *The Power of Place: Urban Landscapes as Public History* (Cambridge: MIT Press, 1995), 3-13.
[63] Reuben Rose-Redwood, Derek Alderman, and Maoz Azaryahu, "Collective Memory and the Politics of Urban Space: An Introduction," *GeoJournal* 73.3 (2008): 161.
[64]Kenneth E. Foote, *Shadowed Ground: America's Landscapes of Violence* (Austin: University of Texas Press, 2003), 305.
[65] This is the text of the quote: "Here we admit a wrong. Here we affirm our commitment as a nation to equal justice under the law" (President Reagan, Civil Liberties Act, 1988).
[66] World War II is arguably the greatest event of the 20th century for many Americans, and the omission of the Japanese American experience from this narrative must be viewed within this context. For the importance of World War II in American memory, see Howard Schuman and Jacqueline Scott, "Generations and Collective Memories," *American Sociological Review* 54.3 (1989): 362.
[67] LaRoche, "Archaeology, the Activist Community," 620.
[68]LaRoche reminds readers that slaves were amongst the first commodities to be bought and sold on Wall Street. See LaRoche, "Archaeology, the Activist Community," 620.
[69] Franklin Odo, in discussion with the author, October 14, 2012.
[70] There are a number of Civil War monuments within the city which give a biased white-centric view of the conflict, including the aforementioned Confederate

Memorials and Emancipation memorial. A location in proximity to these could perhaps be seen to serve as a counterbalance to this exiting narrative.

[71] The term "contraband camp" refers to camps set up by the Union during the Civil War to provide temporary holding spaces for displaced slaves, see Kate Masur, "'A Rare Phenomenon of Philological Vegetation': The Word 'Contraband' and the Meanings of Emancipation in the United States," *The Journal of American History* 93.4 (2007): 1064.

[72]Allen C. Guelzo, *Lincoln's Emancipation Proclamation: The End of Slavery in America* (New York: Simon & Schuster, 2006), 100.

[73] He commented that, "They're not a pre-historic piece of an animal or a dinosaur, they're a living veteran and people that have died, fought in a real war and they don't feel like they want to be put in the National Museum of the American Indian. They want to be put out there above ground, just like the other three service men, just like the other monuments that are on the National Mall"(representative of the AIVMI in discussion with the author, October 5, 2012).

[74] Shackel, "Public Memory," 659.

[75] Glassberg, "Public History," 13-14.

[76] Patrizia Violi, "Trauma Site Museums and Politics of Memory: Tuol Sleng, Villa Grimaldi and the Bologna Ustica Museum," *Theory Culture Society* 29.1 (2012): 39.

[77] National Japanese American Memorial Foundation, *Patriotism, Perseverance, Posterity: The Story of the National Japanese American Memorial* (Rockville: NJAMF, 2001), 141.

[78] National Japanese American Memorial Foundation ,"Visit the Memorial," accessed November 22, 2013, http://njamf.com/page18/page18.html. Emphasis mine.

[79] Franklin Odo, in discussion with the author, October 14, 2012.

[80] Franklin Odo, in discussion with the author, October 14, 2012.

THE GENDERED APPROACH: TALKING TRAUMA IN NATIONAL MONUMENT DISCOURSES

LIZ MEDOFF

As I write this introduction, I am struck with my own sense of feeling. I have come to the subjects of feeling, history, and public memory in perhaps a unique way. As a person, specifically a woman, who has experienced domestic and sexual trauma, I orient myself to the world in a way that always considers feeling. You could say that this feeling that I do is a "consequence" of trauma, but I fear that attitude limits the knowledge we can access from feelings, perpetuating the mythical binary of "good" and "bad" ones. No feeling is good or bad (although it may feel good and/or bad). The way a feeling *feels* is simply a kind of bodily knowledge that we haven't yet learned to fully understand.

Thinking about my own felt experience in this world orients me towards issues of gendered violence in the mass media. For example, in November 2011, a scandal broke in State College, PA. Assistant football coach Jerry Sandusky was indicted on 42 counts of sexual abuse of minors; others were indicted and, like head coach Joe Paterno, forced to resign for covering up Sandusky's crimes. The community response to the news was mixed, which is by no means unusual—frequently, perpetrators of atrocity are supported by their communities at first because fellow citizens are slow to process shock into anything but denial; riots broke out to protest the news that Paterno was being forced to resign. However, what I wish to highlight here is the other side of the story, that of the victims, which presents the abhorrent fact of childhood sexual abuse.

Similarly, the United States Military has for years been stifling scandalous reports of rampant sexual violence against its female service members. In February 2011, fifteen women and two men, all survivors of sexual assault in the military, filed a lawsuit against the Pentagon regarding its handling of the violence.[1] Women in the military face a pronounced risk of sexual violence at the hands of fellow soldiers, which is often ignored (and in some cases all but sanctioned) by superiors.[2]

Implicit in this project is an overall critique of violence; I am not pro-military. However, each soldier is in fact a human individual and not the Military-Industrial Complex itself. Each soldier—male or female—has made a commitment to the United States that ought to be reciprocated with a commitment to its soldiers' wellbeing. Instead, we again face the fact of sexualized violence, as well as the dismissal of it. In an abysmally clear illustration of this mentality, Fox News pundit Liz Trotta was quoted as asking, "What did they [women in the military] expect?"[3]

That each of the culpable institutions is steeped in unyielding, patriarchal binaries of shame and heroism is no coincidence. These environments function on gendered notions of strength and weakness, perpetrator and victim. An overarching devaluing of "femininity" or anything perceived as such pervades. In environments like these, often no crime is seen to have been committed in the case of sexual violence—women are asking for what men are always already entitled to.

There's nothing remarkable about the aforementioned examples—if anything, they are microcosms that illustrate widely held beliefs about affect, trauma, and gender in America—sexual violence is something that "only" affects feminine (i.e. "weak") bodies, and we'd better keep quiet about it. The reality is that perpetrators have institutional backing based on male-bodied privilege, which at the same time works to stifle the affective responses of survivors.

Ann Cvetkovich, author of *An Archive of Feelings: Trauma, Sexuality, and Lesbian Public Cultures,* provides a starting point for understanding cultural framings of trauma. She argues,

> Once the causes of trauma become more diffuse, so too do the cures, opening up the need to change social structures more broadly than just fix individual people. Yet as the links between sexual abuse and sexism show, event trauma can play a prominent role in drawing attention to more insidious forms of trauma.[4]

I believe in the "need to change social structures more broadly"; among them is the institution of American public memory. Countless peoples' everyday affective experiences of fear, anxiety, and insidious trauma—the chronic traumatic stress of (invisible) structural violence—are silenced. Is public memory the inverse of insidious trauma? I am interested in national monuments precisely because of their scale and "authority"—they claim a collective voice, which I do not trust. Ample scholarship exists on more organic, less "official" mourning culture but I am less interested in that partly *because* it is less official. I am interested in the problems national public memory of trauma generates—one story privileged over another, memory cannibalizing memory.

But what does this have to do with 9/11? 9/11 presents a myriad of issues that pertain to how emotional experience is processed in the United States. The United Sates has committed immeasurable resources to ensuring that 9/11 is woven into the very fabric of daily life—from "anti-terrorism" legislation to emblazoning everything with the phrase, "Never Forget," to the massive memorial complex at Ground Zero, which is the focus of this chapter. Forgetting is not an option when we are reminded at every turn. 9/11 has officially made it into what one might call the "canon of trauma"—that is, generally speaking, the trauma of 9/11 is one that is acceptable to discuss, almost without question. That we have visual means of reference—terrorism memorials—is no coincidence. Erika Doss, author of *Memorial Mania: Public Feeling in America*, contends that this compulsion to commemorate stems from the need "to control the meaning of terrorism and to manage its traumatic memory,"[5] and I agree; terrorism memorials undeniably serve nationalistic ends, and in the following sections of my chapter I will illustrate how notions of ideal American masculinities populate national memorials, and to what ends. Terrorism discourses allow for narratives of heroism, innocence, and sacrifice to inhabit and gender the popular understanding of trauma; I find this to be especially evinced by something I will call "pathological patriotism," which I will argue is a masculine affect. However, to borrow Cvetkovich's terminology, I believe that "event trauma," like 9/11, can indeed play a prominent role in assessing the more diffuse kinds of insidious trauma I have spoken about already.

In very real ways, the memory of the trauma of 9/11 surrounds us. Not least of which is New York City's 9/11 memorial, *Reflecting Absence*. Memorials are spaces of feeling, not to mention essential symbols of the American public imaginary of grief and mourning as much as history. I am interested in the tensions that exist between memorials as sites of history, but also as sites of complex, diffuse affect. Looking specifically at *Reflecting Absence* as one such site, I will then extrapolate some of the intricacies of American public memory in the larger context. How does affect connect us to history, and how can public memory facilitate or hinder that relationship? To what degree does the re-inscription of gendered narratives of "acceptable" affects undermine our ability to *be affected* by sites of public memory?

Ann Cvetkovich argues that, "questions remain about what counts as a trauma history and whose feelings matter in the national public sphere."[6] That is to say, there is a certain degree of overwriting lived history that takes place within the memorial landscape, a certain preservation of "convenient" discourses and the silencing and discarding of the ones that may be less so. Like popular discourses on the traumatic experience of sexual and domestic violence, terrorism discourses avoid taking stock of the cultural climate in which such violence occurs. Events of terrorism, like events of sexual and domestic violence, are frequently framed as exceptional, and are seen to have no causal relationship to society and culture—mainstream debates about the causes gloss over the socio-political climes in which they breed. It is as if we live in a vacuum, where bad things just *happen*; anxieties surrounding these violent acts flourish and serve ends of social control. If the causes of a violent act cannot be discerned, or even realistically hypothesized in thoughtful discussion, can that violence *and how to prevent it* be meaningfully assessed?

Erika Doss writes thoughtfully about this kind of amnesia. In a critique of the Oklahoma City National Memorial, she notes, "No mention is made of how and why these 168 people died, an absence of context that sustains terrorism as an inexplicable evil rather than the structural project of particular human and historical agents."[7] Despite being ourselves responsible for creating the culture in which violent atrocities like terrorism and assault occur, they are narrated as freak occurrences at best, and at worst, crimes for which the victim was asking.

Did the response to the events at Penn State occur as such because our culture is permissive of sexualized violence? Yes, but even richer to think about are the complexities that arise in discourses surrounding sites of national public emotion, like *Reflecting Absence*, and how they inflect our understanding of and willingness to address trauma—as individuals and as a culture.

And so we begin our journey. First, I present the spatial walk-through of the 9/11 memorial complex as a means to deconstruct the ways in which affect and gender come into play as narrative agents. I offer the possibility that national monuments make visible distinct types of masculine patriotism. Then, I speak about my own personal experience at the complex—as a woman, as a critical writer, and as an American citizen. What follows is an attempt to make plain some of the most complex and nuanced structures of national culture.

Reflecting Absence in Space: Visiting the Memorial Complex

In the complex, enduring aftermath of 9/11, US culture bears the indelible marks of its legacy, such as the "threat of terrorism" and the construction of the identity of the ever-present, any-bodied "terrorist." In an ongoing effort to manage the memory of 9/11, monuments and memorials that center around it shape how its meaning is manipulated and disseminated. In its sanitized minimalism, New York City's official 9/11 monument, *Reflecting Absence*, is quickly becoming one of the richest examples of what Pierre Nora might call the "exterior scaffolding" of memory—that is to say, an attempt to apprehend and fix the memory of the lived experience of 9/11.[8] The memorial complex refigures the myriad experiences of 9/11 into a reading of history that is steeped in images of heroic men, enabling a gendered reading of the memorial that is not distinct to this site, but particularly pronounced within it. In addition to offering the possibility that this gendered reading enables the visibility of new forms of masculine patriotism, I will also argue that it suggests a binarized notion of acceptable and unacceptable feeling, which has implications in how we consider trauma to be worthy or unworthy in a broader cultural sense. Consider this: we live in a culture where, misogyny, homophobia, and fear of vulnerability within the military notwithstanding, it is acceptable for male war veterans to discuss experiences of post-traumatic stress, however, female veterans experiencing post-traumatic stress after sexual assault perpetrated *by fellow soldiers* are routinely shamed or outright threatened into silence. Instead of being united through the experience of battle, our war-wounded have cannibalized each other. And, culturally, we have reinforced this. Yet, our monuments to trauma present excellent opportunities to effect dialogue around these issues. How can public memory lead us to a richer engagement with trauma that is less reliant on such problematic binaries, and instead embraces the spectrum of felt experience? How do monuments work to modulate, restrain, redirect, and also capitalize on the affective flows of visitors? That is, how do monuments facilitate or hinder visitors' relationship with the spectrum of felt experience, and to what ends? By going on a brief tour of the complex, we can begin to assess this and other critical questions.

Visiting *Reflecting Absence* is a bit overwhelming, as it includes a multistep process that requires planning. First, one begins in the virtual space of the memorial website, *911memorial.org*, to register for visitor passes. Spontaneous visitors are not currently allowed at the site; a specific visitation slot and personal information is required so that there is a record of every attendee. Visitors' names and "appointments" are printed on small cards that also feature an image of the memorial site, and a barcode lines the right edge.

On the back of the card is a litany of rules and regulations, including "Visitor Information" such as what kind of ID to show and what kinds of bags (not) to bring, along with the official "Terms and Conditions." This section is significant because of the lengths to which it goes to articulate the authority that the memorial staff reserve over visitors. Included in the list is, "Unlawful transfer or reproduction is grounds for seizure and cancellation"; "Holder agrees to submit to security checks prior to entering the 9/11 Memorial"; a long list of "prohibited items"; orders to obey all safety "signage, instructions, and rules"; and, perhaps the most telling, "The 9/11 Memorial reserves the right to refuse admission, control occupancy, or *eject any person* whose conduct is deemed by the management to be disorderly or who fails to comply with the terms and conditions herein" (emphasis mine). Additionally, each visitor also receives a small map of the memorial site and its accompanying structures (*9/11 Memorial Preview Site*, security area, museum, *Tribute WTC Visitor Center*), which I will henceforth refer to as the "memorial complex."

In order to pick up entrance passes upon arrival at the complex, visitors must go to the 9/11 Memorial Preview Site. The building, which is a repurposed storefront space on Vesey Street, acts as a placeholder until the planned museum opens. Upon entry, visitors are confronted with a detailed photographic and textual history of what happened on 9/11, with a step-by-step retelling, "7:59 A.M.: Flight 11 takes off"; "8:14 A.M.: Flight 175 takes off." Several items taken directly from the planned museum collection, like a fragment of twisted steel from one of the towers, are also on display, ostensibly to give visitors a sense of unadulterated "preserved" history. Approximately half of the building's space is filled with gift shop items, where visitors can buy everything from a $57.00 bow tie featuring an allover "reunite" text print in the signature 9/11 memorial font to commemorative jewelry to coffee table books of full-color photographs of the planes hitting the towers.

Visitors then walk a few blocks to the security screening center, an airport-style security area set in another adapted storefront space. Upon entering, guards instruct people to please have passes and IDs available. Visitors scramble to remove shoes, jackets, and items from pockets as lines move. Just like at an airport, all belongings are sent through x-ray screening processes, and visitors walk through metal detectors. Guards check IDs and passes and usher visitors through. Plastered on every wall are large, full-color photographs of smaller scale 9/11 commemorative objects and events from around the world, creating a temporal collision between the so-called "actual" past presented in the photos and the living, lingering aftereffects of 9/11, among them this heightened security.

Across the street is the memorial site itself. Lines form behind velvet ropes designated for either tours or individual visitors, and personnel in official *9/11 Memorial* gear assist accordingly. They check IDs and passes and allow small groups in every half hour. Large concrete barriers hide the memorial from street view, and although this is a temporary result of the ongoing museum construction, it necessarily creates a sense of distance, as if to restrain the potential affective flows of grief-energy until visitors are "properly" inside. At this stage of construction, visitors must walk around the barriers and up the slight hill of Washington Street to enter the memorial, which begins as a park—trees, benches, open space for cigarette breaks and such—and extends into the now well-known concrete recesses of each tower.

The memorial proper is comprised of two concrete "reflecting pools," nearly an acre each, in the footprint of each fallen tower. Waterfalls line the four sides of each rectangular pool, and then drop approximately 30 feet to a small, square collecting basin where the water is then recycled back into its main supply. Some is diverted to a shallow basin that lines the perimeter at about waist height, in front of which are stoic granite plaques that feature the names of all who died in both the 2001 and 1993 World Trade Center attacks. If visitors wish, they can touch this water; all inevitably get sprayed by the mist carried upwards from the pools.

To finish the memorial complex experience, visitors make their way from the memorial site to the *Tribute WTC Visitor Center*. This is a heavily windowed corner structure at Liberty and Greenwich streets. The Visitor Center houses a plethora of gift shop items which, like the website, range from trivial items like pens and key chains, to more somber items like framed photographs of the rubble of the towers. Every item is in some way commemorative, often bearing the branding of the "9/11 Memorial" text-logo, and it is here that visitors can grasp a strong understanding of the managed memory at play. By literally branding the memory of 9/11, the memorial is able to function as a director, officiating over what gets commemorated and how. A pen is not just a pen—it's a *9/11 pen*; through this constant connection to 9/11 via common, everyday objects, the memorial is extended into one's daily life, encouraging ongoing commemoration.

But whose experiences are we remembering? For example, one book among many available for purchase at the Visitor Center is Joel Meyerowitz's photographic tome, *Aftermath*, a gleaming visual journey into 9/11. Meyerowitz was the only photographer granted full access to Ground Zero, and what has made its way onto his pages perpetuates the memory of male heroism: photograph after photograph of the now-iconic male first responders and others who helped at the scene. This is not to say that Meyerowitz categorically excludes women in his work nor that those male first responders *aren't* heroic and admirable, but rather to illustrate that the visual lexicon of the memory of 9/11 is steeped in images of the strength and courage of *men*, and a particular kind of masculinity. Take, for example, *Fireman at Last Column*. A lone, rugged fireman poses with a hoe amidst the expansive backdrop of the cleared rubble at Ground Zero. Staring directly at viewers, he proudly displays the American flag on his shirtsleeve. Such images do little to complicate widely held notions of the archetypal (and patriotic) male savior.[9] Further, Meyerowitz's images gain increased "official" status as several are slated to be included in the official 9/11 museum's permanent collection.

What kind of narrative does the memorial complex present? I experienced this narrative, and its affective by-products, as one of diminished complexity, eschewing the richness of grief for a more simplistic, nationally favored storyline of masculine hero worship and fear: fear of vulnerability, fear of "terrorists," fear of the loss of memory of 9/11 itself. Because of the scripted, linear way in which it moves visitors through the space, the complex creates an atmosphere of fear and confusion, amplifies it at each step, and seems to disengage from important questions of accountability in order to produce a clean, unified presentation of one of the most contested events in American history.

As Jill Bennett notes in her book *Empathic Vision*, "We need to examine how affect is produced within and through a work, and how it might be experienced by an audience coming to the work."[10] Affect is negotiated at every turn in the memorial complex, in problematic and confounding ways. What does the construction of the memorial complex illustrate about our relationship to responses to trauma and agency? Our response to the traumatic violence of 9/11 has been to (re)build, build, build—after all, the memorial proper doesn't exist on its own, but in concert with all the other structures in the complex. The desire for active restoration of one's environment after a traumatic event is natural, but the sheer scale of the complex—literally blocks—is what underscores the excessive structure of commemoration within which the memorial is set. The construction of the memorial complex suggests the notion that to have *done less*—or built less—would have not just been unbearable, but also unacceptable. The twin towers were once a symbol of a thriving, "fully erect" America, and now the complex fills the void created by the attacks by way of enunciating their memory again and again. The complex, and specifically the footprint design of the memorial, functions to remind visitors that on 9/11, the nation was "feminized," proved vulnerable to tragic ends. It at once provokes and contains those same feelings of vulnerability and disquiet, as a means to suggest the "relief" of masculine "protection."

For a time, there was discussion about leaving Ground Zero as it was, as some felt that was the most "powerful" way to commemorate the violent day on which so many met their end.[11] But monuments are historically about power, and control, about the privileging of one historical perspective over all others. In this case, the look backwards is one whose gaze falls on notions of America as exceptional, innocent, and, perhaps most importantly, *not emasculated.* Instead of a meditation on lost lives and fractured confidence, the sprawl of the memorial complex becomes a space in which one can only be "saved" from the discomfort of vulnerability by the heroism of men.

In our contemporary American culture, we generally shy away from unrestrained emotion, and are distrustful of it as a source of knowledge (knowledge implies the rational, the historical enemy of emotion). Rather than sit with the feelings of uncertainty and loss provoked by a national trauma like 9/11, the nation geared up with a full-on rhetorical assault regarding "fighting back" and "never forgetting." These reactions devalue the felt response provoked by meditative, intentional processing—working *through* and *with* discomfort—in favor of action under the guise of "patriotism," suggesting that to feel, rather than project invulnerability in America, is to lose because to feel is to be "weak." To be "weak" is to be "feminine;" to feel is to be "too gentle," and if "the terrorists" perceive "us" as "not tough enough," "they" will attack "us" again. Not surprisingly, this notion of "feeling through" to which I keep referring could also be thought of as historically feminine, if we think back to one example among many, the Salem witch trials, when having a sense of bodily intuition, or feeling "too much," resulted in the death of thousands of women who were perceived to be minions of the devil. Although we certainly no longer live in quite such a climate, we do live out the legacy of a national culture which historically engages reluctantly with feeling, if at all, lest it be perceived as inferior in any number of ways.

The memorial complex disregards feeling through for industrial construction that articulates a sense of masculine aggression. This kind of "acting out" was famously elaborated by Sigmund Freud,[12] and later Dominick La Capra who relevantly noted, "Victims who are acting out the past are caught in it as if it were an eternal present, compulsively repeating actions related to the crisis, forever revisiting the site of trauma."[13] This becomes a signifier of a more uncomfortable, actually very unresolved America, with nowhere for those affects to pour into except for the frenzy of post-9/11 bedlam like the memorial complex.[14] The literal overbuilding—the blocks-wide radius that the complex occupies—suggests a traumatic repetition that hasn't yet found its way to release. The space reifies and covers over painful affects with those of aggression, anger, and detachment (a hurried moving on without first accounting for what's been lost). This tactic of "overcompensating" operates to *manage* fear and anxiety.

Strangely, the minimalist form of *Reflecting Absence* works simultaneously for and against these aims; the Minimalists were pro-confrontation but anti-intimacy, adding a degree of historical background that complicates the memorial's relationship between its very form and feeling. However, the public's preference for minimalism for its equation to power, unity, and tidy resolution cannot be overstated; in her essay, "Minimalism and the Rhetoric of Power," Anna Chave contends that if Donald Judd's work were a person it would be "the strong, silent type."[15] There is a particular kind of masculinity tied into this notion, and it is entombed in the spirit of power—not only is the "strong, silent type" masculine because of his strength, but he is hyper-masculine because he has power over his feelings and keeps them contained. In contemporary American memorial design, Minimalist styling represents this ideal masculinity and reflects national attitudes about how to contend with (i.e. contain) responses to tragedy. Further elucidating the public's preference for this notion of containment, Chave writes,

> As the male body is understood to be the strong body—with strength measured not by tests of endurance, but by criteria of force, where it especially excels—so the dominant culture prizes strength and power to the extent that they have become the definitive or constitutive descriptive terms of value in every sphere: we are preoccupied not only with physical strength and military strength, but with fiscal, cultural, emotional, and intellectual strength, as if actual force were the best index or barometer of success in any of those spheres.[16]

By force, the ideal male keeps his feelings at bay; we call this emotional strength. By the force of their cool austerity, minimalist memorials reroute the "intimate" responses of grief into other flows of anger and confrontation with "the enemy." In this way, *Reflecting Absence* itself becomes a masculine space.

The complex embodies a sense of desperation—the grandiosity with which the American tendency has infused the memorial seems at odds with the unfixed, ephemeral nature of the traumatic memory it aims to commemorate. In this way, we come to know what I call "pathological patriotism," or what amounts to a need to aggressively assert one's national identity in the face of national trauma, even though that nation's policies may be worthy of criticism. I equate these feelings of nationalism with a disavowal of other kinds of feelings, ones that are perhaps more quickly deemed "sensitive" and therefore feminine: sadness, grief, and perhaps most critically, vulnerability. Rather than engage with such feelings, pathological patriotism incites adamancy, aggression, and violence.

In an American cultural context, pathological patriotism occupies a distinctly masculine position. It incites *reaction*, an assertion of masculine dominance as a means to confront the assault of 9/11. It is worth mentioning that although the formal introduction of Post-Traumatic Stress Disorder into the Diagnostic and Statistical Manual of Mental Disorders-IV has legitimized the experience of trauma in certain important ways (namely helping survivors obtain valuable, therapeutic mental health services), it has also given rise to an attitude that feeling trauma "needs" to be "fixed"—that is, cultural attitudes towards felt responses to trauma imply that the "cure" results when one doesn't feel anymore. But isn't trauma much more complicated than that? Doesn't the joy of survival lie partly in the triumph of feeling over the terror that threatened it?

In addition to embodying this frenetic energy, the memorial complex experience also enacts a rhetoric of fear. We need look no further than the visitor pass, although unease builds at every step of the way, folding in and folding over layers of itself. The vague language of the "Terms and Conditions" obviously acts as a catch-all, as anyone can basically be "ejected" for any reason—smart from a crowd control standpoint—but this also casts anyone "unfavorable" as suspicious and fearful. That is, by making room for *any body*, at any time, for any reason, to be the object of fear and suspicion, a narrative of mistrust and anxiety is bred into the atmosphere of the memorial, perpetuating fear since there is no defined "proper" recipient of that anxiety and thus no constructive recourse.

Yet, special weight is given to the lack of the towers, literally monumentalizing the material absence of them. However, how is this absence positioned? If the memorial itself consists of a frozen moment of trauma (the destruction and absence of the towers), one can never exit from the loop of terror brought about from the memory it conjures, thereby maintaining the anxious affective conditions that re-inscribe the narrative of fear. As Erika Doss contends, "Loss connotes destruction and disappearance, whereas absence suggests vacancy or lack, or 'non-presence' and the anxious possibility of re-appearance."[17] Although the monument functions in many ways to resolve and contain notions of the traumatic, this is one instance where it is left to linger. The decision to preserve the voids appears vengeful, a way to *really never forget* the brutality of 9/11. Alternatively, this facet of the space could be read as hyper-feminine, and visitors may wonder if the voids reference female genitalia. However, it reads more like a caricature of femaleness than a robust engagement with a liminal space that embraces the spectrums of femininities and masculinities equally. Instead of functioning as a space that relishes the so-called "feminine" affects of gentleness and openness, the memorial and its vaginal voids are more apt to connote the shame that is often attached to femininity in US culture.

The voids implore us to remember the violence done to us, and act as a means of perpetuating anxiety about future attacks, consequently enabling an ongoing thirst for revenge and protection. Trauma scholars and psychologists (Judith Herman, M.D. and Bessel A. van der Kolk, M.D., to name just two) have long since noted a response wherein the traumatized individual has violent fantasies of retribution as a means to manage the anxiety and despair that comes with the experience and memory of trauma.[18] However, they also regard this as an unsustainable, unrealistic coping strategy. In his article entitled "The Compulsion to Repeat the Trauma: Re-enactment, Revictimization, and Masochism," van der Kolk articulates this danger, stating that "repetition causes further suffering for the victims or for people in their surroundings."[19] That is to say, the layer of repetition embedded in the complex serves not to heal but instead to dangerously remind the nation to be on guard against, and actively hostile towards, as-yet undefined forces. That one could read retribution as encrypted into the site is not necessarily unique, but just a more recent example of how national monuments function to manage and direct our understanding of and relationship to history.

Because the memorial complex reinscribes the memory of male heroism, valor, strength, and action, the brand of patriotism it stimulates may encourage brash, aggressive, and male-celebratory undertones of national feeling. An unfortunate lost opportunity to challenge the status quo of public feeling in America, the complex symbolizes the thinking that the so-called "more feminine" affective responses of loss, sadness, and vulnerability are not also part of the picture of post-9/11 rebuilding. It enacts erasure at the expense of the complexity of feeling grief and trauma, and processing those felt experiences into useful discussion of national memory. In a sense, public memory is an opportunity to "check in"—that is, to evaluate, take stock, and understand where we are culturally and how we can move forward in light of a traumatic event. However, that requires reckoning with some difficult realities. In her piece entitled, "In the absence of an explanation: the World Trade Center memorial site," Clare Hurley astutely contends,

> It has been said that people get the memorial they deserve, but the victims and survivors of the World Trade Center attacks deserve more than a

> memorial that is little more than a cover-up. They deserve a full and open accounting for the events that took loved ones' lives and caused ongoing trauma; only then can an appropriate memorial be created. Ironically, *Reflecting Absence*, which promises to remain a large, uncomfortable void, like an irritated wound that won't heal, is an unintentionally fitting emblem of the failure to adequately account for the terror attacks of September 11, 2001.[20]

Hurley's comments highlight an important issue regarding national monuments, which is the notion that a sense of openness be a part of the historical context of them. Because the memorial scripts and redirects the felt experience of visiting, one is likely blocked from accessing the release from grief that it might provide as a space of commemoration. *Reflecting Absence* is not an intimate space, nor a space that evokes intimacy in its visitors. Many feel cheated by this, and rightfully so—the memorial complex reads less as a monument to the lives lost on 9/11 and more as one to the wounded ego of a nation reliant on tropes of masculine strength to define its identity.

Visiting *Reflecting Absence* provokes many complex questions about American public memory on the whole, but I am particularly compelled to think about how history and memory, society and affect might collide in these contexts. How can a memorial cultivate the co-feeling necessary for so-called "togetherness" to take place?[21] That is, how is feeling carried across bodies? In an effort to understand how we have ended up with the "monumental masculinity" that pervades our national visual memorial culture, as well as to further elaborate on how affects "catch" and circulate within and around it, in the next section I want to offer my own experience at the memorial complex. Finally, how can public memory of national trauma lead us towards a more nuanced and compassionate understanding of trauma? By considering how we discuss trauma on a national level, we may be able to reconsider how we relate to it on more localized scales, and in turn, foster a dialogue that recognizes and embraces survivors with myriad experiences. What follows is an attempt to parse out what it means to make memory—for ourselves and in culture—in contemporary America.

Affected Visiting: Encountering the Memorial Complex

"When is it important to move on and when is it useful, if painful, to return to the past?"[22]
—Ann Cvetkovich, *An Archive of Feelings*

I visited *Reflecting Absence* shortly after it opened to the general public for the tenth anniversary of the attacks on the World Trade Center. Like most visitors, I started my day at the Preview Site. The place was astonishing in the amount of activity it seemed to house, families and individuals practically piled on top of each other waiting to get a glimpse of the institutionalized versions of the events many of them probably knew so well. I wondered why people were there; I think that institutionalized memory brings some people comfort.

Do people in other countries feel this way about their sites of national memory? I'm angered by the attacks because all acts of violence anger me, but I'm also angry at a government that isn't accountable for its mistakes. To this day, I feel a little awkward about considering what some might call conspiracy theory—*did* our government know about the planned attacks beforehand? In a moment of embarrassment at the preview site, I reminded myself that either way, there's no shortage of problems to consider in terms of how we handle things economically, politically, and socially, and the US Occupy Wall Street activity nearby provided a stark contrast to the romantic tone presented at this juncture of the complex, and demanded the accountability that I, too, recognize is missing.

Progressing into the security area, it was hard to ignore that the place was the very embodiment of frantic, tragic, post-traumatic stress—overburdened workers doing their "patriotic duty" by serving the memorial, eager visitors awash in each others' anxious affective energies. Everyone around me was excited in the way that one can get excited on the way to a funeral, a mixture of sadness and anxiety, and in this case, patriotism amplifying the two. I don't think I felt the way I was supposed to feel, because what I really felt was pity. The photos that lined the walls seemed to yearn for validation, or maybe it was a way to process shock. But the way they were arranged, they weren't conversing with me—they were sermonizing. They yelled, *"This is how you will remember this. This is how you will remember us remembering this."* It is what I call memory curation.

The air of hyper-vigilance in this structure was also undeniable, and carried with it a charge of sadness and institutional anxiety. I was afraid the guard would take away my notebook, but maybe more afraid that he would look at me with dewy, patriotic eyes that implore me to "never forget." What are we remembering? The city breathes the language of trauma now, perhaps more than ever. What is the role of vigilance in memory; in grief; actively trying not to forget?

"'Our country is strong,' we are told again and again. I for one don't find this entirely consoling. Who doubts that America is strong? But that's not all America has to be," writes Susan Sontag.[23] Post-9/11 America is a wound that hasn't healed properly—not an open wound, per se, but one whose scabs and eventual scars never formed quite right; now the skin is shiny and puckered, pulled too tightly to function correctly. In our "post" times—post-9/11, post-traumatic, post-civil autonomy–it is hard to think back to before such "wounds" on the national "body." But with every new memorial we get closer to Sontag's words, "that's not all America has to be." America would do well to engage with a sense of vulnerability, a grappling with difficult truths, in addition to strength. What we have now is a culture of false stability, a meaningless bravado, not to mention a misguided lust for control. To put it in pathological terms, we are in a dangerous stage of what Freud called "repetition" as regards trauma, as opposed to working through it. Rather than integrating the trauma of 9/11, the nation has simply fixated on the frightful images of destruction and death, forever looping those initial moments of terror in an interminable national-psychic wail. These are the images that transcend time and memory. These are the ones that have been picked out and saved.

I imagined myself giving a lecture on feelings in this space. In my best Lecture Voice, I commanded the audience's attention,

> *...Things to Keep in Mind, or, Some Thoughts about How We Feel*
>
> *The affects of grief and mourning are difficult to master, yet it is possible to move beyond them. It involves the reconciliation between past and present, between what was once but is no longer. One must wrestle with this on his or her own terms. The process is painful and often disjointed, and not always graceful. Without this process, however, we close ourselves off to accessing the inherent knowledge that affects provide a kind of bodily awareness that is different than what language alone affords us...*

All of this is tied to a problematic relationship to collective mourning. Our public memory misses the mark—rather than function as a site that facilitates our connections to grief, *Reflecting Absence* circles us around feeling but never quite lands us anywhere. Conversation about the events of 9/11 is limited in scope to hero worship and platitudes for the dead. Rather than mourn, for me this site distracts. I can't connect with the narrative; I am outside of it. I think of Erika Doss writing that the memorial is "steeped in historical denial and metaphors of absence, and mastered by motives of rebuilding and revenge," and I feel even more outside.[24] The way I am aware of my body in relation to this space of feeling is in terms of distance and disconnection from the prescriptive sense of mourning, other feeling bodies, and from the memorial object itself. Denial only works for so long as a strategy of mourning, and I feel like I'm watching a sinking ship.

In a momentary flood of dissociation, I try to make sense of the sound around me, but can't. Reflective surfaces are substituted for the difficulty and upheaval of grief, turning any question of accountability back onto the viewer. Indestructible materials communicate a sense that fragility is unacceptable, even in this case of unbridled tragedy. In the visual rhetoric of remembrance, there is no room for loss, only "rebuilding."

I wonder how this ties into recent reports that the NYPD and grief experts are now less worried about a new rash of terrorist attacks at the memorial, but rather the likelihood that suicides will become a disturbing part of the equation as desperation literally plunges people into the reflecting pools.[25]

Does this memorial represent the mourning of mourning?[26] Mustn't there be a better solution? I'm concerned on two levels: that the memorial inhibits or devalues the range of emotion that can accompany processing of grief and trauma, professing a narrow acceptance of only one *kind* of response (love America, don't ask questions, hate "terrorists"), and that because of that, the memorial creates an environment that may romanticize the notion of ending one's life there. This only further perpetuates gendered notions of valor and the "active" quality of *acting on* suicide versus the "passive" quality of feeling beyond it. In her book *The Cultural Politics of Emotion,* Sarah Ahmed elucidates the problem with the limitations inherent in this kind of binary, arguing that "to be emotional is to have one's judgment affected: it is to be reactive rather than active, dependent rather than autonomous."[27] This sets off alarm bells for me: what does it say about a memorial—a public space *devoted to the acknowledgement of grief*—if part of its effect is to numb the circuits of the mind to the point of bypassing engagement with feeling discomfort, not to mention the question of who is accountable for the tragedy, in favor of death?

I ended my day at the Visitors Center. The layout of the memorial complex is such that I think the center is meant to act as a kind of "capstone" experience, not surprisingly, to help tell you how to feel. I waited outside in what periodically became a very long line, overhearing people anxiously chatter about the items they hope to buy to remember their experience—it's a kind of museum gift shop, really. Upon entering, I was completely enveloped by energized bodies—the place was packed. It's not a large building, and is barely large enough to accommodate the hundred or so people perusing the extensive collection of 9/11 photography books, DVDs, and other "memorabilia." Most striking, however, was the video playing on a large flat screen television, an excerpt of *Rebirth* (2011).

Rebirth's premise is simple and compelling: interview survivors of the attacks and the loved ones of those who perished, once a year for ten years. What results is a sort of portrait of the ways in which people move through grief. Not surprisingly, the film generated an overwhelming response.

I was surrounded by the sniffling, sobbing, heaving, sometimes *wailing* mass of fellow visitors. The space was so cramped that if someone sobbed near me, they heaved *onto my body*. A person next to me wiped a tear from his or her hand, which then brushed mine in momentary wetness. What could I do but *be affected*? I was desperately trying to remain critical enough to continue to interrogate my surroundings, but I was also undeniably moved by the outpour of emotion in the room. Out of the corner of my eye, however, I spotted the movie for sale surrounded by a tower of FDNY Beany Babies and key chains, and was reminded of this very constructed environment of feeling.

Overall, I was puzzled by the terse confrontation of the capitalizing and reproduction of fear and anxiety that the space seems to do on the one hand, and the aversion from other affects on the other. I am still processing what it means to *feel* American.

Bibliography

Ahmed, Sara. *The Cultural Politics of Emotion.* New York: Routledge, 2004.

Bennett, Jill. *Empathic Vision: Affect, Trauma, and Contemporary Art.* Palo Alto: Stanford University Press, 2005.

Brennan, Teresa. *The Transmission of Affect.* Ithaca: Cornell University Press, 2004.

Chave, Anna. "Minimalism and the Rhetoric of Power." *Arts Magazine* 64.5 (1990): 264-81.

Codde, Philippe. "Buried by the History of the Twentieth Century: Trauma and Narrative Containment in Daniel Stern's Holocaust Novels." *Partial Answers: Journal of Literature and the History of Ideas* 5 (2007): 55-56.

Cvetkovich, Ann. *An Archive of Feelings: Trauma, Sexuality, and Lesbian Public Cultures.* Durham: Duke University Press, 2003.

Doss, Erika Lee. *Memorial Mania: Public Feeling in America.* Chicago and London: University of Chicago Press, 2010.

Freud, Sigmund. "Further Recommendations in the Technique of Psychoanalysis: Recollection, Repetition, and Working-Through." In *The Standard Edition of the Complete Psychological Works of Sigmund Freud, Vol. XII*, edited by J. Strachey, 147-56. London: The Institute of Psychoanalysis and The Hogarth Press.

Herman, Judith. *Trauma and Recovery: The Aftermath of Violence—From Domestic Abuse to Political Terror,* 39-42. New York: Basic Books, 1992. 1997.

Hurley, Clare. "In the absence of an explanation: the World Trade Center memorial site." Last modified March 20, 2004. World Socialist Web Site. Last accessed April 1, 2012. http://www.wsws.org/articles/2004/mar2004/wtcc-m20.shtml.

LaCapra, Dominick. *History and Memory after Auschwitz.* Ithaca: Cornell University Press, 1998.

Meyerowtiz, Joel. *Aftermath: World Trade Center Archive.* London: Phaidon Press, 2006.

Nora, Pierre. "Between Memory and History: Les Lieux de Memoir." In *The Nineteenth Century Visual Culture Reader,* edited by Vanessa R. Schwartz and Jeannene Przyblyski, 235-37. New York: Routledge, 2004.

Rebirth. Directed by James Whitaker. New York City: Oscilloscope Laboratories, 2011. DVD.

Sontag, Susan. "The Talk of the Town." *The New Yorker Online.* Last modified September 24, 2011. Accessed January 18, 2014. http://www.newyorker.com/archive/2001/09/24/010924ta_talk_wtc.

van der Kolk, Bessel A. "The Compulsion to Repeat the Trauma: Re-enactment, Revictimization, and Masochism." *Psychiatric Clinics of North America* 12.2 (June 1989): 389-411.

Notes

[1] The Political Notebook, accessed March 03, 2011, http://www.thepoliticalnotebook.com/post/3581967666/a-week-ago-15-women-and-2-men-all-of-them.

[2] Brittany L. Stalsburg, *SWAN Fact Sheet.* "While 1 in 6 civilian women will experience sexual assault, for military women this number climbs to approximately 1 in 3," 2011.

[3] "Fox News' Liz Trotta on Women Raped in Military: 'What did they expect? These people are in close contact,'" *Huffington Post*, accessed February 13, 2012, http://www.huffingtonpost.com/2012/02/13/fox-news-liz-trotta-rape_n_1274018.html.
[4] Ann Cvetkovich, *An Archive of Feelings: Trauma, Sexuality, and Lesbian Public Cultures* (Durham: Duke University Press, 2003), 33.
[5] Erika Doss, *Memorial Mania: Public Feeling in America* (Durham: Duke University Press, 2010), 168.
[6] Cvetkovich, *An Archive of Feelings*, 37.
[7] Doss, *Memorial Mania*, 147.
[8] Pierre Nora, "Between History and Memory," in *The Nineteenth-Century Visual Culture Reader*, eds. Vanessa R. Schwartz and Jeannene M. Przyblyski (New York: Routledge, 2004), 237. Therein, Nora particularly notes that "The less memory is experienced from the inside the more it exists only through its exterior scaffolding and outward signs—hence the obsession with the archive that marks our age attempting at once the complete conservation of the present as well as the total preservation of the past. Fear of a rapid and final disappearance combines with anxiety about the meaning of the present and uncertainty about the future to give even the most humble testimony, the most modest vestige, the potential dignity of the memorable."
[9] See also: images of the father, government, and Judeo-Christian god.
[10] Jill Bennett, *Empathic Vision: Affect, Trauma, and Contemporary Art* (Palo Alto: Stanford University Press, 2005), 7.
[11] Doss, *Memorial Mania*, 144. Worries that rebuilding the towers might trigger more acts of terrorism were brushed off as the whimpers of cowards and traitors—of "giving in" to terrorists. Architects Elizabeth Diller and Ricardo Scofido pleaded, "Let's not build something that would mend the skyline, it is more powerful to leave it void." But local politicians and real estate developers insisted on "recovery through rebuilding," on new and loftier buildings that would serve as economic catalysts and reaffirm American national authority, while simultaneously representing the "absence" of the original buildings and several thousand people.
[12] Sigmund Freud, "Further Recommendations in the Technique of Psychoanalysis: Recollection, Repetition, and Working-Through," in *The Standard Edition of the Complete Psychological Works of Sigmund Freud, Vol. XII*, ed. J. Strachey (London: The Institute of Psychoanalysis and The Hogarth Press), 147-56.
[13] Dominick LaCapra, *History and Memory after Auschwitz* (Ithaca: Cornell University Press, 1998).
[14] Philippe Codde, "Buried by the History of the Twentieth Century: Trauma and Narrative Containment in Daniel Stern's Holocaust Novels," *Partial Answers: Journal of Literature and the History of Ideas* 5 (2007): 55-56.
[15] Anna Chave, "Minimalism and the Rhetoric of Power," *Arts Magazine* 64 (1990): 264-81.
[16] Chave, "Minimalism," 272.
[17] Doss, *Memorial Mania*, 345.
[18] Bessel A. van der Kolk, "The Compulsion to Repeat the Trauma: Re-enactment, Revictimization, and Masochism," *Psychiatric Clinics of North America* 12.2 (June 1989): 389-411 and Judith Herman, "Terror," in *Trauma and Recovery: The*

Aftermath of Violence—From Domestic Abuse to Political Terror (New York: Basic Books, 1997), 40.
[19] van der Kolk, "The Compulsion to Repeat the Trauma," 1.
[20] Clare Hurley, "In the absence of an explanation: the World Trade Center memorial site," last modified March 20, 2004, World Socialist Web Site, accessed April 1, 2012, http://www.wsws.org/articles/2004/mar2004/wtcc-m20.shtml.
[21] Teresa Brennan, *The Transmission of Affect* (Ithaca: Cornell University Press, 2004).
[22] Cvetkovich, *An Archive of Feelings*, 156.
[23] Susan Sontag, "The Talk of the Town," *The New Yorker Online*, last modified September 24, 2011, accessed January 19, 2014, http://www.newyorker.com/archive/2001/09/24/010924ta_talk_wtc.
[24] Doss, *Memorial Mania*, 156.
[25] "At 9/11 Memorial, NYPD and Grief Experts Concerned About Possibility for Suicides," Huffington Post, accessed February 17, 2012, http://www.huffingtonpost.com/2012/02/17/911-memorial-concerns-nypd-suicide-risk_n_1284645.html.
[26] "Feel this and only this."
[27] Sarah Ahmed, *The Cultural Politics of Emotion* (New York: Routledge, 2004), 3.

PROSTHETIC MEMORIES OF FRANKLIN D. ROOSEVELT'S INFANTILE PARALYSIS AS NARRATIVE EMBODIMENTS FOR TRAUMATIC AMERICAN WAR MEMORY

SARA POLAK

In the opening scene of the film *FDR American Badass!* (Garrett Brawith, 2012), Franklin Roosevelt is bitten in his leg by a werewolf when hunting with some friends. The werewolf bite gives him the polio that paralyzes his legs; the werewolf is killed and on inspection turns out to be a Nazi, sent by Hitler and his pack of Nazi werewolves. Roosevelt's staff has Albert Einstein invent a superhero fighting wheelchair in which commander-in-chief and supreme "badass" FDR singlehandedly combats and conquers the Evil in Europe. While obviously an absurd, silly and low-budget film with a ditto plot, *FDR American Badass!* makes a move that occurs regularly in films about World War II and other cultural artifacts that function as sites of American World War II remembrance. Somehow the trauma of the war—particularly the trauma of being attacked by a sneaky (invisible, treacherous) enemy—is projected onto, or, as in this case, is literally embodied by, the president's disability through polio. This chapter aims to show how and why this mechanism works, building on cultural memory and trauma theories formulated by Marianne Hirsch and Alison Landsberg, and complicating Landsberg's concept of prosthetic memory.[1] It uses the concrete case of representing Roosevelt's disability in films, because that is exemplary of what happens in prosthetic cultural memory on a conceptual level. To show how the case of Roosevelt's disability operates as a concrete metaphor with which to address conceptual issues that remain imprecise in Landsberg's approach to prosthetic memory, I will first discuss how Roosevelt's disability has been remembered in American mainstream cultural representations since his death. Then Landsberg's concept of prosthetic memory will be introduced and elaborated on in relation to theories about collective memory, trauma, and postgenerations.[2] Finally, using several cinematic representations of Franklin Roosevelt's physical prosthesis, I will show how, with prosthetic memory, Landsberg has introduced an important concept and a felicitous term, which, however, needs to be complicated and expanded.

Roosevelt's Disability in American Memory

Franklin D. Roosevelt, US president during most of the Great Depression and World War II (1933-1945), had poliomyelitis at age 39 and was, as a result, paralyzed from the waist down. In popular biographies, museum exhibitions, documentaries and other sites of memory much attention is given to the idea that FDR kept his disability a secret.[3] An early and paradigmatic example of this is Hugh Gallagher's bestselling popular biography *FDR's Splendid Deception: The Moving Story of Roosevelt's Massive Disability—And the Intense Efforts to Conceal It from the Public* (1985). This book, like its title, created and reinforced popular narratives about FDR's experience of polio and the resultant disability. Gallagher argues that these experiences were extremely traumatic, with a highly formative effect on his character, and that Roosevelt was very secretive about them. Those narratives have been echoed endlessly in popular culture, for instance in films like *Warm Springs* (Joseph Sargent, 2005), documentaries like *FDR: A Presidency Revealed* (2005), and experiential guided tours like that of the Roosevelt Home in Hyde Park (NY). This essay does not argue for or against claims of how traumatic the disease was or why FDR kept his disability a secret, but questions why these have become such important aspects of FDR in American cultural memory, and how they function as mnemonic prostheses for American national traumas of World War II.

One film in which the representation of Roosevelt's personal trauma is intricately connected with collective American trauma memory is *Pearl Harbor*. Michael Bay's 2001 three-hour box office success (the sixth highest earning picture of 2001), starring Ben Affleck and Kate Beckinsale, was made to remember the sixtieth anniversary of the attack on Pearl Harbor.[4] It is essentially a love story against the backdrop of the attack on Pearl Harbor and the Doolittle Raid—the bombing of Tokyo that was the US's response. Most of the film's plot takes place at the hierarchical level of air force pilots and nurses, but that narrative is regularly interspersed with a subplot of high-level decision-making about war tactics. One of the main characters in this subplot is Franklin Roosevelt (Jon Voight), portrayed as a brave yet compassionate commander-in-chief, who has to drive his risk-obsessed top officers into action. Roosevelt's being in a wheelchair is presented as an essential motivation underlying his energetic decisiveness and courageous determination to take bold action in response to the attacks. The very first introduction of this subplot, occurring 32 minutes into the film, is a shot of

Roosevelt's wheelchair being rolled into a conference room. Thus, *Pearl Harbor* makes use of the presumably common knowledge that Roosevelt was in a wheelchair.

Although clearly Roosevelt's wheelchair is seen nowadays as a well-known emblem by makers of box-office hits like *Pearl Harbor*, Roosevelt's supposed secrecy about it is almost equally famed. When early in July 2013 an eight-second clip of President Roosevelt in his wheelchair surfaced, it became instant world news.[5] No such footage had been available previously, barring a single well-known photograph—clearly posed and consciously distributed—of FDR in his wheelchair taken in 1941. Without actually revealing anything previously unknown, the discovery of the clip made an incredible impact as news, but that is not because it contained any new information. It has been well-known that Roosevelt had had polio ever since it happened, and that he was therefore wheelchair-bound has been common knowledge at least since the 1970s when academic and popular monographs, such as Gallagher's, focusing on FDR's disability, started to appear and receive widespread attention. Before and during Roosevelt's presidency, Americans knew that the president had had poliomyelitis and was an "invalid" as a result. They saw him move to the rostrum before speeches, supported by a walking stick or crutch on one side and aided usually by one of his sons on the other, and in one of his last public speeches, he himself explicitly apologized for addressing the Congress from his chair.[6] Referring so explicitly to his physical invalidity was certainly not Roosevelt's habit, but he was in other ways publicly visible with and because of it. He set up the March of Dimes to further medical research concerned with finding a polio vaccine and helping polio survivors; it is still one of the largest charities in the US.[7] Large celebration dinners and balls were held throughout the nation in celebration of Roosevelt's birthday to raise money for the fight against polio, and he was personally very involved in developing Warm Springs, Georgia, as a polio rehabilitation center. Moreover, campaign biographies actually gave explicit attention to Roosevelt's physical condition, with Earl Looker—a Republican biographer—concluding that Roosevelt was in perfect shape for the presidency, despite his polio history.

Even if many Americans during his presidency must have known about Roosevelt's disability and must have been able to imagine him in a wheelchair, there is a stark contrast between that implicit and indirect knowledge and the public image of FDR that has evolved in the last few decades. In recent representations of Roosevelt, memorial, cinematic or documentary, his wheelchair has practically become his most memorable prop. In movies about World War II made over the last 20 or 30 years, when viewers see a man in a wheelchair enter the scene, they understand immediately that this must be the President of the United States. So, whereas Roosevelt's disability was perhaps less a secret during his presidency than we now tend to think, his wheelchair has come to occupy center stage only relatively recently. In modern representations, Roosevelt's disability is practically always portrayed as a nearly insurmountable personal trauma, which he nonetheless overcame. I will argue here that, as such, Roosevelt's disability and the presumed trauma surrounding it in his private life have come to function as a metaphor for American World War II traumas, and that the silence surrounding FDR's disability is an important enabling factor in this metaphor.

This chapter focuses on the functions Roosevelt's disability and wheelchair have been attributed in cultural memory. I do not mean to argue here that Roosevelt was not secretive about his handicap, or that his suffering from polio and its effects was not personally traumatic for him. Rather, I want to argue that Roosevelt's polio has in various ways become a metaphor for the US's national traumatic memory of being attacked by surprise in World War II, especially in cinema, and that Roosevelt's silence on this matter helped it become so. The political agency of these metaphors lies in the fact that they project nationally shared, but simultaneously highly diverse and indeed often opposing and antagonistic traumatic memories, onto an individual's experiences. Because of this individualization of the trauma—carried, as it were, by an individual who simultaneously represents the nation—and because of the displacement of its cause (from war to polio), Rooseveltian trauma narratives can create or suggest consensus in a way other national memories of war cannot, because they are too heavily tied up with political disputes, historical trauma and conflicting interests. As such, narratives of FDR's polio trauma have come to effectively embody or stand in for narratives of traumatic American war memory, particularly through film.

Prosthetic Memory in a Theoretical Context

Cultural memory, as the Assmanns understand it, concerns memories that are no longer "lived" in society, but are culturally inherited. Such memories become fixed legends or myths, which function as cultural touchstones for a group,

> Cultural memory has its fixed point; its horizon does not change with the passing of time. These fixed points are fateful events of the past, whose memory is maintained through cultural formation (texts, rites, monuments) and institutional communication (recitation, practice, observance). We call these 'figures of memory'.[8]

Roosevelt's presidency is now in the 21st century precisely so far away that it is in the process of becoming part of cultural memory rather than "communicative memory," the counterpoint the Assmanns have formulated, to refer to lived memory in the process of evolving and existing in various forms among different individuals and groups. The fact that Roosevelt's presidency and person are currently at the point of shifting from communicative memory towards a more fixed, ritualized cultural remembrance makes his a particularly intriguing case. At stake here is the question of agency: FDR himself was very keen to exert influence over his long-term cultural remembrance, but 21st century rememberers too apply and appropriate his story to suit purposes remote from FDR's agenda. The place of his wheelchair and the trauma of his paralysis—which, if not a secret, was hardly central to his public image—have changed radically since his death in ways that are informative of how this process works, and where the agency lies. Following memory scholar Jay Winter, I therefore make a distinction between memory and remembrance, where remembrance connotes the ritualized and politically charged quality of practically all acts of collective memory.[9]

Thus, in cultural remembrance, the historical context in which the remembered events happened are not primarily steering the memory's content, but rather the interests relevant at the time of the memory's construction.[10] This is not to say that, when the remembered events happened, no thought was given to how they would "go down in history." Franklin Roosevelt particularly considered that question and was very active and astute at steering how he would be remembered, to the point that some of his own preferred interpretations of his presidency can by now be said to have become cultural memory. Thus, some of Roosevelt's own formulations and favored epigrams have become fixed points in the collective memory of his presidency. For example some of his most widely disseminated and most flattering nicknames, like "Dr. New Deal" and "Dr. Win-the-War" are Roosevelt's own coinages, and the Franklin D. Roosevelt Presidential Library and Museum, which is still leading in giving voice to celebrations of Franklin Roosevelt and his presidency, was Roosevelt's own invention.[11]

Silence, however, also played a central role in Roosevelt's management of his own image—not only with regard to his disability. Through his silence or else his penchant for being vocally buoyant but nonetheless elusive, he carefully molded sites for the (future) public to fill in its own narrative interpretations. One of his most regularly cited phrases is, "I'm a juggler, I never let my left hand know what my right hand does." Additionally, in a letter to a fan who advised him to address the nation over the radio more often, he replied, "For the sake of not becoming a platitude to the public, I ought not to appear oftener. (…) I am inclined to think that in England Churchill, for a while, talked too much, and I don't want to do that."[12] Here, and in some other places, Roosevelt explicitly says he monitors that he is not talking too much. Nowhere does he say that he avoids any topic private or public because it is too painful, traumatic or otherwise unspeakable; nonetheless, understandably, his reservation in speaking about his polio is often interpreted as such, particularly in the context of trauma theory.

Silence has a central role in western trauma theory. As Mieke Bal has argued concisely in her introduction to *Acts of Memory: Cultural Recall in the Present*, "trauma narrative" is inherently a contradictory term. Essentially since Freud, trauma has culturally been regarded as precisely the kind of physical or psychological wound that inhibits its own narration. Whether due to repression or dissociation the defining characteristic of traumatic memory is that it cannot be narrated. The gap in the narrative in turn leads to a gap in the identity of the traumatized, by way of the also Freudian idea that identity consists of the narratives we tell ourselves and each other about ourselves. Thus, trauma both defies and can only be overcome through the construction of a narrative to fill the cavity.[13] Like many other scholars of traumatic memory, notably Dominick LaCapra in *Writing History, Writing Trauma*, Bal particularly stresses the importance of listeners to bear witness to trauma narratives.[14] LaCapra goes on to theorize the need for witnesses to the testimonial narrative and the impact of trauma narratives on witnesses.

Whereas LaCapra focuses on the role of witnesses in healing original traumas, in *The Generation of Postmemory* Marianne Hirsch studies the need for trauma narratives for a particular subgroup of witnesses: those whose parents or otherwise affiliated forebears have experienced traumas they have not themselves lived through—particularly the Holocaust. She argues that this postgeneration of direct children of the Holocaust needs trauma narratives as much as their parents (though in different ways and for different reasons). Hirsch presents an intriguing case of precisely this process and the inherent paradox of the narration of traumatic memory.[15] "Fifty Years of Silence" is an artwork by Tatana Kellner made up of two books containing her father's and mother's Holocaust memoirs written in their own handwriting and native Polish, side by side with her own English translation. As such their narratives are told in the parents' own voices, or in fact in the only replacement for their actual voices in which they could tell it—the artist initially intended to tape-record her parents as they told their stories, but they found they literally could not speak about them or communicate them in vocal form to their daughter. Thus the trauma is both narrated for the benefit of direct and indirect children of survivors, and retains its quality of uncommunicability, in the sense that the parents' trauma is not directly addressed. The silence is both broken and sustained: the books narrate, but do not actually produce sound; they contain the story of the trauma, but fail to communicate it in its original form because the postgeneration cannot actually understand the language, nor truly relate or bear witness to the experience. Yet, Hirsch argues, this silence is productive: if not for the victims themselves, it provides Kellner and by extension the postgeneration at large with a site to work through the trauma of not-having-been-there, of deriving from parents an unrelatable and obliterated history. Thus, the artwork functions as a kind of replacement for actual communicable family history—communicative memory—in a way comparable to a prosthesis for a missing limb. At the center of both of Kellner's books there is a cavity shaped from a plaster cast of her parents' arms (obviously tattooed with their depersonalizing Auschwitz numbers), stressing both the presence of the trauma and the emptiness at the heart of its narration. This arm-shaped emptiness supports the reading of "Fifty Years of Silence" as a sort of metaphorical prosthesis for an actual family history.

Alison Landsberg has introduced the term *prosthetic memory* to describe those kinds of memories that evolve in the modern world of mass migration and mass media. Landsberg argues that as a result of mass migration, and the traumas involved in particular migrations (e.g. Jews escaping the Holocaust, African Americans having been torn away from their families through slavery), and on the other hand the possibilities of the available mass media, prosthetic memory has evolved as a new form of memory. Prosthetic memory is an alternative for memories a person has lived through, or somehow organically inherited from parents or other ethnic or cultural forbears,

> This new form of memory (…) emerges at the interface between a person and a historical narrative about the past, at an experiential site such as a movie theater or museum. In this moment of contact, an experience occurs through which the person sutures himself or herself into a larger history. (…) In the process that I am describing, the person does not simply apprehend a historical narrative but takes on a more personal, deeply felt memory of a past event through which he or she did not live. The resulting prosthetic memory has the ability to shape that person's subjectivity and politics.[16]

Prosthetic memory, then, can be placed in between Assmann's cultural memory, which is more fixed and functions as a cultural point of reference to identify a particular group, on the one hand, and communicative memory, which is negotiated in the social realm of lived experience, on the other. Memory-making through the experience of film or an artwork like "Fifty Years of Silence" is more intensely personal and experiential than learning the *topoi* of cultural memory, but less so than direct experience. Landsberg calls this kind of memory acquired through mass cultural commodities prosthetic for four reasons. Firstly, it is not the product of lived experience or organically inherited. Indeed, even if the cultural artifact in contact with which the memory is produced is not fictional (as it often is), the memory is like a prosthesis in the sense that it is still fake, even if it seems like and serves as a memory of lived experience. Secondly, prosthetic memories are products of sensuous experiences, or as Landsberg somewhat dramatically puts it, "like an artificial limb, [they] are actually worn on the body." Almost as an afterthought, she adds what seems to me essential, "Also, prosthetic memories, like an artificial limb, often mark trauma."[17] Thirdly, like prostheses, they are interchangeable and commodified to fit a mass audience, even if the same movie (exhibition, documentary) can produce different prosthetic memories in different people, and so in that respect do not generate or echo a referential collective or cultural memory in Halbwachs' or Assmann's sense. Finally, Landsberg regards prosthetic memories, like other prostheses, as useful, because "they help condition how a person thinks about the world and [they] might be instrumental in articulating an ethical relation to the other."[18] Thus, prosthetic memories can bridge differences between members of different ethnic or cultural groups. Landsberg argues, for instance, that prosthetic memories of slavery history can be assumed not only by African Americans, and Holocaust memories are appropriated by non-Jews as well.

The point is that the adopted prosthetic memory attains the function of a supporting limb for one's own lost history. Landsberg investigates cases where this loss is incurred through migration or separation from one's natural forebears, including cases in which organic memories cannot be shared satisfactorily because of their traumatic nature for the generation who lived through the past event. However, there is also a potential demand for prosthetic memories in cases where (elements of) traumatic events remain too painful for the postgeneration as well, even if they could be narrated. This is, I believe, the case with particularly uncomfortable aspects of past events, which do not find their way into cultural memory, in this case painful, awkward, or humiliating experiences surrounding World War II, particularly Pearl Harbor. Essentially these are traumas that are not absorbed into narrative memories, because the postgeneration does not want or is unable to bear witness to them. This leaves gaps in cultural memory, and therefore in the movies and other cultural artifacts that provoke prosthetic memories in their spectators. These gaps may be filled with other memories—what Freud would have called *Deckerinnerungen*.[19] Freud explores this concept in the individual. As he explains in his 1899 essay of the same title, screen memories are childhood memories that seem innocent to the point of meaninglessness, but actually both conceal and symbolize repressed memories or desires. This does not, Freud argues, deny the accuracy of the original memory, but it does clarify why particular, often seemingly innocuous, memories are retained: they can easily function as carriers for the actual memory or desire that is screened off. Something similar happens when traumatic war memories are replaced, overlaid or otherwise tangled up with much more gratifying memories of Roosevelt's disability. The memory of Roosevelt's disability is then the innocuous screen: not a fantasy but a real memory of which the historical relevance seems hard to understand in hindsight, except as a foil for something else. As such, these memories of Roosevelt's polio are in a sense prosthetic in two ways: firstly by Landsberg's definition because they are generated through experiential mass media and secondly because they are prostheses for memories that remain distressful to narrate directly.

The concrete narratives of Roosevelt's disease and disability, which always involve actual prostheses (wheelchair, crutches, leg braces), are then exemplary of what happens on a conceptual level: mass mediated narratives about him take on the function of prosthetic memories to their audiences, particularly in the second sense. The silences kept by Roosevelt and his staff provide room for film makers and their audiences to fit metaphorical prostheses, narratives interpreting traumas that are overtly attributed to Roosevelt, but actually standing in for more collective ones. Roosevelt's silence about his wheelchair lends itself well as a prosthetic site for the adaptation of other trauma narratives. And unlike adopting the subject position of the cuckolded American GI or officer around the Pearl Harbor attack, the position of the handicapped but powerful and resilient president is one that is attractive to imaginatively assume. Cinema, Landsberg argues, is especially suited for making this kind of movement, because it is, like lived events, highly experiential and transporting. It is, to modify the Freudian maxim, the royal road to prosthetic memory, but while a commercially successful film can address large parts of Pearl Harbor memory, it needs to avoid others. Michael Bay's *Pearl Harbor* replaces these, in another act of prosthesis, with images of Roosevelt's disability; *Hyde Park on Hudson* and *FDR American Badass!* go even further: they focus so strongly on Roosevelt's personal predicament, that, in connecting it to World War II geopolitics, they can avoid any mention of Pearl Harbor altogether.

Roosevelt's Wheelchair as Cinematic Prosthesis for Pearl Harbor Trauma Memory

The historical Roosevelt understood that the Japanese attacks on Pearl Harbor and other American bases on December 7, 1941 would loom large, but would also be problematic in American memory. As he said in his historic address the next day, December 7, 1941 would be "a date which will live in infamy" and "always will our whole Nation remember the character of the onslaught against us."[20] Of course "Pearl Harbor" has ever since remained a key national American memory—the first point of reference to be invoked following that other day of infamy, September 11, 2001—but only parts of it are habitually referred to in mass culture productions, while others are not. The problem lies not so much in condemning "the character of the onslaught," but in recognizing what it has done to the US and how the US made that possible. In the monograph *A Date Which Will Live, Pearl Harbor in American Memory*, Emily Rosenberg, draws attention to the—much older—trope of the US as a "sleeping giant," an innocent and benign but extremely strong superpower, awoken by a "dastardly attack" (FDR, Pearl Harbor speech, December 8, 1941). In *Pearl Harbor*, the attack and the US's response is portrayed at length and in detail, including much bloodshed and a Japanese general saying, "I fear all we have done is to awaken a sleeping giant," but the film's heroes respond to the pain and humiliation of the attack not with words, but with a silent determination to take revenge; they go to war in a quiet rage. Instead, at a number of key moments when the shock and pain of the attacks are shown at their worst and most unbearable, these are broken off by a cut to Roosevelt in his wheelchair. Such cuts to Roosevelt's wheelchair, and the traumatizing nature of the moments that precede them, suggest that the polio narrative functions as a screen memory, overlaying and mitigating the shock of the actual trauma, within the prosthetic memory, through the use of a concrete prosthesis.

Pearl Harbor may not be a collective trauma on the scale or of the same kind as the Holocaust in Europe, but taken as a *pars pro toto* for a wider range of surrounding events and experiences it is nonetheless a national trauma, painfully undercutting cultural ideologies of self-reliance and American exceptionalism. The national fear of being attacked from the outside, or from the inside by an invisible enemy, and the sudden realization that the enemy may already have infiltrated deeply into their own ranks does not originate in World War II, as Rosenberg shows, but did become a national trauma within communicative memory as a result of it. In *FDR American Badass!* America is attacked by undercover Nazi werewolves—such themes of alien infestations are highly recurrent in American popular culture, be it in the form of Nazi werewolves, zombies or guerilla terrorism. Arguably, however, the absence of collective memory about American Nazi sympathizers in the US, who of course did exist notwithstanding Roosevelt's widely supported hostility to fascist ideologies, suggests that there are domestic issues surrounding World War II that still continue not to be addressed directly in popular culture. Roosevelt's disability, on the other hand, is very easily remembered as a narrative of individual struggle with deservedly glorious outcomes—after all Roosevelt did not conquer his physical impairment, but he did overcome its far-reaching social implications. That his victory is easily claimed as an American victory, representative of national merits, becomes clear for instance from Clinton's speech at the dedication of the Franklin D. Roosevelt Memorial in Washington (DC), "It was that faith in his own extraordinary potential that enabled him to guide his country from a wheelchair. And from that wheelchair, and a few halting steps, leaning on his son's arms or those of trusted aides, he lifted a great people back to their feet and set America to march again toward its destiny."[21] Clinton does not say that the wheelchair was instrumental in "lifting a great people back to their feet," but the neat juxtaposition of the two does carry that suggestion. *Pearl Harbor* represents precisely that take on the function of Roosevelt's wheelchair. His first entrance, showing the wheelchair before its occupant, already signals that the President's disability is attributed an important role in the film, however tentatively it is related to its subject and action. In the same scene, introducing the narrative of the decision-making officials, Roosevelt opens the meeting by saying, "I'm afraid I'm in a bad mood. Churchill and Stalin are asking me what I'm asking you. How long is America going to pretend the world is not at war? (…) But our people think Hitler and his Nazi thugs are Europe's problem."[22] Clearly, at this stage, that is also what the present chief officers think, but Roosevelt sees ahead, and characterizes the enemy in terms of a spreading infection, made worse by America's petrified denial of its global contagiousness. The implicit suggestion is that FDR, after having had polio, is now more proactive in recognizing threats of contagion.

Further into the film, following dramatic footage of the Pearl Harbor attack, including a series of shots of lost or to-be-amputated limbs, Roosevelt is wheeled towards a messenger whom he asks, "How bad…?" This cut and Roosevelt's question, suggesting that he is in some way the direct, physical victim of the attack, conjures up a link between his disability and the invalidity of those anonymous Pearl Harbor veterans. This suggests that Roosevelt embodies the US as a nation under siege and implicitly evokes a sense that Roosevelt is the ideal man for this job because he is experienced, if not directly as a war veteran, then at least as someone who knows what it means to be the bodily site for a fight between good and evil. As such, his particular narrative of conquering disability is both an apt and a politically charged placeholder for what is too devastating about Pearl Harbor to address upfront. The scene seems to argue that trauma is best confronted frankly and straightforwardly as Roosevelt does in *Pearl Harbor*. This is paradoxical, because the scene's own shift to Roosevelt's polio as the focus of attention, suggests that the confrontation with Pearl Harbor is so debilitating that prosthetic narratives are needed to screen off the trauma, even from prosthetic memory.

That reading is later confirmed and elaborated on, first by the combination of Roosevelt's famous war speech (cited above) in voiceover, with more extensive and dramatic footage of Pearl Harbor, linking the Presidential voice to the sheer enormousness of the trauma incurred. Following that documentary-style interlude repeating words and visual images that remain highly familiar in cultural memory, is another scene of a meeting between FDR and his military chiefs of staff. Again, Roosevelt is portrayed as eager to fight back and show America's spirit. Again, body metaphors are used to connect, or indeed metaphorically replace, Roosevelt's body with that of the nation, for instance when FDR invokes a boxing expression: "We are on the ropes, gentlemen." In a sense, at that point the US and Roosevelt personally are cast in the same position of being nearly beaten down physically and mentally, with the difference that Roosevelt has already had time to recover from his injuries, at least psychologically, an experience the military leaders clearly have not yet had, as their panicked response in the meeting signals. In a charismatic and meditative monologue, Roosevelt says,

> Gentlemen, most of you did not know me when I had the use of my legs. I was strong and proud and arrogant. Now I wonder every hour of my life, why God put me into this chair. But when I see defeat in the eyes of my countrymen, in your eyes right now, I start to think that maybe He brought me down for times like these, when we all need to be reminded who we truly are, that we will not give up or give in.[23]

The scene ends dramatically when, in answer to this speech, one of the generals says "what you're asking can't be done." Roosevelt, refusing all help, gets up, walks away from his wheelchair, and replies, "Do not tell ME it can't be done!" Here, the cinematic Roosevelt implies that it is precisely his disability, indeed his prosthesis, which has caused him to be mentally prepared and equipped, unlike the others, for a crisis situation like this. The primary meaning of "in this chair" is "in this wheelchair," but it could also be taken to refer to "this position"; this conflates the office of Presidency with being disabled, underlining that the two are united in one person, and stressing the divine interference at work here. When the cinematic Roosevelt says that, "maybe He brought me down for times like these, when we all need to be reminded who we truly are," he implies that being "brought down" by polio is after all an empowering experience, strengthening one perhaps not physically but psychologically, bucking up a nation in distress. The scene is dramatic and inspires prosthetic memories of the war in Landsberg's sense—perhaps even more so than the shocking Pearl Harbor footage that precedes it. Moreover, it presents a metaphorical vision of the future of America "on the ropes"—like Roosevelt, it will be back to become more powerful than ever.

Roosevelt's final gesture, that of standing up independently by refusing to accept that "it can't be done," is ambiguous. It is a strong and emotive but also a troubling moment: clearly Roosevelt cannot really stand up independently, and his refusal of help makes the gesture more powerful, but also exposes his fragility, not just physically but also psychologically. One of the widespread narratives surrounding Roosevelt's paralysis and his process toward rehabilitation and integration of the disability in his life, is that he utterly refused to acknowledge that he would not walk again. Gallagher and other chroniclers of Roosevelt polio narratives regularly repeat how in social situations FDR often professed that, "with a year or two more of progress he would be able to discard his braces and walk unassisted," and that even in private, he kept assiduously practicing to walk in ways that were realistically unattainable given the condition of his leg muscles.[24] By implication, the suggestion is that denial is also part of what was at stake in the situation of the US after Pearl Harbor. However, this suggestion seems unintentional, which strengthens the idea that Roosevelt's invalidity is a screen memory with enough points of comparison to what is screened off to work well—so well, indeed, that the film makers may not have realized the extent to which the metaphor is a prosthesis, or which trauma it is that is being hidden behind Roosevelt's dramatic gesture.

If narratives of Roosevelt's polio and disability have one thing in common with the one presented in *Pearl Harbor*, it is that they portray the experience of having polio and becoming paralyzed as deeply traumatic on a personal emotional level. They also practically always stress the strength of Roosevelt's morale through this personal crisis and the idea that his suffering contributed both to his extreme resilience in the face of subsequent crises (e.g. the Great Depression, World War II) and his great compassion for others (particularly the victims of the Great Depression and the war). In *Pearl Harbor* Roosevelt is the first to literally stand up against the Japanese, but he is also the one most visibly affected by the news of the deaths of American soldiers.

It is hard to say to what extent and in what way his disease and disability really were traumatic for the actual Roosevelt, but the silence he kept about it does two things: it suggests, in the light of modern western trauma theory that it was indeed very traumatic, so much so that it was on some level impossible for him to speak about. And secondly, it leaves a massive gap that later generations have been eager to fill. This is, on the one hand, the postgeneration's need to know its own history—which is in part what Hugh Gallagher, himself a polio victim and thus a non-familial beneficiary of Roosevelt's cultural heritage, has said drove him to do research for and write *FDR's Splendid Deception.*[25] On the other hand, FDR's reticence provides space for later generations to fill in the prosthetic memories that they need. This duality draws attention to the multidirectional quality of screen memories, which Michael Rothberg has discussed in *Multidirectional Memory*: they are at the center of complex temporal relations between needs and desires of past and present, and "both hide and reveal what has been suppressed."[26] Thus, Roosevelt, consciously or not, left a fertile space for screen memories to be inserted, which exaggerate his importance in remembrance, whereas in the other direction, he offers a useful and relatively easy route for the postgeneration to channel its least comfortable memories of Pearl Harbor.

The Roosevelt in *Pearl Harbor* does refer to his disability but in a way that fits much better into the context of 2001 views of and discourse about disability than in the context of 1941 discourse. Roosevelt's treatment of both his disability and the crisis at Pearl Harbor, as setbacks that are hard to chew, but also provide wisdom and self-reliance, are representative of a modern American self-perception. But they also gloss over an aspect of trauma—both that of Pearl Harbor, and perhaps the trauma of polio—that is harder to address: something is also lost, not all suffering has a cause or can really be turned into something positive even in the long run. Many of those killed at Pearl Harbor died for no good reason at all, because America was collectively too late in recognizing the danger. Similarly, polio and other diseases destroyed many lives before vaccinations were invented, either because their victims died, or because they were excluded from public life and society failed to offer opportunities to give meaning to their lives. Roosevelt was then, and in fact remains, a rare exception. Projecting the trauma of Pearl Harbor onto Roosevelt's personal trauma of polio thus provides a site for working through Pearl Harbor. Doing so also pigeonholes Pearl Harbor with Roosevelt as one of the exceptional—indeed exceptionally American—cases in which suffering is not pointless. In these cases, trauma is presented as enhancing individual talent rather than wasting it.

Hyde Park on Hudson (2012) directed by Roger Michell and starring Bill Murray as FDR makes his handicap functional in similar ways. The film tells the story of the British royal visit to Roosevelt's Hyde Park estate in the Hudson Valley in June 1939, to ask the US for support in resisting the Nazi attacks on Great Britain. This plea for help from America's former colonizer is projected as a symbolic moment in the countries' history, at which the US takes over the role of world hegemony from Great Britain. That element is thickly underscored in the film: the King and Queen constantly fear that they are being made fun of, and their extremely informal reception at Hyde Park hints that they are right to be worried. Roosevelt's private life is highly instrumental here: its informality, the amateurism of his mother's cookery, and the King's bedroom decorated with cartoons of British Redcoats losing the Independence War all signal that America as FDR represents it, is deeply indifferent to the British King and the respectful reception his position once commanded. Roosevelt's wheelchair is instrumental in the show of blithe informality: he receives the King and Queen sitting in a chair, and his requisite "Please forgive me for not getting up" excuses but also stresses the potential disrespect that the informality could be construed to represent. Later, Roosevelt asks the King to push his wheelchair, with the same effect: like the royal couple, viewers cannot be sure whether this is meaningless, indeed pleasant familiarity or impertinence. This coupling, like in *Pearl Harbor*, creates and reinforces a prosthetic memory of a prosthesis; it suggests that Roosevelt's wheelchair contributed not only to Roosevelt's physical mobility, but is also a vehicle in transporting us as witnesses to the experience of America at war, and in transporting America to its post-war position of world hegemony.

The key meeting between FDR and King George follows just after King George has pushed Roosevelt's wheelchair; the president with paralyzed legs and the stuttering King have a highly intimate personal conversation decisive for the bilateral relationship of the US and the UK. Roosevelt is in this situation clearly the one on top, geopolitically, but in a scene that is played out primarily on a personal level. King George tries to express himself, but is caught up by his stutter, and exasperatedly cries out "this goddamn stutter!," to which Roosevelt coolly responds, "this goddamn polio." Roosevelt goes on to explain his personal theory that as long as he ignores his polio other people won't even notice it, saying,

> Let me confess something to you now, as you've been so honest with me. No one ever mentions the fact that I can't use my legs. It's never referred to. Not by anyone. And I used to think it was because they were embarrassed about it. [*gets up out of wheelchair, starts 'walking'*] But now I think it's because it's not what they want to see. Of course, you and I, we think that they see

> everything that we are. All our flaws. Our transgressions our failures. [*laboriously moves over to desk*] But that's not what they're looking to find when they look to us. And God help us if that ever changes. Can you imagine the disappointment when they find out what we really are?[27]

Roosevelt's words here are interestingly juxtaposed with his movements: during this explicit speech about how he keeps his disability implicit, by not drawing attention to it, he draws particular attention to it by trying to walk which the paralysis makes impossible. *Hyde Park on Hudson*'s general take on Roosevelt's genius seems to be that he was a brilliant manipulator of people and appearances. While perhaps in the film Roosevelt's contemporaries do not see his handicap, the movie audience do so all the more except that to them it is not a handicap but another attribute that helps to show the brilliance of his manipulation. Thus, the "walking" that Roosevelt does has a different meaning for the cinematic King George than for us: for King George it is a demonstration of how desperately trying to be physically capable may actually draw more attention to one's invalidity than its acceptance; to us, it suggests Roosevelt's utter ease with consciously projecting whatever image he needs at a particular moment. Roosevelt does not only embody here the particularly American talent at projecting a desirable image, but also on another level mimics his country: as long as he does not mention the war, it is not there, and other than the knowledge that promises are made, the war is absent from the film.

Even more glaringly absent, also from the summary of outcomes following the narrated events in voiceover at the end of the film, are the attacks on Pearl Harbor. On the face of it, *Hyde Park on Hudson* suggests that Roosevelt's silence about his disability was an intentional media strategy, and the pointed absence of any reference to Pearl Harbor seems to perform a similar kind of movement. Of course, the narrated royal visit took place in 1939, well before Pearl Harbor or any concrete threat from the Pacific on American soil, but the fact that it is not referred to in any way nonetheless stresses only America's role in the war as primarily a matter of disinterested moral superiority, diverting attention away from America's beleaguered state in 1941. On the other hand, the final voiceover is very explicit about Roosevelt's own wish to repress the presence of bad news in his personal life. Describing the illness and death of his secretary and former mistress Marguerite LeHand, the narrator says, "When she fell terribly ill, he paid for everything. He even changed his will, giving her half should she outlive him. But to the surprise of nearly everyone, he did not visit her once in the hospital. I asked him why. 'It's a terrible fault of mine,' he said. 'I find it too painful to be around illness.'"[28] Thus in the midst of the film's own silence about the war that America did become engaged in during the years after the

British royal visit in 1939, it does focus on Roosevelt's attempt to negate the existence of disease in his private life. On the one hand, he does what he can, materially, to exorcise it, and on the other he refuses to be confronted with it on an emotional level. Roosevelt's feeling that being "around illness" is "too painful," suggests that it is traumatic for him, reminding him of his own physical frailty. In what follows, the audience see FDR being carried and lifted into his car by assistants. After having installed himself, he says, "Ok boys, take it away!" to press photographers who then start taking pictures of him. Thus the same indirect denial of imperfection is repeated. The narrator ends,

> A year passed. And then another. And another. I watched him grow tired and frail and ill. He tried to hide this from everyone. He knew how to do that. From everyone but me. Everyone still looking to him. Still seeing whatever it was they wanted to see. In a time, not so very long ago, when the world still allowed itself secrets, Franklin Roosevelt was mine.[29]

The narrator, through her presumed understanding of Roosevelt, can literally feel that she owns him, and his full story, because she can fill in the void that he leaves in his silence about his physical inadequateness. She assumes the role of addressee of an implicitly told story, much like the postgeneration exemplified by Hirsch through the "Fifty Years of Silence" art books. This movement mimics that of the American psyche that chooses to fill in a narrative about Roosevelt's disability instead of creating for itself more detailed trauma narratives addressing more painful parts of World War II (such as Pearl Harbor). Thus, *Hyde Park on Hudson* creates prosthetic memories in various senses. Like Roosevelt, despite its claim that the world no longer allows itself secrets, *Hyde Park on Hudson* gives viewers "whatever it [i]s they want to see." A prosthesis within a screen memory to screen off another prosthetic memory that remains harder to chew.

Bibliography

Alter, Jonathan. *The Defining Moment: FDR Hundred Days and the Triumph of Hope*. New York: Simon & Schuster, 2006.

Assmann, Aleida. "Four Formats of Memory: From Individual to Collective Constructions of the Past." In *Cultural Memory and Historical Consciousness in the German-Speaking World since 1500*, edited by Christian Emden and David Midgley, 19-37. Bern: Peter Lang, 2004.

Assmann, Jan. "Collective Memory and Cultural Identity." Translated by John Czaplicka. *New German Critique* 65 (1995): 125-33.

Bal, Mieke. Introduction to *Acts of Memory: Cultural Recall in the Present*, edited by Mieke Bal, Jonathan Crewe, and Leo Spitzer, vii-xvii. Hanover and London: University Press of New England, 1999.

Erll, Astrid. *Memory in Culture*. Translated by Sara B. Young. London, New York: Palgrave Macmillan Memory Studies, 2011.

FDR, American Badass!. Directed by Garrett Brawith. New York City: Screen Media Films, 2012. DVD.

FDR: A Presidency Revealed. Directed by David C. Taylor. New York City: History Channel, 2005. TV.

Freud, Sigmund. "Screen Memories." In *The Standard Edition of the Complete Psychological Works of Sigmund Freud*, Volume 3 (1893-1899), 301-22. Translated and edited by James Strachey and Anna Freud. London: The Hogarth Press, 1962.

Gallagher, Hugh Gregory. *FDR's Splendid Deception: The Moving Story of Roosevelt's Massive Disability and the Intense Efforts to Conceal It from the Public*. St. Petersburg, FL: Vandamere Press, 1985.

Halbwachs, Maurice. "From *The Collective Memory*." In *The Collective Memory Reader*, edited by Jeffrey Olick, Vered Vinitzky-Seroussi and Daniel Levy, 139-49. Oxford: Oxford University Press, 2011.

Hirsch, Marianne. *The Generation of Postmemory: Writing and Visual Culture After the Holocaust*. New York: Columbia University Press, 2012.

Houck, Davis, and Amos Kiewe. *FDR's Body Politics, The Rhetorics of Disability.* College Station, TX: Texas A&M University Press, 2003.

Hyde Park on Hudson. Directed by Roger Michell. 2012. Universal City, CA: Universal Studios Home Entertainment, 2013. DVD.

LaCapra, Dominick. *Writing History, Writing Trauma.* Baltimore: The Johns Hopkins University Press, 2001.

Landsberg, Alison. *Prosthetic Memory: The Transformation of American Remembrance in the Age of Mass Culture*. New York: Columbia University Press, 2004.

Lippmann, Theo, Jr. *The Squire of Warm Springs: F.D.R. in Georgia 1924-1945.* Chicago: Playboy Press, 1977.

Looker, Earle. *This Man Roosevelt.* New York: Brewer, Warren and Putman, 1932.

Pearl Harbor. Directed by Michael Bay. Burbank, CA: Touchstone Pictures, 2001. DVD.

Roosevelt, Franklin Delano. Speeches, 1933-1945. Miller Center Presidential Speech Archive. http://millercenter.org/president/speeches#fdroosevelt.

Roosevelt, Elliott, ed. *FDR: His Personal Letters, 1928-1945*. New York: Duell, Sloane and Pearce, 1950.

Rosenberg, Emily. *A Date which Will Live: Pearl Harbor in American Memory*. Durham & London: Duke University Press, 2003.

Rothberg, Michael. *Multidirectional Memory: Remembering the Holocaust in the Age of Decolonization*. Stanford, CA: Stanford University Press, 2009.

Stein, Sally. "The President's Two Bodies: Stagings and Restagings of FDR and the New Deal Body Politic." *American Art* 18-1(2004): 32–57.

Walsh, David Austin. "Ray Begovich: How I Found Rare Footage of FDR in a Wheelchair." George Mason University History News Network, July 15, 2013. Accessed September 16, 2013. http://hnn.us/article/152604.

Warm Springs. Directed by Joseph Sargent. New York City: HBO Home Video, 2005. DVD.

Winter, Jay. *Remembering War: The Great War between Memory and History in the Twentieth Century*. Ann Arbor, Michigan: Sheridan Books, 2006.

Notes

[1] Alison Landsberg, *Prosthetic Memory: The Transformation of American Remembrance in the Age of Mass Culture* (New York: Columbia University Press, 2004), 2-3.

[2] Jan Assmann, "Collective Memory and Cultural Identity," trans. John Czaplicka. *New German Critique* 65 (1995): 125-33; Mieke Bal, Introduction to *Acts of Memory: Cultural Recall in the Present*, eds. Mieke Bal, Jonathan Crewe, and Leo Spitzer (Hanover and London: University Press of New England, 1999), vii-xvii; Marianne Hirsch, *The Generation of Postmemory: Writing and Visual Culture After the Holocaust* (New York: Columbia University Press, 2012).

[3] This is chronicled and discussed amongst others in Davis Houck and Amos Kiewe's *FDR's Body Politics, The Rhetorics of Disability* (College Station, TX: Texas A&M University Press, 2003).

[4] *Pearl Harbor*, directed by Michael Bay (Burbank, CA: Touchstone Pictures, 2001), DVD.

[5] David Austin Walsh, "Ray Begovich: How I Found Rare Footage of FDR in a Wheelchair," George Mason University History News Network, July 15, 2013, accessed September 16, 2013, http://hnn.us/article/152604, retrieved 16 September 2013).

[6] Franklin Roosevelt, Address to Congress on Yalta (1 March, 1945), Speeches, 1933-1945, Miller Center Presidential Speech Archive, retrieved September 16, 2013, http://millercenter.org/president/speeches#fdroosevelt.

[7] March of Dimes, http://www.marchofdimes.com/mission/a-history-of-the-march-of-dimes.aspx.

[8] Assmann, "Collective Memory and Cultural Identity," 125-33.

[9] Jay Winter, *Remembering War: The Great War between Memory and History in the Twentieth Century* (Ann Arbor, Michigan: Sheridan Books, 2006), 150.

[10] Maurice Halbwachs, "From *The Collective Memory*," in *The Collective Memory Reader*, eds. Jeffrey Olick, Vered Vinitzky-Seroussi, and Daniel Levy (Oxford: Oxford University Press, 2011), 144.
[11] Jonathan Alter, *The Defining Moment: FDR's Hundred Days and the Triumph of Hope* (New York: Simon & Schuster, 2006), 272; for a brief history of the FDR Library, see the Library's website: http://www.fdrlibrary.marist.edu/library/onedefinitelocality.html.
[12] FDR to Mary Norton, March 24, 1942, in *FDR: His Personal Letters, 1928-1945*, ed. Elliott Roosevelt (New York: Duell, Sloane and Pearce, 1950).
[13] Bal, Crewe & Spitzer, *Acts of Memory*, vii-xvii.
[14] Dominick LaCapra, *Writing History, Writing Trauma* (Baltimore: The Johns Hopkins University Press, 2001).
[15] Hirsch, *The Generation of Postmemory*, 87-93.
[16] Landsberg, *Prosthetic Memory*, 2.
[17] Landsberg, *Prosthetic Memory*, 20.
[18] Landsberg, *Prosthetic Memory*, 21.
[19] Sigmund Freud, "Screen Memories," in *The Standard Edition of the Complete Psychological Works of Sigmund Freud*, Volume 3, trans. James Strachey (London: Hogarth Press, 1962), 301-22.
[2020] Franklin Roosevelt, Address to Congress Requesting a Declaration of War (December 8, 1941), Speeches, 1933-1945, Miller Center Presidential Speech Archive, retrieved September 16, 2013, http://millercenter.org/president/speeches#fdroosevelt.
[21] Bill Clinton, 2 May 1997, cited in *FDR's Body Politics*, 3.
[22] *Pearl Harbor* [33:00].
[23] *Pearl Harbor* [2:09:30].
[24] Hugh Gregory Gallagher, *FDR's Splendid Deception: The Moving Story of Roosevelt's Massive Disability and the Intense Efforts to Conceal It from the Public* (St. Petersburg, FL: Vandamere Press, 1985), 64.
[25] Gallagher, *FDR's Splendid Deception,* xi.
[26] Michael Rothberg, *Multidirectional Memory: Remembering the Holocaust in the Age of Decolonization* (Stanford, CA: Stanford University Press, 2009), 13-14.
[27] *Hyde Park on Hudson*, directed by Roger Michell (2012; Universal City, CA: Universal Studios Home Entertainment, 2013), DVD. [51:30].
[28] *Hyde Park on Hudson* [1:26:51].
[29] *Hyde Park on Hudson* [1:27:56].

Part Four:

9/11 and the Canonization of Trauma

HEALING THE NATION, MEMORIALIZING TRAUMA: GROUND ZERO AND THE CRITIQUE OF EXCEPTIONALISM IN THE RECENT AMERICAN NOVEL

RODICA MIHĂILĂ

A decade after the 9/11 terrorist attacks, more than one hundred novels involving the event directly or indirectly have been published in the US alone. Some are novels by canonical writers like John Updike, Don DeLillo, Philip Roth, Thomas Pynchon and Cormac McCarthy, some are more or less successful debut novels, and an impressive number of such novels are written by immigrants or from the perspective of immigrants and expatriates, especially from Europe, Asia and Africa.

A considerable body of critical work by scholars across the world explores 9/11-related literary and cultural texts from a multitude of critical perspectives.[1] The present chapter attempts to contribute to that work by examining various forms of memorializing the 9/11 terrorist attacks in the recent American novel so as to point out to what extent memorializing national trauma functions both as successful therapy, contributing to the nation's healing, and as a direct or oblique critique of American exceptionalism.

The theoretical frame of my discussion is provided by my working definition of trauma and the main goals of trauma therapy, which suggests how trauma can be worked through, and by my inquiry into the double strain of American exceptionalism, its bright and its dark face, for the nation's healing depends largely on restoring confidence in America as the Good Empire and at the same time on accepting the idea that the US "cannot be absolved from possible involvements" in the primary causes that triggered the 9/11 attacks.[2]

Whether called ideology of "consensus,"[3] creed, ethos or myth, exceptionalism has informed the nature of American nationhood, being the vehicle by which the idea of the uniqueness of the American experience, the claim to liberal democracy and cyclic self-renewal of a truly "visionary nation,"[4] its messianic belief in its role-model for the rest of the world and its mission as redeemer have all endured.

The 9/11 terrorist attacks struck at the heart of American exceptionalism and of what the American dream was expected to be in the new century, targeting main symbols of US economic, political and military power which have made for the rise of the "American Empire" as the power center of the emerging globalized world. Under such circumstances, the cataclysmic events of September 11, 2001 and their aftermath, the war on terror, could not fail to produce a massive trauma shared by the whole nation, which turned the US into a collective victim and marked a pivotal moment in US history and in the world order.

"As a nation," observes Kathleen Nader, "we shared shock/disbelief, horror, fear, sadness, grief, despair, anger, rage, worry, stress, and/or the need to take action. In addition, we have each been affected in an individual way by this tragedy."[5] These are all symptoms of what Dominick LaCapra in his *Writing History, Writing Trauma* (2001) defines as "historical trauma"—trauma which refers to specific, often human-made, historical occurrences that involve losses such as the Holocaust, slavery, apartheid, the dropping of the atom bomb on Japanese cities, etc.[6] Contrary to Cathy Caruth's opinion that trauma—irrespective of its type—is non-symbolizable and cannot be worked through because of the "collapse of witnessing" and "the impossibility of knowing that first constituted it,"[7] LaCapra argues that historical trauma, which is more likely to be a nationally shared trauma, is produced by events that can be located, therefore such a trauma can be "worked through," even if it can never be completely erased. As he puts it,

> working-through does not mean total redemption of the past or healing its traumatic wounds (...) But at least in trauma's historical dimension, we can work to change the causes of this cause insofar as they are social, economic, and political and thereby attempt to prevent its recurrence as well as enable forms of renewal.[8]

Working through a trauma, the practitioners of psychosocial healing tell us, means "to acknowledge the experience—that is, remember it and tell the truth about it—and then integrate it into a sort of personal or collective rebirth."[9] In other words, trauma therapy implies a three-stage process: remembrance, telling the truth about the experience, and rebirth. My attempt to explore ways in which the recent American novel strives to make sense of America's traumatic experience and to address the complex issue of healing starts from Ground Zero, the site of the former WTC complex, the national shrine erected to memorialize the 9/11 trauma and to contribute to the healing of the nation's wounds.

Designed by architects Michael Arad and Peter Walker, the 9/11 Memorial occupies more than half of the 16-acre site of Ground Zero, being the only one to acquire iconic status among the more than 700 other 9/11 memorials across the country. In 2003, the international competition for its design attracted over 5,200 submissions from 63 nations. Called "Reflecting Absence," the memorial is a tribute to the victims, a "reminder of the absence" of the nearly 3000 people who lost their lives in the terrorist attacks at the WTC site, at the Pentagon, near Shanksville, Pa. and in the WTC bombing of February 1993. The functions of remembrance, as well as the affirmation of hope and renewal, are performed in the Memorial Plaza by the grove of sweet gum and swamp white oak trees, staging nature's "annual cycle of rebirth"[10] around the two pools with the largest manmade waterfalls cascading down their side walls in the footprints of the twin towers, and with the wide ribbons of the names of "the absent" surrounding them. The same functions are performed by the bold architecture of the five buildings of the reconstructed WTC complex, featuring the diamond-shaped 104-story Freedom Tower (1WTC), the tallest building in the Western Hemisphere, with a symbolic height of "1776" feet—a reminder of the enduring power to reinvent itself of an America that Jefferson used to call "The Empire of Liberty."

The goals of trauma treatment (remembrance of the experience, telling the truth about it and individual/collective rebirth) are clearly phrased in the *Memorial Mission Statements*, "May the lives remembered, the deeds recognized, and the spirit reawakened be eternal beacons, which reaffirm respect for life, strengthen our resolve to preserve freedom, and inspire an end to hatred, ignorance and intolerance."[11] We recognize in this statement the lofty founding moral principles at the core of the *Declaration of Independence* which made America exceptional ("that all men are created equal, that they are endowed by their Creator with certain unalienable Rights, that among these are Life, Liberty and the pursuit of Happiness"), and we also recognize the ideals of American multiculturalism, which at the time of the attacks had already been proclaimed an identity model for the 21st century globalized world. But there is another face to exceptionalism, one that became more visible especially after the outbreak of the "war on terror" with its "us vs. them" ideology, when the escalation of the exceptionalist logic by the neo-conservatism of the Bush administration, the failure of the New Economy, and the combination of arrogance and narcissism that led to the country's blindness to its own history, have been diagnosed by many as signs of exceptionalism's self-destructiveness. Speaking about recent projections of America's being-in-the-world and the new world order, Godfrey Hodgson discovers this "Other, dark exceptionalism"[12] in the "missionary persuasion" of American politics.[13] Acknowledging the cataclysmic Ground Zero experience, the necessary step in trauma healing implies facing the "Jekyll and Hyde" nature,[14] "the double-edged sword"[15] or the double strain of American exceptionalism—which alone can lead to a collective rebirth. This is what the novel can do best.

Even when it focuses on the incipient stages of individual trauma and "retreat into domestic detail,"[16] as it often does, exploring the double strain of exceptionalism, the post-9/11 novel attempts to map out a new space of America's endurance as "a wish-fulfillment dream" and "a way of imagining,"[17] a new space of "romance with America,"[18] "a transgenerational state of fantasy"[19]—a space for hope, change and action, for "America's Promise" coming true again.[20] This is not a space of consensus, but one of common humanity and hope, shaped by a utopian vision of the ethical relations between us and them, between us and us. Problematic as it may be, this ethical space of vision is a tentative site of "collective rebirth," of nation healing—apparently, the only one left.

In my previous critical inquiries into literary and cultural texts dealing with 9/11, I have focused on what I called "the ethical turn" in the post-9/11 novel, on the way the novel approached the binary opposition "us vs. them" ignited by the war on terror. I have circumscribed my reading of novels such as Jonathan Safran Foer's *Extremely Loud & Incredibly Close*, John Updike's *Terrorist*, and Don DeLillo's *Falling Man* within the boundaries of the responsibility for the Other,[21] and of a critique of American exceptionalism which addresses the fractures of democracy in America's multicultural society and reaffirms hope in the possibility—(fragile and remote as it may be)—of a new beginning, triggering the cyclic renewal of the paradigm of exceptionalism.

As the focus of the critique of America is moving from the multicultural to the transnational and global perspective, that is, from the inward perspective of American multiculturalism to the outward one of an emerging cosmopolitanism marking the shift from the "stories of the immigrant encounter"[22] to what Caren Irr calls the "world"/"global" novel,[23] the emphasis on the ethical relations between Self and Other is shifting toward the complex interrelation between cultures and the globalization of fear and anxiety. A number of novels, especially after 2008, the end of the Bush era, have opened America to the world, exploring the world in America and America's being-in-the-world—in other words, they take a transnational turn, which places American literature within a new global imaginary. Among such novels, which combine the perspectives of the immigrant narrative and of the world novel are Joseph O'Neill's *Netherland* (2008), Teddy Wayne's *Kapitoil* (2010), and more recently, Amy Waldman's *The Submission* and

Teju Cole's *The Open City*. In my critical inquiry I will address the last two, which are debut novels released in 2011.

An unequivocal concern with memorializing and healing the 9/11 trauma gives substance to *The Submission*, the debut-novel of Amy Waldman, a former correspondent for *The New York Times*.[24] The novel historicizes 9/11 and its immediate aftermath, for "history makes its own truths, new truths," as one of the characters observes,[25] and, at the same time, it offers an alternate history of the Ground Zero memorial, which raises serious questions about the effects of 9/11 and its aftermath on the American society, about what it means to memorialize, about "the politics of memorial"[26] and the way to healing, and about America's being-in-the-world. Waldman could have easily given her novel the title she gave to the documentary about the failed memorial project in the epilogue of the book: "America in argument with itself."[27]

The story itself is the best illustration of the shift of the post-9/11 American novel from the narratives of immigrant encounter stressing the opposition us/Americans vs. them/Muslims to the world/global novel, from a hyphenated American identity to a cosmopolitan one. The novel starts two years after the attacks, with a vote to select the winner of a national competition for the design of the Ground Zero memorial from the more than 5,000 blinded submissions. When the jurors open the selected submission titled "The Garden," they discover in stupor that the winner is a Virginia-born architect named Mohammed Khan, an American Muslim. "It's Maya Lin all over again. But worse,"[28] exclaims one juror, in reference to the Vietnam Memorial, designed by Maya Lin, a Chinese American undergraduate student at Yale, who won a "blind" design competition in 1981, generating fierce controversy. What follows after the winner's name leaks to the press is a storm of pro and anti-Islam protests, rallies of the victims' families, and outraged comments in the press. The novel brilliantly anticipates the storm of protests unleashed in the spring of 2011 over the planned construction of a Muslim Cultural Center in Lower Manhattan, two blocks away from Ground Zero. The memorial is supposed to "heal" (the word "heal"/"healing" is repeated fourteen times in the first 40 pages alone), which means "bringing people together."[29] But America appears more divided than ever. When one of the jurors suggests that having a Muslim design the memorial "could be a healing gesture," he is reprimanded, "The families will feel very offended. This is no time for multicultural pandering."[30] The fights and disputes over the memorial expose various fractures and failed promises of democracy: racism, ignorance of the Other, and the demonization of the Muslim, uncertainty about what is an American, the fate of illegal ("undocumented") immigrants, the denial of the victims' equal right to be remembered, the machinations of the press.

Can a national memorial heal the nation? The question receives a cynical answer, "She didn't understand her own country (…); it would take more than a new memorial to unite it."[31] Acknowledging the truth and telling it, indispensable in trauma healing, are made possible in this novel through de-aestheticizing the immigrant's ideal of America. One such case is that of US-born Abdul, whose parents, Asma and Inam Haque migrated from Bangladesh for they "idealized America,"[32] for, as Asma said in defence of Khan's "Garden" Memorial, echoing the symbol of America as "garden of the world," "I think a garden is right, (…) because that is what America is—all the people Muslim and non-Muslim, who have come and grown together. How can you pretend we and our traditions are not part of this place?"[33] But Abdul, whose father was one of the "undocumented" WTC victims and whose mother was stubbed to death in New York for speaking in support of Khan's design of the memorial, no longer wants to return to America, despite his American citizenship. The dominant counter-narrative de-aestheticizing America belongs to the American Mo Khan, son of Iranian immigrants, born and raised an American, a prototype of a young successful American, who leaves America in profound disappointment never to return. He chooses to be now "a global citizen, American only in name."[34]

And yet, the promise of trauma healing as personal/collective rebirth is kept alive by the idea of the endurance of American exceptionalism. In the novel's epilogue, twenty years after his Garden design for the Ground Zero memorial was dropped and he left America, Khan, living now in Mumbai, is given the highest international recognition as one of America's leading architects. The Museum of New Architecture in New York hosts a retrospective of his career described as "a tribute to his blaze of work, most of it in the Middle East, India, or China, over the past twenty years."[35] The caption of one of his "Garden" drawings reads, "He withdrew his submission in the face of heated political opposition, but the controversy brought his talent to the international stage."[36] This is exceptionalism re-visited. "It was a quintessentially American story—that you could profit even by losing…"[37] The collective rebirth is made possible by America's exceptionalism, its inexhaustible power of renewal. Although Khan is "stuck in the past" by the truth of his art, "the country had moved on, self-corrected, as it always did, that feverish time mostly forgotten."[38]

We recognize here the pattern of the cyclical rebirth of America as a utopian project, which is possible because the idea and ideal of America always has the capacity of endless regeneration. That is so since, as Bercovitch explained, American exceptionalism is not only an ideology of consensus but also the ideology of a never-ending change.[39] Does it mean the nation was healed? In an inspired inquiry into the relationship between traumatic memory, America's exceptionalism and the symbolism of Virgin Land and Ground Zero, Donald Pease, who described exceptionalism as "a transgenerational state of fantasy (…) [which] bears traces of transgenerational trauma"[40] draws attention to the fact that "[the] virgin land produced historical continuity by suppressing the traumatic memory of lawless violence," while "the events of 9/11 demanded the recovery of this traumatic memory so as to reverse the national people's relation to violence and to inaugurate a new global order."[41]

Khan designed *the Garden* as a site of remembrance and healing, where trauma therapy implied "rapprochement through architecture"[42]—healing through rapprochement between cultures, through meddling elements of Western and Islamic art. He "considered it incomplete otherwise."[43] His memorial, as a "lieu de mémoire,"[44] was grounded in the idea that successful trauma therapy requires not only the recovery of traumatic memory, but also knowledge of the Other, responsibility for the Other. As such, his Garden stands as a viable solution for memorializing 9/11 trauma at a time when the on-going globalization of anxiety and terrorism-induced trauma has made the world increasingly skeptical of America's capacity to provide the much-needed healing—even though, significantly, the 9/11 Memorial at Ground Zero, eventually designed by an Israeli-American architect, is a powerful reaffirmation of America's faith in its exceptional destiny. After all, the diamond-shaped Freedom Tower—the jam in the World Trade Center crown is taller than the collapsed twin towers and much taller than Empire State Building.

My critical inquiry into the recent American novel leads to the conclusion that, as the novel opens to the world shifting gradually from a dominant multicultural to a transnational perspective, the therapy of recovering traumatic memory is more closely associated with the therapy of getting to know the Other.

Ground Zero and, by extension, New York City as a site of recovery of traumatic memory of violence, and at the same time a place of knowing the otherness of the new world order takes the stage in another debut novel of 2011, *Open City* by Teju Cole,[45] a Nigerian American writer living in New York. Cole's novel offers an even wider panorama of the world in America and America in the world. Julius, the narrator and protagonist of the novel, comes to post-9/11 New York as an intern in the psychiatry department of the Columbia Presbyterian Hospital, working on "a clinical study of affective disorders in the elderly."[46] Born in Lagos to a German mother and a Nigerian father, Julius has always felt an outsider, an eternal Other. The narrative is built in the neo-picaresque tradition, using Julius' numerous wanderings through the city as means to connect with people and their individual stories and as triggers for excursions into the past and reflections on the history of multicultural, cosmopolitan New York, on America's history and its role in today's world, on Europe's future and on Julius's own African youth.

He is a typical *flâneur* in the tradition of Baudelaire and he describes the city as "lived experience," in the same way as Bachelard views architecture in *The Poetics of Space*.[47] With a wide cultural horizon and an introspective mind Julius thinks incessantly, nourishing his thoughts with the most unexpected references to social and critical theory, art, literature, music, philosophy and history, and he reads a lot of sophisticated books such as Roland Barthes's *Camera Lucida* and Kwame Anthony Appiah's *Cosmopolitanism*—a transparent allusion to his own way of looking at things and to his own cosmopolitan spirit. While the universe of his mind is truly cosmopolitan, his life experience is that of a world of immigrants. Most of the people he meets and talks to are immigrants, "victimized Other[s],"[48] current or former victims of some form of oppressive power: professor Saito, a Japanese American taken to internment in an Idaho camp back in 1942; a Liberian imprisoned for more than two years in a US Immigration and Customs Enforcement detention facility in Queens; a Haitian shoe-shiner in Penn Station; Moji, a woman he knew as a girl in Nigeria; Farouq, an angry Moroccan Ph.D. student running an Internet and telephone shop in Brussels, whose political ideas are eaten by "a cancerous violence;"[49] and Khalil, another Arab in Brussels, a Marxist and an extremist, for whom "America is a version of Al-Qaeda."[50] He himself is a migrant, but one who is almost exclusively preoccupied with the migrant's inner/subjective experience and the isolation that dislocation imposes on him. *Open City* stands alone among the post-9/11 novels in that it memorializes trauma almost exclusively from the perspective of the migrant's subjective experience of the city set against his experience and knowledge of the larger world. The *flâneur*'s eye offers profound insights into a changing world, into a nation's struggle to regain a sense of direction after the shattering experience of 9/11 and into the nightmare of history revealed in the palimpsestic quality of New York, a city "written, erased, rewritten."[51]

With his mind's eyes, Julius sees the city rising on numerous layers of extreme suffering and violence, which marked its history and the history of America. He memorializes 9/11 trauma by placing Ground Zero, the "empty space (...) the ruins of the World Trade Center,"[52] in a New York transformed into a vast memory-site of American history, "the place had become a metonym of its disaster (...) not the site of the events of 9/11 but (…) 9/11 itself, the date petrified into broken stones."[53] It reminds him that the 9/11 attack on the WTC "was not the first erasure on the site,"[54] and he goes back in history to evoke the "bustling network of little streets" which "had been all obliterated in the 1960s to make way for the World Trade Center,"[55] and before those, "the old Washington Market, the active piers, the fishwives, the Christian Syrian enclave that was established here in the late1800s (...) And, before that?"[56] Before that there was once the Negro Burial Ground, where "the bodies of some fifteen to twenty thousand blacks, most of them slaves,"[57] had been buried. His imagination travels even further back to the times before the Europeans discovered the Virgin Land of the so-called Indians and raped the "virgin," before the slave traders first set foot on the American land. In doing so, he admits he also "wanted to find the line that connected [him] to [his] own part in these stories."[58]

In memorializing the 9/11 trauma, *Open City* goes far beyond the boundaries of American history, for Ground Zero finds its place among all the other "lieux de mémoire" pointing to the violence and nightmare of history—from the massacre of the Indian tribes to the atrocity of slavery, of racism, of the Holocaust and of such dictators as Hitler, Stalin, Pol Pot and Idi Amin, "But atrocity is nothing new, not to humans not to animals. The difference is that in our time it is uniquely well organized (...) And this late contribution, the absence of bodies. No bodies were visible, except the falling ones, on the day America's ticker stopped."[59]

Like Junot Díaz in *The Brief Wondrous Life of Oscar Wao* (2007) or Leslie Marmon Silko in *Almanac of the Dead* (1991), Cole is among those writers for whom rewriting American history, starting with the pre-Columbian times, has been part trauma therapy, part search for their own origins as well as a subversive critique of US exceptionalism.

The novel ends with another famous site of memory, the Statue of Liberty, a landmark of America's exceptionalism, reminiscent of the hopes of millions of immigrants in search of the American dream. The intended parallel with the WTC twin towers, another symbol of America's power, is unmistakable. The double strain of American exceptionalism, the ambiguous message it sends to the present world is symbolized by the flame of the torch that used to make of the Statue a lighthouse, a guiding "beam" for the ships, but, at the same time, especially in bad weather, the very same light would disorient the birds, who end up by finding their death crashed against the Statue. The closing sentence of the novel reports the death of "175 wrens (...) all dead of the impact, although the night just past hadn't been particularly windy or dark."[60] Symbolic of the death of the hopes of many newly arrived immigrants, the death of the birds is also symbolic of the trauma which in various forms has marred the American dream.

In *Open City*, American exceptionalism fails the test of multiculturalism, but Cole refers here to the early, radical version of multiculturalism, which defines diversity as difference, and difference as unbridgeable otherness. When Julian attends the performance of Mahler's Ninth Symphony at Carnegie Hall, "almost everyone, as almost always at such concerts, was white."[61] The homogeneous "all-white spaces" stand apart from the hybridity of the city. The unbridgeable otherness is all there. As Julian ponders, "it never ceases to surprise me how easy it is to leave the hybridity of the city and enter into all-white spaces, the homogeneity of which, (...) causes no discomfort to the whites in them."[62] In spite of all this, the novel clearly points to a shift from a view of America based on parochial multiculturalism toward a transnational approach which opens America to the world, blurring the borders of continents and countries, of history and time—an America which promises to endure.

Three pages before the end of the novel, Cole introduces an explicit reference to the endurance of American exceptionalism, of America as a "transgenerational ideal." Coming out of Carnegie Hall through one of its emergency exits leading straight to the fire escape outside the building, a frightened Julius finds himself locked out on a stormy night. When finally, "with relief and gratitude," he finds a door to let him go inside, he looks straight up and much to his surprise, despite the rainy night and the habitual pollution of the city, he sees stars in the sky, and he knows that,

> in the dark spaces between the dead, shining stars, were stars I could not see, stars that still existed, and were giving out light that hadn't reached me yet, stars now living and giving out light but present to me only as blank interstices. Their light would arrive on earth eventually, long after I and my whole generation and the generation after me had slipped out of time, perhaps long after the human race itself was extinguished. To look into those dark spaces was to have a direct glimpse of the future.[63]

The enduring idea of America as the land of promises and hopes is symbolized by this starlight that "would arrive in due time, and cast its illumination on other humans, or perhaps on other configurations of our world, after unimaginable catastrophes had altered it beyond recognition."[64]

We recognize here the pattern of cyclical rebirth of America as a utopian project, which is possible in spite of "traces of transgenerational trauma,"[65] because the idea of America as promise always "re-emerges in regenerated forms."[66] Therefore, the Ground Zero memorial, with its 400 trees and the two pools in the footprints of the twin towers, continuously fed by the largest manmade waterfalls cascading down their side walls, memorializes the 9/11 trauma by placing it in the never ending cycle of nature's rebirth and change.

Bibliography

9/11 Memorial. *Memorial Mission Statements*. Accessed November 20, 2013. http://www.911memorial.org/mission-statements-0.

Arad, Michael, and Peter Walker. "Reflecting Absence." Accessed November 20, 2013. http://www.wtcsitememorial.org/fin7.html.

Bachelard, Gaston. *The Poetics of* Space. Translated by Maria Jolas. Boston: Beacon Press, 1994.

Bercovitch, Sacvan. *The Rites of Assent. Transformations in the Symbolic Construction of America.* New York, London: Routledge, 1993.

Breithaupt, Fritz. "Rituals of Trauma: How the Media Fabricated September 11." In *Media Representations of September 11*, edited by Steven Chermak, Frankie Y. Bailey and Michelle Brown, 67-81. Westport, CT: Praeger, 2003.

Byrt, Anthony. "Teju Cole interview—the long version." *New Zealand Listener*, June 1, 2012. Accessed November 20, 2013. http://www.listener.co.nz/culture/books/teju-cole-interview-the-long-version/.

Caruth, Cathy, ed. *Trauma: Explorations in Memory*. Baltimore: Johns Hopkins University Press, 1995.

Cilano, Cara, ed. *From Literature to Schisms. 9/11 and After in Fiction and Film from Outside the U.S.* Amsterdam/New York: Rodopi, 2009.

Cole, Teju. *Open City*. New York: Random House, 2011. Kindle edition.

Fluck, Winfred. "American Studies and the Romance with America: Approaching America through Its Ideals." In *Romance with America? Essays on Culture, Literature, and American Studies*, edited by Johannes Voelz and Laura Bieger, 87-104. Heidelberg: Universitätsverlag Winter, 2009.

Gray, Richard. "Open Doors, Closed Minds: American Prose Writing at a Time of Crisis." *American Literary History* 20.3 (2008): 128-50.

Gross, Andrew, and Maryann Snyder-Korber, eds. *Amerikastudien*: *Trauma's Continuum—September 11th Reconsidered* 55.3 (2010).

Gutlove, Paula, and Gordon Thompson, eds. *Psychosocial Healing: A Guide for Practitioners*. Cambridge, MA: Institute for Resource and Security Studies, 2003.

Hodgson, Godfrey. *The Myth of American Exceptionalism.* New Haven: Yale University Press, 2009.

Irr, Caren. "Toward the World Novel: Genre Shifts in Twenty-First-Century Expatriate Fiction." *American Literary History* 23.3 (2011): 660-79.

Karabell, Zachary. *A Visionary Nation. Four Centuries of American Dreams and What Lies Ahead*. New York: Harper Collins, 2001.

Keniston, Ann, and Jeanne Follansbee Quinn, eds. *Literature after 9/11*. New York: Routledge, 2008.
Koh, Harold Hongju. "On American Exceptionalism." *Stanford Law Review 55* (2003): 1479-1527.
LaCapra, Dominick. *Writing History. Writing Trauma*. Baltimore: The Johns Hopkins University Press, 2001.
Levinas, Emmanuel. *Totality and Infinity*. Translated by Alphonso Lingis. Pittsburgh, Pa: Duquesne University Press, 1969.
Lipset, Seymour Martin. *American Exceptionalism. A Double-Edged Sword*. New York: W.W. Norton & Co, 1997.
Nader, Kathleen. "Terrorism: September 11, 2001. Trauma, Grief, and Recovery." *Gift From Within*. September 21, 2001. Accessed May 26, 2012. http://www.giftfromwithin.org/html/PTSD-after-9-11-Trauma-Grief-and-Recovery.html#1.
Nora, Pierre. "Between Memory and History: *Les Lieux de Memoire*." Translated by Marc Roudebush. *Representations* 26 (Spring 1989): 7-24.
Obama, Barak. "Acceptance Speech." *DNC*. August 28, 2008. Accessed November 20, 2013. http://uspolitics.about.com/od/speeches/.
Pease, Donald. *The New American Exceptionalism*. Minneapolis: The University of Minnesota Press, 2009.
Waldman, Amy. *Submission*. London: Windmill Books, 2011.

Notes

[1] Some of the best examples are such book-length collections of essays as: Ann Keniston and Jeanne Follansbee Quinn, eds., *Literature after 9/11* (New York: Routledge, 2008); Cara Cilano, ed., *From Literature to Schisms. 9/11 and After in Fiction and Film from Outside the U.S.* (Amsterdam/New York: Rodopi, 2009) and the special issue of *Amerikastudien*: *Trauma's Continuum—September 11th Reconsidered* 55.3 (2010, guest editors Andrew Gross and Maryann Snyder-Korber).
[2] Fritz Breithaupt, "Rituals of Trauma: How the Media Fabricated September 11," in *Media Representations of September 11*, eds. Steven Chermak, Frankie Y. Bailey and Michelle Brown (Westport, CT: Praeger, 2003), 70.
[3] Sacvan Bercovich, *The Rites of Assent. Transformations in the Symbolic Construction of America* (New York, London: Routledge, 1993), 13.
[4] Zachary Karabell, *A Visionary Nation. Four Centuries of American Dreams and What Lies Ahead* (New York: Harper Collins, 2001).
[5] Kathleen Nader, "Terrorism: September 11, 2001. Trauma, Grief, and Recovery," *Gift from Within*, September 21, 2001, accessed May 26, 2012, http://www.giftfromwithin.org/html/PTSD-after-9-11-Trauma-Grief-and-Recovery.html#1.
[6] Dominick LaCapra, *Writing History. Writing Trauma* (Baltimore: The Johns Hopkins University Press, 2001), 43-85.

[7] Cathy Caruth, ed., *Trauma: Explorations in Memory* (Baltimore: Johns Hopkins University Press, 1995), 11.
[8] LaCapra, *Writing History. Writing Trauma*, 117-18.
[9] Paula Gutlove and Gordon Thompson, eds., *Psychosocial Healing: A Guide for Practitioners* (Cambridge, MA: Institute for Resource and Security Studies, 2003), 1.
[10] Michael Arad and Peter Walker, "Reflecting Absence," accessed November 20, 2013, http://www.wtcsitememorial.org/fin7.html.
[11] 9/11 Memorial, *Memorial Mission Statements*, accessed November 20, 2013, http://www.911memorial.org/mission-statements-0.
[12] Godfrey Hodgson, *The Myth of American Exceptionalism* (New Haven: Yale University Press, 2009), 130.
[13] Hodgson, *The Myth of American Exceptionalism*, xii.
[14] Hodgson, *The Myth of American Exceptionalism*, 130.
[15] Seymour Martin Lipsit, *American Exceptionalism. A Double-Edged Sword* (New York: W.W. Norton & Co, 1997).
[16] Richard Gray, "Open Doors, Closed Minds: American Prose Writing at a Time of Crisis," *American Literary History* 20.3 (2008): 134.
[17] Bercovitch, *The Rites of Assent*, 12.
[18] Winfred Fluck, "American Studies and the Romance with America: Approaching America through Its Ideals," in *Romance with America? Essays on Culture, Literature, and American Studies*, eds. Johannes Voelz and Laura Bieger (Heidelberg: Universitätsverlag Winter, 2009), 89.
[19] Donald Pease, *The New American Exceptionalism* (Minneapolis: The University of Minnesota Press, 2009), 38.
[20] Barak Obama, "Acceptance Speech," *DNC*, August 28, 2008, accessed November 20, 2013, http://uspolitics.about.com/od/speeches/a/obama_accept.htm.
[21] Emmanuel Levinas, *Totality and Infinity*, trans. Alphonso Lingis (Pittsburgh, Pa: Duquesne University Press, 1969).
[22] Gray, "Open Doors, Closed Minds," 141.
[23] Caren Irr, "Toward the World Novel: Genre Shifts in Twenty-First-Century Expatriate Fiction," *American Literary History* 23.3 (2011): 660-79.
[24] Amy Waldman, *The Submission* (London: Windmill Books, 2011).
[25] Waldman, *The Submission*, 26.
[26] Waldman, *The Submission*, 368.
[27] Waldman, *The Submission*, 368.
[28] Waldman, *The Submission*, 20.
[29] Waldman, *The Submission*, 14.
[30] Waldman, *The Submission*, 21.
[31] Waldman, *The Submission*, 352.
[32] Waldman, *The Submission*, 291.
[33] Waldman, *The Submission*, 296.
[34] Waldman, *The Submission*, 286.
[35] Waldman, *The Submission*, 369.
[36] Waldman, *The Submission*, 369-70.
[37] Waldman, *The Submission*, 370.
[38] Waldman, *The Submission*, 370.

[39] Bercovitch, *The Rites of Assent*, 12.
[40] Pease, *The New American Exceptionalism*, 38.
[41] Pease, *The New American Exceptionalism*, 173.
[42] Waldman, *The Submission*, 370.
[43] Waldman, *The Submission*, 370.
[44] Pierre Nora, "Between Memory and History: *Les Lieux de Mémoire*," trans. Marc Roudebush, *Representations* 26 (Spring 1989): 7-24.
[45] Teju Cole, *Open City* (New York: Random House, 2011, kindle edition).
[46] Cole, *Open City*, 7.
[47] Gaston Bachelard, *The Poetics of Space*, trans. Maria Jolas (Boston: Beacon Press, 1994).
[48] Cole, *Open City*, 104.
[49] Cole, *Open City*, 107.
[50] Cole, *Open City*, 121.
[51] Cole, *Open City*, 59.
[52] Cole, *Open City*, 52.
[53] Cole, *Open City*, 52.
[54] Cole, *Open City*, 58.
[55] Cole, *Open City*, 58.
[56] Cole, *Open City*, 58.
[57] Cole, *Open City*, 58.
[58] Cole, *Open City*, 59.
[59] Cole, *Open City*, 58. In an interview, Cole explains that his book explores in an "oblique way" nightmares of history such as 9/11 and World War II, to which he had some kind of personal connection. For instance, the idea of Brussels which declared itself "open city" in 1940 in front of German invaders, the internment of Japanese Americans in 1942, his mother's war experience in Germany, Farouq's reflections on the Israeli-Palestinian conflict. See Anthony Byrt, "Teju Cole interview – the long version," *New Zealand Listener*, June 1, 2012, accessed November 20, 2013, http://www.listener.co.nz/culture/books/teju-cole-interview-the-long-version/.
[60] Cole, *Open City*, 259.
[61] Cole, *Open City*, 251.
[62] Cole, *Open City*, 251.
[63] Cole, *Open City*, 256.
[64] Cole, *Open City*, 256.
[65] Pease, *The New American Exceptionalism*, 38.
[66] Fluck, "American Studies and the Romance with America," 89.

WRITING POST-TRAUMATIC MEMORIES, WRITING THE CITY: JONATHAN SAFRAN FOER'S *EXTREMELY LOUD & INCREDIBLY CLOSE*

AUDREY BARDIZBANIAN

The terrorist attacks of September 11, 2001 caused such shock and devastation that they can be characterized as the defining tragedy of our time. As Slavoj Žižek notes about 9/11 events, in *Welcome to the Desert of the Real*, "[i]t is not that reality entered our image: the image entered and shattered our reality."[1] Marita Sturken argues that the US lost their innocence at the moment of the collapse and also points out that the term "Ground Zero," which originally referred to complete nuclear destruction, suggests "a starting point, a tabula rasa."[2] This radical alteration of the world after the World Trade Center disaster has led many critics to characterize the event itself as traumatic[3] and to portray the New York City urban landscape as what French historian Pierre Nora called a "site of memory" (*lieu de mémoire*).[4] Within this context, the terrorist attacks of 9/11 have given rise to a revival of the need to bear witness through different media and especially through images, in their various forms, in keeping with Frances Guerin and Roger Hallas's claim that "the compulsion to bear witness to 11 September in and through images has become ever-present in this first decade of the new millennium."[5]

After tackling the Holocaust in his debut novel *Everything Is Illuminated* (2002), Jonathan Safran Foer ventured to represent, in his 2005 novel *Extremely Loud & Incredibly Close*,[6] the traumatic events of September 11, and to interlace them with those of the Allied fire-bombing of Dresden that took place at the end of World War II. Using experimental narrative techniques, Foer therein focuses on visual language and mediation, issues that have become crucial to representations of trauma and memory, and more particularly loss and mourning. In this sense, the writer seems to be less concerned with treating the events of 9/11 as they occurred than with depicting the consequences of that tragic day for the main protagonist, a nine-year-old boy named Oskar Schell.[7] The novel follows Oskar's urban adventures through New York City, a literal and psychological journey that he undertakes to cope with the traumatic loss of his father, who died in the terrorist attacks of 9/11.This chapter will first explore how such urban landscapes are portrayed as powerful sites of memory, in Foer's second novel, and how the experimental form of the narrative conveys the complexity of trauma. I will then focus on the multifaceted depiction of New York City and on the way reality and myth become closely interrelated, through the main protagonist's symbolic quest and the narration of urban space. Finally, I will analyze the way in which post-traumatic memories and visual imagery reflect each other throughout the novel. This study will thus endeavor to demonstrate how Jonathan Safran Foer, while treating deeply personal experiences, also deals with collective trauma through his work, thereby bearing witness to this tragic event within both a particular and a universal framework.

From Urban Memories to Narrative Creativity

Relying on Geoffrey Hartman's works on landscape and place as well as on Pierre Nora's concept of "sites of memory," Anne Whitehead points out, in *Trauma Fiction*, that the issue of space in relation to memory has become crucial in contemporary trauma theory and particularly focuses on the link between trauma and landscape in her analysis of Anne Michaels's *Fugitive Pieces*.[8] In the case of Jonathan Safran Foer's *Extremely Loud & Incredibly Close,* the readers are faced with the representation of what we might rather call "*cityscapes*,"[9] and more precisely, with the performance of urban memory through the cityscape of New York, as being intimately bound up with the tragedy motivated by the 9/11 attacks. Nevertheless, as we shall see, this cityscape is not the only one that strategically appears in the novel.

The different sites of memory that are depicted in *Extremely Loud & Incredibly Close* reflect the complex structure of the novel, in which the action develops by means of three different intertwining narrative threads into an intricate web of trauma experiences. The main narrative focuses on the picaresque journey of nine-year-old Oskar Schell through the boroughs of New York City, during which he tries to come to terms with his father's death in the attacks on the World Trade Center. Oskar's narrative is structured around the quest motif, which begins when he comes across a mysterious key in an envelope labelled "Black" among his father's belongings. As Ilka Saal has observed, "[t]he separate phases of the quest-journey present various didactic stages enabling Oskar to cope with traumatic loss and to mature in the process."[10] With only a tambourine for company,

Oskar travels to all corners of the city in search of the matching lock to his key.[11] The ensuing treasure hunt is driven by the boy's need to soothe his painfully lively imagination and fulfil an insatiable desire to recreate his father's image as accurately as possible. In depicting the various mechanisms that Oskar sets up in order to gain mastery over his trauma, Foer uses all the traditional elements of the quest, namely "the call to action, the dangers incurred, the helpers who assist in the effort but may also hinder it, and finally the last ordeal that leads the quester to his goal."[12] This motif is epitomized from the beginning of the novel, when Oskar narrates how he used to play a game with his father, called "Reconnaissance Expedition."[13] This particular segment of the novel can be seen as a tool to try and understand how the novel functions as a whole, and how to make sense of the interweaving between form and content. During one of these "expeditions," his father gives him a map of Central Park without providing him with any evidence. Oskar desperately tries to interpret the different objects he finds, but is progressively kept in the dark, "The more I found, the less I understood."[14] When connecting the dots on the map of Central Park that indicate the places where he digs up an object, he observes, "I could connect them to make almost anything I wanted, which meant I wasn't getting closer to anything."[15]

The random structure of the dots seems to mirror the ostensible arbitrariness of the structure of the novel. In this respect, Mitchum Huehls has pointed out that there seems to be no logic behind the different functions of each of the formal experiments,

> [B]oth in the novel's photographs and in its overall performativity, there is an equivocation: sometimes a thing is what it is, and at other times it represents something other than itself. Lacking an internal and consistent logic, this undecidability has given reviewers good cause to chastise Foer. And yet, I would like to entertain the possibility that such undecidability might be the point.[16]

This "undecidability" also seems to be the focal point of the novel as a whole: as Oskar digs up several objects in Central Park, he is desperate to know which of them represent clues and wonders how he can ever be right without further indication. The only reply Oskar gets from his father is that "'[a]nother way of looking at it would be, how could you ever be wrong?'"[17] The fact that there is neither a right nor a wrong interpretation of the things Oskar discovers as he progresses in his quest could also apply to the reading of the narrative itself, which would therefore have no predetermined interpretation or meaning. Thus, if "undecidability" is the clue, then the reader's participation in "connecting the dots" of the novel's structure seems to be firmly required, in order to try and make sense of its content and unconventional form.

Mirroring Oskar's narrative, testimonies written by the child's grandmother are interwoven with his grandfather's letters to his son—Oskar's father, killed in the terrorist attacks—that gradually disclose to the readers another site of memory, referring to the Dresden air raids in 1945. While Oskar's narrative builds and progresses,[18] his grandparents' voices only seem to testify to the very failure of working through their trauma and to their entrapment in perpetual "melancholia."[19] Indeed, throughout the novel, we see them struggle in vain to put their experience of the Dresden bombing into words, thus reflecting what Shoshana Felman and Dori Laub have termed, to describe the devastating aspect of the Holocaust, "the crisis of witnessing,"[20] a situation in which "[t]he survivor (…) is not truly in touch either with the core of his traumatic reality or with the fatedness of its reenactments, and thereby remains entrapped in both."[21]

This "paralysis," this very impossibility to tell, is best embodied in the figure of Oskar's paternal grandfather, Thomas Schell Sr., who, in a literal sense, is unable to share his traumatic experiences with others because he suffers from aphasia. His loss of speech stands for his inability (unwillingness?) to cope with his traumatic past. Indeed, in one of his letters—all of them remaining unsent—to his son Thomas (Oskar's father), he writes, "if I could tell you what happened to me that night, I could leave that night behind me, maybe I could come home to you, but that night has no beginning or end, it started before I was born and it's still happening."[22] Likewise, Oskar's paternal grandmother attempts to type out the story of her life (in chapters entitled "My Feelings") but does so without a typewriter ribbon, producing reams of blank pages that are visually present in the novel, but which eventually remain indecipherable to anyone but her.[23] Hence, despite the characters' great urgency to communicate, the various letters and memoirs they compose merely convey the impossibility of communicating their traumatic past and of remaking the world that has been destroyed for them twice: in Dresden and in New York.

In this regard, Oskar's grandparents seem to express the "frozen and wordless quality of traumatic memories,"[24] as identified by Judith Lewis Herman, and therefore to emphasize the problematic relation between trauma and language.[25] Their inability to articulate horrific experiences lies precisely in the lack of pre-existing schemata that could provide a prior scheme of knowledge and thus possibly absorb the traumatic experience and integrate it. Indeed, as Bessel Van Der Kolk and Onno Van Der Hart have underlined, "[t]raumatic memories are the unassimilated scraps of overwhelming experiences, which need to be integrated with existing mental schemes, and be transformed into narrative language."[26] However, the failure of Oskar's grandparents' attempts at "writing the disaster"[27] points to the difficulty (impossibility?) of uttering the pain that seems to paralyze them both.

The two events, distant in time and presented fragmentarily by the three traumatized narrators, thus coincide in many respects, as temporal parallelisms and narrative fragmentation are linked, in a reflective manner, to the different pathological effects suffered by the grandson and his grandparents. By interweaving the bombings of the World Trade Center with those of Dresden, Foer highlights that vulnerability and suffering are not unique to New York. The writer thereby places 9/11 "outside the reach of facile political recuperation," according to Kristiaan Versluys.[28] Yet, if *Extremely Loud & Incredibly Close* introduces a political critique about the implications of terrorism and historical trauma, one should not consider it a realist novel dealing with 9/11, but rather a "conscious artifact,"[29] drawing from magical realism techniques,[30] by which the desolate cityscape is not only transformed into a mythical environment, but is also given spiritual insight through the child's urban and psychological wanderings.

New York City, between Realism and Myth

What seems to characterize Foer's attempt to make the reader depart from a mere realistic approach to life, is the quest that Oskar undertakes through the metropolis, a place that becomes imbued with mystery and enchantment as the story unfolds. This self-made mythology is best highlighted through the parable of the Six Borough, which is a bedtime story Oskar's dad tells his son the night before "the worst day."[31] According to the tale, New York had a sixth borough, which was "separated from Manhattan by a thin body of water whose narrowest crossing happened to equal the world's long jump record."[32] The holder of this record made the leap as part of an annual party and "[f]or those few moments that the jumper was in the air, every New Yorker felt capable of flight."[33] Reflecting on the use of the term "jumper," David Brauner has drawn a parallel between "the athlete" and "those who leapt to their deaths from the twin towers," observing that "the collective fantasy of flight of the assembled crowd alludes to the crowds of New Yorkers who witnessed the collapse of the towers while fleeing from the scene and also anticipates Oskar's photographic montage in which a jumper from one of the towers miraculously levitates rather than descending."[34] If this fairytale may stand for further instruction from Thomas Jr. to his son and for another pattern of the latter's extensive quest, its combination with Oskar's own vision of the 9/11 events in hindsight can thus be considered as a metaphor for the nine-year-old child's attempt to grapple with his own trauma.

In *The Uses of Enchantment*, Bruno Bettelheim, a psychoanalyst and a survivor of the Holocaust who was particularly concerned with how children were affected by traumatic events, discussed the emotional and symbolic importance of fairytales in children's coping with their psychological troubles and saw them as "examples of both temporary and permanent solutions to pressing difficulties,"[35] noting that "[i]t is here that fairy tales have unequaled value, because they offer new dimensions to the child's imagination which would be impossible for him to discover as truly on his own. Even more important, the form and structure of fairy tales suggest images to the child by which he can structure his daydreams and with them give better direction to his life."[36] In this regard, the internalization of the fairytale schemata by Oskar could be seen as the gift of working through loss offered by his father before his death, thanks to the bedtime stories he kept recounting to him.

If the fable of the Sixth Borough, associated with Oskar's trauma and overactive imagination, has further been compared by other critics to the story of Peter Pan,[37] it also works as a parable about history and truth. Indeed, Oskar's father tells his son that the Sixth Borough started drifting away and finally ended up in Antarctica, but that the New Yorkers of that time were able to hold on to a small piece of the island, which turned out to be Central Park. The reader eventually learns that the former Sixth Borough is now floating around the planet with "a gigantic hole in the middle of it where Central Park used to be."[38] As the story unfolds, Oskar repeatedly interrupts his father's narrative to question its authenticity, "'Was there *really* a sixth borough?'"; "'Dad?' 'Yes?' 'I know there wasn't really a sixth borough. I mean, objectively.'"[39] However, Oskar will not receive any proper answer from his father, who only tells his son, "'Well, you won't read about it in any of the history books, because there's nothing—save for the circumstantial evidence in Central Park—to prove that it was there at all.'"[40] The question of authenticity and reality, which permeates Foer's fictional work, is openly addressed by the famous physicist Stephen Hawking, who, as a fictional character in the story, reminds Oskar—to whom he finally sends a proper reply, in response to his multiple requests—that, *"[t]he fragile balance depends on things we'll never be able to see, hear, smell, taste or touch. Life itself depends on them. What's real? What isn't real? Maybe those aren't the right questions to be asking. What does life depend on?*"[41]

The "hole" that, according to the parable, lies in the middle of the Sixth Borough is thus highly allegorical and seems to function as a trope in the novel. Indeed, it is not only reminiscent of the "black hole," which is well-known for being one of Stephen Hawking's main subjects of study, but it also refers to the "psychic hole," an expression used by the psychoanalyst Ilany

Kogan to describe the experience of the second-generation descendants of the Holocaust as follows,

> The patient experiences this 'hole', which represents a part of his parents' history which has disappeared, as a persistent wound in his psyche or a gap in his emotional understanding. This 'psychic hole' does not belong to the category of 'blankness'—negative hallucination, blank psychosis, blank mourning, all connected to what Green (1986) calls the problem of emptiness or of the negative. The 'psychic hole' I am talking about is more similar to the 'black hole' in the world of physics, a body which sucks into itself everything that gets close to it because of the forces of gravitation.[42]

Just as this "psychic hole" "sucks into itself everything that gets close to it," so Oskar's trauma takes the shape of a hole within himself, "That secret was a hole in the middle of me that every happy thing fell into."[43] Indeed, on the fateful day, Oskar found a number of messages on the answering machine from his father, calling from the burning towers. When it rang a last time, Oskar was too paralyzed to pick up the phone, a "traumatizing 'betrayal' [that] has saddled the boy with a crushing sense of guilt."[44] The child, therefore, spends his time giving himself bruises and indulging compulsively in a series of inventions (such as birdseed suits to jump from burning buildings; skyscrapers that move downward instead of elevators going up), in order to soothe his pain.

This "repetition compulsion,"[45] symptomatic of Oskar's traumatized mind, can also be observed following the boy's plan to visit all the New Yorkers by the name of Black, in the hope of finding the lock that matches the key—a metaphor for the doorknobs that are visually present in the novel, and that would give access to his father's past. In his analysis of the fable of the Sixth Borough, Matthew Mullins has described the novel as "depict[ing] a seemingly lost unity that was never truly lost at all. (…) There can be no one-to-one, allegorical or archetypal comparison for Manhattan and the fabled Sixth Borough, but Foer paints a picture of a once-unified world that only *appears* to be no longer unified, when, in fact, the heart of that world remains common and available to all people."[46] Likewise, Oskar's quest participates in conveying a global image of community prevailing in the novel. In this respect, *Extremely Loud & Incredibly Close* seems to emphasize the unbreakable bond that lies within and between nations, through the many helpers[47] Oskar comes across in his peregrinations, most of them being connected by a common experience of trauma. Oskar's picaresque wanderings through the metropolis can thus be seen as having a redemptive value and as celebrating the diversity of New York City itself, as Kristiaan Versluys underlines,

> While Oskar crisscrosses the city and visits places he has never been before, there is redemptive value in the fact that his life touches those of other New Yorkers, however briefly. (…) The variety of the city itself produces epic momentum and psychic uplift. (…) Oskar's travels over the five boroughs of New York (…) signify, if not a resacralization of the territory, at least its reoccupation, after it has been usurped by 9/11 terrorists. In the upbeat spirit of his dead father, Oskar's exploration of his native ground is an act of reconquest and reaffirmation: firsthand proof that the terrorists have failed to break the city's stride.[48]

However, Oskar's exploration of New York City does not seem to be such "an act of reconquest and reaffirmation" of history and of himself, when considering the presence of visual images in the novel that have come to characterize the nine-year-old's post-traumatic memories and his own struggle with the event.

Visual Memory and the Reversal of History

Extremely Loud & Incredibly Close graphically reproduces images that are imprinted on Oskar's mind during the traumatic years following his father's death. As Foer emphasizes, "[t]o speak about what happened on September 11 requires a visual language. My singular motivation was to create the most powerful book I could."[49] Indeed, photographs are scattered throughout the novel, some of which Oskar did not take himself, others which represent mental snapshots depicting persons or scenes he encountered during his search for the lock.[50] Because of this "avant-garde tool-kit,"[51] the novel was met with mixed reactions, as some book reviewers found these postmodern experiments[52] to be completely inappropriate for representing 9/11.[53] Yet, as many literary critics have made clear, there is more to the concept of trauma in the novel than initially meets the eye.

Extending the findings of trauma theory on visual studies, many critics, such as Susan Sontag, Marianne Hirsch, Ulrich Baer, or Barbie Zelizer, have pointed out photography's therapeutic functions and limitations in managing trauma. In this respect, Marianne Hirsch has emphasized the link between photography and temporality as a way to understand the events of 9/11,

> If still photography is the visual genre that best captures the trauma and loss associated with September 2001—the sense of monumental, irrevocable change that we feel we have experienced—it is due to the photograph's temporality. (…) To photograph, we might say, is to look in a different way—to look without understanding. Understanding is deferred as it is to trauma, enabling photography to help us understand the traumatic events of September 11.[54]

In the case of Oskar and his grandfather, to whom most of the pictures of the novel are related, photography does not seem to function as a therapeutic tool, since the pictures, eventually, do not help them cope with their trauma. Although Susan Sontag contends that photography provides a way for attempting to grasp the traumatic event, she does argue that "[photographs] are not much help if the task is to understand. Narratives can make us understand. Photographs do something else: they haunt us."[55] Photography thus seems to function in a similar way to the traumatic mind, as victims are haunted by traumatic flashbacks that elude understanding. Indeed, in the words of Cathy Caruth, "[t]o be traumatized is precisely to be possessed by an image or event. (…) The flashback or traumatic re-enactment conveys, that is, both *the truth of an event*, and *the truth of its incomprehensibility*."[56]

In this sense, just as in Art Spiegelman's *In the Shadow of No Towers*, images and layout are used to virtually represent the traumatized victim's mind. As such, although their most obvious function is to chronicle the events in Oskar's life, all of these intercalated pictures and images also have a symbolic meaning that transcends their seemingly documentary function. In a most performative manner, Oskar shows the reader, at one point, some of the pictures collected in his diary *Stuff That Happened to Me*. While in bed, he writes, "I flipped through it for a while, wishing that I would finally fall asleep."[57] The following fifteen pages are composed of images from his scrapbook,[58] after which he eventually tells us that "[he] got out of bed."[59] The images displayed in this passage derive from various media and include, among others, a rack full of keys, a design for a paper airplane, mating tortoises, fingerprints, and photographs of astronauts. The immediacy generated by these images seems to cater to a desire for direct witnessing—an essential aspect regarding the visual display of images of 9/11 to the public—that actively involves the reader's attention. Most of these images are directly connected to Oskar's experiences that are either recounted later in the novel or that are already alluded to at that point, and are thus closely related to Oskar's verbal narrative.[60]

In spite of the apparent complementarity of the visual and verbal representations of one and the same experience, their obvious dissociation within the novel tends to disrupt the narrative unity and thus requires greater attention from the reader in order to be able to link them together into a coherent meaning. In this respect, the foreshadowings and flashbacks created through the images that appear in Oskar's scrapbook can be seen as metaphors for the workings of memory itself, thus suggesting at the same time that the meaning of past experiences is not definite but can be created anew through imagination. Indeed, as Birgit Däwes has argued, "[a]ll of these images underline the processes of both individual and collective memory as multi-faceted and complex, working in series or unique moments, repetitions, flashbacks, as well as by non-linear association."[61]

Among the images composing Oskar's diary, a picture that keeps recurring throughout the novel—and the one that provides a primary illustration of New York City and the attacks of 9/11—is the one of a man falling from the World Trade Center.[62] *Extremely Loud & Incredibly Close* is not the only novel in which falling bodies are used to represent the tragic events of 9/11. Other novels such as Don DeLillo's *Falling Man*, Frédéric Beigbeder's *Windows on the World* or Art Spiegelman's *In the Shadow of No Towers*, explore the centrality of these "iconic figures" in the representations of 9/11 and also point to the failures of knowledge related to their literary treatment.[63] In this regard, when Oskar finds a picture of the falling man on the internet, the young boy wants to believe that the man in the picture is his father, so that he can finally have closure and work through his trauma,

> I want to stop inventing. If I could know how he died, exactly how he died, I wouldn't have to invent him dying inside an elevator that was stuck between floors, which happened to some people, and I wouldn't have to imagine him trying to crawl down the outside of the building, which I saw a video of one person doing on a Polish site, or trying to use a tablecloth as a parachute, like some of the people who were in Windows of the World actually did. There were so many different ways to die, and I just need to know which was his.[64]

Oskar's inventions and obsession with death can thus be seen as an oblique way to relate to the loss of his father and at the same time to come closer to him. According to Birgit Däwes, the images of the falling body have come to symbolize the collective memory of 9/11 as a whole, "well-known, widely accessible, and overwhelmingly unambiguous on the one hand, and radically manifold or re-readable on the other."[65] Indeed, as the final pages of the novel show, Oskar does not succeed in elucidating the conditions of his father's death, which eventually remains a mystery to him,

> Was it Dad?
> Maybe.
> Whoever it was, it was somebody.
> I ripped the pages out of the book.
> I reversed the order, so the last one was first, and the first was last.
> When I flipped through them, it looked like the man was floating up through the sky.[66]

Oskar's desire to reverse time is visually expressed by the presence of a flipbook at the end of the novel, showing images from the nine-year-old's scrapbook that he reinserts in reverse order—so that "[they] would have been safe"[67]—making the man fly back safely into the building when the pages are flipped forward. The novel's conclusion and Foer's choice to end his novel not in words but in images have been much commented by literary critics. Mitchum Huehls thinks that the final pages of the novel bring "their cinematic temporality to the reader's own fingertips and mak[e] the novel performatively coextensive with Oskar's journal,"[68] while according to Philippe Codde, they emphasize "not only the radical inaccessibility of the past, but also the impossibility of closure."[69]

In this respect, one could argue that the novel's conclusion does not give a solution to the narrative, but merely appears to be another invention of the little boy's traumatized mind. As Laura Frost notes, "[t]he flip-book creates a narrative out of the arrested, unrelenting presentness of the snapshot. It attempts to break the frame of photographic stillness by inventing a new ending (which is, by inversion, its beginning) for the falling man."[70] Oskar's imagined historical reversal can be interpreted, in other words, as another productive way of working through his trauma, thus suggesting that the child remains caught in "discontinuous still time."[71]

The reversal of history conveyed through Oskar's back-to-front flicker book is foreshadowed by the grandmother's dream that makes the destruction caused by the fire-bombing of Dresden magically undone, "I had been dreaming about where I came from. (…) In my dream, all the collapsed ceilings re-formed above us. The fire went back into the bombs, which rose up and into the bellies of planes whose propellers turned backward, like the second hands of the clocks across Dresden, only faster."[72] In juxtaposing the two characters' attempts at reversing history, Foer draws a clear parallel between the grandmother's dream and her grandson's wish to go back in time by using the fifteen photographic frames of the falling man, while tying the two historical events together. Although the grandmother knows that her redemptive vision is only a dream, just as Oskar knows that his father's rescue and coming back to life can only take place in his imagination, what these rewritings of history aim at is, as David Brauner has demonstrated, "to challenge the conventional view of history as inevitable, fixed, predetermined, objective; to posit, through the imagining of alternative histories, an idea of history as provisional, precarious, indeterminate and subjective."[73] However, as the critic goes on to argue, "they may, paradoxically, have the opposite effect: rewinding and replaying these events might reinforce a teleological view of history by apparently implying that each stage of history is one link in a causal chain that cannot be broken, a linear route from which there are no diversions or exits, only the possibility of reversing."[74]

By transgressing the pre-established dimensions of time and space, Foer thus attempts to re-conceptualize and transform the unbearable into an imaginative art form, as a way, paradoxically, "to 'return to the Real,'" "to regain firm ground in some 'real reality,'" as Slavoj Žižek puts it.[75] In this regard, Oskar's own interpretation of the events in trying to make sense of his father's death can be considered as a "counter-memory"[76] to media's overpowering visual narrative, therefore adding another layer of complexity to the whole structure of the novel, where the boundaries between reality and fiction become blurred. For, as Jean Baudrillard has underlined, "[r]eality and fiction are inextricable, and the fascination with the attack is primarily a fascination with the image (both its exultatory and its catastrophic consequences are themselves largely imagery)."[77]

Conclusion

As I have shown in this chapter, *Extremely Loud & Incredibly Close*'s intricate narrative form exposes the complexity of trauma and directs the reader's attention to the processes of understanding rather than to the novel's plot. Oskar's peregrinations through New York City in search of the missing lock convey his attempt at overcoming his fears and coping with the loss of his father. By interlacing two generations and depicting the different cityscapes as devastated and wounded sites of memory, the novel as a whole can be read as a way to "universaliz[e] grief,"[78] while at the same time suggesting that this very grief can be soothed in the tightening of personal attachments. Through the brilliant visual interplay between words and images, Jonathan Safran Foer therefore reveals that memory and trauma, both personal and collective, form an ineluctable part of the human experience.

Bibliography

Adams, Tim. "A Nine-year-old and 9/11." *The Observer*, May 29, 2005. Accessed October 10, 2010. http://www.guardian.co.uk/books/2005/may/29/fiction.features.

Almond, Steve. "The Boy Who Knew Too Much. The Young Oskar—and his Creator, Jonathan Safran Foer—Show Off Their Skills, With Mixed Results." *Boston Globe*, April 3, 2005. Accessed May 3, 2012. http://www.boston.com/ae/books/articles/2005/04/03/the_boy_who_knew_too_much/?page=full.

Baer, Ulrich. *110 Stories: New York Writes after September 11*. New York and London: New York University Press, 2002.

—. *Spectral Evidence: The Photography of Trauma*. Cambridge, MA and London: The MIT Press, 2002.

Baudrillard, Jean. *The Spirit of Terrorism and Requiem for the Twin Towers*. Translated by Chris Turner. London and New York: Verso, 2002.

Bettelheim, Bruno. *The Uses of Enchantment: The Meaning and Importance of Fairy Tales*. London: Thames and Hudson, 1976.

Blanchot, Maurice. *The Writing of the Disaster*. Translated by Ann Smock. Lincoln, Nebraska, and London: University of Nebraska Press, 1995.

Bowers, Maggie Ann. *Magic(al) Realism*. London and New York: Routledge, 2004.

Brauner, David. "Fantasies of Flight and Flight of Fancy: Rewriting History and Retreating from Trauma in *The Plot Against America*." In *Philip Roth*, edited by David Brauner, 186-217. Manchester and New York: Manchester University Press, 2007.

Caruth, Cathy, ed. *Trauma: Explorations in Memory*. Baltimore and London: The Johns Hopkins University Press, 1995.

Codde, Philippe. "Philomela Revised: Traumatic Iconicity in Jonathan Safran Foer's *Extremely Loud & Incredibly Close*." *Studies in American Fiction* 35.2 (2007): 241-54.

Collado-Rodríguez, Francisco. "Trauma, Ethics and Myth-Oriented Literary Tradition in Jonathan Safran Foer's *Extremely Loud & Incredibly Close*." *Journal of English Studies* 5-6 (2005-2008): 47-62.

Däwes, Birgit. "On Contested Ground (Zero): Literature and the Transnational Challenge of Remembering 9/11." *Amerikastudien/American Studies* 52.4 (2007): 517-43.

Faber, Michel. "A Tower of Babble." *The Guardian*, June 4, 2005. Accessed November 16, 2011. http://www.guardian.co.uk/books/2005/jun/04/featuresreviews.guardianreview22.

Felman, Shoshana, and Dori Laub. *Testimony: Crises of Witnessing in Literature, Psychoanalysis, and History*. New York and London: Routledge, 1992.

Foer, Jonathan Safran. *Everything Is Illuminated*. London: Penguin Books, 2002. 2003.

—. *Extremely Loud & Incredibly Close*. London: Penguin Books, 2005. 2006.

Foucault, Michel. "Nietzsche, Genealogy, History." In *Language, Counter-Memory, Practice: Selected Essays and Interviews by Michel Foucault*, edited by Donald F. Bouchard, 139-64. Ithaca, New York: Cornell University Press, 1977.

Frost, Laura. "Still Life: 9/11's Falling Bodies." In *Literature after 9/11*, edited by Ann Keniston and Jeanne Follansbee Quinn, 180-206. New York and London: Routledge, 2008.

Greenberg, Judith. *Trauma at Home: After 9/11*. Lincoln, Nebraska, and London: University of Nebraska Press, 2003.

Guerin, Frances, and Roger Hallas. *The Image and the Witness: Trauma, Memory and Visual Culture*. London and New York: Wallflower Press, 2007.

Herman, Judith Lewis. *Trauma and Recovery: From Domestic Abuse to Political Terror*. New York: BasicBooks, 1992. 2001.

Hirsch, Marianne. "I Took Pictures: September 2001 and Beyond." In *Trauma at Home: After 9/11*, edited by Judith Greenberg, 69-86. Lincoln, Nebraska, and London: University of Nebraska Press, 2003.

Hudson, Gabe. "Everything Is Interrogated." *Village Voice*, March 22, 2005. Accessed September 25, 2010. http://www.villagevoice.com/2005-03-22/books/everything-is-interrogated/.

Huehls, Mitchum. "Foer, Spiegelman, and 9/11's Timely Traumas." In *Literature after 9/11*, edited by Ann Keniston and Jeanne Follansbee Quinn, 42-59. New York and London: Routledge, 2008.

Hutcheon, Linda. *A Poetics of Postmodernism: History, Theory, Fiction*. New York and London: Routledge, 1988.

Huyssen, Andreas. *Present Pasts: Urban Palimpsests and the Politics of Memory*. Stanford, California: Stanford University Press, 2003.

Kakutani, Michiko. "A Boy's Epic Quest, Borough by Borough." *New York Times*, March 22, 2005. Accessed April 2, 2013. http://www.nytimes.com/2005/03/22/books/22kaku.html?_r=0.

Kirn, Walter. "Everything Is Included." *New York Times Book Review*, April 3, 2005. Accessed May 6, 2012. http://www.nytimes.com/2005/04/03/books/review/0403cover-kirn.html?_r=0.

Kogan, Ilany. *The Cry of Mute Children: A Psychoanalytic Perspective of the Second Generation of the Holocaust*. London and New York: Free Association Books, 1995.

LaCapra, Dominick. *Writing History, Writing Trauma*. Baltimore and London: The Johns Hopkins University Press, 2001.

Mullins, Matthew. "Boroughs and Neighbors: Traumatic Solidarity in Jonathan Safran Foer's *Extremely Loud & Incredibly Close*." *Papers on Language and Literature* 45.3 (2009): 298-324.

Nora, Pierre. "Between Memory and History: Les Lieux de Mémoire." *Representations* 26 (1989): 7-24.

Rycroft, Charles. *A Critical Dictionary of Psychoanalysis*. London: Penguin Books, 1968. 1995.

Saal, Ilka. "Regarding the Pain of Self and Other: Trauma Transfer and Narrative Framing in Jonathan Safran Foer's *Extremely Loud & Incredibly Close*." *Modern Fiction Studies* 57.3 (2011): 453-76.

Siegel, Harry. "Extremely Cloying & Incredibly False." *New York Press*, April 13, 2005. Accessed June 2, 2013. http://nypress.com/extremely-cloying-incredibly-false/.

Sontag, Susan. *Regarding the Pain of Others*. New York: Farrar, Straus & Giroux, 2003.

Spiegelman, Art. *In the Shadow of No Towers*. New York: Pantheon Books, 2004.

Sturken, Marita. *Tourists of History: Memory, Kitsch, and Consumerism from Oklahoma City to Ground Zero*. Durham and London: Duke University Press, 2007.

Uytterschout, Sien, and Kristiaan Versluys. "Melancholy and Mourning in Jonathan Safran Foer's *Extremely Loud & Incredibly Close*." *Orbis Litterarum* 63.3 (2008): 216-36.

Uytterschout, Sien. "An Extremely Loud Tin Drum: a Comparative Study of Jonathan Safran Foer's *Extremely Loud & Incredibly Close* and Günter Grass's *The Tin Drum*." *Comparative Literature Studies* 47.2 (2010): 185-99.

Versluys, Kristiaan. "A Rose Is Not a Rose Is Not a Rose: History and Language in Jonathan Safran Foer's *Extremely Loud & Incredibly Close*." In *Out of the Blue: September 11 and the Novel*, edited by Kristiaan Versluys, 79-119. New York: Columbia University Press, 2009.

Wardi, Dina. *Memorial Candles: Children of the Holocaust*. London and New York: Routledge, 1992. 2000.

Whitehead, Anne. *Trauma Fiction*. Edinburgh: Edinburgh University Press, 2004.

Zelizer, Barbie. "Photography, Journalism, and Trauma." In *Journalism After September 11*, edited by Barbie Zelizer and Stuart Allan, 48-68. London and New York: Routledge, 2002.

Žižek, Slavoj. *Welcome to the Desert of the Real! Five Essays on September 11 and Related Dates*. London and New York: Verso, 2002.

Notes

[1] Slavoj Žižek, *Welcome to the Desert of the Real! Five Essays on September 11 and Related Dates* (London and New York: Verso, 2002), 16.

[2] Marita Sturken, *Tourists of History: Memory, Kitsch, and Consumerism from Oklahoma City to Ground Zero* (Durham and London: Duke University Press, 2007), 167.

[3] It should be noted that trauma is a word of Greek origin meaning *wound*, and dictionaries mostly define it as, "[a] structural damage to the body caused by the impact of some object or substance; (…) any totally unexpected experience which the subject is unable to assimilate; (…) any experience which is mastered by uses of defences," Charles Rycroft, *A Critical Dictionary of Psychoanalysis* (London: Penguin Books, 1995), 187. However, trauma has become, over the last decades, an overused term, that has come to define "[l]oosely, inaccurately, but frequently, any distressing or upsetting experience, regardless of whether it has lasting effects or not," Rycroft, *A Critical Dictionary of Psychoanalysis*, 188. In this respect, some critics, such as Andreas Huyssen, have expressed scepticism over the transposition of psychoanalytical categories of trauma onto the public, historical sphere where remembrance takes place, "The focus on trauma is legitimate where nations or groups of people are trying to come to terms with a history of violence suffered or violence perpetrated. But the transnational discourse of human rights may give us a better handle on such matters than the transfer of psychoanalysis into the world of politics and history," Andreas Huyssen, *Present Pasts: Urban Palimpsests and the Politics of Memory* (Stanford, California: Stanford University Press, 2003), 9. When considering the literature of 9/11, it should nevertheless be observed that most of the writers have built their responses to the event around such concepts as "collective trauma" and "absence," which have become key terms in dealing with the Twin Towers attacks, as Ulrich Baer has contended, "The 110 authors create an index to measure the absences that now define New York City: absences initially confined to Ground Zero but quickly rippling outward to ever-wider circles of the bereaved, and ultimately affecting everyone who distrusts simple answers, ready-made and precision-bombed solutions, and the arrogant and foolish certainty of having the correct response to a severe collective trauma," Ulrich Baer, *110 Stories: New York Writes after September 11* (New York and London: New York University Press, 2002), 2.

[4] See Pierre Nora, "Between Memory and History: Les Lieux de Mémoire," *Representations* 26 (1989): 7-24.

[5] Frances Guerin and Roger Hallas, *The Image and the Witness: Trauma, Memory and Visual Culture* (London and New York: Wallflower Press, 2007), 5.

[6] *Extremely Loud & Incredibly Close* was adapted into a film by the same name, which was directed by Stephen Daldry and released on December 25, 2011.

[7] Oskar Schell is modeled on various young literary characters, such as Holden Caulfield, the protagonist of J.D. Salinger's *The Catcher in the Rye* (1951), and Oskar Matzerath, the protagonist of Günter Grass's *The Tin Drum* (1959). These intertextual references have been criticized by some reviewers, such as Steve Almond or Michiko Kakutani who has argued that the main protagonist of *Extremely Loud & Incredibly Close* "comes across as an entirely synthetic creation, assembled out of bits and pieces of famous literary heroes' past. Like J. D. Salinger's Holden Caulfield, Oskar wanders around New York City, lonely, alienated and on the verge, possibly, of an emotional breakdown. Like Günter Grass's Oskar Matzerath in *The Tin Drum*, he plays a musical instrument (in his case, a tambourine) while commenting on the fearful state

of the world around him. And like Saul Bellow's *Herzog*, he writes letters to people he doesn't know," Michiko Kakutani, "A Boy's Epic Quest, Borough by Borough," *New York Times*, March 22, 2005, accessed April 2, 2013, http://www.nytimes.com/2005/03/22/books/22kaku.html?_r=0/. For a comparative analysis of Jonathan Safran Foer's *Extremely Loud & Incredibly Close* and Günter Grass's *The Tin Drum*, see Sien Uytterschout, "An Extremely Loud Tin Drum: a Comparative Study of Jonathan Safran Foer's *Extremely Loud & Incredibly Close* and Günter Grass's *The Tin Drum,*" *Comparative Literature Studies* 47.2 (2010): 185-99.

[8] See Anne Whitehead, "'Ground that will remember you': trauma and landscape in Anne Michaels's *Fugitive Pieces*," in *Trauma Fiction*, ed. Anne Whitehead (Edinburgh: Edinburgh University Press, 2004), 48-78.

[9] Francisco Collado-Rodríguez has used this term to qualify Foer's depiction of the urban topography of New York in *Extremely Loud & Incredibly Close*. See Francisco Collado-Rodríguez, "Trauma, Ethics and Myth-Oriented Literary Tradition in Jonathan Safran Foer's *Extremely Loud & Incredibly Close,*" *Journal of English Studies* 5-6 (2005-2008): 57.

[10] Ilka Saal, "Regarding the Pain of Self and Other: Trauma Transfer and Narrative Framing in Jonathan Safran Foer's *Extremely Loud & Incredibly Close,*" *Modern Fiction Studies* 57.3 (2011): 457.

[11] Later on in the novel, Oskar befriends his upstairs neighbor, the elderly Mr. Black, and enlists his help in the quest. Eventually, Mr. Black steps down in favor of the mysterious figure of "the renter" who will turn out to be Thomas Schell, Oskar's long-lost grandfather.

[12] Kristiaan Versluys, "A Rose Is Not a Rose Is Not a Rose: History and Language in Jonathan Safran Foer's *Extremely Loud & Incredibly Close*," in *Out of the Blue: September 11 and the Novel*, ed. Kristiaan Versluys (New York: Columbia University Press, 2009), 103.

[13] Jonathan Safran Foer, *Extremely Loud & Incredibly Close* (London: Penguin Books, 2006), 8.

[14] Foer, *Extremely Loud & Incredibly Close*, 10.

[15] Foer, *Extremely Loud & Incredibly Close*, 10.

[16] Mitchum Huehls, "Foer, Spiegelman, and 9/11's Timely Traumas," in *Literature after 9/11*, eds. Ann Keniston et al. (New York and London: Routledge, 2008), 50.

[17] Foer, *Extremely Loud & Incredibly Close*, 9.

[18] According to Ilka Saal, Oskar's narrative "eventually allow[s] him to work through his trauma and to regain a strong sense of self," Saal, "Regarding the Pain of Self and Other," 457. Yet, as we will see, the end of the novel seems to prove the opposite.

[19] Since Dominick LaCapra's reintegration of the Freudian terms "acting out" or *melancholia* and "working through" or *mourning* in the field of trauma studies, this dichotomy has become the theoretical groundwork for examining trauma in literature. See Dominick LaCapra, *Writing History, Writing Trauma* (Baltimore and London: The Johns Hopkins University Press, 2001), 65-67. For an analysis of the various narrative strands in *Extremely Loud & Incredibly Close*, in terms of Freud's concepts of melancholia and mourning, see Sien Uytterschout and Kristiaan Versluys, "Melancholy and Mourning in Jonathan Safran Foer's *Extremely Loud & Incredibly Close*," *Orbis Litterarum. Orbis Litterarum* 63.3 (2008): 216-36.

[20] Shoshana Felman and Dori Laub, *Testimony: Crises of Witnessing in Literature, Psychoanalysis, and History* (New York and London: Routledge, 1992), xvii.
[21] Felman and Laub, *Testimony: Crises of Witnessing*, 69.
[22] Foer, *Extremely Loud & Incredibly Close*, 208.
[23] Foer, *Extremely Loud & Incredibly Close*, 124.
[24] Judith Lewis Herman, *Trauma and Recovery: From Domestic Abuse to Political Terror* (New York: BasicBooks, 2001), 37.
[25] For an analysis of language in *Extremely Loud & Incredibly Close*, see Versluys, "A Rose Is Not a Rose Is Not a Rose," 79-119.
[26] Bessel Van Der Kolk and Onno Van Der Hart, "The Intrusive Past: the Flexibility of Memory and the Engraving of Trauma," in Cathy Caruth, ed., *Trauma: Explorations in Memory* (Baltimore and London: The Johns Hopkins University Press, 1995), 176. Relying on the theory of Pierre Janet, Bessel Van Der Kolk and Onno Van Der Hart define "narrative memory" and "traumatic memory" as follows, "…in contrast to narrative memory, which is a social act, traumatic memory is inflexible and invariable. Traumatic memory has no social component; it is not addressed to anybody, the patient does not respond to anybody; it is a solitary activity. In contrast, ordinary memory fundamentally serves a social function, illustrated by Irène's telling people about the death of her mother as an appeal for help and reconnection," Van Der Kolk and Van Der Hart, "The Intrusive Past," 163.
[27] I refer here to Maurice Blanchot's famous expression "the writing of the disaster." See Maurice Blanchot, *The Writing of the Disaster*, trans. Ann Smock (Lincoln, Nebraska, and London: University of Nebraska Press, 1995).
[28] Versluys, "A Rose Is Not a Rose Is Not a Rose," 82.
[29] This expression is taken from Collado Rodríguez, "Trauma, Ethics and Myth-Oriented Literary Tradition," 48.
[30] For a detailed study of magical realism, see Maggie Ann Bowers, *Magic(al) Realism* (London and New York: Routledge, 2004).
[31] Foer, *Extremely Loud & Incredibly Close*, 12.
[32] Foer, *Extremely Loud & Incredibly Close*, 217.
[33] Foer, *Extremely Loud & Incredibly Close*, 218.
[34] David Brauner, "Fantasies of Flight and Flight of Fancy: Rewriting History and Retreating from Trauma in *The Plot Against America*," in *Philip Roth*, ed. David Brauner (Manchester and New York: Manchester University Press, 2007), 212.
[35] Bruno Bettelheim, *The Uses of Enchantment: The Meaning and Importance of Fairy Tales* (London: Thames and Hudson, 1976), 6.
[36] Bettelheim, *The Uses of Enchantment*, 7.
[37] According to Sien Uytterschout and Kristiaan Versluys, "[t]he theme of the Sixth Borough combined with Oskar's earlier express wish to stunt his growth is reminiscent of the story of Peter Pan. (…) The story of Central Park, in other words, can be seen as a metaphor for the inescapability of adulthood." For a more detailed analysis, see Uytterschout and Versluys, "Melancholy and Mourning," 229.
[38] Foer, *Extremely Loud & Incredibly Close*, 222.
[39] Foer, *Extremely Loud & Incredibly Close*, 217-21.
[40] Foer, *Extremely Loud & Incredibly Close*, 217.
[41] Foer, *Extremely Loud & Incredibly Close*, 305.

[42] Ilany Kogan, *The Cry of Mute Children: A Psychoanalytic Perspective of the Second Generation of the Holocaust* (London and New York: Free Association Books, 1995), 156. Oskar has also been compared to a "child of the Holocaust" by the literary critics Sien Uytterschout and Kristiaan Versluys, who have defined him as a "memorial candle"—an expression used by Dina Wardi to designate the children of survivors who are "given the burden of participating in [their] parents' emotional world to a much greater extent than any of [their] brothers or sisters"—because of his resemblance to his father and grandfather. See Uytterschout and Versluys, "Melancholy and Mourning," 232-33; and Dina Wardi, *Memorial Candles: Children of the Holocaust* (London and New York: Routledge, 1992, 2000), 6.
[43] Foer, *Extremely Loud & Incredibly Close*, 71.
[44] Philippe Codde, "Philomela Revised: Traumatic Iconicity in Jonathan Safran Foer's *Extremely Loud & Incredibly Close*," *Studies in American Fiction* 35.2 (2007): 244.
[45] Versluys, "A Rose Is Not a Rose Is Not a Rose," 103.
[46] Matthew Mullins, "Boroughs and Neighbors: Traumatic Solidarity in Jonathan Safran Foer's *Extremely Loud & Incredibly Close*," *Papers on Language and Literature* 45.3 (2009): 318. For an analysis of "community" in Foer's *Extremely Loud & Incredibly Close,* see Mullins, "Boroughs and Neighbors," 298-324.
[47] Among the many helpers Oskar comes across in his quest, A. R. Black (the old man who accompanies the young boy for six and a half months in his adventures) has a significantly larger role in the narrative. Abby Black, the "incredibly beautiful" woman who lives in "the narrowest house in New York" (Foer, *Extremely Loud & Incredibly Close*, 90-91), will also turn out to be instrumental in solving the mystery of the key.
[48] Versluys, "A Rose Is Not a Rose Is Not a Rose," 114.
[49] Jonathan Safran Foer, in Gabe Hudson, "Everything Is Interrogated," *Village Voice*, March 22, 2005, accessed September 25, 2010, http://www.villagevoice.com/2005-03-22/books/everything-is-interrogated/.
[50] Oskar's pictures only appear in the chapters of which he is the narrator, not in those containing his grandparents' letters.
[51] Walter Kirn, "Everything Is Included," *New York Times Book Review*, April 3, 2005, accessed May 6, 2012, http://www.nytimes.com/2005/04/03/books/review/0403cover-kirn.html?_r=0.
[52] For a thorough study on postmodernism, see Linda Hutcheon, *A Poetics of Postmodernism: History, Theory, Fiction* (New York and London: Routledge, 1988).
[53] See, among others, Tim Adams, "A Nine-year-old and 9/11," *The Observer*, May 29, 2005, accessed October 10, 2010, http://www.guardian.co.uk/books/2005/may/29/fiction.features; Michel Faber, "A Tower of Babble," *The Guardian*, June 4, 2005, accessed November 16, 2011, http://www.guardian.co.uk/books/2005/jun/04/featuresreviews.guardianreview22; Harry Siegel, "Extremely Cloying & Incredibly False," *New York Press*, April 13, 2005, accessed June 2, 2013, http://nypress.com/extremely-cloying-incredibly-false/.
[54] Marianne Hirsch, "I Took Pictures: September 2001 and Beyond," in *Trauma at Home: After 9/11*, ed. Judith Greenberg (Lincoln, Nebraska, and London: University of Nebraska Press, 2003), 71-72.

[55] Susan Sontag, *Regarding the Pain of Others* (New York: Farrar, Straus & Giroux, 2003), 89.
[56] Caruth, *Trauma: Explorations*, 4-5, 153.
[57] Foer, *Extremely Loud & Incredibly Close*, 52.
[58] Foer, *Extremely Loud & Incredibly Close*, 53-67.
[59] Foer, *Extremely Loud & Incredibly Close*, 68.
[60] The design for a paper plane (Foer, *Extremely Loud & Incredibly Close*, 56), for instance, refers to Oskar and his father's attempts at building such a plane (Foer, *Extremely Loud & Incredibly Close*, 70), while the picture of a tennis player lying on his back (Foer, *Extremely Loud & Incredibly Close*, 64), which is probably taken from the newspaper Oskar's father read the evening before he died, is explicitly mentioned at the beginning of the novel (Foer, *Extremely Loud & Incredibly Close*, 13).
[61] Birgit Däwes, "On Contested Ground (Zero): Literature and the Transnational Challenge of Remembering 9/11," *Amerikastudien / American Studies* 52.4 (2007): 537.
[62] Foer, *Extremely Loud & Incredibly Close*, 59, 62, 205.
[63] For a detailed analysis of the falling bodies in *Extremely Loud & Incredibly Close*, see Laura Frost, "Still Life: 9/11's Falling Bodies," in *Literature after 9/11*, eds. Ann Keniston et al. (New York and London: Routledge, 2008), 180-206.
[64] Foer, *Extremely Loud & Incredibly Close*, 257.
[65] Däwes, "On Contested Ground (Zero)," 537.
[66] Foer, *Extremely Loud & Incredibly Close*, 325.
[67] Foer, *Extremely Loud & Incredibly Close*, 326.
[68] Huehls, "Foer, Spiegelman, and 9/11's Timely Traumas," 43.
[69] Codde, "Philomela Revised," 250.
[70] Frost, "Still Life," 194.
[71] Frost, "Still Life," 193.
[72] Foer, *Extremely Loud & Incredibly Close*, 306-307.
[73] Brauner, "Fantasies of Flight and Flight of Fancy," 211.
[74] Brauner, "Fantasies of Flight and Flight of Fancy," 211.
[75] Žižek, *Welcome to the Desert of the Real*, 19. According to Slavoj Žižek, "[t]he Real which returns has the status of a(nother) semblance: *precisely because it is real, that is, on account of its traumatic/excessive character, we are unable to integrate it into (what we experience as) our reality, and are therefore compelled to experience it as a nightmarish apparition*," Žižek, *Welcome to the Desert of the Real*, 19, emphasis in the original.
[76] I refer here to Michel Foucault's famous concept of "counter-memory," that he defines as "a transformation of history into a totally different form of time," Michel Foucault, "Nietzsche, Genealogy, History," in *Language, Counter-Memory, Practice: Selected Essays and Interviews by Michel Foucault*, ed. Donald F. Bouchard (Ithaca, New York: Cornell University Press, 1977), 160. For a more detailed definition of the term, see Foucault, "Nietzsche, Genealogy, History," 160.
[77] Jean Baudrillard, *The Spirit of Terrorism and Requiem for the Twin Towers*, trans. Chris Turner (London and New York: Verso, 2002), 28-29.
[78] Versluys, "A Rose Is Not a Rose Is Not a Rose," 82.

THE SPECTATOR-SURVIVOR: *UNITED 93* AS MEMORIAL CINEMA

ALLISON WHITNEY

> "Total war takes us from military secrecy (the second-hand, recorded truth of the battlefield) to the overexposure of live broadcast. For with the advent of strategic bombing everything is now brought home to the cities, and it is no longer just the few but a whole mass of spectator-survivors who are the surviving spectators of combat."[1]
> —Paul Virilio, *War and Cinema*

Paul Greengrass' 2006 film *United 93*, a reenactment of the highjacking of United Airlines Flight 93 (UA93)[2] and the response of aviation authorities on 9/11, presents itself as a memorial to the heroism of the passengers and crew, who resisted the highjackers and helped ensure their plane never reached its intended target. While most accounts of UA93, from television movies to popular songs, emphasize the experience of those on board the aircraft, substantial portions of *United 93* have a different focus, enacting a procedural drama about both civilian and military air traffic control systems and their struggles to manage this unprecedented incident. Many of the performers in these reenactments are non-professional actors: real pilots portray the pilots, real controllers staff the control rooms, and in eleven cases, individuals involved in the real events, including military personnel with the North East Air Defense Sector (NEADS), air traffic control (ATC) workers, and Federal Aviation Administration (FAA) officials, portray themselves in the film, literally re-enacting their personal memories from the day. While this casting strategy, which Greengrass has used elsewhere, seems to support a bid for historical authenticity, it also suggests another side to the film's memorial strategy—to enact, record, and allow audiences to participate in an act of memorial spectatorship, one built around the specifically modern position of the spectator-survivor.

In *War and Cinema*, Paul Virilio explains that with the advent of aerial bombardment, spectacles of war were re-located from the battlefield to the cities, while the concurrent growth of the mass media allowed the visual experience of war to extend beyond those immediately affected by conflict. In modern warfare, the spectator becomes a new kind of combat survivor, and *United 93* draws upon audiences' traumatic memories of spectatorship from watching news coverage on 9/11, and connects the psychological impact of those experiences with the paralysis of aviation systems in the face of an attack designed to stymie emergency protocols and undermine strategies for mitigating risk. As I will explain, ATC, FAA and NEADS sequences consist largely of people monitoring screens, be they radar, computer, or television monitors. The viewer of *United 93* watches people in the act of watching, and is invited to map their own spectator-survivorship onto these figures in the diegesis.

United 93 presents both its own production and its audiences' spectatorship as memorial acts, drawing upon both collective memory of mass-media images of urban destruction, and the accompanying anxieties about the integrity of modern infrastructure. *United 93* valorizes the resourcefulness of those on board UA93, but it also emphasizes the position of the onlookers, whose emotional states of confusion arise not only from their shock at scenes of death, but also from a breakdown of trust in the expert systems that underlie the powers, and dangers, of modernity. I argue that *United 93* memorializes 9/11 by allowing its audience to remember the cognitive dissonance experienced by the spectator-survivor, who watched as major symbols and systems of American modernity, from the New York skyline to the invisible networks of civilian and military air control, quite literally collapsed before their eyes. In addition to memorializing the dead, the film creates an artifact that documents spectator-survivorship, while offering future viewers a sense of exactly how the national consciousness was ruptured by 9/11.

Memorial Production

Any film that offers historical reenactments engages in a memory project, but *United 93*'s temporal proximity to 9/11, barely five years after the event, made its purposes somewhat difficult to discern. For example, in her *New York Times* review, Manohla Dargis admitted that "I haven't a clue" as to why the film was made.[3] In *Firestorm: American Film in the Age of Terrorism*, Steven Prince explains that *United 93*, and its 2006 contemporary, Oliver Stone's *World Trade Center*, had difficulty finding an audience, as, "Many viewers had no desire to see a film about a terrible event that they felt they already knew too well. Documentary films, in a sense, did not face this problem because viewers implicitly understood why these would be produced."[4] Indeed, *United 93* is not presented as a documentary, but it does make multiple claims of historical accuracy, such as using *The 9/11 Commission Report* as a primary source, consulting with family members of victims on script development, and casting "real" people in the reenactments. Of course, reenactment takes many forms in nonfiction filmmaking, from asking a documentary subject to repeat an action for the camera, to the necessarily artificial direction to "act natural," to what we see in *United 93*, where much of the film's claim to authenticity stems from the fact that several of the key players portray themselves.

Greengrass used a similar approach in casting *Bloody Sunday* (2002), a reenactment of the 1972 massacre of protesters by British soldiers in Londonderry, Northern Ireland. In that film, numerous witnesses and participants portray themselves, the majority of the extras were from Londonderry, and professional soldiers were cast in the military roles.[5] In her essay on *Bloody Sunday*, Aileen Blaney explains how the film's found-footage aesthetics allows the film to present itself "as counterfeit historical document, and thereby encourages the viewer to experience it as a cultural or 'prosthetic' memory."[6] Of course, the thirty-year interval between the event and its reenactment places a particular set of pressures on the performers to recall the events, and also on the audience, who may have no memory of the 1972 incident. Meanwhile, for the re-enactors and audience of *United 93*, the crisis was still in recent memory, and the mainstream culture was still awash in 9/11 images. If we compare *United 93* to other reenactment films, such as the television productions *Flight 93* (Peter Markle, 2006) and *Flight 93: The Flight That Fought Back* (Bruce Goodison, 2005), Greengrass' choice to place so much emphasis on ATC, FAA and NEADS re-enactors, rather than family members of the victims, makes his film stand apart. In *United 93*, the "prosthetic memory" is specifically oriented to the experiences of the people who operate modern systems of safety and control.

Trust and Modernity

Greengrass states in multiple interviews that in addition to honoring the crew and passengers of UA93, his film explores our relationship to systems of modernity, and explains how the highjackers' capacity to paralyze such systems created not just an immediate threat, but triggered much deeper levels of trauma and anxiety in American society. In a *Film Comment* interview by Gavin Smith, Greengrass explains, "I hope what comes out is the idea of the fragility of our modernity, our democracies, our technological systems."[7] Given the foci of the film, it would seem that by "technological systems" he is referring specifically to aviation infrastructure, in both its civilian and military manifestations. Indeed, the film organizes its diegesis very carefully around this infrastructure, consisting almost entirely of interior shots, and limiting itself to a very few narrative spaces—once the plane takes off, all scenes take place within aircraft, air traffic control centers, or military facilities.[8] In the introduction to his interview with Greengrass, Smith explains how the insular qualities of the film stem from a formal principle where, with the exception of the opening cityscapes, the film only uses "camera positions that can be justified by the conceivable presence of a human observer—we never see the exterior of the plane once it's airborne, and the devastation of the Twin Towers is seen only from the remove of the Newark Airport control tower and the television screens in the various control rooms."[9] As a consequence of this narrow focus, many critics have suggested that *United 93* is merely a procedural drama, whose goal is a straightforward exposition of how aviation systems struggled to handle the crisis, and that while the film offers an effective suspense drama, it fails to engage in political critique, or any other productive discourse. For example, Simon Cooper and Paul Atkinson include *United 93* among texts that "refuse the political" and "emphasize a narrow field of action and heroism at the expense of any wider examination or contextualization of the events of 9/11."[10] Similarly, Lance Rubin compares United 93 with many television programs, including *24* and *Alias* that also decontextualize their events while they "implicitly support the dominant discourse on the 'war on terror'."[11]

Indeed, *United 93* does not offer any direct exposition of 9/11's larger context, in that it explicates neither the historical circumstances that preceded the event, nor any of its subsequent political, social, or military fallout. However, these factors are in many respects extraneous to the film's ambition as a memorial artwork—to affirm a collective memory (or impart such a memory to future viewers) of a uniquely modern state of terror brought about by a suspension of the capacity to trust in modern systems. Greengrass' film suggests that in order to understand 9/11, one must grasp this moment of confusion brought on by the act of observing systemic collapse.

On one level, the film's focus on the authorities' failure to respond effectively to the crisis might seem to offer a point of contrast, one that magnifies the bravery and efficacy of the passengers and crew, thereby enhancing their heroic narrative. For example, Manohla Dargis' review in the *New York Times* finds it a "sober reminder of the breakdown in leadership on the morning of Sept. 11."[12] While the film does indeed trace the perils of miscommunication, viewing the film as an indictment of leadership underplays its more interesting meditation on modernity, where even the most powerful leaders are bound by systemic structures. While we might have common-sense ideas about our reliance on modern systems—when there is a power failure, we realize how much we depend on electricity—*United 93* demonstrates the psychological effect of living within, and at the mercy of, such intricate structures. In *The Consequences of Modernity*, Anthony Giddens explains how for modern people, the relationship with modern infrastructure requires a particular kind of trust, specifically in abstract and expert systems.[13] Giddens describes how the rapid technological and philosophical changes of modernity provided people with great privileges, but that modernity is also a "double-edged phenomenon," for as our powers increase, so does the potential for danger and destruction.[14] For example, high-speed transportation opens up vast economic, personal, civic, and social possibilities, but it also introduces new potential for accidental death or injury, mass-destruction in warfare, and as we have come to realize, environmental degradation. Further, modern systems are necessarily large—a rail system needs to traverse large spaces to be effective—and require levels of technical and logistical complexity that render them increasingly "abstract," in that their physical and conceptual scale surpasses any individual's understanding or control. In order to mitigate the risks, modern societies establish "expert" systems, "systems of technical accomplishment or professional expertise that organize large areas of the material and social environments in which we live today."[15]

Of course, in any society, people depend on one another's specialized knowledge and expertise, and members of any community need to trust one another. However, in the pre-modern context, those trust relations were based largely in personal relationships and accountability; if the local carpenters build a structure and it falls down, then they are accountable for their shoddy work. The community feels it can trust the carpenters' work because they know the people they apprenticed under, and they have a personal connection to them. In modernity, however, one's relationship to the carpenter's work, or indeed any structure or system, becomes "disembedded," meaning that social relations are removed from the equation. Giddens offers the example of the simple act of "sitting in a house"—an act that, for a modern person, requires one to trust in a vast network of expert systems that the house will not collapse, burn down, poison or electrocute its occupants.[16] Of course, pre-modern housing came with its own contingencies, but Giddens would argue that in those cases, one's trust that the roof would not cave in was founded on a sense of personal connection and accountability—one feels safe in a structure built by craftspeople you know personally, made with materials whose sources are clear (the wood came from the forest, the stones from the field), and constructed through processes that are relatively transparent, for while you may not be a carpenter, the processes of carpentry are neither unfathomable nor invisible. In modernity, mechanisms of disembedding, where the individual is separated in space and time from such processes, requires that one trust in institutions and practices that are unknown and unknowable: factory-made materials produced in distant locations, unseen engineers and architects and the schools and professional associations that train and certify them, myriad laws and building codes and the people who enforce them, and the vast systems that ensure safe supplies of electricity, water, gas, and other dangerous, but essential, amenities.

When one begins to contemplate how something as simple as turning on a light switch requires that one trust not only the electricians who wired the house, but the organizations who trained and licensed them, the manufacturers of every wire, switch, fuse, socket, and light bulb, the professionals who establish, maintain, and oversee the electrical grid, the power-generation companies, and so forth, modernity's "double-edged" qualities can appear quite terrifying. Consider how the archetypal modern activity of flying in an airplane, itself a highly unnatural activity, requires individuals to trust their lives to vast systems and realms of expertise of which they have little or no direct knowledge. Even a passenger who is knowledgeable about aviation, such as an aeronautical engineer, still has to trust in expert knowledge, as they are not likely also a meteorologist, an air traffic controller, a mechanic, a parts manufacturer, an aviation lawyer, and a Federal Aviation Authority administrator. If we extrapolate and consider the number of abstract systems that sustain modern infrastructure, it becomes clear that "*the nature of modern institutions is deeply bound up with the mechanisms of trust in abstract systems*."[17]

Modern trust is not without conflict, for, as Giddens explains, ambivalence lies "at the core of all trust relations."[18] A degree of danger lies beneath the trust relationship—one trusts that the airplane will land safely, but there remains the knowledge that a crash is possible. Therefore, we enter a bargain with modernity—where we accept a level of risk, i.e. a set of contingencies that can be calculated and predicted. Giddens contrasts the notion of risk with the pre-modern idea of "fate," where misfortune was regarded as part of a larger cosmic vision, as opposed to a matter of probability. Modern systems are designed based on data-driven calculations of risk, which is part of what allows people to overcome the psychological barriers to undertaking inherently unnatural activities, such as flying at altitudes where the air is too thin to breathe, or traveling at speeds that are beyond the body's structural capacities.

United 93's lengthy procedural sequences draw attention to how modern people enact these trust relations, making it all the more terrifying when the highjackers disrupt our capacity to trust by introducing unanticipated risk factors. For example, Greengrass explains that as his actors were rehearsing, specifically those playing the passengers on UA93, they began to comment that the experience of going through an airport, and particularly its security systems, places you in a position of "obedience": "In order to have our supremely sophisticated systems, whether they're aviation or whatever, it takes a high degree of processed obedience from us."[19] Understanding that the exercise of authority at airport security, even before the routinely-critiqued "security theatre" of the post-9/11 era, entails a level of coercion, this revelation of "obedience" is significant to the film's project. In some respects, obedience is premised on a level of trust, as in "if I follow this rule, I trust that I will be spared certain consequences," but the term obedience also speaks to the power imbalance inherent in such relations, and therefore resonates with the ambivalence that we feel toward all abstract systems in modernity. The act of flying in an airplane, where it is very clear that we are dependent on such systems for our survival, makes the enactment of modern trust relations seem all the more fearsome.

Our ambivalence about modern trust relations is probably best understood in our relationship to military institutions, whose nuclear arsenals manifest the darkest side of modernity's double edge. While the sequences involving NEADS were, like other parts of *United 93*, based on *The 9/11 Commission Report*, Greengrass did take some creative license. The first scene at NEADS uses a fictional premise, showing the military preparing for a training simulation just as the crisis begins. The simulation scenario, where a Russian force is penetrating the Air Defense Identification Zone in Alaska, is clearly based on a Cold War scenario. As they rehearse for a war long past, the film underlines their lack of preparedness for a 9/11-style attack, and suggests how the entire physical, communication, and command infrastructure of both American and global military systems and alliances could not handle 9/11 because it did not fit into their paradigms of modern conflict.

As the film progresses, it emphasizes not only how much we depend on systems, but also how the people working within them are just as limited by their structures. For example, the film emphasizes the difficulty in transmitting accurate information among government agencies and the military, making it impossible for them to strategize effectively. As the highjacking reports start to reach NEADS, their first question is whether this is part of the training simulation, but as its real-world status becomes clear, they struggle to respond, precisely because this scenario had never been simulated. As they try to improvise, it becomes clear that a modern system of such complexity and power as the US military cannot take action that has not been preconceived.[20] One of the ways the film illustrates this problem is the way it continually refers to transponder codes. In several instances, military and civilian controllers ask if planes have "squawked 7500," i.e. transmitted the transponder code that pilots use to signal a highjack. The standard procedures for highjack situations, which were refined in the 1980s, operated on the assumption that the pilot remains at the controls, that the highjackers want the authorities to hear their demands, and that they hope to survive the incident. Of course, the 9/11 highjackers were aware of these assumptions, and used them to their advantage.

The continual inquiries about "7500" might seem like a small detail, but this matter of the transponder codes is one of the elements of *United 93* that is actually fictionalized. In the real event, the highjackers simply turned off their transponders, making it extremely difficult for the authorities to track their movements. Greengrass' decision to change this historical detail serves several functions, including enhancing the suspense by allowing controllers to panic at planes' plunging altitudes and unsafe speeds, but it also draws attention to the fact that there was no transponder code to describe 9/11, as the highly regulated aviation system, where every rule and practice is designed to mitigate risk, was incapable of conceptualizing this new attack strategy.[21] Indeed, *The 9/11 Commission Report*, responding to reports that the FAA had been incompetent, defends both civilian and military authorities and their attempts to improvise, never having "handled a highjacked aircraft that tried to disappear" nor anticipated the "transformation of commercial aircraft into weapons of mass destruction."[22]

As the transponder drama makes clear, modern trust relations depend on prescribed narratives of crisis events, whose risk factors have been calculated by expert systems. Indeed, every aviation regulation represents an accident, mechanical problem, or tendency of human failure. For example, in the 1980s, air passengers were instructed that in the event of a highjack, their survival depended not on resistance, but on compliance—a truism that one of the passengers repeats in *United 93* in the initial stages of the attack. The 9/11 highjackers were counting on the passengers to follow this script, but the scenario changed on UA93 for two reasons: the departure was delayed so it could not reach its target on time, and the passengers had ready access to air- and cell phones, allowing them to discover the plot from their friends and family. While the passengers and crew of UA93 were undeniably courageous, the film does not suggest that they were uniquely brave, but rather, because they were among the first to figure out how the highjack narrative had changed, they were able to determine which trust relations had been suspended, and to take unprecedented action to mitigate a new constellation of risks.

Giddens' differentiation of modern "risk" from pre-modern "fate" resonates with the film's narrative structure, and particularly in the way it introduces characters. Other films about UA93, including *Flight 93*, devote considerable attention to the crew and passengers before they board the flight, including biographical profiles and details of personal skills that would become relevant during the incident, such as flying experience, medical training, or martial-arts proficiency. By emphasizing the special talents of select passengers, these films imply that it was a matter of fate, that the right people were somehow destined to be on UA93, and that their sacrifice was in aid of a loftier goal, to save the would-be victims at the intended target in Washington. While Greengrass does highlight individuals' courageous actions, *United 93* avoids such lengthy preambles, emphasizing instead the randomness of air travel, and the fact that the flight was selected to suit the highjackers' strategic calculations, rather than some cosmic plan.

As a memorial text, *United 93* encourages the viewer to remember 9/11 as a profoundly disturbing event, not only because of the loss of life, but also because it confirmed our ambivalence about the abstract systems that are the foundation of modern physical and social infrastructure. By introducing unforeseen factors, the highjackers enacted a uniquely modern nightmare, where systems that provide perspectives, opportunities, and experiences that have huge symbolic import in modernity—the airplane and the skyscraper—are turned against us. By focusing as much on aviation control systems as the drama on board the aircraft, *United 93* makes viewers realize that their feelings of confusion and helplessness were in fact systemic—they went all the way to the top. Indeed, the film makes references to both Vice President Cheney and President Bush, and their inability to adapt quickly enough to take decisive action.[23]

Memorial Spectatorship

United 93 draws direct connections between the spectator-survivor and aviation infrastructure in the ways it uses television news footage. While of course there were many eyewitnesses in New York and Washington, many of whom photographed their experiences, for the majority of people, 9/11 was a television event. Furthermore, by the time *United 93* was released, even direct eyewitnesses had been subjected to years of continual media broadcast of traumatic images of urban destruction. Compared with other 9/11 films, *United 93* is sparing in its use of television footage, but it is also very conscious of, and carefully thematizes, the experience of watching.

In the opening sequence, the film lays out its major formal strategies, such as the ever-moving camera, but it also offers shots of New York City from an aerial perspective. The film begins with the sound of a Muslim prayer over a dark screen, followed by shots of two of the highjackers in their hotel room, in the wee hours of the morning. These are followed by an aerial shot of a nighttime cityscape, shown from a straight-down, bird's eye view position. The image appears to be of Times Square, but the unusual angle makes the location unclear, especially since movie images of Times Square usually capitalize on its spectacular signs, rather than its street layout. After several more images of the highjackers, there is a second aerial shot, this one from an oblique angle, flying over the city. Again, while it is New York, the shot does not include any of the city's more iconic buildings, marking a departure from the long tradition of skyline establishing shots in films about this city. On one level, these shots represent one of the 9/11 targets, but they also allow New York to represent Western urban modernity in a more general sense. Further, these shots remind the viewer of how the very act of looking at the New York skyline in the aftermath of 9/11, whether in person or in the media, is marked by the conspicuous absence of the World Trade Center, for as Andreas Huyssen notes, the Twin Towers came to represent "home in the metropolis" as they were the most quickly identifiable features of the skyline.[24]

Of course, *United 93*, unlike many other 9/11 movies, is not really a New York story. The city is only seen from the distant perspective of Newark Airport, or through the abstractions of ATC screens, while the film's titular subject, UA93, was intended for a target in Washington D.C., most likely the Capitol. And yet, these aerial shots help to connect the film's discourses on systems, trust, and modernity's disembedding functions to a larger history of aviation, modern warfare, and the abstraction of the city. In *Aerial Perspective: The Earth as Seen from Aircraft and Spacecraft and Its Influence on Contemporary Art*, Margret Dreikausen carefully differentiates vertical perspective, looking straight down, from oblique perspective, looking out from the very high angle offered by an aircraft. While an oblique angle "gives a sense of wide-open space" and allows architectural forms to remain recognizable, the vertical angle has a tendency to flatten the landscape and render it abstract, to the point where structures "become geometric shapes and resemble an architect's blueprint."[25] The opening sequence of *United 93* interlaces the highjackers' morning preparations with both types of perspective. First, from the vertical perspective, it emphasizes the city's grid structure, flattening its vertical immensity and its identifiable features, and emphasizing its interlocking systems of vehicular movement and electrification. Second, it shows the city from an oblique angle, from the uniquely modern perspective of an aircraft, in an image that at once romanticizes the beauty of the architecture, and mourns its destruction.

The process of abstraction Dreikausen describes is consistent with Virilio's discussion of aerial perspective in *War and Cinema*, where he examines the intertwined histories of the cinema, flight, and modern technologies and philosophies of warfare. Virilio explains how in the wars of the 20th century, weapons and representational systems (including photography, cinema, radio, radar, and other electronic communications) allowed for greater distances between combatants, and between the scene of war and those observing and acting upon it, where "face to face confrontation was supplanted by instant interface, and geographical distance by the notion of real time."[26] He offers an anecdote about a pilot who has two views of the landscape below, an ocular view from looking out the window, and a radar view relayed through his instruments, but he hesitates as to which one is truly "real."[27] Flight technologies and their capacities for surveillance, aerial photography, mapping, weapon guidance and detection systems, all contribute to a process of derealization, where tactics, soldiers, and targets become increasingly both abstracted and specularized. These regimes of vision and power generate a way of experiencing war where everyone becomes a spectator-survivor, and Virilio explains that this mode of spectatorship was quickly integrated with practices of war remembrance. For example, in the proliferation of war museums established after 1945, often located at the sites of battles or military installations, there would be conventional displays of artifacts, as well as samples of newsreel footage, but they also featured combined diorama and projection facilities, where "visitors were shown into huge, windowless rooms resembling a planetarium or a flight (or driving) simulator. In these *war simulators*, the public was supposed to feel like spectator-survivors of the recent battlefield." [28] These installations encouraged memorial practices where reenactment and spectatorship converge.

United 93 devotes a great deal of screen time to screens themselves, with virtually all the scenes outside the aircraft taking place in rooms devoted to video, radar, and computer screens. In his introduction to the *Film Comment* interview, Smith notes, "*United 93* can be said to present the events of 9/11 strictly as a series of abstractions unfolding on the radar screens and monitors of air-traffic-control centers."[29] While of course the film does cut back and forth among the various control centers to UA93, providing the viewer with concrete information that the controllers can only deduce, it is significant that most of the figures in the film are themselves spectator-survivors, whose experience of the event is at once direct and distanced. Not unlike the "war simulators" of the post-World War II era, *United 93* draws explicit connections between reenacted scenes of screen-watching, and audiences' memories of viewing traumatic events on television. With the exception of a CGI sequence where ATC workers in Newark watch from their windows as planes strike the World Trade Center, *United 93*'s images of urban destruction are taken from real television news footage. There are relatively few of these images, especially when we compare *United 93* to its contemporaries, but just as the shots of the city from the air in the opening sequence draw upon viewers' memories of the skyline, the film's use of news images, and the traumatic experience of seeing them, requires the viewer both to fill in the blanks with their personal memories, and to reflect on their own spectatorship. As the authorities begin to turn on televisions in their control rooms, these images also come to mediate the editing transitions from one control center to the next, emphasizing both their collective shock and paralysis, but also suggesting that direct, unmediated perception is no longer even a possibility.

Indeed, when the first plane, American Airlines 11, hits the North Tower, none of the ATC workers, not even those in Newark who can see the skyline from their windows, witness the event directly. A controller notes that the plane has vanished from his screen "around Manhattan," while the military also notes its disappearance, but neither has any explanation for the event. A minute and a half later, we see a shot from Newark tower of smoke coming from the city, from a camera position peering around a controller's shoulder. The buildings remain in very soft focus as people gradually notice the smoke, saying "look at the Trade Center" and "that's a lot of smoke" as one of them reaches for binoculars. Once the camera shares the binoculars' point of view, the focus gradually adjusts, but even as the image sharpens, the controller cannot make sense of what he is seeing. Subsequent shots show people telephoning colleagues to look out the window, or relaying reports from pilots about smoke from the North Tower. While viewers of *United 93* would have been familiar with footage of American 11's crash that surfaced in the days after the attack, the film avoids any such direct representation, instead emphasizing how the system, calibrated to monitor and mitigate known risks, was literally unable to observe this catastrophic event.

Several FAA officials repeat the rumor, reported on CNN, that a light plane had hit the building, prompting the FAA and NEADS alike to tune large display screens to CNN. When they turn on the television at the FAA headquarters at Herndon, Virginia, the first image is a close-up of the fire in the North Tower, prompting speculation about what caused it. Again, while several people comment that the hole in the building is too big to be caused by a light plane, they are unable to definitively connect it to American 11's disappearance because their systems are unable to produce a coherent picture from their abstracted information. A similar chain of events begins with United 175, also disappearing from radar, then being picked up by Newark ATC, who spot it first as a radar blip, on a screen positioned conspicuously over the window framing the Trade Center. As they try to make sense of the radar readings, one controller looks out the window and spots the plane in the distance. They watch it flying low toward the city, in a blurry CGI image, but the film cuts to real television footage at the moment of impact with the South Tower. Of course, by the time United 175 approached Manhattan, countless cameras were trained on the Towers, but this transition to television footage emphatically contrasts (and connects) witnesses' direct vision of the event with the mediated version experienced by the mass of spectator-survivors. The very next shot is of the simultaneous response of everyone at NEADS, exclaiming in shock as they watch the identical footage on CNN. The moment of the second impact, which Greengrass describes in his DVD commentary as the "dead center" of the film, uses television footage as the literal shared experience of the various air traffic control systems, and by extension, the entire viewing public. In "Black Screens, Lost Bodies: The Cinematic Apparatus of 9/11 Horror," Laura Frost notes the widespread circulation of images of 9/11 witnesses, gazing at scenes of destruction with shocked expressions.[30] She describes these images as substitutions, standing in for the scenes of violence being observed, but in the case of *United 93*, the film lingers on reenactors' faces, especially those who are portraying themselves, in a manner that aligns these individuals, and the stymied systems they represent, with the spectator's personal memories of spectator-survivorship.

The ensuing sequences, where each component of the air control system tries, and fails, to interpret and share their information, plays the blatant television images of destruction off the now-meaningless abstractions that visualize abstract systems. The final scenes at NEADS and Herndon both emphasize their state of shock, while mapping their paralysis onto the act of watching television, an act of spectatorship that signals a new reality of war. The last scene at NEADS concludes with a shot of CNN's coverage of the fire at the Pentagon, with Colonel Marr (Gregg Henry), on the telephone, saying, "Yes sir, that's the question. What are we going to do now?" The next scene, which concludes the Herndon sequence, ends with FAA Director Ben Sliney (as himself), after taking the unprecedented step of closing American airspace, pointing at the CNN screen and saying, "We're at war with someone, and until we figure out what to do about it, we're shutting down. That's it, we're finished." As Sliney begins this sentence, the continually mobile camera focuses on him, but as he points at the screen, the camera pans left, following his sightline to the television projection, with its image of the burning city. Systems whose fail-safes rely on consistency, rigidity, and carefully calculated risk, are forced into such a state of paralysis that once they declare their inability to act, the film leaves them, and devotes the last 30 minutes to the events on UA93, concluding at the moment of the crash.

United 93 asks its spectator-survivors to feel for the individuals who died, and also to mourn their romanticized associations with the city of New York, such as when one passenger turns to another to reminisce about Manhattan, calling it the "Emerald City." However, the film also memorializes 9/11 by reminding the viewer of a deeper sort of dread, where the benefits of speed, power, and instantaneous communication that come with modern systems require us to suppress our fears of such systems, and to accept our inability to fully control or comprehend them. One of the reasons that UA93 received so much cultural attention is because, in many respects, it was one of the few expressions of agency on 9/11—although they did not survive, the passengers and crew were able to understand the implications of what was happening, and to take action. In *United 93*, the film concludes with the passengers breaking into the cockpit, and trying to wrest control from the highjackers. Forensic data suggests that this may not have actually happened—that the highjackers themselves may have crashed the plane, realizing that not only were they off course, but possibly that it was only a matter of time before the passengers overpowered them. Regardless, the passengers' attempts to regain control offer a much-desired narrative of agency in the midst of helplessness. In Laura Frost's essay on images of people jumping from the windows of the World Trade Center, she explains, "Unlike the passengers on United 93, which sources such as the *9/11 Commission Report*, A&E's

drama *Flight 93*, and the film *United 93* narrated as a proactive deed of heroism, the falling people present a catch-22."[31] This catch-22 concerns how we interpret the agency of those who jumped to their deaths, either as an act of desperate panic, or as a conscious choice to die on their own terms, rather than simply to wait for the fire to engulf them, or the building to collapse. *United 93* clearly valorizes the passengers' resistance, but it also acknowledges the hopelessness of their situation. Much like the people trapped in the World Trade Center, the passengers on UA93 cannot extricate themselves from the system—they have accepted a bargain with modernity, and once accepted, it is impossible to truly opt out.

In the film's final seconds, there are several shots from the cockpit windows, showing the horizon teetering as the passengers struggle for the controls, leading up to the last shot, a vertical perspective on the landscape as the plane plummets to the ground. While this image expresses the finality of the plane's trajectory, where there is literally no more sky, it also recalls the vertical perspective from the beginning of the film, where the point of view offered by aviation technology renders the world below in abstract terms. While the colors and substance of the farmland are different from its urban counterpart, the perspective of the passengers, and perhaps of the aircraft itself, renders the earth in the same flattened, abstract, and geometric terms that pervade the logic of modern warfare. When *United 93* shares the doomed passengers' final perspective with its viewers, it turns spectator-survivorship into memorial practice. Just as the "war simulators" of the post-World War II era conflated spectatorship and reenactment, *United 93* concludes with the viewer surviving an un-survivable act of profoundly modern vision, reminding us that modernity is both fragile and intractable.

Bibliography

The 9/11 Commission Report: Final Report of the National Commission on Terrorist Attacks Upon the United States. New York: W.H. Norton & Co., 2004.

Blaney, Aileen. "Remembering Historical Trauma in Paul Greengrass's *Bloody Sunday*." *History and Memory* 19.2 (Fall/Winter 2007): 113-38.

Bloody Sunday. Directed by Paul Greengrass. 2002. Burbank, CA: Warner Home Videos, 2014. DVD.

Cooper, Simon, and Paul Atkinson. "Graphic Implosion: Politics, Time, and Value in Post 9/11 Comics." In *Literature after 9/11*, edited by

Ann Keniston and Jeanne Follansbee Quinn, 60-81. New York: Routledge, 2008.

Dargis, Manohla. "Defiance under Fire: Unbounded Bravery in Unfriendly Skies." *New York Times* (1923-Current file), April 28, 2006: E1. Proquest Historical Newspapers *The New York Times* (1851-2006). Accessed August 11, 2009.

Dreikausen, Margret. *Aerial Perception: The Earth as Seen from Aircraft and Spacecraft and Its Influence on Contemporary Art*. Cranbury, NJ: Associated University Press, 1985.

Flight 93. Directed by Peter Markle. Miami, FL: MTI Home Video, 2006. DVD.

Flight 93: The Flight That Fought Back. Directed by Bruce Goodison. Silver Spring, MD: Discovery Channel. 2005. TV.

Frost, Laura. "Black Screens, Lost Bodies: The Cinematic Apparatus of 9/11 Horror." In *Horror after 9/11: World of Fear, Cinema of Terror*, edited by Aviva Briefel and Sam J. Miller, 13-39. Austin: University of Texas Press, 2011.

—. "Still Life: 9/11's Falling Bodies." In *Literature after 9/11*, edited by Ann Keniston and Jeanne Follansbee Quinn, 180-206. New York: Routledge, 2008.

Giddens, Anthony. *The Consequences of Modernity*. Stanford: Stanford University Press, 1990.

Huyssen, Andreas. *Present Pasts: Urban Palimpsests and the Politics of Memory*. Palo Alto, CA: Stanford University Press, 2003.

Prince, Steven. *Firestorm: American Film in the Age of Terrorism*. New York: Columbia University Press, 2009.

Rubin, Lance. "'We're the Culture that Cried Wolf': Discourse and Terrorism in Chuck Palahniuk's *Lullaby*." In *Literature after 9/11*, edited by Ann Keniston and Jeanne Follansbee Quinn, 161-79. New York: Routledge, 2008.

Smith, Gavin. "Mission Statement: Paul Greengrass Discusses the Creative Process Behind His Reconstruction of the Worst Day in Modern American History." *Film Comment* 42.3 (May/June 2006): 24-28.

United 93. Directed by Paul Greengrass. Universal City, CA: Universal Studios Home Entertainment, 2006. DVD.

Virilio, Paul. *War and Cinema: The Logistics of Perception*. Translated by Patrick Camillier. London: Verso, 1989.

World Trade Center. Directed by Oliver Stone. 2006. Los Angeles: Paramount Home Entertainment, 2007. DVD.

Notes

[1] Paul Virilio, *War and Cinema: The Logistics of Perception*, trans. Patrick Camillier (London: Verso, 1989), 66.
[2] For the sake of clarity, I will use the abbreviation UA93 to refer to the real-life aircraft, since both "United 93" and "Flight 93" are easily confused with film titles.
[3] Manohla Darghis, "Defiance under Fire: Unbounded Bravery in Unfriendly Skies," *New York Times,* April 28, 2006: E1.
[4] Steven Prince, *Firestorm: American Film in the Age of Terrorism* (New York: Columbia University Press, 2009), 7.
[5] Aileen Blaney, "Remembering Historical Trauma in Paul Greengrass's *Bloody Sunday,*" *History and Memory* 19.2 (Fall/Winter 2007): 127.
[6] Blaney, "Remembering," 131.
[7] Gavin Smith, "Mission Statement: Paul Greengrass Discusses the Creative Process Behind His Reconstruction of the Worst Day in Modern American History," *Film Comment* 42.3 (May/June 2006): 28.
[8] In comparison, other dramatizations of UA93 place much more attention on the experience of family members on the ground, specifically their telephone conversations with loved ones on the aircraft.
[9] Smith, "Mission Statement," 26.
[10] Simon Cooper and Paul Atkinson, "Graphic Implosion: Politics, Time, and Value in Post 9/11 Comics," in *Literature after 9/11*, eds. Ann Keniston and Jeanne Follansbee Quinn (New York: Routledge, 2008), 77.
[11] Lance Rubin, "'We're the Culture that Cried Wolf': Discourse and Terrorism in Chuck Palahniuk's *Lullaby*," in *Literature after 9/11*, eds. Ann Keniston and Jeanne Follansbee Quinn (New York: Routledge, 2008), 171.
[12] Darghis, "Defiance," E1.
[13] Anthony Giddens, *The Consequences of Modernity* (Stanford: Stanford University Press, 1990), 83.
[14] Giddens, *The Consequences of Modernity*, 7.
[15] Giddens, *The Consequences of Modernity*, 27.
[16] Giddens, *The Consequences of Modernity*, 27.
[17] Giddens, *The Consequences of Modernity*, 83.
[18] Giddens, *The Consequences of Modernity*, 89.
[19] Smith, "Mission Statement," 28.
[20] I should note that in the aftermath of 9/11, it became clear that intelligence and government agencies did in fact have knowledge of Osama Bin Laden's plans to attack American targets by highjacking civilian aircraft. However, as many investigations make clear, including *The 9/11 Commission Report,* that information was not effectively communicated, nor were safeguards put in place. Therefore, as far as NEADS, the FAA, or air traffic controllers were concerned, this highjacking scenario was entirely unanticipated.
[21] Since 9/11, the transponder signal to indicate this new form of suicide-highjacking has been 7500 followed by 7700, the code for life-threatening emergency.

[22] *The 9/11 Commission Report: Final Report of the National Commission on Terrorist Attacks Upon the United States* (New York: W.H. Norton & Co., 2004), 31.
[23] As I mentioned, some critics have complained that *United 93* lacks political engagement. While the film is less overt in its political messages than some other 9/11 films, it is interesting that the few references to George W. Bush either report him as inaccessible, or, in the film's epilogue, they note that late in the crisis, he did give authorization for the military to destroy civilian aircraft. However, this order was not relayed to pilots, for fear of an accidental shoot-down. Given the political environment at the time of the film's release, it is interesting that its final statement suggests that the most practical and moral decision is to second-guess the President's defense strategies.
[24] Andreas Huyssen, *Present Pasts: Urban Palimpsests and the Politics of Memory* (Stanford: Stanford University Press, 2003), 160.
[25] Margret Dreikausen, *Aerial Perception: The Earth as Seen from Aircraft and Spacecraft and Its Influence on Contemporary Art* (Cranbury, New Jersey: Associated University Presses, 1985), 18.
[26] Virilio, *War and Cinema*, 72.
[27] Virilio, *War and Cinema*, 76.
[28] Virilio, *War and Cinema*, 48.
[29] Smith, "Mission Statement," 26.
[30] Laura Frost, "Black Screens, Lost Bodies: The Cinematic Apparatus of 9/11 Horror," in *Horror after 9/11: World of Fear, Cinema of Terror*, eds. Aviva Briefel and Sam J. Miller (Austin: University of Texas Press, 2011), 20.
[31] Laura Frost, "Still Life: 9/11's Falling Bodies," in *Literature after 9/11*, eds. Ann Keniston and Jeanne Follansbee Quinn (New York: Routledge, 2008), 188.

ARTICULATION AND EVASION: HISTORICAL TRAUMA AND IMAGE IN *EXTREMELY LOUD & INCREDIBLY CLOSE*

BRITTANY HIRTH

Jonathan Safran Foer's novel, *Extremely Loud & Incredibly Close* (2005), illustrates how quickly trauma is transmitted and shared in an urban space. Foer's narrative centers around a child that loses his father to the terrorist attacks on September 11. As Oskar attempts to cope with the loss of his father, he undertakes a "mission," or what he believes is a scavenger hunt that his father left for him to complete. Oskar traverses much of New York City on his mission, and meets a variety of people who were also touched by traumatic events. The novel centers on the story of a boy who attempts to cope with death by literally retracing what he thinks are his father's last steps through the city, but a metaphorical tracing of other people's traumas is also discernible as Oskar collects each of their stories. On another level, the city is also the site where Oskar meets his long-lost grandfather who brings with him traumatic stories of having survived World War II. Across generations and through the very city's five boroughs, Foer brings together past and present historical traumas.

In this chapter, I place Marianne Hirsch's "postmemory" in conversation with Michael Rothberg's "multidirectional memory" to elucidate how the city provides a space to think about the recent trauma of 9/11. Hirsch's postmemory defines the transmission of trauma across generations as a consequence of traumatic recall, or the issue of defining the present in relation to a troubled past.[1] Rothberg implies that Hirsch's postmemory is a version of multidirectional memory, where Hirsch sees a paradox between continuity and rupture of traumatic memory, Rothberg views the same memory paradox as a point of entry for the "multidirectional confluence of disparate historical imaginaries."[2] Hirsch's postmemory results from the return of past trauma to the present: a return that implies one must come to terms with various ruptures and breaks induced by a trauma that inhibits dominant memory of the event. However, where Hirsch finds an uneasy oscillation between the past and present, Rothberg finds new entry points to compare divergent accounts of historical events, in the hopes of working toward a more productive understanding of traumatic history. Both Rothberg and Hirsch are invested in understanding what the present moment can reveal about the past, and what the past might reveal about the current moment. Their respective memory structures allow me to explain the transference of generational, traumatic experience (postmemory) in a city space, and the cultural understanding of the event (multidirectional memory). Both models of memory factor the past into the present for comparative understanding. In other words, rather than viewing the familial transmission of traumatic events, the "living connection," as approximate and affective but "not memor[y],"[3] as Hirsch claims, we can view this generationally transmitted trauma as additional narratives for comparative representation of a fraught historical past. Comparing a multitude of traumatic accounts from the past in the present can lead to a more comprehensive representation of history than articulating a dominant, collective memory; a multitude of traumatic accounts is especially vital for contemporary traumas for which representation may not yet be accessible, like 9/11.

Foer's setting of New York City, in the novel, draws into question the representation of past historical traumas, such as Hiroshima and Dresden—two personal accounts of World War II that are given in Foer's novel about 9/11. The father and grandfather characters exemplify how trauma is generationally transmitted to their (grand)son through "postmemory," while Rothberg's "multidirectional memory" exemplifies the city as the site for the exploration of many historical traumas through the lens of the present moment. Just as Rothberg advocates, 9/11 analysis and representation is informed by the way past World War II traumas were previously represented.

While Hirsch and Rothberg are important for exploring why New York City is poignant for Foer's setting, adding Cathy Caruth's theory of latency demonstrates why *Extremely Loud & Incredibly Close* is not explicitly a representation of 9/11. Like Rothberg's "multidirectional memory," Foer utilizes the Dresden and Hiroshima bombings within his narrative in order to write about 9/11. However, Foer selects a number of images to reproduce within his text that stand-in for various characters and traumas that arguably do not represent 9/11; even "The Falling Man" image contained within the novel is a manipulated version of Lyle Owerko's original photograph.[4] Caruth's theory of latency clarifies that a traumatic experience requires a waiting period before the effects can be articulated.[5] Foer's novel, written four years after 9/11, demonstrates that the event is not accessible in the current moment. But as the author reveals, the various images and historical traumas that readers associate with an event, stand-in for representation in the interim: city sites and the stories of its inhabitants culminate into a cultural commentary about representing 9/11, collectively and through the lens of past traumatic events.

Grieving through City Sites and Artifacts

Extremely Loud & Incredibly Close offers a three-part narrative that encompasses the lives of nine-year-old Oskar and his grandparents. The main storyline comes from Oskar's point of view as he grieves the loss of his father, who died on September 11 in the North Tower's restaurant, Windows on the World. Oskar attempts to understand the event surrounding his father's death through a "mission": he believes his father left him a clue when he discovers a slip of paper that contains the word "Black," and a key in a vase that his father stored inside his closet. Recognizing "Black" as a last name, Oskar decides to meet every person he can with that last name in New York City's five boroughs to discover what the key unlocks. In the course of his travels throughout NYC, Oskar meets a variety of people named Black who listen to the boy's traumatic narrative about 9/11 and they, in turn, tell Oskar about their personal losses and traumas.

The scavenger hunt mission allows Oskar to cope with the loss of his father through the material object of the key. Oskar decides that his father must have left the key as a clue for a larger final message—his father had a penchant for scavenger hunts with Oskar in Central Park, what Oskar calls "Reconnaissance Expeditions."[6] The key fixation relates to what Marita Sturken writes in *Tourists of History*, that "processes of grief often involve a need for a material trace of the dead." Sturken explains that in the absence of material remains of the dead, objects such as photographs, empty coffins, and other material artifacts provide a "corporeal presence to mediate the absence of the dead."[7] For Oskar, the key provides the corporeal presence of his father that he requires for the grieving process, as the symbolic funeral that his family performed for the father seems absurd to Oskar who emphasizes that they did not bury anyone; "It's just an empty box," he observes, as he enumerates that his father's remains are "on rooftops, and in the river, and in the lungs of millions of people around New York."[8] Oskar does not accept the empty coffin as sufficient closure and, instead, processes his grief through the key as the last material remnant of his father.

The grieving process takes Oskar on a journey that traverses the urban space of New York City, and all of its five boroughs. The boroughs, and its people, become the sites for Oskar to transmit the traumatic memory of his father and 9/11 to others, while the others who receive Oskar's story also convey their own traumas to Oskar. For example, A.R. Black listens to Oskar's story about the key and his father, and tells Oskar about the traumatic loss of his wife—he has not left the apartment in the twenty-four years after her death. For every person that Oskar questions, he records their stories in his journal, *Things That Happened to Me*, and he inserts pictures to accompany the stories. These pictures add the aura of "documenting" the stories and of memorializing significant aspects of the interviewed people's lives and of his father, a point I return to later. Many of the people that Oskar encounters during his search have experienced loss, and one character even references the civilian deaths on 9/11. In one scene of the text, Oskar learns that he is unable to question a woman about his key because she died on 9/11: the woman's neighbor tells Oskar that she was a waitress at Windows on the World. While most of the interviewed people do not have a direct connection to 9/11, they still connect to Oskar's trauma and offer him their stories of loss and mourning.

One "Black," in particular, crosses the generational and familial gap, as the last person that Oskar speaks to finally reveals what the key is for; William Black recognizes the description of the vase that contained the key, and tells Oskar that the key was accidentally sold in the vase: the key opens Black's late father's safe-deposit box. William Black had been searching for the key for two years without success. Oskar brings closure to William, with the key, as William was also unable to deal with the sudden death of his father, who had died two months after being diagnosed with cancer. Oskar and the key provide closure for William, who will finally know what his father left him in the safe-deposit box. In turn, William provides the same closure for Oskar, who notes that William is the same age that his father would have been, so Oskar explains to William that he was home the last time that his father called from the burning World Trade Center. Oskar was unable to answer the phone call at the time and asks William to forgive him for "not being able to tell anyone."[9] Aside from the closure of finally telling someone that he was unable to answer his father's final call from the burning North Tower, William also gives Oskar some additional memories of his father by describing what he remembered about Oskar's father when he purchased the vase from William's estate sale. In the urban space of NYC, the story reaches full-circle as William Black is the husband of Abby Black, one of the first people that Oskar converses with on his key mission. Since Oskar's key does not provide the intended closure at the end of the novel, letters become the material mediation for the loss of the father.

As Sturken claims, the grieving process requires material objects to reconcile the absence of the dead. Foer's novel additionally employs the process of letter writing for characters to alleviate suffering. William Black says that his father wrote letters to everyone he ever knew when he was diagnosed with cancer—leaving behind words for others to read when he was gone. But Oskar's grandfather also wrote letters. The grandfather left when his wife became pregnant, and, for years on end, he wrote letters to his unborn son that were never mailed, with the exception of only one letter. The grandfather's letters are instrumental to the grieving process: Oskar tells the grandfather that he wants to bury something in his father's coffin because "it's the truth…that he's dead."[10] Oskar's acceptance of his father's death toward the end of the novel involves placing material into the coffin for the death to be "true." The grandfather's letters fill his son's coffin in the absence of his body—the body of words from the past becomes the material "body" that they can bury.

Sites of Traumatic Transmission

New York City's sites become the spaces for mimetic trauma, as the Empire State Building becomes one site for imagining 9/11 trauma in the novel. As Oskar stands on the observation deck, he narrates that, "even though [he] knew the view was incredibly beautiful, [his] brain started misbehaving, and the whole time [he] was imagining a plane coming at the building, just below [them]."[11] As Dora Apel writes in *Memory Effects*, "The art of secondary witnessing is thus based on a constant return to a past that is always beyond our grasp. Secondary witnessing ends in a kind of crisis, a greater sense of traumatic history's elusiveness, but also of its pervasiveness and its imminence, driving the compulsion toward reenactment or mimetic approximation."[12] Secondary witnessing in which a person's experience of trauma can be passed to another through storytelling or photographs clarifies why Oskar displays apprehension about being in the Empire State Building because, to him, a tall building equates with potential air attack: Oskar heard his father's last messages from the burning Trade Center. Oskar plays and replays the messages often, and from hearing the anxiety in his father's voice, Oskar, too, fears that a plane will crash into the floor below him.

The height of the Empire State Building and the panoramic view of New York City provide the space for Oskar to visualize what the September 11 attacks must have been like for the people in the towers. He visualizes that the plane would hit the floor below him, and the corresponding experience of panic and fear. He imagines,

> the last second, when [he] would see the pilot's face, who would be a terrorist. I imagined us looking at each other in the eyes when the nose of the plane was onc millimeter from the building (…) there would be an enormous explosion, and the building would sway, almost like it was going to fall over, which I know is what it felt like from the descriptions I read on the Internet, although I wish I hadn't read them.[13]

From the description of the plane hitting the building, Oskar goes on to explain the imagined last minutes of people's lives in the building. He describes the smoke and the people screaming; the people who had been trapped and their experience of heat so intense that their skin blistered; he thinks about whether he would jump or not; and if he could have made a phone call, he questions who he would have wanted to speak to last.[14] From the phone messages his father left and the personal accounts he read on the internet, Oskar becomes a secondary witness to the trauma, a trauma that is exemplified as he imagines the attacks on the tower while looking at "the gigantic hole where the World Trade Center was."[15] Oskar's trauma of imagining a plane attack is triggered by the loss of his father, as Oskar often repetitiously replays those last phone messages. Bringing to mind Sturken's claim about Ground Zero becoming the site of "intense emotional investment" and the "site of memory and mourning,"[16] Oskar utilizes the view of Ground Zero as a site for "postmemory" as he recalls what his father likely experienced in his last minutes. However, Oskar transfers the imagined last minutes of his father's life to other victims. While the father's death has transmitted a fear of plane attacks to Oskar, in this scene in the novel, the transmission of this trauma is what allows Oskar to think about and connect to other 9/11 victims. In this scene, in which Oskar fears a plane hitting the Empire State Building, he thinks about the chaos surrounding the other victims of 9/11 and what they must have felt in their last moments. The postmemory of his father's death allows Oskar to envision the 9/11 experience, and it is this postmemory that permits Oskar to work toward representing a collective depiction for the other victims of 9/11; after all, when Oskar seeks understanding of his father's death, he contemplates an image, "The Falling Man," another 9/11 victim. Oskar applies his postmemory, the traumatic recall of his father's death, toward comprehending the entirety of the event. In other words, Oskar's personal loss of his father allows him to envisage the 9/11 experience for other victims—the personal experience becomes a launching-point for understanding collective 9/11 memory.

In this scene in the novel in which Oskar contemplates the possibility of a plane hitting the Empire State Building, the tour guide begins listing facts about the building that include the detail that "a World War Two bomber crash[ed] into the seventy-ninth floor in 1945."[17] The Empire State Building serves as a connection to the past as the site of a World War II American accidental plane crash that is the precursor event to the American civilian planes crashing in the World Trade Center. Oskar, as a secondary witness to 9/11 through his father's death, mimetically fantasizes that the same might happen to him. The city and its sites provide Oskar the space to contemplate and connect the past historical events to his current trauma surrounding 9/11.

Multidirectional Memory, Postmemory and Traumatic Representation

The Oklahoma City bombing was the most recent event of a terrorist attack on American soil before 9/11.[18] As such, Sturken claims that when 9/11 happened, there was an "instant effect on how the Oklahoma City bombing was viewed, almost immediately redefining it as 9/11's smaller and less significant precursor."[19] The capacity for a present event to potentially erase or obscure a past one is the work that Michael Rothberg does with "multidirectional memory." Rather than concentrate on "privative" facets of memory, Rothberg advocates using the past in "productive" modes of consideration for the past. In other words, collective memory does not need to be "competitive memory,"[20] in which traumatic events struggle for public consciousness. In competitive memory models, events such as the Holocaust and other traumatic, historical moments compete for collective memory and public consciousness. Instead of viewing history as innately competitive for public memory, the "multidirectional" model questions what past historical events can expose about the present. Questions that follow the "multidirectional" model include: can the Holocaust, or other World War II events, inform us about 9/11? Can 9/11 analysis explain or illuminate additional traumatic aspects of World War II or a new way of interpreting those events?

In Foer's novel, World War II events collectively represent the trauma of recent disaster. As Rothberg claims, memory is "multidirectional" and is "subject to ongoing negotiation, cross-referencing, and borrowing."[21] This "multidirectional" approach to memory allows interpretation of 9/11 both in the current perspective of terrorism but also in the previous modes of war-related trauma. In a sense, Foer borrows the bombing scenes of World War II to negotiate representation of the newer 9/11 trauma. Accordingly, the anecdotes of Hiroshima and Dresden appear as a template for thinking through the unimaginable event of 9/11, as World War II events are a familiar part of cultural memory. But, describing previous wars and scenes of war-related violence is not a unique representation of the current tragedy. Relying on historical anecdotes to represent 9/11 illustrates the atrocity of war-related violence, through the "multidirectional memory" of World War II. Rothberg further suggests that multidirectional memory is the "back-and-forth movement of seemingly distant collective memories in and out of public consciousness."[22] Multidirectional memory accounts for how we can interpret the "unthinkable" 9/11 events through the common memory of World War II war scenes. But, at the same time, reproducing scenes that recall World War II imagery does not directly confront the moment of contemporary terrorism.

Throughout Foer's novel, his text is accompanied by many photographs and images. Often the photographs correspond to what Oskar writes in *Things That Happened to Me,* and depict everyday items such as turtles, New York buildings, or doorknobs, but none of these images are explicitly 9/11 centered, with the exception of "The Falling Man" that appears in several chapters. Aside from photographs that are not centered on 9/11, Foer's evasion of representing 9/11 is apparent in the overt war scenes. Instead of grappling with depicting scenes of America being attacked or bombed by other countries, Foer includes scenes of war enacted by America. Interestingly, Foer opts to describe historical scenes in which America performs the bombing, rather than depict the scene in which America is bombed: Foer graphically details the Dresden and Hiroshima bombings that, historically, were executed by American forces. In searching for a moment that reveals the vulnerability of America in a moment similar to 9/11, Foer could have described the moment of Pearl Harbor as the World War II event, but he seemingly avoids the scenes of American destruction by depicting the atrocity that America is capable of abroad rather than depicting the atrocity that can happen within American borders. Arguably, Foer offers a new insight into traumatic memory, namely that articulating trauma from the standpoint of the perpetrator is inherently more accessible. Foer seems to offer this insight through accessing the graphic details of Dresden bombings, but exemplifies the difficulty of articulating traumatic experience from the perspective of a victim when he does not include depictions of Pearl Harbor or 9/11.

The explicit moment of the Hiroshima atomic bomb appears in interview form. For "show and tell" Oskar brings an interview of a mother detailing the loss of her daughter. In this moment, the interviewer on the recording is asking objective questions such as "Did you see the mushroom cloud?," "But the cloud spread over the city?," and "Can you describe the black rain?"[23] The one question that the interviewee, Tomoyasu, directly answers is that she did not see the mushroom cloud. After all the rest of the interviewer's questions about the cloud or rain, Tomoyasu persists in continuing the story of trying to find her daughter in the city. After Tomoyasu's perseverance in narrating the story of searching for her daughter, a victim of the Hiroshima bomb, the interviewer eventually asks the basic question that reacts to Tomoyasu's story: "You were holding her in your arms all that time?"[24] But, this acknowledgement of the story being told only occurs after Tomoyasu sidestepped each of the objective questions and proceeds to relate her trauma narrative. Five of the six questions asked by the interviewer do not relate, or open the conversation for, the affected woman to talk about the plight of trying to locate her daughter, and yet, that is the story that is divulged. This interviewer tries to direct the line of questioning towards the moment of bombing in talking about the mushroom cloud or the black rain, but the survivor avoids narrating the moment of the bomb being dropped. Although the Hiroshima survivor interview is a trauma narrative of war-related violence and a fictional reproduction of a historical event, the actual moment of the Hiroshima bombing is eluded, in that instead of fictionally detailing the flash of the bomb, mushroom cloud, or black rain, those moments are obscured for the personal story of losing a daughter. In both instances, Foer avoids depicting the moment of bombing for both World War II and 9/11, and substitutes articulating violence by concentrating on the traumatic aftermath.

The Hiroshima moment appears in the 9/11 novel under an interesting pretense. Oskar, without explanation, has this testimony in his possession and he brings it to school to share with his classmates. Oskar, who does not speak of his father to anyone except his mother, picks this specific interview. The historical event of Hiroshima is the backdrop and catalyst for the mother, baring her moment of tragedy about the death of her daughter. As an inversion to Oskar's situation, this mother reveals her sorrow over the death of her daughter through the direct confrontation of emotion that Oskar is not capable of verbalizing about the loss of his father. Oskar uses the Hiroshima testimony as a template to publically and indirectly express the loss of his father. Oskar also uses the space of the classroom to enact secondary witnessing the Hiroshima trauma: when he stops playing the interview, several of the girls are crying.

Another scene in which Oskar employs the past to elucidate his present trauma occurs when he attempts to gain closure of the recent 9/11 tragedy by filling the metaphorical hole with words from the past. Oskar digs up the coffin that does not contain the body of the father who died in one of the towers—because like many real 9/11 victims' families, Oskar and his mother buried an empty coffin. Oskar and the grandfather fill the coffin with the letters that the grandfather wrote to his son, but never sent, over the years. By the novel's end there is the metaphorical significance of filling the empty coffin with recycled words that fill this void. Oskar does not deliver an explicit speech to say goodbye but figuratively uses the words of the past to gain closure since he cannot form his own speech in the present moment.

Similar to the metaphorical significance of Oskar's using someone else's words to gain closure, the Dresden bombing narrates destruction in ways that Foer does not illustrate about 9/11. The Dresden bombing is represented in letter form by the grandfather who writes about the bombing to his unborn son. The grandfather spends little of the narrative actually describing the moment of the bombing. He expresses the sense of chaos and the sentiment that it felt as if it lasted weeks, but nothing specific about the bombing, planes, or actual moment of impact is explicitly described. The letter details the grandfather's traumatic personal experience of his desperate search for his girlfriend. While the grandfather attempts to make the journey to his girlfriend's house, he details all that he is witnessing in terms of human carnage. The Dresden survivor is on a quest to find a loved one that is ultimately discovered to have died in the bombing and attention is focused on dying humans and peeling flesh but not on the actual act of bombing.

However, while these moments of World War II historical events produce representation through character memory, the inclusion of these events also elides 9/11 representation while serving as a template to embody the same kind of crisis; specifically this is seen through Oskar who plays the testimony of a parent losing a child amid chaos and destruction instead of verbalizing the experience himself. The entire novel operates by not revealing all: history can serve as exemplification of current trauma but it does not directly re-present the event. Hiroshima is recalled through a recorded testimony, an interview that Oskar plays in the present, but the interview does not contain details of the actual bomb. Dresden is revealed through a letter but the grandfather writes mostly about the zoo animals he shot instead of the bomb victims. And, 9/11 is incorporated through phone messages left by the father calling from the burning tower; but, even those phone messages elude 9/11, as the father does not indicate that he is calling from the burning building.

These stories of bombings and 9/11, contain one unifying thread: each one of the characters is on a mission to find a loved one in the midst of chaos created from war-related violence. Tomoyasu searches for her daughter amid the Hiroshima aftermath, the grandfather attempts to search for his girlfriend through the Dresden wreckage, and Oskar tries to metaphorically find his father in post-9/11 New York through his key mission. Each of the characters undertakes a journey but ultimately comes up empty-handed and suffers the loss. In each case, the story is also a trauma narrative that delves into issues of personal mourning and coping with death against the framework of traumatic, historical events. Explicitly, the characters' personal trauma narratives all have a source based in reality (all these historical events did happen) but the fictional character stories also avoid representing the historical event. Memory is incorporated as the mode of storytelling; but just as with memory that is innately selective, these survivors select recapping bodily injuries and the loss of the love object that emphasize the emotional impact of tragic historical events rather than objectively representing the historical occurrence. World War II events, and specifically Hiroshima's atomic bomb, echo the current moment of 9/11 in the novel, especially in the sense that the empty remains of the terrorist attack on the towers, Ground

Zero, "a name pulled from history," refers to the destruction caused by nuclear bombs.[25]

In *The Generation of Postmemory*, Hirsch defines "postmemory" as the "*structure* of inter- and transgenerational return of traumatic knowledge and embodied experience. It is a *consequence* of traumatic recall but (unlike posttraumatic stress disorder) at a generational remove."[26] "Postmemory" appears in the novel between the grandfather's and father's transmissions of trauma to their (grand)son. The grandfather's Dresden experience traumatizes and renders him mute, as he experiences aphasia, and he leaves his family, as he claims he does not know how to live after what he saw. In the letter that the grandfather writes to his unborn son about the Dresden bombing, the letter contains circles of the mistakes and notable words in red pen, a reading habit of Oskar's father (Oskar's father circles mistakes in the newspapers he reads). Aside from the tiny, textual clue that this is the only letter that the grandfather sent to his son, it is the material object that connects the grandfather to his son, both victims of "bombings." The text reveals that the grandmother gave her son the "only letter [the grandfather] ever sent. He was obsessed with it, always reading it. I don't know what you wrote, but it made him go and look for you."[27] The Dresden letter is a similar object facilitating the grieving process for Oskar's father that the key is for Oskar: Oskar's father develops a fascination with the letter and searching for his Dresden victim father in the same way that Oskar becomes obsessed with the key and finding a final message from his dead father.

Oskar and the grandfather also connect through their traumas. Not realizing that his grandmother's "renter" is his grandfather, who came back when he read his son's obituary, Oskar tells his grandfather about his struggle with his father's death and what he has done with the key mission. In response, the grandfather writes a note to Oskar that he cannot speak because "something is broken"[28]; this is the most the grandfather elaborates about his trauma that is not in a letter. Symbolically, the traumatic aftereffect is transferred and recognized between two characters through a similar traumatic event, albeit not the exact same one. Recognizing traumatic experience in each other across the span of World War II to 9/11, the grandfather and Oskar traverse the generations in burying the grandfather's World War II, and later, letters in Oskar's 9/11 victim father's coffin. Interestingly, all of Oskar's photographs are taken with his grandfather's camera, an object he inherited from his grandmother, as his grandfather left during his wife's pregnancy.

Historical Representation for the Current Event: Photographs and Memory

Historical events can facilitate the explanation of current traumatic events through familiar scenes of past trauma, but explaining the present through the past is not a unique representation for the exceptional event—never before have American civilian planes been operated to "bomb" and kill American civilians.

Much of the critical work written on this novel contends with the photography aspect and the rationale for the multitude of images that Foer adds to his story. Sturken writes that,

> photographs seem to have played a dominant role in the response to 9/11, far more than the television images. Unlike the television images which defined the media spectacle, the photograph seems to aid in mediating and negotiating a sense of loss. In the first months after 9/11, in addition to the proliferation of photojournalism, there was a frenzy of amateur picture taking in New York and an obsession with looking at images.[29]

Sturken suggests that the pictures of New York City sights and make-shift memorials that sprang up are the effect of coping with the loss of the towers and people. The documentation impulse that surrounded 9/11correlates with the images that Oskar snaps of the city's structures and people that he later places in his journal; Oskar essentially documents what he has seen and copes with loss through this act. Oskar's pictures "prove" the authenticity of the narrative and add an element of "realism" to the novel—or that Foer is attempting to recreate the media frenzy of documenting 9/11. The documentation impulse is similar to what Roland Barthes observes in *Camera Lucida*, that photographs are evidence of the person or object's existence, that "the thing has been there."[30] However, these photographs which authenticate that "this has happened" are only superficially created documentation through the written narrative; it is the written words that solidify that these experiences belong to Oskar when they are referenced throughout the story. But while these pictures attest to a fictionalized but realistic realm, the very relationship between text and image unravels this very notion. The "realistic" photographs are not from the same year, place, or any other unifying element and do not support the narrative in a literal way, therefore, these photographs are not mere illustrations of the narrative.

Other scholars have suggested that photographs can become an appropriate means of expressing the inexpressible. Specifically for this novel, Philippe Codde suggests that the images are a "disruptive means of conveying the inability to articulate the traumatic experience of 9/11."[31] For

Codde, these photographs become the delicate and appropriate means of representing the traumatized mind in which the disruptive photographs exemplify the mind's search for an appropriate method of explaining the source of trauma. In this case, Codde refers to the observation made by Bessel van der Kolk and Onno van der Hart that traumatic experiences often escape representation on the linguistic level, and tend to be stored in the mind as a series of images. Particularly, Codde extends the clinical perception of how the mind stores trauma to account for why Oskar collects pictures. Children tend to interact with their world visually. In addition to the idea that pictures fill the pages as a demonstration of the distressed mind filling in the gaps of representation with images, the images also reflect a child's specific reaction to trauma.

Lisa Farley also emphasizes that children mitigate traumatic history through visual aspects, in particular, drawings. Children's interaction with the visual underscores the key aspect of memory: historical rupture is impossible to witness. Farley's solution to recalling an impossible history relies on psychoanalysis to explain the "unconscious of history."[32] The imaginative struggle of memory is to "transform the rawness of history's repeated irruptions into the symbolic realm, [that is] needed to make meaning of absence."[33] The squiggle game that children engage with to mitigate trauma, for Farley, "may be evidence of how we make from the stray fragments of the past a meaningful historical narrative (…) the ultimate act of creativity, the art of history.[34] Farley connects how children draw unrelated squiggles, talk through the process of drawing the squiggle, and start to make meaning of their traumatic experience. For Farley, the "squiggle game"[35] metaphorically describes how memory draws fragments of the past into a comprehensible narrative.

In the novel, it is possible that Oskar's unrelated pictures, fragments of the past, are drawn into a representation of 9/11 as he processes his father's death. In line with Farley's interpretation of the "squiggle game," Codde argues that Foer organizes his book with a series of images precisely to illustrate a child's struggle for representation; like traumatized children that elect to relate traumatic experiences through drawing, Oskar creates a "convincing representation of trauma" through the collection of his images.[36] But these pictures are more than an illustration of a child's inability to express the loss of a parent or the event of September 11—this imagery creates a distraction from these very issues. It is not that the loss of his father is inexpressible for Oskar or even inaccessible as he represents the loss of his father through other media and non-verbal means. Oskar's photographs are not an expression of emotional pain, but a distraction from loss.

A more nuanced analysis of the photographs exposes more than the collective impulse to pictorially document 9/11 or the support of a plot through photography. More importantly, these photographs undermine the severity of the characters' traumatic narratives. Moments of characters writing are a major component of this novel as Oskar writes letters to various strangers in his journal while his grandfather writes letters to his unborn son. It is mainly through epistolary and journal writing that character suffering is revealed. While the written word reveals the various kinds of trauma that each character has endured, the pictures and visual typography are a distraction from the story. In his journal, Oskar verbally divulges bruising himself while choosing pictures such as rocks or tennis players to appear alongside the same train of thought. These photographs quite literally interrupt the narrative as they are full-page, placed in the middle of chapters, and made up of ordinary scenes. The intensity of the narrative that reveals Oskar's bruising is nullified by the pictures that document the everyday. In other words, the scenes of major character trauma are not reinforced with pictures of the events, aftermath, or people involved; the parts that describe moments of atrocity are straightforward and are unsupported by photographs. These mundane photographs that appear alongside the narrative remove some of the intensity of the stories, given that these photographic choices can potentially confuse the reader.

These photographs are one of the more persistent means of avoidance in the novel, as these pictures do not illustrate 9/11 or suggest that 9/11 has even happened. Of the images that are reproduced, seven *could have been* taken in New York: two pictures of the New York skyline, Brooklyn Bridge, the Coney Island "Cyclone," the Empire State observation deck, and a still-frame of the news report about the Staten Island Ferry crashing into the pier. The only image that is conclusively taken in New York is the screen caption of a local NYC news report. The place where these pictures were taken is not cited on the copyright page, and most likely many are not exclusively taken in New York settings: the skyline photographs could be any metropolitan setting, the close-up of the bridge is not necessarily Brooklyn Bridge and even the up-close picture that shows that the roller coaster is labeled "Cyclone" could be any of the "Cyclone" coasters that exist in the country. But regardless of whether these pictures are taken in New York settings or not, they are not outwardly associated with 9/11, nor are they explicitly post-9/11. The copyright page indicates that only a handful of photographs are from 2001. Certainly some of the other images, like the Museum of Natural History illustration, birds, gems and windows, are not pictures of post-9/11 New York. The only exception to the novel's series of unrelated photographs is the image of "The Falling Man"—an image undeniably taken in New York and capturing a moment from 9/11.

But perhaps these pictures must be mundane to reinforce the chaos of personal tragedy and the overarching national tragedy of 9/11. Instead of clarifying or reinforcing the narrative, these pictures have the ability to dislocate the reading practice, but more importantly, the reader. As these pictures preempt their mention in the text, the reader is forced to confront the picture without context first and then later read about the various photographed items; the assumption is that the reader will recognize the textually mentioned picture that occurs after the picture has already appeared in the novel. Thus, the pictures force the reader to always be drawing connections from one passage to the next in the attempt to understand what the various photos stand for. This way of composing the novel, in which pictures precede the narrative, imitates a working-through of an experience and the challenge of finding the words and images to represent it. Symbolically, the chaos of the non-chronological narrative that is further confused with unsystematic imagery does appropriately model the realistic, public disorientation after 9/11. In a way, the disorderly nature of the photographs demonstrates what Sicher and Skradol have observed about 9/11, namely "the Hitchcock moment of horror that is actually happening; intrusion of the real into fiction."[37] In the novel, real photographs are "intruding" on Foer's fiction. The pictures obscure the narrative voice of Oskar's journal as the reader is confronted with both emotionally intense fictional narration and real, unrelated photos.

From the plethora of 9/11 photos that could have been selected for inclusion in this novel, only the image of "The Falling Man" appears; there are not any pictures of towers burning, papers pouring down from the skies, or firefighters surveying rubble. Instead, the one image that Foer includes is of an unidentified man falling to his death. Through his creative choice to exclude certain images, Foer seems to purposively not display images from 9/11. The selection of "The Falling Man" avoids depicting death and destruction since the falling man is not yet dead as he plummets downward—he is still alive at the moment the picture is taken. Moreover, the building's destruction is not shown either as the backdrop of the picture shows an intact portion of the tower; the impending destruction of both person and building is not exposed in this moment. Of the many images, Foer debatably chose the image that does not reveal disaster.

Conceivably, Foer elects "The Falling Man" image not only to avoid the moment of depicting the destruction of 9/11, but because this image also symbolizes helplessness. Andrea D. Fitzpatrick writes extensively on images of falling and September 11 in her article, "The Movement of Vulnerability:

Images of Falling and September 11th." She delves into the issue of vulnerability and the metaphorical significance of a falling body. Of "The Falling Man" image she writes,

> Drew's seventh frame hit a nerve with the public in the sense of agency, perhaps even dignity, conveyed by the position of the man's body, which appeared so directional; this pierced viewers affectively. Junod details how this element—utterly contradictory in the face of such calamity—was not lost on viewers: 'Some people who look at the picture see stoicism, willpower, a portrait of resignation; others see something else—something discordant and therefore terrible: freedom' (Tom Junod qtd in Fitzpatrick) (…) The power or courage that graced the man's position is, for some, also that which equates his body's movements with a suicidal 'choice' to jump, with despair at its utmost.[38]

Throughout her article, Fitzpatrick considers what vulnerability means not only on the individual level, but the larger implications that these images of falling have revealed about a "nation wounded" characterized by constituted images of "defeat."[39] Her analysis of the photograph reveals the conflicting interpretations that can arise from a viewer's perception. It is a "portrait of resignation" (as Tom Junod claims in his article, "The Falling Man") in that the falling man is brave for electing to jump and take a sense of agency into his hands. Or, for others, this image epitomizes a moment of defeat and despair as the man has been forced out of a burning building. But this seventh frame is not the image that Foer selects for the novel. Rather than depicting the image that was heavily circulated in the media, in which the man is resolutely headfirst, Foer elects a photo illustration based on a photograph by Lyle Owerko—the frame in which the man's body position is free falling like an inverted parachute.[40] The "jumpers" of 9/11 were ruled homicides by the New York Medical Examiner's office; they were thereby placed into the category of victims and not suicidal agents. In this sense, Foer selects the photograph that displays the status of a victim as the man cannot control his body's position in the descent. This moment of helplessness as the body takes the position of an inverse parachute is starkly contrasted with the picture of the falling cat that takes the form of a parachute in its fall—a posture that allows cats to survive falling from heights. As an emphasis of vulnerability, Foer juxtaposes the image of a cat that is capable of surviving a fall with the helplessness of the human body that physically cannot take that form.

Ostensibly, this frame of the man's descent is chosen for its symbolic vulnerability, but Foer also chooses the photograph that is somewhere between life and death. This image of the falling man as a moment of despair, as Tom Junod points out, correlates with Foer's modes of representation in the novel. "The Falling Man" models Oskar's despair over his father and his struggle to gain closure. Oskar's concentration on the picture of "The Falling Man" is what allows him to fixate on the moment of his father's death in imagining what his father's last moments must have been like, but it also circumvents the actual image of his father as Oskar imagines his father through "The Falling Man" image. Whenever Oskar wants to learn about his father's death, he googles words like "people jumping from burning buildings" and looks at the images of people falling from the towers.[41] Oskar also refers to the photograph in psychologically difficult situations. In one moment in which he is socially self-conscious in front of another character, Oskar says, "Because the string was still around my neck, when she leaned in to look at the key, her face came incredibly close to my face. We were frozen there for a long time. It was like time was stopped. I thought about the falling body."[42] Part of Oskar's coping with the loss of his father is to undertake a "key mission," as aforementioned, he journeys all over New York looking for people named Black. In this moment, Oskar is questioning Abby Black about the key; since Oskar claims to be "in love" with Abby, it would be a safe guess to assume that his self-consciousness is due to the sudden crush he develops. Interestingly, in this moment in which he is anxious, Oskar reflects back on the image of "The Falling Man."

Similarly, Oskar visits the owner of the key, William Black, as already mentioned. He finally realizes that the key is not a new piece of information that he was hoping to discover about his father, but a key that belonged to William Black's father and was mistakenly sold in a vase that Oskar's father purchased. At the end of the key search, Oskar realizes that he is empty-handed and relates that he "started thinking about the pixels in the image of the falling body, and how the closer you looked, the less you could see."[43] It is as though the up-close image of "The Falling Man" and the suggestion that "the closer you looked at the figure the less you can actually see" becomes the metaphor for Oskar and his search for his father's last moments before his death through his key mission. The image of "The Falling Man" serves as signification of the loss of the father as Oskar consistently examines this image in his journal; in moments that he wishes to think through the trauma of losing his father, Oskar thinks about "The Falling Man." But this image is merely a representation of his father. "The Falling Man" image symbolizes the loss of his father but also signifies the incomprehensibility of articulating this loss, as Oskar looks to another 9/11 victim in the attempt to understand his father's death. The incomprehensible loss of the father persists through the text that is scattered with eighteen images of "The Falling Man."

The image of "The Falling Man" has become iconic, but in the weeks and months after 9/11, the image was removed from mainstream media. Foer's inclusion of the image signifies that even though the picture, and its implications of death, is disturbing or even offensive to some, it must be viewed. Oskar mentions that, in his fictional google searches, the videos in which he can see the falling body are on a foreign site. Oskar states, "They were on a Portuguese site, where there was all sorts of stuff they weren't showing here, even though it happened here (…) it makes me incredibly angry that people all over the world can know things that I can't, because it happened *here*, and happened to *me*, so shouldn't it be *mine*?"[44] As Foer's mouthpiece, Oskar implies an important point: if 9/11 happened in America, why did images of "The Falling Man" stop disseminating in American media? One reason for the removal is that many people were concerned about privacy issues for the victims' families. At the same time, American media has a history of censoring images of the country's own dead. Susan Sontag suggests that media outlets stopped circulating many images of 9/11 because of "good taste." She contends, "With our dead, there has always been a powerful interdiction against showing the naked face."[45] Sontag exemplifies how American media rarely broadcasts the faces of their dead soldiers to an American audience. However, many 9/11 images, whether they depicted faces or not, were not printed in newspapers or shown on TV. Perhaps, aside from good taste, the media removed these images precisely because these victims are not soldiers but civilians. Similar to how photographs of the murdered are not commonly circulated, so too, the photos of these 9/11 victims are not circulated either. But this is Foer's point exactly: if the experience happened in America, why not allow the American public to confront these images? Importantly, Foer's novel, like many American novelists "censor" the event by not depicting a fictional unfolding of towers collapsing. Instead, American novelists like Safran Foer, Don DeLillo, and Jay McInerney choose to craft their narratives in New York, post 9/11. In opposition, the French author Frédéric Beigbeder centers his novel, *Windows on the World*, in one of the collapsing towers. However, for American distribution, Beigbeder's novel was subject to censorship of his more extreme scenes of apocalyptic sex between a couple trapped in the burning building and the lines in which he compares the burning of 9/11's civilians to Auschwitz's victims. Fascinatingly, a French author crafted the scene of destruction in ways that the American authors did not; but, even for the American market, the scenes of extremism were edited for the English language version.

Foer, unlike many media sources, readily reproduces the vulnerable image of "The Falling Man" to make his readers look at the photograph of a victim that was not readily disseminated. However, in one place in the novel the image is blurred to the point of being unrecognizable, and the end of the novel features fifteen photographs of "The Falling Man" in a series to serve as a flipbook to visually float the man back to safety. Even at the level of the photograph, Foer attempts to represent the event, but his character, Oskar, avoids contending with the magnitude of the atrocity as the character crafts the flipbook that nullifies that the event has happened. In this sense, Foer has moments in which 9/11 is indirectly represented but the tragedy of the event is also avoided. More importantly, while Foer boldly chooses to reprint this image several times in the course of his novel, it is not the image that created a terrible media stir. Instead, Foer selects the image that is merely based upon a photograph; the author manipulates the image of "The Falling Man" so that it is virtually unrecognizable as an "authentic" image from 9/11 thereby confronting the image only to later unravel that confrontation with a blurred version of the image.

Foer's novel takes place after 9/11 but does not attempt to reveal much of the disaster; instead, Foer recreates 9/11-esque moments from past historical trauma—in this sense, 9/11 is represented and eluded. Even in the photography aspect of the novel, the one image from 9/11 is "The Falling Man," but this is arguably not going to become the "iconic" image that 9/11 is associated with in later years—perchance because of the victimization that the image displays. Instead, Marianne Hirsch exemplifies what an "iconic" image of 9/11 might become. She claims that,

> four photographers interviewed on the Charlie Rose program agreed that the [9/11] icon would be the picture of the three firemen raising the flag on top of the rubble because it echoes the famous prize-winning photograph of American GI's raising the flag at Iwo Jima. In their search for the one lasting iconic image, they were looking for the conventional, the coded, not the new.[46]

Hirsch suggests that these photographers select an image that reminds them of Iwo Jima as a preference for the familiar rather than embodying a new image for the recent tragedy. She aptly questions: "Is this familiarity reassuring, inscribing this event into a known visual register and thus a known history? And does it thus perhaps shield us from the shock of the suddenness and unexpectedness of the devastation?"[47] The answer, at least for this novel, is seemingly, yes. The photographers are comfortable selecting an image that reminds them of another traumatic moment in American history; they select an "iconic" image analogous to an image of World War II, not because these two events are explicitly comparable but, because the image recalls a predictable familiarity. Or, I would argue, the choice of a familiar image is because World War II is distanced decades from the present moment. The Iwo Jima image, in particular, and World War II photographs, in general, have been seen and studied for decades and are the opposite of the "new" destruction of 9/11. Similarly, Foer is doing the same with recalling common everyday images. Instead of including images of the new and sudden destruction of 9/11, Foer selects familiar and everyday sights of New York, or images that can stand in for New York. But, Hirsch's point is that the photographers selected an image of the already "known." These photographers were using the visual template of World War II to select an image for 9/11 in the same way. Thus, instead of articulating the experience of 9/11, Foer returns to the "coded, not the new" of World War II's Hiroshima and Dresden. The personal accounts that Oskar reads on the internet and the pictures he views about 9/11 certainly form an interactive and communal account of the event in keeping with Hirsch's point that the "capabilities of the Web as a collective repository of images and texts deriv[ed] from official and personal archives" generates a "place for collective memory and cultural exchange."[48] But, if the collective memory of images from 9/11 and the written accounts help to *understand* the event and its traumatic effects on Oskar, these images and testimonies of trauma within the novel do not *represent* 9/11.

9/11 Representation as the Event Requiring Latency

Extremely Loud & Incredibly Close, written in 2005, ostensibly models what Cathy Caruth claims is the latency of traumatic history. As Caruth rereads Freud, she states, latency is the "period during which the effects of the experience are not apparent." She further exemplifies that with unexpected and shocking moments based upon which, "the experience of trauma, the fact of latency, would (…) seem to consist, not in the forgetting of a reality that can hence never be fully known, but in an inherent latency within the experience itself."[49]

The observation that a moment of shock requires a delay in understanding the traumatic moment is applicable to Foer's novel that eludes commenting on, or verbalizing the experience of, the 9/11 terrorist attack. In many ways, Foer echoes the theory of "latency," or that the effects are not yet apparent, by fictionalizing 9/11 through other historical events—the 9/11 moment is avoided through narrative and visual techniques. My analysis of Foer's novel illuminates the common turn for many 9/11 novelists of avoiding the event entirely, or representing the event through the past. Foer fictionalizes a detailed account of two World War II bombings: Hiroshima and Dresden. These two scenes of bombing are able to stand in as "accessible" events through the language of fiction; the narrative reveals a "multidirectional" reaction to 9/11 that relies on reproducing other historical "traumas" to represent this contemporary incident. The moments of World War II's Hiroshima and Dresden are surrogate events to stand in for 9/11. World War II bombings become the comprehensible templates: the novel's representation of other historical events exposes not only the overarching theme about the inability to represent 9/11 in the proximal years after the event, but also reflects how a return to history, and the familiarity with it, can serve as exploration of a contemporary tragedy. However, representing a new event through former historical tragedies does not directly represent 9/11.

Inevitably, Jonathan Safran Foer tells a story that confronts individual and national shock through a series of imitations for an unprecedented, violent event. Kristiaan Versluys argues that "the whole task of Safran Foer's novel is to describe a normalcy that has been brutally interrupted."[50] And Foer does just this in crafting a narrative that interrupts, undermines, and contradicts itself in its storytelling of post-9/11 New York. Foer represents the current disaster through a return to past catastrophic events. The use of images in the novel can be read as a commentary on their role in the construction of a collective memory of 9/11, attuned to Rothberg's claim that collective memory is "the relationship that [different social] groups establish between their past and their present circumstances."[51] Perhaps on a metaphorical level, Foer is recalling 9/11 through the images in this novel. The pictures are non-specific and may stand in for a variety of representations as "9/11" or 9/11's "collective memory." However, as many scholars have written, 9/11 was a heavily, and visually, recorded phenomenon. If Foer was pushing towards signifying the event through the mind of a traumatized child, why are there not more 9/11 specific images? Perhaps 9/11 representation in this novel, through a child's viewpoint, begins in these nondescript images. As Oskar works through the traumatic loss of his father, and understanding the larger impact of 9/11 on his NYC community, he utilizes these images to stand in for his currently available representation. Similar to the traumatized children who articulate their traumas through drawing, Oskar attempts to represent 9/11 through his familiar sights—his childlike past memories of turtles and doorknobs can latently stand in for current 9/11 representation.

September 11 is the moment of an unexpected attack, but in the realm of history it is not an unprecedented event. World War II bombings conveyed through the grandfather's traumatic Dresden "postmemory" and the Hiroshima victim's interview, represent the similar devastation that 9/11 created in American lives, but also serves as a kind of grounding historiography. For many scholars, 9/11 is the moment in which the unthinkable happened—the targets were the very icons of America. The staging of Hiroshima and Dresden in the novel can stand in for 9/11 and avoid the direct commentary on the 9/11 tragedy that is not yet accessible in the few years after the event in which Foer is writing. Potentially, Foer was not ready to represent 9/11 a mere four years after the event, given that this novel dovetails with the notion of the latency of the traumatic. In this sense, Foer overtly borrows events from a familiar history and even narrative tradition, as Kurt Vonnegut utilizes Dresden, first, as a surrogate event in lieu of Vietnam in *Slaughterhouse-Five*. The novel's images, like the narrative, dislocate the reader from making one to one correlations such as these images or this story stands in for a community's or an individual's recovery from 9/11. Text and image collaborate in this novel to purposefully not represent 9/11. Instead, the role of memory is one of remembering a kind of traumatic history in representing 9/11 through World War II; or, the idea that this event can be fittingly represented through familiar, past scenes of traumatic history, for now. Instead of describing 9/11 from the standpoint of past history, or a disaster movie, Foer's novel demonstrates that latency is necessary to reconsider an original representation for 9/11, as a unique historical event.

Bibliography

Apel, Dora. *Memory Effects: The Holocaust and the Art of Secondary Witnessing*. New Brunswick: Rutgers University Press, 2002.

Barthes, Roland. *Camera Lucida: Reflections on Photography*. Translated by Richard Howard. New York: Farrar, Straus, & Giroux, 1980.

Caruth, Cathy. *Unclaimed Experience: Trauma, Narrative, and History*. Baltimore: Johns Hopkins University Press, 1996.

Codde, Philippe. "Philomela Revisited: Traumatic Iconicity in Jonathan Safran Foer's *Extremely Loud and Incredibly Close*." *Studies in American Fiction* 35.2 (2007): 241-54.

Farley, Lisa. "Squiggle Evidence: The Child, the Canvas, and the 'Negative Labor' of History." *History and Memory* 23.2 (2011): 5-39.

Fitzpatrick, Andrea D. "The Movement of Vulnerability: Images of Falling and September 11th." *Art Journal* 66.4 (2007): 84-102.

Foer, Jonathan Safran. *Extremely Loud & Incredibly Close*. New York: Houghton Mifflin Co., 2005.

Hirsch, Marianne. "I Took Pictures: September 2001 and Beyond." In *Trauma at Home: After 9/11*, edited by Judith Greenberg, 69-86. Lincoln: University of Nebraska Press, 2003.

—. *The Generation of Postmemory: Writing and Visual Culture after the Holocaust*. New York: Columbia University Press, 2012.

Hoth, Stefanie. "From Individual Experience to Historical Event and Back Again: '9/11' in Jonathan Safran Foer's *Extremely Loud & Incredibly Close*." *Kulturelles Wissen und Intertextualität: Theoriekonzeptionen und*

Fallstudien zur Kontextualisierung von Literatur, edited by Marion Gymnich, Birgit Neumann and Ansgar Nünning, 283-300. Trier: Wissenschaftlicher Verlag Trier, 2006.

Rothberg, Michael. *Multidirectional Memory: Remembering the Holocaust in the Age of Decolonization*. Stanford: Stanford University Press, 2009.

Sicher, Efraim, and Natalia Skradol. "A World Neither Brave Nor New: Reading Dystopian Fiction after 9/11." *Partial Answers: Journal of Literature and the History of Ideas* 4.1 (2006): 151-79.

Sturken, Marita. *Tourists of History: Memory, Kitsch, and Consumerism from Oklahoma City to Ground Zero*. Durham: Duke University Press, 2007.

Sontag, Susan. *Regarding the Pain of Others*. New York: Farrar, Straus & Giroux, 2003.

Versluys, Kristiaan. *Out of the Blue: September 11 and the Novel*. New York: Columbia University Press, 2009.

Notes

[1] Marianne Hirsch, *The Generation of Postmemory: Writing and Visual Culture after the Holocaust* (New York: Columbia University Press, 2012), 5-6.

[2] Michael Rothberg, *Multidirectional Memory: Remembering the Holocaust in the Age of Decolonization* (Stanford: Stanford University Press, 2009), 271.

[3] Hirsch, *The Generation of Postmemory*, 33.

[4] Lyle Owerko took the photograph that was featured on the cover of *Time* magazine's September 11, 2001 issue. A Canadian photographer, who frequently composes photographs of urban imagery, Owerko was sitting in his Tribeca neighborhood home in NYC when he heard the first plane crash into One World Trade Center (the North Tower). Owerko went downstairs to the street-level and began snapping a multitude of pictures; he was able to capture the moment that the second plane hit Two World Trade Center (the South Tower). According to Evan Mitsui Manmeet Ahluwalia of CBC News, in the article "The 9/11 Cover that Captured the World," Owerko called his moment-of-impact photograph "a spectacular witness image." While the image of the second plane's impact is the photograph most commonly associated with Owerko, he also took many pictures of the 9/11 "jumpers" who leapt from the burning buildings. The iconic image from Owerko's "jumpers" is the picture of a man free-falling, mid-descent. Much speculation of the man's identity surrounded this photograph, as it is the most clearly defined image from Owerko's set of "jumper" photographs.

[5] Cathy Caruth, *Unclaimed Experience: Trauma, Narrative, and History* (Baltimore: Johns Hopkins University Press, 1996), 17.

[6] Jonathan Safran Foer, *Extremely Loud & Incredibly Close* (New York: Houghton Mifflin Co., 2005), 8.

[7] Marita Sturken, *Tourists of History: Memory, Kitsch, and Consumerism from Oklahoma City to Ground Zero* (Durham: Duke University Press, 2007), 178.

[8] Sturken, *Tourists of History*, 169.
[9] Foer, *Extremely Loud & Incredibly Close*, 302.
[10] Foer, *Extremely Loud & Incredibly Close*, 321.
[11] Foer, *Extremely Loud & Incredibly Close*, 244.
[12] Dora Apel, *Memory Effects: The Holocaust and the Art of Secondary Witnessing* (New Brunswick: Rutgers University Press, 2002), 188.
[13] Foer, *Extremely Loud & Incredibly Close*, 244.
[14] Foer, *Extremely Loud & Incredibly Close*, 244-45.
[15] Foer, *Extremely Loud & Incredibly Close*, 245.
[16] Sturken, *Tourists of History,* 168.
[17] Foer, *Extremely Loud & Incredibly Close*, 248-49.
[18] The Oklahoma City Bombing occurred on April 19, 1995. According to the FBI's description of the day's events, an ex-Army soldier, Timothy McVeigh, concocted a homemade bomb from fertilizer and other chemicals. McVeigh parked his rental trunk, containing the bomb, outside the Alfred P. Murrah Federal Building and at 9:02 am, he detonated it. The bomb killed one hundred and sixty-eight people, including nineteen children, and injured almost six hundred other people. The blast of the bomb destroyed over three hundred buildings in the sixteen-block radius. The term "homegrown terrorist" was introduced to describe McVeigh, and photographs of the blast site were consistently compared to the wreckage of a war-zone. In 1995, six years before the events of September 11, The Oklahoma City Bombing was named the deadliest act of terrorism committed in America.
[19] Sturken, *Tourists of History,* 167.
[20] Rothberg, *Multidirectional Memory*, 3.
[21] Rothberg, *Multidirectional Memory*, 3.
[22] Rothberg, *Multidirectional Memory*, 17.
[23] Foer, *Extremely Loud & Incredibly Close*, 188.
[24] Foer, *Extremely Loud & Incredibly Close*, 189.
[25] Sturken, *Tourists of History,* 167.
[26] Hirsch, *The Generation of Postmemory*, 6, emphasis in the original.
[27] Foer, *Extremely Loud & Incredibly Close*, 277.
[28] Foer, *Extremely Loud & Incredibly Close*, 257.
[29] Sturken, *Tourists of History*, 188.
[30] Roland Barthes, *Camera Lucida: Reflections on Photography*, trans. Richard Howard (New York: Farrar, Straus, & Giroux, 1980), 76.
[31] Philippe Codde, "Philomela Revisited: Traumatic Iconicity in Jonathan Safran Foer's *Extremely Loud & Incredibly Close*," *Studies in American Fiction* 35.2 (2007): 254.
[32] Lisa Farley, "Squiggle Evidence: The Child, the Canvas, and the 'Negative Labor' of History," *History and Memory* 23.2 (2011): 6.
[33]Farley, "Squiggle Evidence," 8.
[34] Farley, "Squiggle Evidence," 32.
[35] The analyst D. W. Winnicott developed the "squiggle game" (1968) in which the analyst would start a doodle and then hand the paper over to the child patient to continue drawing. Winnicott and the patient would pass a drawing back-and-forth, always adding to the drawing, and talk through the process of contributing to the

drawing. The idea is to open communication of early life relationships through this visual aspect of drawing.
[36] Foer, *Extremely Loud & Incredibly Close*, 249.
[37] Efraim Sicher and Natalia Skradol, "A World Neither Brave Nor New: Reading Dystopian Fiction after 9/11," *Partial Answers: Journal of Literature and the History of Ideas* 4.1 (2006): 151.
[38] Andrea D Fitzpatrick, "The Movement of Vulnerability: Images of Falling and September 11th," *Art Journal* 66.4 (2007): 91.
[39] Fitzpatrick, "The Movement of Vulnerability," 86.
[40] Stefanie Hoth, "From Individual Experience to Historical Event and Back Again: '9/11' in Jonathan Safran Foer's *Extremely Loud & Incredibly Close*," in *Kulturelles Wissen und Intertextualität: Theoriekonzeptionen und Fallstudien zur Kontextualisierung von Literatur*, eds. Marion Gymnich, Birgit Neumann and Ansgar Nünning (Trier: Wissenschaftlicher Verlag Trier, 2006), 296.
[41] Foer, *Extremely Loud & Incredibly Close*, 256.
[42] Foer, *Extremely Loud & Incredibly Close*, 97.
[43] Foer, *Extremely Loud & Incredibly Close*, 293.
[44] Foer, *Extremely Loud & Incredibly Close*, 256, emphasis in the original.
[45] Susan Sontag, *Regarding the Pain of Others* (New York: Farrar, Straus & Giroux, 2003), 70.
[46] Marianne Hirsch, "I Took Pictures: September 2001 and Beyond," in *Trauma at Home: After 9/11*, ed. Judith Greenberg (Lincoln: University of Nebraska Press, 2003), 85.
[47] Hirsch, "I Took Pictures," 85.
[48] Hirsch, *The Generation of Postmemory*, 240.
[49] Caruth, *Unclaimed Experience,* 17.
[50] Kristiaan Versluys, *Out of the Blue: September 11 and the Novel* (New York: Columbia University Press, 2009), 101.
[51] Rothberg, *Multidirectional Memory*, 2.

GENDER AND THE NOSTALGIC BODY IN POST-9/11 FICTION: CLAIRE TRISTRAM'S *AFTER* AND MOHSIN HAMID'S *THE RELUCTANT FUNDAMENTALIST*

JENN BRANDT

Attempting to assess and understand individual identities and collective cultures alongside globalization, Claire Tristram's *After* (2004) and Mohsin Hamid's *The Reluctant Fundamentalist* (2007) focus on the narrative use and function of "Othered" bodies—specifically those considered transgressive, terrorist, and/or tortured—in response to 9/11 and the War on Terror. As a literary subgenre, *transgressive fiction* contains characters going against the norms of society, often using illicit or taboo means to break away from, and expose, the hypocrisy of contemporary culture. This chapter explores the use of transgressive bodies in the narrative structure of Claire Tristram's *After* and Mohsin Hamid's *The Reluctant Fundamentalist* as they subvert recognizable stereotypes in an effort to problematize notions of identity and nation that have been ignored or oversimplified in discourses of 9/11. Using the body as a vehicle for nostalgia, both novels upend stereotypical notions of gender, sex, class, and nation as a means to address disparities between individual experience and collective memory. Rather than romanticize an imagined past, both *After* and *The Reluctant Fundamentalist*, through their respective narrative techniques, destabilize the process of nostalgia through the transgressive behaviors of their characters. In doing so, these novels address the question of how nostalgia might be appropriated by fiction in order to expose social and political debates that form gendered and national identities in response to trauma.

In *The Body in Pain: The Making and Unmaking of the World*, Elaine Scarry writes of torture, "What assists the conversion of absolute pain into the fiction of absolute power is an obsessive, self-conscious display of agency."[1] Claire Tristram's debut novel *After* explores this notion of torture as agency and its relationship to narrative, trauma, and memory through the sexual encounter of two unnamed narrators. Referred to only as "the widow"[2] and "the Muslim," the novel shifts back and forth between each character's point-of-view as the two engage in a sexual liaison that takes place over the course of one day. Hoping to escape the pain of the first year anniversary of her husband's death at the hands of Islamic extremists,[3] the widow arranges to take a Muslim lover. The Muslim, a married man haunted by his own traumatic memories of terror, agrees to the affair, in part, due to his decreased sense of masculinity in an Islamophobic post-9/11 America. My reading of *After* explores the gendered relationship between terrorism and sexuality as demonstrated through the sexual, and at times violent, interactions of Tristram's characters. In attempting to reenact the horror of her husband's death through intercourse, the widow not only appropriates a masculine identity, but in doing so, becomes a "terrorist" herself as she binds, tortures, and sodomizes the Muslim. I contend that Tristram's masculinization of the widow and feminization of the Muslim serve as a commentary on the nostalgic return to traditional gender roles endorsed by the American media in the wake of September 11, 2001.

Like Tristram's *After*, Mohsin Hamid's *The Reluctant Fundamentalist* also takes place over the course of one evening and centers around the politically charged exchange between the Pakistani narrator, Changez, and an un-named American stranger. Educated at Princeton and working for an American firm on September 11, 2001, at the time of the narrative Changez has since given up his "American dream," returning to his home country and taking part in anti-American protests. Changez and the American meet up one evening in Lahore, Pakistan, and although the two appear to be strangers, the exact circumstances of their encounter are unclear. As Changez recounts his personal narrative to the American, he frequently hails him as "you," drawing the reader into the text and making the reader implicit in the exchange. The "you" is both singular and plural, as it not only implicates the individual reader, but also textually refers to "you" as American and "you" as America. As suspense builds and tension increases, the narrative reaches an abrupt conclusion that finds the American confronting Changez, as he (the American) is either reaching for his business card or a gun.

Through the structure of the novel's narrative and the open-ended nature of its conclusion, *The Reluctant Fundamentalist* interrogates the reader and challenges his/her assumptions regarding terrorism and the Other. As Hamid has discussed, "To try to imagine what a future could be that isn't desperately nostalgic is the great political challenge that I see for this time and it is the reason why the novel ends on a sad note."[4] In examining the implications of the novel's ending as it relates to the reader, my analysis brings the discussion back to this political challenge and explores the novel's treatment of nostalgia as it relates to personal agency and the transgressive potential of bodies in Hamid's text.

Theorizing Nostalgia and Trauma

Marianne Hirsch and Valerie Smith argue that while nostalgic narratives are often dismissed as conservative and escapist, feminist narratives can "resituate the politics of nostalgia by recuperating devalued, marginalized, or repressed cultural formations."[5] While women are often the "keepers" of private and family histories, cultural history and public memory are most often the record of men. Therefore, it is important to consider the gendered implications of cultural memory, as "gender is an inescapable dimension of differential power relations, and cultural memory is always about the distribution of and contested claims to power."[6] Cultural memory, then, becomes a stage for the performance of power differentiations along lines of privilege, and reconsidering the role of women and gender, as well as race and sexuality, illuminates new possibilities in re-mapping cultural relationships to the past.

As demonstrated by *After* and *The Reluctant Fundamentalist*, cultural memory becomes "what we need it to be in times of incomprehensible suffering—part reality and part fiction, depending on memory's most familiar tropes of race, gender, and nationhood."[7] Both Tristram and Hamid were keenly aware of the strong undercurrent of nostalgia that carried along much of the post-9/11 discourse. In drawing attention to the ways in which nostalgia functioned in national narrative responses to 9/11, in their works, both authors use physical bodies as metaphors for nostalgia as they expose the ways in which outdated and traditional stereotypes of gender, sex, and class work to form nationalistic responses to terrorism. Coupled with this use of character bodies, the narration in both *After* and *The Reluctant Fundamentalist* emphasizes post-9/11 literature's thematic preoccupation with addressing figurative and literal border crossing as a way of exposing the gender, racial, class, and national divisions made prominent by the terrorist attacks of September 11, 2001. The question, then, becomes how literature of 9/11 can appropriately use nostalgia to make apparent the need to reexamine historical and cultural "norms" in response to trauma, globalization, and the resulting imperative to rethink dominant codes of national narratives.

In many ways, nostalgia is a manifestation of the resistance to the change inherent with globalization.[8] In the article "Nostalgia as a Feature of 'Glocalization,'" Moonyoung Lee writes,

> When a society undergoes a radical transition, when the familiar system of norms and order has collapsed but new norms and a new type of order are not yet established, when politics, economics, and other aspects of life are in a state of chaos, people experience an asthenia that is strong and real. This is a most important factor, beckoning to lost time and space, encouraging them to come into the present. That is, the experience of this asthenia presentizes nostalgia.[9]

In this sense, nostalgia mimics trauma in the way in which it temporalizes the past as a mitigating factor in both the present and the future. The two phenomena work in tandem, where the disruptive mnemonics of trauma are softened by nostalgia's façade of safety. A "radical transition" such as 9/11, while perhaps not entirely collapsing the entirety of established norms and order, certainly calls the permanence of such systems into question. Further, this "presentisizing" of nostalgia gives both temporal and spatial dimensions to the nostalgic effect, as the condition presses a longing for not only a particular time in history, but also a particular place. In regards to gender, the relationship between nostalgia and trauma highlights the contested positioning and/or historical erasure of "minority" groups along lines of race, gender, and sexuality.

Where nostalgia becomes most powerful is in its shift from a longing and desire for a particular time and space in relation to personal experience, into one adopted for political and nationalistic purposes by a fabricated collective memory. It is this danger of nostalgia that is addressed in both *After* and *The Reluctant Fundamentalist*. In *Ethics and Nostalgia in the Contemporary Novels*, John Su argues that nostalgic narratives can offer a "palpable image of human needs that are not being met. If nostalgia does not necessarily assist individuals in articulating solutions to these needs, it at least enables them to register the needs themselves."[10] The ethical significance of literature that addresses nostalgia is that it allows readers not only to assess their own needs that may or may not be met, but to also question the real and imagined needs of others that nostalgia attempts to bring to light. This awareness becomes crucial in considering the relationship of gender to schisms of national and cultural differences, particularly in times of crisis when nostalgia often becomes a measure by which the present is held to an imagined past.

Nostalgia, Trauma, and the Body

Both *After* and *The Reluctant Fundamentalist* employ narrative structure as a means of engaging readers in the process of evaluating the effectiveness of nostalgia in response to political and personal trauma. Physical bodies become central to this examination in the sense that they serve as tangible models for the ways in which valuation is dependent upon gendered, geographic, political and economic variations. Thus, bodies become not only the site for nostalgia in these novels, but also highlight the hierarchical properties of bodies in relation to difference. Narratively, this is achieved in *After* through the alternating point of view of the widow and the Muslim. In *The Reluctant Fundamentalist* this is most readily seen in Changez's narrative of his time in the United States and his "reading" of Erica, his unrequited love. Further, in *The Reluctant Fundamentalist*, narrative becomes a collaborative effort through Hamid's use of dramatic monologue, where Changez's narration and constant hailing of "you" draws the reader into the action of the text. In both novels, the interpretative process of reading is crucial in breaking down barriers between the reader and the text, which serves as an access point in the reconsideration of other barriers and territories, such as the self and the Other, the familiar and the unknown, and the individual and the collective.

In discussing the narrative technique of *The Reluctant Fundamentalist*, Hamid explains, "One reason for having this formal structure is that by creating half a conversation, a conversation of which you only hear one half, and where the other party of the conversation is only present as an echo, a space opens up in the novel, a vacuum that the reader is invited to fill."[11] The space opened up by the address of Changez is one where the reader becomes an active participant in the text. This "half conversation," which is only one side of the story, draws attention to the biases that divide two sides of a debate. In this case, it opens a space for not only considering non-Western ways of interpreting 9/11, but also serves as a call to action for the reader to investigate his/her own assumptions and biases that mediate his/her understanding of 9/11. The result, as Hamid notes, is: "When you read *this* book [*The Reluctant Fundamentalist*], you are at least partly reading yourself."[12] This reading of oneself is important, as nostalgia plays into an understanding of not only events in the novel, but the reader's *own* nostalgia is also a part of the interpretive process of the self.

Within the novel Hamid makes this clear when Changez comments, "I watched him [the American 'you'] watch me, trying to understand what he was looking for."[13] In its structure, the entire novel is a meditation on post-9/11 US-Pakistani foreign relations, a cat-and-mouse game where, despite outward appearances of congeniality, neither side can be entirely sure of the other's motivations or intentions. Further, as Changez explains to the American, "I am, after all, telling you a history, and in history, as I suspect you—an American—will agree, it is the thrust of one's narrative that counts, not the accuracy of one's details."[14] Therefore, it is up to the reader to decide not only the validity of Changez's tale, but also the outcome of Changez and the American's encounter. The ending of the novel allows for the possibility of multiple outcomes: neither of them has an ulterior motive and the two part ways on friendly terms; Changez has set up the American, and their waiter has been following them for malicious purposes; or, the American is reaching for a gun, having been sent by the US government to "silence" Changez. One's interpretation of the novel's ending, then, becomes not only an exercise in literary analysis, but more importantly, an insight into one's own biases, assumptions, and thoughts on the War on Terror in the aftermath of 9/11.

Tied into this response is the notion of nostalgia and the way it factors into readers' expectations of not only literature, but one's identity post-9/11. Questions of identity in relation to nostalgia are explored through the plots of *After* and *The Reluctant Fundamentalist*, where both works use the nostalgic body to address questions of gender, nation, and memory in response to terrorist activity. *After* draws attention to binaries of gender and ethnicity through the stereotyping of its main characters, "the widow" and "the Muslim." Although Tristram fleshes out the characters through their interactions, she labels, rather than names, them, drawing attention to the oversimplification of identity in response to terrorism. In *The Reluctant Fundamentalist*, gender and nationality are linked not only with Changez's companion, who is masculinized by his frequent comparison to an American soldier, but also through the character of [Am]Erica, the recipient of Changez's unrequited love.

Changez first introduces Erica into his narrative in the novel's second chapter. A fellow Princeton graduate, the two meet while vacationing with friends in Greece the summer before Changez begins work at the valuation firm Underwood Sampson. Changez is immediately infatuated with Erica, and slowly attempts to develop their friendship into a romance upon their return. This courtship is complicated, however, by Erica's grief over her childhood love, Chris, who succumbed to cancer the previous year. Chris's death sends Erica into a depression that is deepened by 9/11. As a metaphor for America, Erica's relationship with Chris is indicative of the supposed "loss of innocence" that the United States suffered on September 11, 2001. This longing for a simpler time, embodied by their childhood romance, becomes a key way in which Hamid uses bodies as a site for nostalgia in the novel. Comparing her grief to homesickness, Erica tells Changez, "I kind of miss home, too. Except my home was a guy with long, skinny fingers."[15] More than just a person, Chris comes to symbolize for Erica a virtuous time and place in her life—the home and safety of childhood. As such, her grief is infused with a mixture of naiveté and innocence that go hand-in-hand with the romanticized nostalgia of first love.

Erica's love for an idealized, youthful past is characterized by the ghost of Chris and brought to the surface by 9/11. Hamid writes, "The destruction of the World Trade Center had, as she [Erica] said, churred up old thoughts that had settled in the manner of sediment to the bottom of a pond; now the waters of her mind were murky with what had previously been ignored."[16] Chris's death, which initiates Erica to the reality of "impermanence and mortality," is magnified and intensified on a national scale by the events of September 11.[17] Therefore Erica and the nation's grief are enmeshed in the novel, and in both instances, they suggest the danger and power of nostalgia.[18] Memories and the past take on an inappropriate significance, and in Erica's case, she eventually is no longer able to function in the present. Her disappearance at the end of the novel suggests a certain unknowability of what will become of America post-9/11, and her outcome is similar to the novel's conclusion in that it is open to the reader's interpretation.

Nostalgia, Trauma, and Gender

Although Erica is not technically a widow, she does mirror some of the traits of Tristram's widow in *After*. Both women mourn their lost loves, with Erica representing the historic "good" widow. She is portrayed as virtuous, pure, and forever faithful to Chris, living in his memory and nothing more. This version of widowhood aligns with the American media's portrayal of the "9/11 widows" (women who lost their husbands as a result of the terrorist attacks of September 11), who in the months following the event were exploited for their grief. As Jennifer Gardner Trulson remarks in her memoir *Where You Left Me*,[19]

> [W]idows were on every talk show and news update, petitioning Congress and City Hall to preserve, redesign, or sanctify Ground Zero. Apparently, we were a hot trend, the new black. We had cachet—at least as far as the media and politicians were concerned. Paraded around State of the Union addresses, honored at charity functions, and remembered at Super Bowl games, the 9/11 widows became every politician's or social climber's favorite accessory.[20]

While Tristram's widow begins *After* embodying this type of widowhood, part of her transgression in the novel is her transformation into the historic stereotype of the "bad" widow. Her misery over her husband's death is warped into her sexual encounter with the Muslim, and, as she becomes voracious and sexual in her interactions with him, she finds herself rebelling against the script of grief that she has been forced to enact. Thus, through fiction and the gendered body, Tristram provides a counter-narrative to the one perpetuated by the mainstream American media in the wake of 9/11.

After's and *The Reluctant Fundamentalist*'s use of their female characters to explore gendered and national stereotypes reflects many of the observations about nostalgia, gender, and 9/11 that Susan Faludi addresses in *The Terror Dream: Fear and Fantasy in Post-9/11 America.* Faludi, whose work argues against what she sees as an increasing marginalization of feminism, investigates the ways in which the media, in the wake of 9/11, retreated to a promotion of outdated myths of marriage, motherhood, and masculinity. She writes, "In the aftermath of the attacks, the cultural troika of media, entertainment, and advertising declared the post-9/11 age an era of neofifties nuclear family 'togetherness,' redomesticated femininity, and reconstituted Cold War manhood."[21] Faludi suggests that these myths are themselves part of America's history, and are (re)cycled through cultural discourse during times of domestic "threat" from both real and imagined outside forces.

The "myths" of gender, trauma, and nation suggested by Faludi were echoed by other scholars post-9/11. Diana Taylor notes, "The attacks immediately triggered the same old scenario: evil barbarians, threatened damsels, and heroic males drawn from a repertoire of frontier lore."[22] As many feminist scholars argued, the response to the national trauma was gendered and racialized along nostalgic tropes related to myths of "how the West was won." In recycling the lore of America's frontier, not only were individual bodies implicated, but the national "body" also took on gendered and racial dimensions. As Sarah Ahmed reminds us, "the soft national body is a feminised body, which is 'penetrated' or 'invaded' by others."[23] The risk of this "softness" is "not only the risk of being feminine, but also of becoming 'less white,' by allowing those who are recognised as racially other to penetrate the surface of the body."[24] As a result, the gendered aspects of trauma are experienced on the personal and collective level.

Both *After* and *The Reluctant Fundamentalist* take up many of the aforementioned gendered "themes." Like the 9/11 widows, the widow in *After* has been forced to deal with her grief in the public eye. The premise of the novel is that rather than face the onslaught of questions and concerns from family and the media on the anniversary of her husband's death, she decides "to do something so unexpected, so clearly outside the role that she had been forced into by her circumstances" and seeks out a Muslim lover.[25] The two rendezvous at a beachside hotel and, over the course of the evening, the widow attempts to work through her grief as she engages in various sexual interactions with the Muslim, many of which involve her attempts to humiliate him. In initiating this encounter, the widow begins the process of breaking out of the "role" and (as she later refers to it) "script" of the good widow in consorting with the Muslim, whom she has cast as the "enemy."

On her website, Tristram writes, "My goal in writing *After* was to explore, through fiction, the fictions we tell ourselves to make us feel we are better than our enemies."[26] This desire for personal fictions relates to Faludi's assertions regarding America's cultural need for myths. It also connects to Changez's assertion in *The Reluctant Fundamentalist* regarding the "thrust" of one's narrative being more important than the accuracy of details. In both novels, narrative structure functions not only at the level of plot, but also as a way to reposition characters and readers in relation to the enemy. Specifically, "personal fictions" are considered on a corporeal level in these narratives as they are expressed through the body. Sex, particularly, is transgressive in the case of the widow, as it goes against the expectations and stereotypes of the honorable widow, chaste and forever bound to the fidelity of her marriage vows.

Therefore, in her sexual torture of the Muslim, *After*'s widow attempts to "rewrite" her position as widow and victim through an appropriation of both terrorist and masculine identities. At first she hopes to find closure by reenacting the last night she and her husband spent together, but instead is shocked to find herself physically responding to the Muslim in ways she never had with her husband. His desire to please her sexually does not fit in with her plan. Not only does he not follow her reenactment expectations, but he actually ends up making her feel good physically. In this way, the event mimics Susannah Radstone's reading of 9/11 and proves traumatic "not because of its inherently shocking nature but due to the unbearable or forbidden fantasies that it prompts."[27] Disturbed because things are not progressing the way she had hoped (i.e., a cathartic re-creation of the last night she spent with her husband), the evening takes a violent turn after the two return from a dinner where the widow is recognized and the Muslim is discriminated against. As a result of her "outing" at the dinner, where she is publically seen cavorting with the "enemy" instead of being dour and dutiful, the widow begins to embrace her new role as the "bad" widow. Back in their hotel room, the widow blindfolds the Muslim, binding his ankles together with his belt and his wrists together with a wire hanger. She then proceeds to scratch at and slap him with another wire hanger before stimulating him anally with her fingers. She finishes her "torture" of the Muslim by forcing him to call home and leave a message for his wife, making him repeat the last words her husband had left in a message for her before he was killed. The novel ends with the two parting the following morning, attempting to regain a sense of normalcy in the face of what has happened.

Regarding torture, Scarry writes, "it is in part the obsessive display of agency that permits one person's body to be translated into another person's voice, that allows real human pain to be converted into a regime's fiction of power."[28] The widow, through her sexual assault of the Muslim, explores this "fiction of power" as she expresses her frustrations over her husband's death at the hands of religious fanatics, as well as her own repressed feelings of gender inequality from her roles of wife and widow. Further, the body becomes the means through which the widow attempts to make meaning of the event; she must "rewrite" it through the body in order to make sense of it. As the novel states, "It seemed that for this anniversary she [the widow] felt a need to inhabit every body, to understand every player."[29]

After returning from dinner, the widow begins this "inhabitation" by shaving her body in a "purifying ritual" similar to those of Islamic suicide attackers and the Pashtun tribesmen of Afghanistan who engage in a ritualistic removal of body hair before going into battle. Satisfied with her transformation, the widow turns her attention to the Muslim who, lying on his stomach in his bound state, appears "womanly" to the widow.[30] As she explores his body with her fingers the widow demands that he repeat after her "I like this" and "don't stop," demonstrating Scarry's assertion that the vocalization of the torturer's desire by the tortured becomes a necessary part of torture's fictionalization of agency, as well as the ways in which senses other than sight contribute to the meaning making of an event. When the Muslim reveals that her actions make him feel like a woman, the widow calls him a "cunt," and thinks,

> This is what men think when they make love to us (…) Wanting to hurt her, invade her, rip her apart. And my lover's only purpose is to allow it. This is what this man thought of me, at the moment of his orgasm. This is what my husband thought of me at the moment of his orgasm. Wanting to penetrate. And look how he asks for it![31]

Through her actions, the widow attempts to embody the multiple agents of her grief. When she first begins to torture the Muslim with the coat hanger, she is thinking of the ways violence was inflicted on her husband, solely because he was American and Jewish. That is, the Muslim is her victim at first purely because of his religion and because he looks "Arab." During the process, however, she begins to regard him as a "woman" and, in doing so, appropriates a masculine identity that allows her to not only take on the gendered identity of her husband's murderers, but also the sexual identities of the Muslim and her husband. She equates the "invasion" of America by the terrorists to the sexual invasion that women experience during intercourse. The widow's assertion "look how he asks for it," suggests the possibility for US cultural and political policies that "opened" America up for attack. At the same time, she is also able to reflect on her own gendered and sexual identity as well as the Muslim's and her husband's.

While the sexual relationship between Changez and Erica in *The Reluctant Fundamentalist* is devoid of the violence seen in *After*, it does share a striking similarity. Just as the Muslim appropriates the identity of the widow's husband in *After*, Changez plays a similar role by pretending to be Chris while having sex with Erica.[32] Reflecting on his actions he remarks, "Probably this was why I had been willing to try to take on the persona of Chris, because my own identity was so fragile. But in doing so—and by being unable to offer her an alternative to the chronic nostalgia inside her—I might have pushed Erica deeper into her own confusion."[33] Changez's willingness to play a dead man reflects not only his desire to be with Erica, but his larger need to "fit in" in America. He attributes his failure in both acts to his fragile sense of self and crisis of identity.

Nostalgia, Trauma, and Nation

Like Erica's turmoil over Chris, Changez's crisis of identity is magnified and made prominent by the events of September 11. Watching the events unfold on television while in the Philippines on business, Changez is shocked to find himself "smiling" when confronted with footage of the attacks on the World Trade Center.[34] Resentment inside had been building in him over time, and 9/11 forces Changez to confront many of the underlying feelings of guilt and inequality he had been experiencing. This discomfort with himself and his surroundings is solidified when Changez returns home to Pakistan for a visit and finds that he has adopted an American gaze, thinking, "I was shamed. *This* was where I came from, this was my provenance, and it smacked of lowliness."[35] This shame echoes his earlier reflection that,

> Four thousand years ago, we, the people of the Indus River basin, had cities that were laid out on grids and boasted underground sewers, while the ancestors of those who would invade and colonize America were illiterate barbarians. Now our cities were largely unplanned, unsanitary affairs, and America had universities with individual endowments greater than our national budget for education. To be reminded of this vast disparity was, for me, to be ashamed.[36]

Changez finds himself caught between the disparity of wealth separating his ancestral and adopted homes, and his identity is in crisis as he struggles to make sense of the shocking global inequalities that he finds himself straddling. This leads to his own nostalgia, which makes it difficult for him to return to New York and Underwood Sampson after his holiday in Pakistan. Changez expresses his resistance to the totalizing monopoly of the United States through the body when he returns to work with a beard. He refuses to shave—despite being warned about the impression of Islamic militancy he is giving off—not because of any particular religious convictions, but because he enjoys the unease it causes his American co-workers and neighbors. His beard challenges Underwood Sampson's model of diversity as Changez attempts to upset their gaze of him in the same way his gaze of Pakistan was tainted when he returned home.

The breakdown of identities is crucial in understanding the ways in which bodies are sorted into types in both *The Reluctant Fundamentalist* and *After*. As Hamid has explained, his intention was "to create very recognizable types and subvert them along the way."[37] Similarly, in discussing her novel, Tristram writes, "I think of it [*After*] as a love story, with tragic characters, a woman and a man who are unable to shed the identities that divide them, even after those identities no longer have any meaning."[38] Both authors, aware of the constructed nature of character types and identity, shed light on the ways in which trauma affects the ways in which one views him/herself, and does not necessarily correspond to how others perceive those with whom they come in contact.

As her "name" suggests, throughout the novel, the widow is defined by her relationship to her husband and his death. Like Erica in *The Reluctant Fundamentalist*, the widow is consumed by her grief, and the absence of her husband becomes the focal point of her existence. In her interactions with the Muslim, however, the widow is forced into the realization that in many ways her identity was dependent upon her husband even before his death. She confesses to the Muslim, "My husband used to tell me what to think about everything. I'm not complaining. I loved him. But without him I find I don't know what to think about things."[39] This confession comes before the widow tortures the Muslim, but subsequent to their first round of intercourse. The slow, thoughtful advances of the Muslim contradict the widow's memory of sex with her husband, where they "always used a condom as well as a diaphragm" when he would "pound" and "plow" her.[40] Sex with her husband was another means by which patriarchal oppression operated in the widow's life. This realization in part leads to the widow's later sexual aggression toward the Muslim, where her treatment of him is as much a displacement of her rage against her husband as it is toward his assailants. The barrier between men and women—signified by the diaphragm and condom that she and her husband always used—is removed in part when she becomes the "bad" widow and sleeps with the Muslim using only a diaphragm for protection. In this way, the widow has full access to the Muslim's body (which she did not have with her husband), but the Muslim does not have full access to hers. Where before the widow defined herself in terms of her husband, taking on a passive identity sexually and otherwise, with the Muslim she begins to shed that identity.

As Tristram notes, the identities of her characters lose their meanings as the result of acts of terror. No longer a wife, the widow attempts to adapt to the new identity that has been given to her. In discussing her new status, the widow slips into a "script" she reiterates many times, "I started taking Zoloft. I put on a lot of weight, it made me fat, but God, I survived."[41] This speech is one that the widow has repeated many times for various interviews and the news media and represents the stoic front she has put on for the cameras. This performance mirrors Faludi's discussion of the 9/11 widows, where she argues that the role of the widow was key in strengthening myths of post-9/11 domesticity and femininity. Faludi writes, "The widows the media liked best were the ones who accepted that their 'job' now was to devote themselves to their families and the memory of their dead husbands."[42] The widow in *After* serves a similar function, where her personal grief is expected to express the grief of the nation. Her story is acceptable as long as she accepts her role and remains the dutiful, lugubrious widow that the nation expects.

As a fellow diner tells the widow, "You're a pillar. An absolute pillar. We all lean on you."[43] The widow's grief is cheapened and de-personalized as it becomes a symbol and fodder for public consumption. The 9/11 widows, Faludi argues, often became complicit in a similar type of nostalgia, serving as national models for mourning, because refusing to do so meant becoming a pariah, nearly as vilified as the terrorists.[44] "Widows who didn't contribute to the 'wonderful story' found themselves dropped from the media dance card," Faludi writes. "Widows who openly flouted its terms were treated far worse—they found themselves objects of widespread censure."[45] This speaks to the widow's desire to "escape" on this anniversary, not only from the prying eyes of the outside world, but also from the person she has become as a result of trauma. In meeting with the Muslim she is attempting to redefine her identity differently from the one that has been given to her. In choosing the Muslim solely for his religion and "Arab" appearance, she still, however, identifies herself in relation to the outside world rather than from her own self definition.

As a response to 9/11, the desire on the part of some to return to "traditional" gender roles was a reaction to not only the initial attack, but to continued US fears regarding Islam. Coupled with this emasculating Islamophobia was the nostalgic need to reinvigorate the image of the American hero, a bastion of strength and testosterone-filled masculinity. His counterpoint was embodied by an outdated femininity that placed women in the home and in need of male protection. This Islamophobia—which functioned as a way to deflect America's own feelings of emasculation as a result of 9/11—is another means by which the traumatized body is explored and used in both *After* and *The Reluctant Fundamentalist*. Despite the fact that neither of them is particularly religious, both the Muslim and Changez find their relative positions in society challenged in the wake of terrorism due to their religion.

Changez's position at Underwood Sampson—itself a metaphor for the power of the United States—reflects the global politics to which Changez has become increasingly resistant. On the surface, Underwood Sampson, like the United States, gives the appearance of diversity, acceptance, and equality. Closer inspection, however, reveals the underlying parameters of acceptable multiculturalism. Changez recalls,

> Two of my five colleagues were women: Wainwright and I were non-white. We were marvelously diverse (. . .) and yet we were not: all of us, Sherman included, hailed from the same elite universities—Harvard, Princeton, Stanford, Yale; we all exuded a sense of confident self-satisfaction; and not one of us was either short or overweight.[46]

While Underwood Sampson's hiring process appears to be a model of affirmative action, Changez soon realizes the company's outward show of diversity is in actuality a façade that masks an alarming homogeneity of privilege. Changez and his colleagues reflect the fact that despite changing demographics in America, there is still a strong underlying class system in place. This division reflects Changez's identity crisis and his family's fallen financial status in Pakistan, which he likens to the "old European aristocracy in the nineteenth century, confronted by the ascendance of the bourgeoisie."[47] Changez's status ascendancy in New York pre-9/11 coincides with the decline of his family's wealth. In occupying these dual positions, Changez becomes a model for the class struggle brought to prominence by globalization, and gives a body to the unequal progress of geographical development.

This division in the access of resources is recognized immediately by Changez, who remarks, "nothing had prepared me for the drama, the *power* of the view from their [Underwood Sampson's] lobby. This, I realized was another world from Pakistan."[48] As a symbol for both America and capitalism in the novel, Underwood Sampson's motto "focus on the fundamentals" speaks to the degree in which everything—including bodies—can be seen as a commodity. Not surprisingly, Changez's dissatisfaction with America corresponds with his decline in performance at Underwood Sampson. Underwood Sampson's valuation of companies resembles the way in which Changez sees the United States wreaking havoc and "legitimizing through its actions the invasion of weaker states by more powerful ones."[49] In both cases, the emphasis on maximized productivity has either a positive or negative affect on bodies as it sees "value" determined by a strict code of capitalism at the expense of other qualities of assessment. Those that achieve under this model fit the hierarchy of privilege embodied by the "diversity" of Underwood Sampson. As a result, both domestically and internationally, the status quo is upheld through the structures of global markets and class systems.

After's Muslim, on the other hand, finds himself defined by the stereotypes and preconceived notions of an Islamophobic United States. His "valuation," while not economic, is physical, as it depends on his appearance as a body marked by difference. Despite his protests, "I am not an Arab. I am Persian. There are great historical differences. And I am not particularly religious. Really, I'm the most secular sort of Muslim you're ever going to meet," he still cannot escape the bigotry of others.[50] While the Muslim has a clear picture of his own self-identity, like Changez, he cannot escape the ways in which his identity has been redefined by the context of the recent terrorist activities. Although he does not consider himself particularly religious, outside forces have turned his religion into a defining feature. Much of this has to do with the appearance of his body, which to ignorant American eyes code him as Arab. His failed attempts at explaining the historic and political differences between Arabs and Persians fall on deaf ears to Americans, as they have been visually "trained" by popular public rhetoric to divide bodies into simplified categories of "us" and "them." *After* narratively breaks free from this binary by portraying the Muslim as a dynamic character with his own traumatic past with respect to terrorism. By alternating the point of view of the novel between the perspectives of the widow and the Muslim, *After* not only fleshes out the characters, but also allows the reader to inhabit multiple perspectives of the same event, demonstrating that there is no final version of "history." This resembles the narrative goals of Hamid's *The Reluctant Fundamentalist*, where Changez suggests that history is only as factual as its storyteller. Further, by making the widow a less sympathetic character than the Muslim, Tristram also uses fiction to allow readers to question their own assumptions and biases in a way that is comparable to the structure of the dramatic monologue in *The Reluctant Fundamentalist*.

Similar to the widow, as well as the characters in *The Reluctant Fundamentalist*, the Muslim is also haunted by memories of terror and random acts of violence. Although not particularly political, as a young man in Tehran he participated in a rally where his best friend was shot and killed only inches from him. Describing the memory of the day as a "chronic pain," the Muslim replays the event in his mind so many times over the course of the years that eventually "what really happened and what he remembered happening were insinuated with each other beyond all reckoning."[51] Although he does not immediately recognize the widow when they first meet, he later agrees to their tryst, in part, because he feels their traumas have somehow brought them together. Rather than seek retribution as the widow does, the Muslim hopes that the encounter will make him feel whole again.

He also, to a certain extent, agrees to their meeting due to an increased feeling of emasculation as a result of the negative portrayal of Islam in the aftermath of the terrorist attack. Like the widow, he too finds himself being defined by outside forces that in actuality have nothing to do with him. Reflecting on his "new" identity, he thinks, "Women apart from his wife had stopped paying attention to him just after the crisis in his country had come to a satisfactory conclusion, after Americans were out of danger once more. Overnight he had lost his mystery and his aura of the forbidden and had become bland, unattractive, sexless."[52] Both before and after the "crisis," the Muslim recognizes that he is sexually objectified through a Western gaze that marks him as "Other." Before the terrorist attack he imagines himself to have been regarded as mysterious and exotic, and he sees this as positive. The arbitrary nature of this description is revealed, however, when he realizes that he is now seen as the opposite: "bland, unattractive, sexless." The widow, while not entirely regarding him as sexless, targets him because of the post-crisis gaze that marks him as an enemy. While he is still exotic and Othered, this "marking" has now taken on a negative connotation. The Muslim's new identity is tied together with the "conclusion" of his country's recent crisis, suggesting that one of the ways in which the novel's terrorist event was resolved was to sexually demarcate those who did not fit the "appearance" of a "true" American.

This new identity not only marks the Muslim sexually, but in other ways as well. His wife, sensitive to the changing cultural climate, displays a large "Proud to Be an American" bumper sticker on the family car and insists on keeping their daughters home from school on the anniversary of the attack. Her actions demonstrate the ways in which bodies marked by ethnicity and religion have been forced to modify the ways in which they interact with the public sphere in response to terrorist activity. While many Americans were afraid to travel or be in large public spaces in the weeks and months after 9/11 for fear of another outside attack, there were just as many Americans who feared domestic terror based on their religious beliefs, skin color, or other obliquely coded "differences."

This fear is echoed in *The Reluctant Fundamentalist*, where Changez remarks, "As a society, you were unwilling to reflect upon the shared pain that united you with those who attacked you. You retreated into myths of your own difference, assumptions of your own superiority."[53] These myths and assumptions translate into a form of nostalgia that functions to create divisions rather than bring people together. Changez, himself, becomes a victim of this mentality upon his return to Pakistan. While, on the one hand, he fantasizes about an imaginary life with Erica, in reality he is teaching at a local university, organizing students and speaking out against the United States. Not only is he caught between two worlds, but his conflicting desires demonstrate nostalgia's physical and mental dislocation of the individual. Changez's nostalgia becomes a means of articulating his dissatisfaction with both his past and present situation, and suggests an unspoken desire to merge his two homes together in order to become whole. Hamid uses Changez to demonstrate the destructive power of nostalgia as not exclusive to the US, but as a universal phenomenon that needs to be addressed given the altered landscapes which have resulted from globalization.

Narrative, Trauma, and Transgressive Bodies

The relationship between space and nostalgia is further explored in *After* and *The Reluctant Fundamentalist* through narrative explorations of bodies and difference. In *Narrative Bodies: Towards a Corporeal Narratology*, Daniel Punday writes, "Narratives will explicitly or implicitly define different types of spaces organized by bodily access: inaccessible spaces, spaces that can be occupied physically, spaces accessible by surrogate means, spaces accessible by sensory or artificial perception."[54] Although they employ seemingly opposing techniques, both *After* and *The Reluctant Fundamentalist* seek to address trauma's relationship to space and the body, mediated through nostalgia. *After* provides the point-of-view of the widow and the Muslim and gives readers unique access into the minds of both sides of an event. Therefore, in the sexual interactions of the widow and the Muslim, not only does the reader have unique access to bodily experiences that are typically prohibited, but, through the narrative structure, the reader is given access to the experience from the perspective of both characters, who in this scenario are cast as victim and victimizer. *The Reluctant Fundamentalist*, on the other hand, limits the narrative perspective and takes the implied American reader and interrogates him through Changez's tale. While the effects and techniques are different, both take up Su's challenge for a deployment of nostalgia that "encourages an imaginative exploration of how present systems of social relations fail to address human needs, and the specific objects of nostalgia—lost or imagined homelands—represent efforts to articulate alternatives."[55] Both novels, using the body as a means to articulate nostalgia, provide alternate means of responding to national narratives and reactions to terrorism. The transgressive use of bodies is suggestive of differing modes of resistance to overarching dictates of nation, gender, and collective memory in the wake of trauma.

In *After*, the widow's violation of the Muslim is a physical and figurative transgression of the body into an area traditionally considered inaccessible. While this sexual taboo is particularly inviolable in Islam (anal sex is considered *haaram*, or "forbidden"), the male anus is generally coded "off-limits" by conservative, Western heteronormative conventions of sexuality. In entering this "forbidden territory," the widow's acts serve as a metaphor for the vulnerability of America in the aftermath of terrorist attacks and the invasion of a country that once seemed impenetrable. Working outside the script of heteronormativity (and the sexual routines each had established in their respective marriages), both the widow and the Muslim are confused as to how to react to the situation mentally, and both are surprised to find their bodies sexually responding to the event. To a certain extent, the violence of their encounter is part of what makes it so enjoyable. Their confusion over their reactions corresponds to the collective response to 9/11, where despite being horrified by the events, for many there was the desire and repeated need to air and watch the footage of the planes hitting the towers and their subsequent collapse (and to a lesser extent, this was later demonstrated by the number of "pilgrimages" made to Ground Zero).

In a similar way, Changez's response to the collapse of the towers—his smile—is transgressive in that it goes against the script of how one was expected to react to a tragedy like 9/11. Instead of feeling grief, Changez began to regard himself as "a modern-day Janissary, a servant of the American empire at a time when it was invading a country with a kinship to mine and was perhaps even colluding to ensure that my own country faced the threat of war."[56] The historical Janissaries were military units of slaves and prisoners of war forced to serve the Ottoman Empire in exchange for a salary, privilege, and benefits. These original Janissaries were Christian by birth, but were converted to Islam in order to prove their loyalty to the Turks. In having Changez refer to himself as "a modern-day Janissary," Hamid reverses religious and national affiliations as a way to draw attention to the arbitrary nature of labels and the often-hollow meanings behind nationalistic and religious affiliation. Like the title of the novel, this term also plays into the perceived connotations that surrounded responses to 9/11. Before reading the novel, most would assume that as a "reluctant fundamentalist," the story chronicles Changez's hesitant evolution into a radical Muslim. The reality, that Changez is reluctant in his conversion to the fundamentals of the capitalism focused on by Underwood Sampson, draws attention to the militancy of both ideologies, while revealing the biases involved in both sides of the debate. It also draws attention to the fact that "fundamentalists" can be secular, yet still opposed to American imperialism.

As a surrogate, fictional means of understanding 9/11, *After* employs a similar technique. In giving the reader access to a single event through the points of view of the widow and the Muslim, the reader perceives the event as both the victim and the victimizer, or more importantly, how the lines between these two constructs are blurred. Additionally, the transgressive actions of both characters—particularly the widow's—are used to question the potential for traumatic resistance. In appropriating a terrorist persona, the widow's violation of the Muslim reveals both the power and impotency of terrorist activity. Although there is an initial shock and impression, it does not take long for a renewed sense of normal to emerge. While there is an immediate impact to the widow's actions, by the next morning the Muslim "looked in the mirror and touched his throat and wondered at how a wound so insignificant could have caused him to fear for his life. The marks on his back, so biting and cruel at the time of their creation, had resolved into a rash of scabbed-over marks that itched but did not pain him."[57] The body thus acts as a site of "healing," and brings up the question of the lasting impacts of terrorism.

Perhaps the cruelest part of the widow's torture is when she forces the Muslim to leave a phone message for his wife. The only time the novel narratively breaks from the perspective of the widow and the Muslim is a short bit where the reader experiences the Muslim's wife's reaction to her husband's call. She wakes up in the middle of the night to the message and is confused as to what is happening to her husband. Trying to rationalize the messages, "Her mind twisted away from either outcome and she found herself thinking, inexplicably, of her husband's voice at another time, and of a conversation, so long ago now, before their marriage."[58] Like the other characters in the novel, the Muslim's wife also tries to rewrite what has happened in a way that reconciles with her ideas and beliefs about her husband and her marriage. This becomes another way in which Tristram allows readers to experience yet another angle from which to view terror and its relationship to memory and fiction. Further, in making the Muslim speak her words in leaving a message for his wife, the widow is abusing another "prisoner"—the Muslim's wife. As Scarry writes about the affects of torture,

> Even where the torturers do not permanently eliminate the voice through mutilation or murder, they mime the work of pain by temporarily breaking off the voice, making it their own, making it speak their words, making it cry out when they want it to cry, be silent when they want its silence, turning it on and off, using its sounds to abuse the one whose voice it is as well as other prisoners.[59]

In passing on the message of her husband's final words[60] to her, the widow is not only "punishing" the Muslim, but is attempting to transfer her pain and identity on to another woman, another wife. The affect of this voice message becomes the main concern for the Muslim once he realizes that he has already begun to physically recover.

Similar to the scratches that heal quickly, the Muslim soon repairs this wound and mentally creates a fiction to account for his altered identity in the aftermath of his rendezvous. Driving home, "by the time the road turned east a plausible lie had come to him. By the time he reached his home he almost believed it."[61] Narrative becomes the means by which the Muslim is able to reconcile what has transpired and will be the way in which he accounts for, and heals, the trauma that has been inflicted, not only on him, but also on his wife.

Interestingly, though, the one scar that he will carry with him is mental, and is translated through the body and relates to his earlier trauma. As the Muslim prepares to leave he glances at the sleeping widow and,

> Her fingers opened and closed (…) He watched the fingers, unable to help himself, feeling himself invaded by her once more. That brief, spastic movement of her blood-covered fingers imprinted itself on his mind, and he knew that he would never again remember with complete accuracy the one thing he was certain of in the death of his friend, which was the way his friend's fingers had opened and closed in the dirt.[62]

Here embodiment functions through the imprinting of one traumatic memory over the other. It is the movement of her body—her fingers—that once again "invade" him, carrying the meaning of not only her actions from the night before, but connecting them to an earlier trauma from which the Muslim has never entirely healed. The widow rewrites (his)tory and it becomes *her* story. This connection reveals the way in which trauma, like nostalgia, is not only of the moment, but a conflation of the past and present that shapes the future. Although dependent on outside forces, memories become the most intimate of fictions, expressed, written, and housed by the body.

In *The Reluctant Fundamentalist*, this is not only true with Erica's memories of Chris, but becomes the similar case for Changez. Where he differs, though, is his ability to admit that he might have been wrong about his assessment of Erica and the feelings he believes they shared. The last time he sees Erica at the hospital a nurse tells him, "You're the one who upsets her [Erica] most. Because you're the most real, and you make her lose her balance."[63] The nurse's assessment that Changez is too "real" speaks not only to Erica's condition, but also metaphorically for America's response to immigration, diversity, and the affects of globalization brought to prominence by September 11. This causes Changez to come to the conclusion that Erica's preoccupation with the past has taken on an importance and meaning greater than anything she believes she can experience in the present, causing her to create a "fiction" of existence that she cannot break from. In a way, though, this is also his own fiction, as he is not entirely sure what has happened to her or what her true feelings for him ever were.

After Erica's disappearance, Changez keeps looking for clues as to what might have happened to her, and hoping that she might reappear in his life. Eventually he reads a copy of her novella, hoping that through her fiction Erica will reveal herself to him. Instead, Changez is forced to admit,

> When I put down the manuscript, it was not with the conviction that Erica was either alive or dead. But I had begun to understand that she had chosen not to be a part of my story; her own had proven too compelling, and she was—at that moment and in her own way—following it to its conclusion, passing through places I could not reach.[64]

The fact that he could not "find" Erica or himself in her work suggests there is more to Erica than Changez had been willing to acknowledge. In accepting that she had chosen not to be a part of his "story," Changez yet again reminds readers that his monologue is only his version of events, only one side of a multifaceted tale. Therefore, [Am]Erica's fate is not up to Changez and is still unknown at the end of the novel. What is clear is that Changez no longer has access to this mental or physical space.

Despite the inaccessibility of [Am]Erica, at the end of the novel, Changez comes to the conclusion,

> [I]t is not always possible to restore one's boundaries after they have been blurred and made permeable by a relationship; try as we might, we cannot reconstitute ourselves as the autonomous beings we previously imagined ourselves to be. Something of us is now outside, and something of the outside is now within us.[65]

This statement reflects not only Changez's situation, but also that of the widow and the Muslim in *After*. Although both novels deal with terrorism on a political scale, they stress the role of relationships—between national and physical bodies—as the means through which trauma is processed. Nostalgia is often a part of this process, as it most often manifests as a desire to return to a time and place before terror struck. Unfortunately, this memory of a past time and place is inextricably tainted by traumatic events, which make it seem disproportionately more authentic and appealing.

Conclusion

In response to trauma, then, how might nostalgia be put to constructive use? As *After* and *The Reluctant Fundamentalist* suggest, nostalgia is most useful when it is used as a tool for critical reflection as opposed to a model for resolution. The novels structurally carry out this mandate as they force readers to reexamine their own biases, blind spots, and beliefs and their relationship to national narratives in times of crisis. Further, on the level of plot, both texts stress a reconsideration of the hierarchical properties of bodies in terms of gender, religion, nation, and class as a way of highlighting the organizing principles of value emphasized by the dominance of global capital markets. As Changez's boss tells him, "Power comes from *becoming* change."[66] The actions of the characters in these novels, although transgressive in their behavior, do speak for the potential for agency and resistance, and suggest that *what* that change will be must be determined by the conditions of the present and not by an imagined past.

Bibliography

Ahmed, Sarah. *The Cultural Politics of Emotion*. New York: Routledge, 2004.

Douthat, Ross G. "After Tragedy." *National Review* 11 (2005): 48-50.

Faludi, Susan. *The Terror Dream: Fear and Fantasy in Post-9/11 America*. New York: Metropolitan Books, 2007.

Hamid, Mohsin. *The Reluctant Fundamentalist*. Orlando, FL: Houghton Mifflin Harcourt, 2007.

—. "Slaying Dragons: Mohsin Hamid Discusses the Reluctant Fundamentalist." *Psychoanalysis & History* 2 (2009): 225-32.

Gardner, Trulson Jennifer. *Where You Left Me: A Memoir*. New York: Gallery Books, 2011.

Harvey, David. "The Body as an Accumulation Strategy." *Environment and Planning D: Society and Space* 4 (1998): 401-21.

Hirsch, Marianne, and Valerie Smith. "Feminism and Cultural Memory: An Introduction." *Signs: Journal of Women in Culture and Society* 1 (2002): 1-19.

Lee, Chana Kai. "Memories in the Making and Other National Fictions." *Signs: Journal of Women in Culture and Society* 1 (2002): 438-39.

Lee, Moonyoung. "Nostalgia as a Feature of 'Glocalization': Use of the Past in Post-Soviet Russia." *Post-Soviet Affairs* 2 (2011): 158-77.

Perri, Lynne. "Two Tangled Webs of Infidelity." *USA Today*, May 27, 2004. Accessed February 23, 2014.

http://usatoday30.usatoday.com/life/books/reviews/2004-05-26-affair-books_x.htm.

Punday, Daniel. "A Corporeal Narratology?." *Style* 2 (2000): 227-42.

—. *Narrative Bodies: Toward a Corporeal Narratology*. New York: Palgrave Macmillan, 2003.

Radstone, Susannah. "The War of the Fathers: Trauma, Fantasy, and September 11." *Signs: Journal of Women in Culture and Society* 1 (2002): 457-59.

Scarry, Elaine. *The Body in Pain: The Making and Unmaking of the World*. New York: Oxford University Press, 1985.

Su, John. *Ethics and Nostalgia in the Contemporary Novel*. Cambridge: Cambridge University Press, 2005.

Taylor, Diana. "Ground Zero." *Signs: Journal of Women in Culture and Society* 1 (2002): 448-50.

Torres, Alissa. *American Widow*. New York: Villard Books/Random House, 2008.

Tristram, Claire. *After*. New York: Farrar, Straus and Giroux, 2004.

—. "After-Word." Accessed July 18, 2010. www.clairetristram.com/afterward.html.

Žižek,Slavoj. *Welcome to the Desert of the Real!: Five Essays on September 11 and Related Dates*. New York: Verso, 2002.

Notes

[1] Elaine Scarry, *The Body in Pain: The Making and Unmaking of the World* (New York: Oxford University Press, 1985), 27.

[2] In *After*, Tristram chooses not to capitalize the "w" in widow, which demonstrates the subordinated nature of her label, as she is not only referred to in relation to her husband, but her "name" is not even capitalized.

[3] While the exact nature of the terrorist attack is never made clear in the novel, the details provided suggest a conglomeration of actual events, such as the terrorist attacks of September 11, 2001 and the murder of journalist Daniel Pearl on February 1, 2002.

[4] Mohsin Hamid, "Slaying Dragons: Mohsin Hamid Discusses the Reluctant Fundamentalist," *Psychoanalysis & History* 2 (2009): 233.

[5] Marianne Hirsch and Valerie Smith, "Feminism and Cultural Memory: An Introduction," *Signs: Journal of Women in Culture and Society* 1 (2002): 9.

[6] Hirsch and Smith, "Feminism and Cultural Memory," 6.

[7] Chana Kai Lee, "Memories in the Making and Other National Fictions," *Signs: Journal of Women in Culture and Society* 1 (2002): 439.

[8] Here it is useful to consider David Harvey's 1998 notion of globalization in relation to the body, where he writes of the process, "Different bodily qualities and modes of valuation (including respect for the bodily integrity of the laborer) achieved in

different places are brought into a spatially competitive environment through the circulation of capital" (410).

[9] Moonyoung Lee, "Nostalgia as a Feature of 'Glocalization': Use of the Past in Post-Soviet Russia," *Post-Soviet Affairs* 2 (2011): 162.

[10] John Su, *Ethics and Nostalgia in the Contemporary Novel* (Cambridge: Cambridge University Press, 2005), 175.

[11] Hamid, "Slaying Dragons," 225.

[12] Hamid, "Slaying Dragons," 232.

[13] Mohsin Hamid, *The Reluctant Fundamentalist* (Orlando, FL: Houghton Mifflin Harcourt, 2007), 7.

[14] Hamid, *The Reluctant Fundamentalist*, 118.

[15] Hamid, *The Reluctant Fundamentalist*, 28.

[16] Hamid, *The Reluctant Fundamentalist*, 83.

[17] Hamid, *The Reluctant Fundamentalist*, 114.

[18] Commenting on the relationship between the body and nostalgia in *The Reluctant Fundamentalist*, Hamid notes, "The stripping away of Erica's weight, and eventually clothing, I guess is a kind of nostalgic anorexia: A refusal to feed on the future or present." Mohsin Hamid, Interview by Jenn Brandt, Skype, January16, 2012.

[19] See also *American Widow* (2008), Alissa Torres's graphic memoir of her first year after the death of her husband, Eddie, a Cantor Fitzgerald employee who died in the World Trade Center on September 11, 2001.

[20] Jennifer Trulson Gardner, *Where You Left Me* (New York: Gallery Books, 2011), 27.

[21] Susan Faludi, *The Terror Dream: Fear and Fantasy in Post-9/11 America* (New York: Metropolitan Books, 2007), 3-4.

[22] Diana Taylor, "Ground Zero," *Signs: Journal of Women in Culture and Society* 1 (2002): 449.

[23] Sarah Ahmed, *The Cultural Politics of Emotion* (New York: Routledge, 2004), 2.

[24] Ahmed, *The Cultural Politics of Emotion*, 3.

[25] Claire Tristram, *After* (New York: Farrar, Straus and Giroux, 2004), 29.

[26] Claire Tristram, "After-Word," accessed July 18, 2010, www.clairetristram.com/afterword.html.

[27] Susannah Radstone, "The War of the Fathers: Trauma, Fantasy, and September 11," *Signs: Journal of Women in Culture and Society* 1 (2002): 458.

[28] Scarry, *The Body in Pain*, 18.

[29] Tristram, *After*, 156.

[30] Tristram, *After*, 156.

[31] Tristram, *After*, 160.

[32] Changez narrates this encounter, "'Then pretend,' I said, 'pretend I am him.' I do not know why I said it; I felt overcome and it seemed, suddenly, a possible way forward" (105). Hamid identifies this scene is one of the three main "bodily developments" in the novel, remarking, "The coupling of Changez and Erica is a physically, biologically fraught encounter, at first. And eventually they get around that quite literally by feeding Erica's nostalgia" (Personal interview).

[33] Hamid, *The Reluctant Fundamentalist*, 148.

[34] Hamid, *The Reluctant Fundamentalist*, 72.

[35] Hamid, *The Reluctant Fundamentalist*, 124.
[36] Hamid, *The Reluctant Fundamentalist*, 34.
[37] Hamid, "Slaying Dragons," 234.
[38] Claire Tristram, "After-Word," accessed July 18, 2010, www.clairetristram.com/afterword.html.
[39] Tristram, *After*, 128.
[40] Tristram, *After*, 78.
[41] Tristram, *After*, 69.
[42] Faludi, *The Terror Dream*, 93.
[43] Tristram, *After*, 119.
[44] Slavoj Žižek makes a similar observation in *Welcome to the Desert of the Real!: Five Essays on September 11 and Related Dates* (New York: Verso, 2002), 13-14, where he notes, "Another case of ideological censorship: when firefighters' widows were interviewed on CNN, most of them gave the expected performance: tears, prayers (…) all except one, who, without a tear, said that she does not pray for her dead husband, because she knows that prayer will not bring him back. Asked if she dreams of revenge, she calmly said that that would be a betrayal of her husband: had he survived, he would have insisted that the worst thing to do is to succumb to the urge to retaliate (…) there is no need to add that this clip was shown only once, then disappeared from the repetitions of the same interviews."
[45] Faludi, *The Terror Dream*, 104.
[46] Hamid, *The Reluctant Fundamentalist*, 38.
[47] Hamid, *The Reluctant Fundamentalist*, 11.
[48] Hamid, *The Reluctant Fundamentalist*, 37.
[49] Hamid, *The Reluctant Fundamentalist*, 131.
[50] Tristram, *After*, 81.
[51] Tristram, *After*, 32.
[52] Tristram, *After*, 18.
[53] Hamid, *The Reluctant Fundamentalist*, 168.
[54] Daniel Punday, *Narrative Bodies: Toward a Corporeal Narratology* (New York: Palgrave Macmillan, 2003), 121.
[55] Su, *Ethics and Nostalgia in the Contemporary Novel*, 5.
[56] Hamid, *The Reluctant Fundamentalist*, 152.
[57] Tristram, *After*, 181.
[58] Tristram, *After*, 172.
[59] Scarry, *The Body in Pain*, 54.
[60] The message that the widow forces the Muslim to repeat is, "Darling. Honey, hon. I don't know when we'll see each other again. I love you. Always remember that no matter what happens" (Tristram, *After*, 164-65).
[61] Tristram, *After*, 189.
[62] Tristram, *After*, 180.
[63] Hamid, *The Reluctant Fundamentalist*, 133.
[64] Hamid, *The Reluctant Fundamentalist*, 167.
[65] Hamid, *The Reluctant Fundamentalist*, 174.
[66] Hamid, *The Reluctant Fundamentalist*, 97.

CONTRIBUTORS

Dr Adam Brown is a Lecturer in Media Studies at Deakin University, Australia, and works as a volunteer at the Jewish Holocaust Centre in Melbourne. He is the author of *Judging "Privileged" Jews: Holocaust Ethics, Representation and the "Grey Zone"* (Berghahn, 2013) and co-author of *Communication, New Media and Everyday Life* (Oxford University Press, 2012). Intensely interested in animal and human rights issues, Adam's interdisciplinary research has spanned Holocaust representation across various genres, surveillance and film, mediations of rape, digital children's television, and board game culture. Academia profile: http://deakin.academia.edu/AdamBrown.

Audrey Bardizbanian is a PhD student in English studies at the University of Paris-Sorbonne Paris IV in Paris, France. Her research focuses on the writing of traumatic memory and the representations of disaster in the works of Jonathan Safran Foer, Daniel Mendelsohn, and Art Spiegelman. She is particularly interested in historical traumas related to the Holocaust and 9/11 and in their inscription in literary and artistic forms.

Jenn Brandt is the Director of Women's and Gender Studies and an Assistant Professor of English at High Point University. Her work focuses on gender, politics, and popular narratives of literature, television, film.

Danielle Christmas is a PhD candidate in English at the University of Illinois at Chicago, with the support of a Mellon/ACLS Dissertation Completion Fellowship (2013-2014) and a United States Holocaust Memorial Museum Fellowship (2013-2014). Her dissertation, "Auschwitz and the Plantation: Labor and Social Death in American Holocaust and Slavery Fiction," concerns how representations of Holocaust and slavery perpetrators contribute to American socioeconomic discourses. She has taught and published on topics ranging from American narratives of Nazi fugitives to the "Hottentot Venus" Saartje Baartman. Most recently, her article on William Styron's *Sophie's Choice* and *The Confessions of Nat Turner* will appear in the journal *Twentieth-Century Literature* (2014). You can find out more about Danielle's work at her website, www.daniellechristmas.com.

Brittany Hirth is an Instructor and PhD candidate in Literature at The University of Rhode Island. Her research interests include trauma theory, aesthetics of the postmodern, and the use of image and ekphrasis in contemporary literature. Her specialization is contemporary American literature, and her dissertation reintroduces the theoretical concept of the absurd into the analysis of war literature. The courses she offers center on fictional trauma narratives, survivor accounts and first-hand testimony, and the memoir genre. Additional interests include representation of the Holocaust, Vietnam War accounts, and apocalyptic literature.

Kate Parker Horigan is Assistant Professor in the Department of Folk Studies and Anthropology at Western Kentucky University. She completed her PhD in English at The Ohio State University in 2013, and her MA and undergraduate degrees at Tulane University in New Orleans in 2006 and 2005, respectively. She is currently working on a manuscript titled "'They probably got us all on the news': Personal Narratives and Public Trauma in Post-Katrina New Orleans."

Emma Login is a PhD student from the University of Birmingham (U.K.), conducting research in Conflict Archaeology under the supervision of Dr John Carman. Her research traces the development of war memorialization in the UK, France and the US from its beginnings in the 1860s through to the present. Using this wider temporal perspective, it examines changing attitudes towards war memorials and in particular the ways in which they are reused and re-appropriated many years after the conflict itself has ended. She has recently completed a 6-month research project in the United States, examining the evolution of processes of war memorialization within an American context.

Liz Medoff received her Master of Arts in the department of Visual and Critical Studies at The School of the Art Institute of Chicago, where she is currently an instructor. Her scholarly-creative research practices focus on trauma and representations of it, specifically in instances of large-scale American monuments and memorials. She has presented work across the United States.

Rodica Mihăilă is Professor of Literature and American Studies and founder of the American Studies undergraduate and graduate programs at the University of Bucharest. She has served as visiting professor at several universities in the United States. Her publications include books, anthologies, articles and studies on topics ranging from American poetry to post-Cold War

Transatlantic cultural relations. She is also a well-known translator of English and American literature and Founding President of the Romanian Association for American Studies.

Dana Mihăilescu is an Assistant Professor of English/American Studies, at the University of Bucharest, Romania. She earned her PhD in Philology at the University of Bucharest in January 2010, with a dissertation entitled *Ethical Dilemmas and Reconfigurations of Identity in Early Twentieth Century Eastern European Jewish American Narratives*. Her main research interests include Jewish American Studies, trauma and witnessing, ethics and memory, oral and written testimonies of Holocaust survivors. She has published articles on these topics in international journals of specialty such as *American Imago, European Review of History, East European Jewish Affairs, Journal of Jewish Identities, Images: A Journal of Jewish Art and Visual Culture* and she has also co-edited a volume of literary and cultural studies, *Romanian Culture in the Global Age* (2010).

Golnar Nabizadeh, PhD is a Lecturer at The University of Western Australia teaching in the areas of modernist literature and film. She has published on pedagogy and cultural studies, and is currently working on an edited collection of papers on children's literature and visual texts for the *Journal of Graphic Novels and Comics*. She is also working on a monograph entitled *Departure and Arrival: Loss and Mourning in Literary Migrant Narratives.* Her broader research interests include trauma and memory studies, cultural mourning, photography and transnational literature.

Roxana Oltean is Associate Professor in the English Department, the Faculty of Foreign Languages, The University of Bucharest, and holds a PhD in Philology. She has published articles in international journals of American literature and culture, and two books on transatlantic and global imagology in the works of Henry James (*Spaces of Utopia in the Writings of Henry James*, 2005 and *Eternal America. Henry James and the Globalizing Imagination*, 2007, both with the University of Bucharest Press). She teaches courses in American utopian models, in Transatlantic Relations and in nineteenth century American literature and culture, and her main areas of expertise and publication include the cultural and ethical impact of globalization, the transatlantic imaginary, and utopian spaces and representations. She was a Fulbright scholar in 2001-2002 at Pennsylvania State University, doing research on Henry James, nineteenth-century literature and the utopian tradition.

Elisabeth Oyler is a graduate student at the University of St. Thomas working towards her M.A. in English. She is interested in the development of memory, particularly second-generation Holocaust literature and literature of the Black Arts Movement. She presented a paper titled "Illuminating Histories: Multidirectional Memory in W.G. Sebald's *Austerlitz*" in 2012, and continues to study the way multidirectional memory can be used to better understand trauma. She was the Editorial Assistant for the *Victorian Periodicals Review* in 2014. In addition to her studies, Elisabeth works at Walden University's Writing Center as a Writing Instructor and Webinar Coordinator, advising students one-on-one throughout the writing process, teaching writing seminars, and coordinating the Center's robust schedule of group seminars.

Sara Polak is an advanced PhD researcher at the Leiden University Centre for the Arts in Society and lecturer in modern American literature at the English Department of Leiden University. Her PhD project focuses of Franklin D. Roosevelt as a cultural icon in American memory, and particularly on his own fabrication of himself as an icon. She teaches twentieth century American literature and contemporary transnational and migration literature with a strong focus on memory and trauma theory. Her publications include an article on Roosevelt's autofabrication in his own (first ever) presidential library in Hyde Park, NY ("Roosevelt in zijn eigen museum" ("Roosevelt in His Own Museum"), published in *Tweede Levens: personen en personages in geschiedenis en literatuur* (*Second Lives, Persons and Personas in History and Literature)*, Amsterdam University Press, 2011), and an oral history about the memory of the Dutch slavery history and heritage (*Meerstemmig Verleden*, Amsterdam: KIT Publishers, 2011).

Mihaela Precup is an Assistant Professor in the American Studies Program at the University of Bucharest, Romania, where she teaches American visual and popular culture, film studies, and American literature. Her main research interests include American graphic narratives, trauma and autobiography studies, and family photography. Her most recent publications are *The Graphic Memoir. An Introduction* (The University of Bucharest Press, 2013) and *Mourning Women. Post-mortem Dialogues in Contemporary American Autobiography* (The University of Bucharest Press, 2014).

Anna Sajecki, a second year English literature PhD at the University of Alberta, is currently researching her project on the cultural history of highway building in Canada. She is a collaborator on the Edmonton Pipelines Project: Narrating Digital Urbanism. With Edmonton Pipelines, she is one of the editors of a publication called Vertical Suburbia, to be submitted for publication with University of Alberta Press. She recently completed a residency with the Leighton Artists' Colony at Canada's premiere artistic institution, The Banff Centre. Her short essay on J.G. Ballard and exhaust will be published in 2015 with Fordham University Press, in a collection of essays called *Fueling Culture: Energy, History, Politics.*

Allison Whitney is an Assistant Professor of Film and Media Studies in the Department of English at Texas Tech University. She holds a PhD in Cinema and Media Studies from the University of Chicago, and her research interests include studies of film and technology, representations of aviation and space exploration in popular culture, and studies of American film genres.

Sostene Massimo Zangari holds a PhD in English from the University of Milan, Italy. He has worked extensively on Herman Melville and ethnic American literature. He has published articles on Richard Wright and Michael Gold. He is co-author of *Americana. Storie e culture degli Stati Uniti* (2012), a narrative dictionary of American culture. He is a member of the editorial board of the journal *Enthymema.* He is currently teaching English at Politecnico University in Milan.

INDEX